U.S.-UK NUCLEAR COOPERATION AFTER 50 YEARS

Significant Issues Series
Timely books presenting current CSIS research and analysis of interest to the
academic, business, government, and policy communities.
Managing Editor: Roberta Howard Fauriol

About CSIS
In an era of ever-changing global opportunities and challenges, the Center for
Strategic and International Studies (CSIS) provides strategic insights and practical
policy solutions to decisionmakers. CSIS conducts research and analysis and develops policy initiatives that look into the future and anticipate change.

Founded by David M. Abshire and Admiral Arleigh Burke at the height of the
Cold War, CSIS was dedicated to the simple but urgent goal of finding ways for
America to survive as a nation and prosper as a people. Since 1962, CSIS has
grown to become one of the world's preeminent public policy institutions.

Today, CSIS is a bipartisan, nonprofit organization headquartered in Washington, D.C. More than 220 full-time staff and a large network of affiliated scholars
focus their expertise on defense and security; on the world's regions and the
unique challenges inherent to them; and on the issues that know no boundary in
an increasingly connected world.

Former U.S. senator Sam Nunn became chairman of the CSIS Board of Trustees
in 1999, and John J. Hamre has led CSIS as its president and chief executive officer
since 2000.

CSIS does not take specific policy positions; accordingly, all views expressed
herein should be understood to be solely those of the author(s).

About Chatham House
Chatham House (The Royal Institute of International Affairs) is an independent
body that promotes the rigorous study of international questions and does not
express opinions of its own. The opinions expressed in this publication are the
responsibility of the authors.

Chatham House, 10 St. James's Square, London SW1Y 4LE
Tel: +44 (0) 20 7957 5704
Fax: +44 (0) 20 7957 5710
Web: www.chathamhouse.org.uk

The CSIS Press
Center for Strategic and International Studies
1800 K Street, N.W., Washington, D.C. 20006
Tel: (202) 775-3119   Fax: (202) 775-3199
E-mail: books@csis.org   Web: www.csis.org

U.S.-UK NUCLEAR COOPERATION AFTER 50 YEARS

Edited by Jenifer Mackby and Paul Cornish

Introduction by John J. Hamre and Robin Niblett

Produced in association with Chatham House

THE CSIS PRESS

**Center for Strategic
and International Studies**
Washington, D.C.

Significant Issues Series, Volume 30, Number 3
Cover design by Robert L. Wiser, Silver Spring, Md.
Cover photograph: The UK submarine HMS *Vanguard* leaving Port Canaveral,
    Florida, October 10, 2005, to test launch a Trident II D5 missile. By Lt. Stuart
    Antrobus RN. Royal Navy. © Crown Copyright.

12 11 10 09 08   5 4 3 2 1

ISSN 0736-7136
ISBN 978-0-89206-530-1

Library of Congress Cataloging-in-Publication Data
U.S.-UK nuclear cooperation after 50 years / edited by Jenifer Mackby and Paul
Cornish.
     p. cm. — (Significant issues series, 0736-7136 ; v. 30, no. 3)
   Includes bibliographical references and index.
   ISBN 978-0-89206-530-1 (pbk. : alk. paper) 1. Nuclear weapons—Government
policy—United States. 2. Nuclear weapons—United States. 3. Nuclear weapons—
Government policy—Great Britain. 4. Nuclear weapons—Great Britain. 5. United
States—Military relations—Great Britain. 6. Great Britain—Military relations—
United States. 7. United States—Military policy. 8. Great Britain—Military policy.
I. Mackby, Jenifer. II. Cornish, Paul. III. Title: United States-United Kingdom nuclear
cooperation after 50 years. IV. Title. V. Series.
   UA23.U784 2008
   355.02'170941—dc22
                                                  2008022027

CONTENTS

ABBREVIATIONS AND ACRONYMS

ABM	antiballistic missile
ABM Treaty	Anti-Ballistic Missile Treaty (1972, amended in 1974)
AEA	Atomic Energy Act (1946)
AEC	Atomic Energy Commission
AF&F	arming, fuzing, and firing
AMEL	ARG Master Equipment List
ANF	Allied Nuclear Force
AWE	Atomic Weapons Establishment (successor [1987] to AWRE)
AWRE	Atomic Weapons Research Establishment (1950)
BMD	ballistic missile defense
CDT	Combined Development Trust
CP	control point
CPC	Combined Policy Committee
CPX	command post exercise
CSA	chief scientific adviser
CTBT	Comprehensive Nuclear Test-Ban Treaty
DAHRT	Dual Axis Hydrodynamic Radiographic Test
DOD	Department of Defense
GLCM	ground-launched cruise missiles
H&S	health and safety
HLG	High Level Group (NATO)
HUAC	House Un-American Activities Committee
ICBM	intercontinental ballistic missile
INF Treaty	Intermediate Nuclear Forces Treaty (1987)
IRBM	intermediate-range ballistic missile
JCAE	Joint Committee on Atomic Energy
JOWOG	Joint Working Group
LANL	Los Alamos National Laboratory

LINAC	linear accelerator
LLNL	Lawrence Livermore National Laboratory
LRTNF	long-range theater nuclear forces
LTBT	Limited Test Ban Treaty
MCNP	Ministerial Committee on Nuclear Policy
MDA	Mutual Defense Agreement (1958)
MIRV	multiple independently targetable reentry vehicle
MOD	Ministry of Defence
MRBM	medium-range ballistic missile
NATO	North Atlantic Treaty Organization
NDRC	National Defense Research Committee
NESE	Nuclear Explosive Safety Evaluation
NGF	next generation fuze
NIF	National Ignition Facility
NNWS	nonnuclear weapon states
NPR	Nuclear Posture Review
NPT	Nuclear Non-Proliferation Treaty
NTS	Nevada Test Site, the
NWS	nuclear weapon states
OSRD	Office of Scientific Research and Development
PINEX	pinhole imaging neutron experiment
PNI	Presidential Nuclear Initiatives (1991–1992)
PSA	Polaris Sales Agreement
PSI	Proliferation Security Initiative
RRW	reliable replacement warhead
RSP	render safe procedures
SALT I	Strategic Arms Limitation Treaty (1972)
SALT II	Strategic Arms Limitation Treaty (1979)
SBSS	science-based stockpile stewardship
SDI	Strategic Defense Initiative
SDR	Strategic Defence Review
SI	System International
SLBM	submarine-launched ballistic missile
SORT	Strategic Offensive Reductions Treaty (2002)
SSBN	strategic nuclear submarine
SSP	Stockpile Stewardship Program
START	Strategic Arms Reduction Talks
START	Strategic Arms Reduction Treaty
STF	shore test facility
TLPP	Temporary Lightning Protection Pole
TNW	tactical nuclear weapons, range of less than 500 kilometers
TTBT	Threshold Test Ban Treaty
WRSE	weapon recovery safety evaluation

ACKNOWLEDGMENTS

This volume involved a transatlantic effort of collaboration among 38 authors. We owe a debt of gratitude to all of them, as well as to the many interviewees who provided an insightful glimpse of history. The visionary not listed in the table of contents is Clark Murdock, director of the CSIS Project on Nuclear Issues (PONI), who conceived the project. Senior PONI mentors Linton Brooks, Frank Miller, and Robert Joseph gave unstintingly of their time to provide valuable advice on the project and to review PONI chapters. CSIS Press director James Dunton, Roberta Fauriol, and Emma Davies are especially commended for guiding the text through the publishing process. Mary Marik skillfully served as copy editor and principal compositor. The staff at CSIS who helped with fact-finding and research are greatly thanked: Mark Jansson, interview coordinators Jessica Yeats and Tara Callahan, and Matt Squeri. Ian Gottesman of CSIS provided essential technical assistance with the audio files of the oral histories. (Audio files are available at www.csis.org/isp/poni/us-uk.)

Chatham House and the Atomic Weapons Establishment coordinated the effort on the UK side in a most sophisticated fashion: Molly Tarhuni at Chatham House and Owen Price at AWE are especially appreciated.

CSIS and Chatham House are most grateful for the support provided to this project by the Defense Threat Reduction Agency, the National Nuclear Security Administration, BAE Systems, Rolls-Royce Submarines, and the Atomic Weapons Establishment.

INTRODUCTION

JOHN J. HAMRE AND ROBIN NIBLETT

As the United States and the United Kingdom commemorate the five decades of their special nuclear relationship embodied in the 1958 Mutual Defense Agreement (MDA), it is fitting that through transatlantic collaboration a research institute in each country examines that history. The Center for Strategic and International Studies, in Washington, D.C., and the Royal Institute of International Affairs, Chatham House, London, enlisted senior and former senior officials, scientists, academics, and members of industry who have been involved in the implementation of the MDA to recount their experiences in retrospective and prospective essays and oral histories. The resulting volume of histories, analyses, and anecdotes provides valuable reading for an understanding of how the two nations were drawn together by a common threat during a turbulent era.

Indeed, our shared resolve to defeat Nazi Germany and, subsequently, to resist the expansion of Soviet communism fashioned a bond between the two English-speaking transatlantic allies that now seems virtually indissoluble. It has survived despite a number of obstacles, including a halt in the scientific collaboration that spurred the Manhattan Project; the Suez crisis; and sharp disagreements over scientific, political, and technical issues. Each of the chapters in this book deals with a significant issue from the history of the nuclear relation-

---

John J. Hamre is president and chief executive officer of CSIS and Robin Niblett is director of Chatham House.

ship. The chapters describe the dramas leading up to the signing of the MDA, the period of political partnership and technical collaboration since, and future challenges facing the relationship in a radically changed security environment.

Because the expertise about the nuclear era resides in senior officials and scientists who have retired or are facing retirement, this project also commissioned young nuclear experts to interview them and to write essays about the MDA. Their essays and abstracts of the oral histories (with, among others, Des Browne, UK secretary of state for defence; James Schlesinger, former U.S. secretary of energy; and Harold Brown, former U.S. secretary of defense) are included in this collection.

The volume is part of the CSIS Project on Nuclear Issues, which aims to build and sustain a networked community of young nuclear experts from the military, policy, academic and industrial sectors. Thus, this volume comprises past, present, and future leaders of the two countries who tell the story of a distinct transatlantic relationship, a liaison that has no parallel.

Part One

THE CHRONOLOGY

Manhattan Project participants (left to right): Sir William Penney, credited as the "father of the British atomic bomb"; Beatrice Langer, data technician; Emil Konopinski and Lawrence Langer, both former physics professors at Indiana University. Photo courtesy of Los Alamos National Laboratory Archives.

THE SPECIAL NUCLEAR RELATIONSHIP

A HISTORICAL CHRONOLOGY

JOHN SIMPSON AND JENIFER MACKBY

During the past seven decades, the nuclear relationship between the United States and the United Kingdom has been both remarkable in its duration and unique in its nature.[1] It has been inherently atypical because the two countries have cooperated on what most observers regarded as the "ultimate weapon" of the second half of the twentieth century. In a little more than two years their secret joint venture produced two unique bomb designs that ultimately changed history. Although cooperation between the United States and the United Kingdom began in the common struggle against Germany, it strengthened considerably under the threat presented by the Soviet Union. Yet its path was never preordained, and it has demanded continuous attention by both states. The British started out ahead on the nuclear discovery path in 1939 and suppressed the U.S. requests to join their effort, yet the United States soon surpassed Britain and then almost closed the door on collaboration. It is only due to the quirks of circumstance, personalities, and historical events that the situation changed into one of reciprocal sharing, or symbiotic kinship embodied in the Mutual Defense Agreement (MDA) of 1958.[2] The agreement was most recently extended in 2004 until 2014. This book is a testament to the MDA's 50th anniversary as well as the future it holds.

When Winston Churchill came to power in 1940, Franklin D. Roosevelt, Britain's "warm-hearted friend," occupied the White House. Churchill invented the concept of a U.S.-UK "special relationship" in his "Iron Curtain" speech in Missouri on March 5, 1946, to argue for the perpetuation of the wartime military relationship. "Neither the sure prevention of war, nor the continuous rise of world organization will be gained without what I have called the fraternal association of the English-speaking peoples," he said. "This means a special relationship between the British Commonwealth and Empire and the United States." [3] Specifically, he envisaged a close relationship between military advisers, exchanges of officers at technical colleges, similar weapons, and the joint use of naval and air force bases possessed by either country around the world. [4]

While the basis of the U.S.-UK nuclear relationship has formally never been reciprocity, in practice this has always been significant and is central to its understanding. Initially, the United Kingdom provided uranium from its stocks to the U.S. nuclear weapons program and bases for U.S. nuclear strike aircraft as well as collaborated in the gathering of raw data about the USSR's nuclear activities. By 1958 the United Kingdom had its own operational strategic nuclear deterrent capability but had also gained access to U.S. nuclear weapons for use in wartime. With the MDA it was able to acquire U.S. weapon engineering expertise to supplement its own thermonuclear design knowledge, including design of warheads, as well as nuclear materials and weapon components that could be most economically manufactured in the United States, strategic nuclear delivery systems, testing facilities, and information on antimissile systems.

The MDA also enabled the United Kingdom to buy a U.S. nuclear submarine propulsion plant for its first nuclear submarine, have it at sea much sooner than a purely national effort would have allowed, and eventually integrate missile submarine operations through joint targeting. For its part, the United States acquired a European base for its Polaris submarines, the use of bases in the United Kingdom and elsewhere in the world, a complementary scientific perspective, support for its foreign policy goals, and increased influence on the world stage.

Despite its dependence on the United States for some materials, components, and its test site, the United Kingdom persisted throughout this period in maintaining both an independent design capability for its nuclear warheads and ultimate operational control over its strategic nuclear forces. Unlike all its European neighbors other than France, it chose not to rely solely on the U.S. extended deterrence guarantees provided through NATO. Although it assigned its strategic forces to NATO's Supreme Allied Commander in Europe (SACEUR) for use in the event of an attack on Western Europe by the USSR in concert with the United States, ultimate operational control remained with the prime minister. As Henry Kissinger observed, the special relationship "owed no little to the superb self-discipline by which Britain succeeded in maintaining political influence after its physical power had waned. . . . Britain's influence was great precisely because it never insisted on it; the 'special relationship' demonstrated the value of intangibles."[5]

Just how did this transatlantic special nuclear relationship evolve?

WARTIME NUCLEAR ALLIANCE

Research on uranium 235 for a weapon started in the United Kingdom in 1939, through émigré European scientists such as Rudolf Peierls and Otto Frisch who had been forced to flee the Continent's fascist regimes and seek refuge in Britain. Many of these expatriates played pivotal roles in building the atomic bomb. In addition, two French scientists had brought to the United Kingdom the world's supply of another important nuclear material, heavy water. In 1941 their work led to the report of the British Maud Committee, which described how an atomic bomb might be made from uranium 235 or plutonium. The report was passed to the United States with the recommendation that "the present collaboration with America should be continued and extended especially in the region of experimental work."[6]

Exchanges of nuclear information took place, and visiting U.S. scientists were impressed with British work on the bomb.[7] Although the U.S. primary interest in atomic energy had hitherto been focused on atomic energy as a power source, the Maud report stimulated the recognition that such a militarily influential weapon would in the future underpin the leading role of the United States and Britain in world affairs.[8] However, when President Roosevelt suggested to Churchill in October 1941 a coordinating effort to pursue the atomic bomb, Churchill's somewhat tardy response was to indicate only a "readiness" to collaborate—specifically, on an exchange of information—as the United Kingdom appeared to be far ahead of the United States. The United States then launched a full-scale effort, the Manhattan Project, drawing on tremendous resources and quickly surpassing the state of UK development.

By mid-1942 the United Kingdom realized that it had been left behind and proposed a partnership with the United States on atomic weapons, but by then the Americans no longer perceived a need for UK assistance. Thus, "the British could not proceed on their own and were cut off completely from the American project."[9] Nevertheless, through the Quebec Agreement of August 1943, the majority of those who had been working on atomic energy in the United Kingdom moved to Chalk River in Canada and to the United States, where they contributed considerably to both the atomic bomb and gaseous diffusion programs in the context of the Manhattan Project. These scientists included William Penney, Sir James Chadwick, James Tuck, and Geoffrey Taylor, some of whom played important roles in the Trinity test. The Combined Policy Committee (CPC) with Canada was created to coordinate allied nuclear activities, and the Combined Development Trust (CDT) was set up to monopolize access to the world's known sources of uranium in Africa.

In September 1944 Churchill and Roosevelt signed the Hyde Park aide-mémoire confirming that "full collaboration between the United States and the British Government in developing [nuclear energy] should continue . . . unless and until terminated by joint agreement." Both this and the Quebec Agreement were executive agreements signed by the president without the knowledge of Congress. Thus, when Congress legislated on U.S. management of its nuclear program following the end of the war, it did so in ignorance of the full nature of the UK role in the Manhattan Project and these U.S.-UK executive agreements.

MCMAHON ACT OF 1946

The resulting 1946 Atomic Energy Act, known also as the McMahon Act (after its sponsor, Senator Brien McMahon [D-Conn.]), made it illegal for U.S. citizens to pass on nuclear weapon design and production information to citizens of other states. Penalties included life imprisonment or death. This terminated the existing close cooperation with Britain on aspects of nuclear weapon design. However, this legislation proved open to differing legal interpretations, which enabled some intelligence and uranium supply collaboration to continue. Work also continued on advanced conventional weapons, including potential nuclear delivery systems and advanced submarine designs. Moreover, in the later 1940s, the start of the Cold War led to the decision to allow U.S. strategic bombers to return to bases in the United Kingdom. This led to questions about how the United Kingdom would participate in decisions over the use of these bases to mount nuclear attacks on the USSR, given the inevitable nuclear retaliation upon the UK homeland. By 1957 the Strategic Air Command and the Royal Air Force (RAF) arranged joint delivery of nuclear weapons against the USSR and its allies.[10]

A December 1947 meeting of the CPC, labeled the Modus Vivendi, identified nine nonweapon areas of potential Anglo-American nuclear information exchange under the 1946 act. In return, the United States was allocated most of the 1948 and 1949 African uranium ore production, and the United Kingdom accepted that the Quebec Agreement (stipulating that neither country would use the bomb without the consent of the other) was no longer operative. In March 1948 the United Kingdom told the United States that it was going to press ahead with a national nuclear weapon program. By November 1948, the United States proposed an integrated U.S.-UK program along the lines of the 1943–1945 program, with about 20 bombs stockpiled in the United Kingdom for its use. The United States believed that production of nuclear weapons for the United Kingdom should take place in the United States.

In 1949 the Soviet Union tested its first bomb. The UK national nuclear weapon program was gathering momentum by then and, following the uncovering of Klaus Fuchs as a spy for the Soviet Union and the appointment of a former communist, John Strachey, as the UK minister for war, further U.S.-UK discussions stalled. Attempts were made in June 1951 to alleviate U.S. concerns over alleged laxities in UK security procedures, and some collaboration continued on the U.S. use of UK air bases for possible nuclear attacks on the USSR and nuclear intelligence. Little progress was possible elsewhere largely because of the differing views held by the U.S. Atomic Energy Commission (AEC) and Department of Defense (DOD) over the scope for collaboration under the 1946 McMahon Act.

The United Kingdom pressed ahead with its first nuclear test in October 1952 in the Monte Bello Islands off the coast of Australia. In January 1953 Churchill met with the newly elected U.S. president, Dwight D. Eisenhower, to explore earlier ideas of supplying the United Kingdom with a small stock of nuclear bombs in return for an integration of the two states' nuclear research, development, and production programs. The meeting was not a success for Churchill. Thus, the United Kingdom decided to build additional nuclear reactors and expand its uranium enrichment capacity. The first operational nuclear bomb was delivered to RAF Wittering for training purposes in 1953.

1954 ATOMIC ENERGY ACT

In 1953 pressures from a number of sources led the Eisenhower administration to ask Congress to amend the 1946 McMahon Act. The resulting 1954 Atomic Energy Act was a compromise that permitted the United States to share data with NATO allies on the military characteristics and yields of U.S. nuclear weapons but not weapon design information. This enabled the allies to carry U.S. nuclear weapons on their own delivery systems. It also allowed for exchanges with other states on the peaceful applications of nuclear energy. Both activities were to take place through bilateral military and civil "agreements for cooperation."

In June 1955 parallel U.S.-UK civil and military agreements were signed in Washington. The civil agreement permitted the supply of uranium 235 for civil purposes, and the military agreement allowed for an expanded dialogue on intelligence issues and planning for nuclear attack and defense, including data to enable UK medium bombers to carry U.S. nuclear weapons.

An agreement for the transfer of U.S. submarine technology on nuclear propulsion systems to the United Kingdom was reached in June 1956. Members of the Joint Committee on Atomic Energy (JCAE) requested the president not to sign it in order to force the United Kingdom to disclose data on its Magnox reactors, but in November 1956 Eisenhower authorized the exchanges to proceed, in part to repair relations following the October 1956 Suez crisis. This action symbolized the change in the internal balance of power between the Eisenhower administration and Congress over nuclear issues, with the president asserting his authority over Congress in interpreting the 1954 act.

SUEZ AND AFTER: MOVING TOWARD CLOSER U.S.-UK NUCLEAR COOPERATION

Following the Suez debacle in October 1956, President Eisenhower and Prime Minister Harold Macmillan, newly elected in January 1957, launched a repair of UK-U.S. relations at a meeting in Bermuda in March 1957. They discussed arrangements for the United Kingdom to acquire U.S. Corporal missiles, with their warheads to be held under U.S. custody in peacetime.[11] The two agreed that the United States would build and transfer Thor missiles to the United Kingdom without charge, with the RAF to staff, support, and maintain them.[12] The United States was to supply the warheads and maintain custody over them. The 1954 act would have to be modified if the United States provided the United Kingdom detailed information on the storage and safety of the warheads.

By the start of 1957, the RAF had a fleet of Canberra jet bombers in service in Germany and was engaged in inducting its new fleet of advanced jet-powered medium V-bombers into service in the United Kingdom. As the United Kingdom now had both strategic nuclear weapons and aircraft to deliver them, an agreement was reached at the Bermuda summit to initiate joint nuclear war planning[13] and extend intelligence exchanges.

Because the United Kingdom had limited facilities for the production of fissile materials, the rapidly increasing numbers of the United Kingdom's nuclear-capable aircraft would soon outnumber its small numbers of nuclear weapons. Negotiations therefore started on Project E, under which both the Canberra and the United Kingdom's first new medium bomber, the Valiant, would have access to U.S. Mark 7 kiloton bombs stockpiled at UK bases. In parallel, discussions took place in the NATO context on arrangements to provide NATO countries, including the United Kingdom, with U.S. nuclear bombs, missile warheads, demolition charges, and artillery shells for tactical and battlefield use on their own delivery systems. Decisions on their use in time of war were to be taken by the SACEUR.

Informal discussions also started in September 1957 on providing the United Kingdom with U.S.-manufactured fissile material to increase the output of UK-owned bombs. The United Kingdom needed to obtain supplies of highly enriched uranium (HEU) to avoid the expense of building and operating a second enrichment plant;[14] however, this too would require an amendment to the 1954 act.[15]

Meanwhile, over Malden Island in the Pacific in May and June 1957, the United Kingdom tested three air-dropped megaton nuclear devices. Although these megaton devices failed to reach the intended yield, the tests were carried out under intense pressure because the United Kingdom wanted to ensure that a proven thermonuclear design had been achieved before a moratorium on nuclear testing was imposed. The three nuclear weapon states had been discussing since 1954 restricting the further development of nuclear weapons by a ban on testing. This was driven in part by the increasing radioactive fallout in the atmosphere and the international and domestic protests it had generated.

By June 1957 the United States, now well ahead of the other two nuclear weapon states in weapon design, publicly advocated a ban on both testing and manufacture of nuclear weapons. In July it proposed a test suspension while these bans were being negotiated. This placed the United Kingdom in a difficult position: it had not yet perfected a thermonuclear weapon design, it had very few operational weapons, and it had only limited supplies of fissile materials. The United Kingdom therefore made clear that it could only support the U.S. proposals if the United States offered assurances of independent access to a limited stockpile of modern, well-engineered nuclear weapons prior to the implementation of a test ban.

SPUTNIK AND THE 1958 ATOMIC ENERGY ACT

The October 1957 launch of Sputnik provoked a transforming effect akin to that of September 11, 2001, on U.S. public and congressional opinion. It was perceived that the United States was falling behind in the nuclear arms race because the Sputnik booster, acting as an intercontinental ballistic missile, could deliver nuclear weapons to North America. Sputnik and the new Soviet technological challenges in antimissile defenses and antisubmarine weapons provided a critical political boost to enhance Anglo-American cooperation.[16] Macmillan sent a telegram to Eisenhower on October 10, 1957, suggesting that the United States and United Kingdom pool all their resources to meet this threat and envisioning a "grand plan" for "cooperation with the Americans in nuclear matters and over ballistic missiles and other weapons."[17] Eisenhower responded by suggesting an urgent meeting with Macmillan to re-examine "the whole pattern of Western cooperation."

Macmillan arrived in Washington on October 23, 1957. The next day the U.S. National Security Council approved a full exchange of information with the United Kingdom on the military aspects of nuclear energy. The communiqué issued after the meeting included a U.S. commitment to amend its 1954 act, with the United Kingdom accepting a major degree of dependence upon the United States for the future equipment of its nuclear deterrent forces in order to use the resources released to enhance the "common defence."[18] A report prepared by U.S. and UK officials proposed exchanges of intelligence, nuclear material, weapons design information, and data for nuclear weapons training and operational planning. It also called for the United States to supply the United Kingdom with complete U.S. weapons systems, with custody of warheads to be retained in U.S. hands and joint decisionmaking systems for use.[19] The report recommended a technical committee of experts to fully "blueprint" these ideas for rapid implementation and report findings by December 20, 1957.[20]

Transatlantic exchanges then took place on what this blueprinting should cover. The exchanges were accompanied by the firing on November 8 of the United Kingdom's Grapple X thermonuclear test device (with a 1.8 megaton yield) in the Pacific Ocean off Christmas Island, thus demonstrating unequivocally that the United Kingdom had mastered the principles of radiation implosion. The United Kingdom listed as its priorities for cooperation the use of atomic test facilities, atomic warheads, supplies of fissile materials, defense against ballistic missiles, and ballistic missiles.[21] The U.S. view, which prevailed, focused on five areas: materials, weapons, power propulsion for military purposes, delivery systems, and biochemical and radiological warfare. The United States suggested that it should immediately sell uranium 235 to the United Kingdom for its civil research and power programs, thus releasing UK enrichment capacity for military production.[22] The resultant plutonium would be bought back for use in U.S. weapons. At the time the United States had no interest in using UK test facilities.[23] In December 1957 Admiral Hyman G. Rickover (known as the "father" of the U.S. nuclear navy) suggested that the United Kingdom purchase a submarine propulsion plant from a U.S. company.[24]

A nuclear subcommittee concerned with weapons and warheads met in Washington in early December and focused on a short UK paper setting out its needs and priorities. Although the UK representatives knew what they were seeking to acquire, neither side was prepared to disclose details of their weapon stockpile, fissile material stocks, and research and development activities. U.S. representatives were legally debarred from doing so by the 1954 act. However, progress was made on the sale of a submarine reactor.[25] Statements of UK objectives identified the extent to which progress depended on amendments to the 1954 act[26] and emphasized its need to avoid building a second enrichment plant producing HEU at double U.S. prices.[27]

1958 ATOMIC ENERGY ACT

In early 1958, Congress started hearings on amending the 1954 act. On January 27, bills incorporating the proposed amendments were introduced in both the House and the Senate and were referred for scrutiny to the JCAE Subcommittee on Agreements for Cooperation.[28] The bills ran into difficulties in two areas: the proposal to swap U.S. HEU for UK plutonium, and the proliferation implications if states other than the United Kingdom were to claim the right to access U.S. nuclear secrets.[29] The situation was exacerbated by rapid movement toward a testing ban, with the UK weapon designers believing that they needed a series of tests in September for a design that could not be neutralized by USSR countermeasures.[30]

Macmillan paid another visit to Washington on June 7–8, 1958, to expedite the process. This resulted in the deferral of the proposal to exchange HEU and plutonium to a later agreement, as well as a formal agreement on "the use of bombs or warheads under joint control" from bases in the United Kingdom.[31] In addition, technical discussions began between the two states on a draft technical annex to the new MDA that would be placed before Congress once the 1958 Atomic Energy Bill had been agreed by Congress. The president finally signed the 1958 Atomic Energy Act on July 2.

Macmillan had meanwhile traded UK support for an October suspension of nuclear testing for a personal assurance by Eisenhower that the United States would provide all necessary information on overcoming the "vulnerability" of UK nuclear weapons and on making smaller and lighter megaton bombs.[32]

THE MUTUAL DEFENSE AGREEMENT

The very next day, July 3, 1958, both countries signed the Agreement for Cooperation on the Uses of Atomic Energy for Mutual Defense Purposes,[33] which set the stage for close nuclear collaboration that continues until the present post–Cold War period. The agreement enabled the United States and the United Kingdom to exchange classified information to improve each party's "atomic weapon design, development, and fabrication capability." It provided for the exchange of classified information for

1. the development of defense plans;

2. the training of personnel in the employment of and defense against atomic weapons and other military applications of atomic energy;

3. the evaluation of the capabilities of potential enemies in the employment of atomic weapons and other military applications of atomic energy; . . . [34]

The agreement also encompassed the development of nuclear delivery systems; research, development, and design of military reactors; and the transfer of "non-nuclear parts of atomic weapons." Further, the agreement covered the export of one complete U.S. submarine nuclear propulsion plant and its enriched uranium fuel, which was installed in the United Kingdom's first nuclear-powered submarine, HMS *Dreadnought*. Subsequently, Rolls-Royce produced British submarine reactors independently. The agreement also stipulated that "there will be no transfer by either Party of atomic weapons."

Moves to implement the agreement started in all the relevant areas, and the necessary amendments to the 1958 act regarding the exchange of materials—U.S. uranium 235, tritium, and lithium for UK plutonium—were placed before Congress on May 7, 1959. The resulting consolidated MDA was of indefinite duration, though there were rather complex provisions for the five types of transfer involved, as different exchanges could be terminated or renewed for periods of five or ten years.[35] Further, under an executive order, Eisenhower delegated powers to the DOD and the AEC acting jointly, and he made the secretary of state responsible for negotiating all agreements for cooperation under the atomic energy acts.

The exchanges of weapon information started at a meeting in Washington on August 27–28, 1958. As might be expected, both sides were uncertain how to proceed on the first day of the meeting. The United Kingdom did not want to reveal too much about its program until it was sure this would be productive, while the U.S. side in theory had to obtain a presidential determination to reveal its own information. The results of the first three-hour meeting were therefore disappointing.

Overnight the United Kingdom decided to offer concepts of its most recent designs, which it did the next morning. The U.S. side called for a recess and then indicated that a full exchange would be possible so long as it could be directly related to problems and weapons the United Kingdom was working on. Late on August 28, Edward Teller, director of the Lawrence Livermore Laboratory, observed that "the re-markable result of the 12 year total separation was that both countries had achieved broadly the same physics understanding, although the greater resources allocated to the United States programmes had given them more sophisticated engineering designs."[36] This initial meeting was followed by a more detailed exchange of information at the Sandia Laboratory in Albuquerque on September 15–17.[37]

The relationship started to focus on the activities of 15 joint work-ing groups (JOWOGs) that addressed specific technical issues of mu-tual interest, such as a lightweight megaton warhead, safety of high explosives, and testing underground and in outer space, to be man-aged through regular stocktake (high-level) meetings. Their continu-ance was predicated on the United Kingdom pursuing an active and independent nuclear research, development, and production program. Stocktake meetings continue to this day with most of the interac-tions taking place at the working level of the two countries' weapons laboratories.

Other elements of the MDA were also being implemented success-fully. HEU was purchased initially from the United States for subma-rine reactors, as was tritium for weapons use, followed later by barter exchange agreements involving UK plutonium from first military and then civil reactors. Under these agreements, 5.37 tons of UK-produced plutonium was sent to the United States in return for 6.7 kilograms of tritium and 7.5 tons of HEU over the period 1960–1979. Some of the UK-produced plutonium was used in 1962 by the United States for a nuclear weapon test of reactor-grade plutonium. Also, the United Kingdom had purchased both nonnuclear weapon material and some components from the United States. Project E and NATO nuclear shar-ing arrangements resulted in nuclear weapons and systems being as-signed to SACEUR. The United States stationed its Polaris submarines at Holy Loch in Scotland and committed to a supply of the next-gener-ation Skybolt air-launched ballistic missiles; thus, the United Kingdom canceled its Blue Streak medium-range ballistic missile.

By early 1962 the nuclear testing moratorium had been breached by the USSR, which freed both the United States and the United King-dom to test again. The major testing activities of the United States were in the atmosphere, and President John F. Kennedy asked the United Kingdom for the use of its Christmas Island testing ground in the Pa-cific for this purpose. Although there was no formal reciprocity, the

United Kingdom started to test underground at Nevada in March 1962 by exploding a weapon assembly code-named Super Octopus, which was followed by a second test on December 2, 1962, while the United States used the UK-owned site for some of its atmospheric tests.[38]

STRAINS IN THE RELATIONSHIP

By the end of 1962, the nuclear activities of the United Kingdom began to narrow as weapon designers were concentrating on only the Skybolt warhead and the WE177 multipurpose bomb, and this inevitably resulted in a decreased interest among U.S. interlocutors. A critical test of the relationship occurred in 1962, when the United States decided to cancel the Skybolt on account of high costs and poor test results. This posed a major challenge to the domestic credibility of the Macmillan government, which depended on the Skybolt for its independent deterrent. Defence Minister Peter Thorneycroft declared, "This missile is at the heart of British defence policy."[39] The crisis was resolved by an agreement negotiated with President Kennedy at Nassau in December 1962 under which the Royal Navy would acquire the Polaris missile from the United States and the missiles would be carried in UK nuclear submarines.[40] The detailed agreement to implement this political deal, the Polaris Sales Agreement (PSA), was completed some months later.[41] This decision, taken just a few months after the Cuban missile crisis, strengthened immeasurably the alliance between the two countries.

The negotiation of the PSA created a duality in the UK-U.S. nuclear relationship that has continued to this day: delivery platforms are built through collaboration between the Royal Navy and the U.S. Navy, and warheads are designed through collaboration between the U.S. and UK nuclear laboratories. Exchanges on penetration aids were not covered by either the PSA or the MDA, which led to future difficulties over collaboration in this area. However, the agreement resulted in two new tasks for Aldermaston: to design a UK warhead for Polaris and a new lay-down thermonuclear weapon for the V-bombers, the WE177B.

The nuclear relationship also fell under some strain in October 1964, when the Conservative government was succeeded by a Labour government headed by Harold Wilson, which publicly committed to abandon the United Kingdom's nuclear deterrent. Although this did not transpire, the United Kingdom canceled the fifth Polaris submarine, suspended its nuclear weapon design activities and its nuclear test program in Nevada, withdrew its conventional and nuclear forces from east of Suez, and refused to provide military support for U.S. activities in Vietnam. As a consequence, the U.S.-UK JOWOG and stocktake interactions diminished. Soon thereafter the United Kingdom, United States, and Soviet Union participated actively in the negotiations leading to the Nuclear Non-Proliferation Treaty, which all three signed in 1968.

TOWARD A STEADY STATE

Concerns in the United Kingdom over the vulnerability of Polaris to Soviet antiballistic missile warheads led to a push for development of the Chevaline[42] "front end" for its missiles. The United Kingdom began explosive tests related to the warheads for them in May 1974, following a nine-year moratorium. During this period Edward Heath's government attempted unsuccessfully to establish a closer nuclear relationship with France. Heath succeeded in persuading President Richard M. Nixon and Henry Kissinger to avoid limiting the scope of the MDA in the ongoing negotiations with the USSR on limitations on offensive and defensive weapons culminating in the Strategic Arms Limitation Treaty and Anti-Ballistic Missile Treaty of 1972. In addition, trilateral negotiations among the United States, the United Kingdom, and the Soviet Union on a nuclear test ban treaty recommenced in 1977, this time lasting until 1981; an expanded multilateral negotiation from 1994 to 1996 would result in the signing of a Comprehensive Nuclear Test-Ban Treaty.

Under the leadership of President Ronald Reagan and Prime Minister Margaret Thatcher, agreement was reached in 1980 for the United Kingdom to purchase the Trident missile. This required both a new UK-designed warhead and new submarines. These developments facilitated putting the MDA on a more secure, long-term footing, with a resulting significantly amended MDA agreed to on June 5, 1984.[43] This provided a ten-year, rather than the previous five-year, term on material exchanges, assuring the United Kingdom of submarine reactor fuel and warhead materials for its Trident program. It also provided coordination of nonproliferation policies and expanded information exchanges to include centrifuge and laser enrichment technologies.[44] Further, information exchanges were given an indefinite duration. Thereafter, the MDA was renewed for ten-year extensions, subject to the termination clauses contained in the agreement.

The Labour government of Prime Minister Tony Blair decided in 2006 to renew the UK nuclear weapons system by extending until the 2040s its missiles made in the United States and replacing the Trident submarines.[45] The Trident warheads are expected to last until 2020, and the British have not decided whether to develop a replacement warhead or extend the life of the current system through a process similar to the U.S. life extension program. Because the system is based on U.S. technology, the two countries will work together on future decisions regarding warheads and missiles. The United Kingdom has also participated since the 1980s in the U.S. ballistic missile defense program.

CONCLUSION

No other states have openly exchanged information and collaborated on nuclear weapon development to the same extent as Britain and the United States. Some would view the MDA as the core of the Anglo-American special relationship. What the United States provided in technological assistance to the United Kingdom on nuclear weapons, it gained in less concrete but powerful terms. Both countries obtained support for their foreign policy goals and exerted influence on each other's nuclear policies.

Through the MDA and the JOWOGs, which continue to this day, both countries profited from a crosscurrent of ideas and information as well as influence in the diplomatic and international security arena. In the absence of testing, the continued cooperation among scientists on designs, computer simulations, and safety and reliability issues as well as the continuation of the Trident program are likely to provide opportunities for the relationship to grow. Some have surmised that, following the difficulties Blair encountered when he supported the United States in the war in Iraq and in light of UK calls for a world free of nuclear weapons, the United Kingdom might be driven to align itself more with the European Union in the future. Nevertheless, with some 11,000 U.S. military personnel stationed in the United Kingdom, shared bases, daily intelligence, nuclear weapons technology and components, as well as strengthened ties among both countries' defense industries, the defense of the United Kingdom and the United States is so intertwined that it is unlikely to be unraveled. It has been and will most likely continue to be an interdependent mutually assured defense.

NOTES

1. Interviews with more than 30 senior governmental and scientific officials conducted in the United States and United Kingdom, abstracts of which are included in this volume.

2. Formally, the "Agreement between the Government of the United States of America and the Government of the United Kingdom of Great Britain and Northern Ireland for Cooperation on the Uses of Atomic Energy for Mutual Defense Purposes," signed July 3, 1958, hereafter referred to as the MDA. The agreement is of indefinite duration although provisions on transfers of materials and equipment include dates that have been extended by amendment every five or ten years.

3. Winston S. Churchill, "The Sinews of Peace" (speech at Westminster College, Fulton, Missouri, March 5, 1946), http://www.nato.int/docu/speech/1946/s460305a_e.htm.

4. Ibid.

5. Henry Kissinger, *White House Years* (Boston: Little, Brown, 1979), p. 90.

6. Margaret Gowing, *Britain and Atomic Energy, 1939–45* (London: Macmillan, 1964), Appendix II.

7. David J. Hawkins, *Keeping the Peace: The Aldermaston Story* (Bath: Bath Press, 2000), p. 5.

8. Andrew Pierre, *Nuclear Politics: The British Experience with an Independent Strategic Force, 1939–1970* (London: Oxford University Press, 1972), p. 20.

9. Margaret Gowing, "Nuclear Weapons and the 'Special Relationship,'" in *The "Special Relationship": Anglo-American Relations since 1945,* ed. Wm. Roger Louis and Hedley Bull (Oxford: Clarendon Press, 1986), p. 119.

10. This was called Project Encircle. See Ken Young, "A Most Special Relationship: The Origins of Anglo-American Nuclear Strike Planning," *Journal of Cold War Studies* 19, no. 2 (Spring 2007): p. 6.

11. Dwight D. Eisenhower and Harold Macmillan, memorandum of conversation, March 22, 1957, Avia 65/909, National Archives, Kew.

12. Dwight D. Eisenhower and Harold Macmillan, memorandum of conversation, and Sir Richard Powell's note for the record, March 22, 1957, Air 2/13373, National Archives, Kew.

13. Young, "A Most Special Relationship," pp. 17–18.

14. "Supplies of Fissile Material," brief by minister for defence, October 7, 1957, PREM 8/1367, National Archives, Kew.

15. Sir H. Caccia (ambassador of the United Kingdom to the United States), telegram no. 1846 from Washington to the Foreign Office, para. 7, September 14, 1957, National Archives, Kew.

16. Harold Macmillan to Dwight D. Eisenhower, telegram, October 10, 1957, PREM 11/246, National Archives, Kew.

17. "Note to the PM and His Comments," October 15, 1957, PREM 11/2554, National Archives, Kew.

18. For the record of the discussions and the communiqué of October 25, 1957, see PREM 11/2329, dated October 28, 1957, National Archives, Kew.

19. Lewis Strauss, Donald Quarles, Sir Edward Plowden, and Sir Richard Powell, "Report to the President and the Prime Minister," August 21, 1957, CAB 21/4754, p. 1, National Archives, Kew.

20. Ibid., pp. 2, 3.

21. "Ambassador from Powell, Ministry of Defence," November 8, 1957, Prem11/2554, National Archives, Kew.

22. Other reports indicate that the uranium 235 was in fact what is now known as low enriched uranium (LEU), that is, HEU enriched to less than 5 percent. A parallel could be drawn between this arrangement and contemporary discussions over the U.S.-India nuclear agreement.

23. "Visit of Powell and Plowden," November 23, 1957, CAB 21/4754, pp. 1–3, National Archives, Kew. The United States did use the UK facilities on Christmas Island in 1962.

24. For a succinct account of these activities, see "American Nuclear Submarine Machinery, Brief by the Admiralty" [for the prime minister's visit to Washington on June 1958], June 6, 1957, CAB 130/147, National Archives, Kew.

25. Sir H. Caccia (ambassador of the United Kingdom to the United States), telegrams no. 2569 and no. 2570 from Washington to the Foreign Office, December 6, 1957, PREM 11/2554, National Archives, Kew.

26. Sir H. Caccia (ambassador of the United Kingdom to the United States), telegram no. 2578 from Washington to Foreign Office, December 6, 1957, PREM 11/2554, National Archives, Kew.

27. The difference was largely a product of the U.S. plants being operated on electricity generated by hydro plants and in the United Kingdom by coal-fired plants.

28. *Atomic Energy Act of 1954—Amendment, House Report,* U.S. Code Congressional and Administrative News, 85th Congress, 2nd Session (1958), vol. 11, p. 2818.

29. See John Simpson, *The Independent Nuclear State: The United States, Britain, and the Military Atom,* 2nd ed. (Basingstoke: Macmillan, 1986), pp. 135–138.

30. Ibid., p. 138.

31. Harold Macmillan, *Riding the Storm: 1956–1959* (London: McMillan, 1971), p. 494.

32. Ibid., pp. 561–562.

33. Cmnd 537, Treaty series no. 41, 1958. See Annex to this volume.

34. Ibid.

35. Cmnd 859, "Amendment to Agreement . . . for Cooperation on the Uses of Atomic Energy for Mutual Defence Purposes," Treaty series no. 65, 1975.

36. See Simpson, *The Independent Nuclear State*, p. 143.

37. Richard Moore, "British Nuclear Warhead Design, 1958–66: How Much American Help?" *Defence Studies* 4, no. 2 (Summer 2004): p. 212.

38. Ibid., pp. 217–219.

39. Richard E. Neustadt, *Report to JFK: The Skybolt Crisis in Perspective* (Ithaca, N.Y.: Cornell University Press, 1999), p. 71.

40. Cmnd 1915, Bahamas Meetings, December 1962. Text of Joint Communiqués.

41. Cmnd 2108, Polaris Sales Agreement, Treaty series no. 59, 1963.

42. Chevaline, designed to degrade the effectiveness of the Soviet radar, was not deployed until 1982.

43. Cmnd 9434, Amendment to the Agreement . . . for Cooperation on the Uses of Atomic Energy for Mutual Defence Purposes, Treaty series no. 4(85), November 1984.

44. Simpson, *The Independent Nuclear State*, pp. xxxiii–xxxiv.

45. See "The Future of the United Kingdom's Nuclear Deterrent" (London, Stationery Office Limited, December 2006, http://www.mod.uk/NR/rdonlyres/AC00DD79-76D6-4FE3-91A1-6A56B03C092F/0/Defence-WhitePaper2006_Cm6994.pdf.

Part Two

HISTORICAL AND TECHNICAL COOPERATION

2

HOW IT ALL BEGAN

THE ATOMIC BOMB AND THE BRITISH MISSION

ALAN B. CARR

For the past five decades, the United States and the United Kingdom have enjoyed a symbiotic defense relationship. Over the years, the two partners have worked closely under the auspices of the 1958 Mutual Defense Agreement (MDA) to develop robust nuclear weapons and innovative delivery systems. However, this special relationship has roots far deeper than MDA.

The journey to atomic partnership between the United States and United Kingdom proved to be a difficult but very rewarding one. In 1943, at the height of World War II, years of diplomatic efforts culminated in the Quebec Agreement. Under the agreement the United Kingdom provided several of Europe's brightest scientists to the Manhattan Project, the U.S. effort to build the world's first atomic bombs. Most of these scientists, collectively known as the British Mission, were British subjects but others had fled to Britain to escape oppression on the Continent. Together, the scientists of the British Mission and British policymakers made valuable contributions to the development of the atomic bomb, prompting General Leslie R. Groves, head of the project, to later write: "I cannot escape the feeling that without active and continuing British interest there probably would have been no atomic bomb to drop on Hiroshima."[1] The MDA of 1958 represented a renewal of this collaboration, a partnership that originally produced two unique bomb designs in just over two years.[2]

DIFFICULT ROAD TO ATOMIC PARTNERSHIP

In the opening decades of the twentieth century, European scientists made many tremendous discoveries on the way to unraveling the secrets of the atom. Men and women from England, France, Germany, Italy, and many other countries formed an international scientific community without borders, and research thrived for many years under these conditions. Unfortunately, this fruitful period was interrupted by the Second World War, and many of Europe's great scientists, a number of whom were Jewish, fled the Continent's fascist regimes, seeking refuge in Britain and the United States. During the next few years, many of these expatriates played pivotal roles in building the atomic bombs.

In 1933, the year Adolf Hitler became chancellor of Germany, a young physicist named Rudolf Peierls left Germany to study in England. Peierls chose to stay in England after his fellowship expired and accepted a professorship at the University of Birmingham in 1937. Two years later another physicist, Otto Frisch, an Austrian, also left Germany and came to Birmingham. In early 1940, only a few months after the outbreak of World War II, Frisch and Peierls coauthored a memo to a British colleague at the university describing an entirely new and devastating type of weapon made possible by the discovery of fission. They wrote: "The attached detailed report concerns the possibility of constructing a 'super-bomb' which utilizes the energy stored in atomic nuclei as a source of energy"; they also noted that the blast would "produce a temperature comparable to that in the interior of the sun."[3] By late March, the memo had reached the highest levels of the British government, which immediately responded by sponsoring a study on the feasibility of building an atomic weapon. A special group called the Maud Committee undertook the assignment and quickly started exploring the possibility of weaponizing the atom.[4]

As the Maud Committee prepared its reports, a small British group led by Sir Henry Tizard went to the United States to share Britain's latest advancements in military technology. Although the United States officially remained neutral in the war, President Franklin D. Roosevelt had clearly demonstrated a personal commitment to Great Britain and the shrinking number of European democracies. The Tizard mission, which arrived shortly after the fall of France, offered information on radar, jet engine technology, and atomic energy.[5] During the visit Tizard and his colleagues discovered that Britain had a clear lead in atomic energy research over the United States, but in late summer 1940, as the Battle of Britain unfolded, the futuristic and uncertain technology of nuclear weapons seemingly possessed little value in combating the Nazi onslaught.

In the months following Tizard's visit, Britain fended off the German air force, but Hitler managed to consolidate his hold on western Europe and went on the attack in the Balkans and North Africa. In July 1941, only weeks after the Germans invaded Russia, the Maud Committee finally completed its work, predicting that under ideal circumstances an atomic bomb could be ready in late 1943 and was "likely to lead to decisive results in the war."[6] The British quickly provided the United States with a copy of the report, which stirred senior U.S. policymakers to action. The director of the Office of Scientific Research and Development (OSRD), Vannevar Bush, and the chairman of the National Defense Research Committee (NDRC), James Conant, successfully petitioned Roosevelt for support and resources in October 1941. The Maud reports succeeded in changing U.S. priorities, but a true atomic partnership remained nearly two years away.[7]

Still holding the atomic lead, Britain now hesitated to become the partner of the United States in a full-scale unified atomic bomb project. The British government endorsed the continued exchange of information but, at the behest of senior scientific advisers, privately insisted upon independent projects. Despite this, the U.S. project rapidly moved forward, spurred on by the Maud Committee's findings and the December 7, 1941, Japanese attack on Pearl Harbor. During the first half of 1942, the U.S. program caught and surpassed its British counterpart, and Bush and Conant now pushed for more secrecy. The United States possessed all the resources to produce an atomic bomb, which looked more and more realistic with every passing day, as well as the expertise necessary for exploiting the atom as an energy source, and Bush and Conant saw little reason to share information with Britain. Roosevelt supported this stance and placed restrictions on the exchange of information. As a result, cooperative exchanges came to a virtual halt in the remaining months of 1942.[8] Britain had lost all hope for an equal partnership in the atomic venture and now hoped to salvage the role of junior teammate.

Much of the information impasse centered on postwar control of atomic energy. Bush and Conant feared that Britain would use U.S. technological innovations for postwar industrial purposes although, in actuality, British leaders had no interest in postwar commercial gain.

The breakthrough finally came in July 1943 when Bush, Secretary of War Henry L. Stimson, and Prime Minister Winston Churchill met in London to discuss the matter. Churchill, after emphasizing that Britain's interests lay only in developing atomic weapons, proposed a series of conditions that would provide the foundation for a formal pact between the two nations.[9]

The "Articles of Agreement Governing Collaboration between the Authorities of the U.S.A. and the U.K. in the matter of Tube Alloys," or the Quebec Agreement as it is more commonly known, was signed August 19, 1943. The United States and the United Kingdom agreed never to use atomic weapons against each other and never to use atomic weapons against or share information with a third party without each other's consent. The agreement also established the Combined Policy Committee to govern the exchange of information. Bush and Conant were glad to find an additional provision as well, which stated: "The Prime Minister expressly disclaims any interests in . . . industrial and commercial aspects beyond what may be considered by the President of the United States to be fair and just and in harmony with the economic welfare of the world."[10]

At last, the atomic partnership had been sealed. Although the United States would play the dominant role in developing atomic weapons, Britain had secured its position as an important and exclusive partner in the endeavor. British leaders immediately began assembling a team of the nation's top scientific minds to send across the sea to the United States. This group, known as the British Mission, would play an important role in the years to come, working side by side with the Americans on one of history's largest, most secret military projects.

COMING TO AMERICA

Almost immediately, members of the British Mission began arriving in the United States. James Chadwick, the leader of the group, arrived in Washington with Peierls the day after the Quebec Agreement was signed.[11] In the year and a half since the attack on Pearl Harbor, the U.S. atomic venture had been transferred to the Army Corps of Engineers and secretly dubbed the Manhattan Project.[12] With an unlimited budget, the highest priority for resources, and Gen. Leslie Groves at the helm, the project had flourished. Major installations were either completed or well under construction in Hanford, Washington; Oak Ridge, Tennessee; and Los Alamos, New Mexico. America's best scien-

James Chadwick, leader of the British Mission (left), and General Leslie Groves. Photo courtesy of Los Alamos National Laboratory Archives.

tists and technicians staffed these unique facilities. Impressed with the Manhattan Project's progress, Chadwick began to collaborate closely with Groves in order to maximize the talent Britain brought to the table.

Britain provided many scientists who boasted a wide range of expertise. Initially, many worked on methods of separating the fissionable isotope of uranium, uranium 235, from its far more abundant sibling, uranium 238. For a short time, several worked on the gaseous diffusion method of separation, but British participation in this effort ended in late 1944. Other teams, such as the one assigned to assist Ernest Lawrence with his electromagnetic method of separation, remained throughout the war.[13] Another team, and by far the most well known of the British contingents, came to the remote outpost of Los Alamos to work on designing the bombs. This cosmopolitan group would make significant contributions to the successful development of the atomic bombs, leaving a legacy of cooperation and productivity that would long outlive the Manhattan Project.

Several scientists arrived in Los Alamos under the auspices of the British Mission. There were the Britons, of course; they included Chadwick, Anthony French, James Hughes, Derrik Littler, William Marley, Donald Marshall, Philip Moon, William Penney, Michael Poole, Harold Sheard, Tony Skyrme, Geoffrey Taylor, Ernest Titterton, and James Tuck as well as many fellow Europeans. Among them were Egon Bretscher of Switzerland; Boris Davison, a native of Russia; the Austrian, Otto Frisch; two Germans, Rudolph Peierls and Klaus Fuchs; Carson Mark, a Canadian; George Placzek of Czechoslovakia; and the

Pole, Joseph Rotblat. Niels Bohr, the great Danish Nobel laureate, also came to Los Alamos occasionally as part of the British Mission, bringing his son and future laureate Aage with him.[14] The two Danes, who served as consultants, offered ideas and contributed to the international atmosphere that resembled the peaceful years prior to World War II.

Although the scientists of Los Alamos welcomed the camaraderie of the incoming Europeans, General Groves remained mildly skeptical of his new guests. Shortly after the Quebec Agreement was signed, Groves asked British officials for a statement ensuring the loyalty of the British Mission scientists. After receiving an "inconclusive" initial response, the British offered a more "definite" one that guaranteed, according to Groves, "that each member had been investigated as thoroughly as an employee of ours engaged on the same type of work." As it turned out, Groves's doubts proved well founded. Fuchs, a German-born communist who had become a naturalized British citizen in 1942, passed secret information to the Soviet Union while in Britain and on several occasions during his time at Los Alamos. Regarding this breach, Groves later penned: "The United Kingdom not only failed us, but herself as well."[15]

BUILDING THE ATOMIC BOMBS

Despite Fuchs's treachery, he remained a very good theoretical physicist who played a prominent though little-known role in developing the atomic bomb. Many of his British Mission colleagues played important parts as well. Shortly after the war, Major Ralph Carlisle Smith, a senior administrator at Los Alamos, wrote: "the British Mission as a group, have substantially complete knowledge of the gun assembly and implosion assembly of fissile material, the actual design of the aerial bombs employing these principles, the possible future developments including the 'Super' or Thermonuclear Reaction type Ordnance," and familiarity with reactors and fissile material processing techniques.[16] The "substantially complete knowledge" possessed by the British Mission came as a direct result of the group's involvement in virtually every aspect of the project.

The British Mission's contribution began with its leader Rudolf Peierls, who took over for Chadwick because the latter's duties required him to remain close to senior U.S. leaders, such as Groves, in Washington. Peierls led not only the British Mission at Los Alamos but also the

Theoretical Division's Implosion Hydrodynamics Group, one of the groups most responsible for developing the implosion weapon, which relied on a symmetrical explosion to compress a core of fissile material to initiate the chain reaction. One of Peierls's best scientists was Fuchs, whom he had personally recruited to join the project. In a July 1949 memo, Ralph Carlisle Smith stated: "Fuchs and Peierls provided two-thirds of the team which handled the hydrodynamics in [the Theoretical] Division which made the implosion development possible. They both contributed heavily to all phases of the weapon development, including implosion and Super."[17] Just as implosion was becoming increasingly important to the overall success of the project Peierls and Fuchs arrived, providing expertise in an area of critical need.

Peierls, who was dubbed "the most effective group leader in the Theoretical Division" by his division leader, Hans Bethe, was not the only wartime laboratory group leader among the British contingent.[18] Frisch, his collaborator at the University of Birmingham, served as the leader of the Critical Assemblies Group, another group central to the implosion effort. Bretscher led the Super Experiments group, which explored the feasibility of a thermonuclear or hydrogen bomb and, toward the end of the war, George Placzek led the Composite Weapon Group in the Theoretical Division, which explored the possibility of designing a core for the implosion system that used both plutonium and uranium.[19]

Many other British Mission scientists, who "were almost without exception men of outstanding caliber," played key roles as well.[20] Tuck, for example, who had already been awarded the Order of the British Empire by King George VI for his work on shaped explosive charges, was instrumental in proposing the high explosive (HE) lens system for the implosion device.[21] Tuck, along with the brilliant Hungarian mathematician John von Neumann and physicist Seth Neddermeyer, argued that a lens system could redirect the force of the initial HE explosion evenly on the bomb's fissile core, maximizing the explosion's impact. This crucial innovation became a standard feature on many early atomic weapons. Tuck also proposed a unique design for the implosion bomb's initiator, a component intended to improve the nuclear efficiency of the weapon. During his wartime career at Los Alamos, he even studied possible methods of igniting a hydrogen bomb.[22] So innovative was the work of Tuck and his colleagues that they jointly submitted two patents for implosion assembly components. Other

British Mission scientists followed suit. As of January 1946, the laboratory's docketed patent cases included five of Frisch's inventions, two of Titterton's, and several innovations developed by small teams that included Bohr, Frisch, Peierls, Titterton, and Tuck.[23]

As the summer of 1945 approached, preparations for the field test of the "gadget," as the implosion device was known, kicked into high gear. Some of the British Mission scientists would play a part in the event, dubbed the Trinity test, and still more would witness it. Geoffrey Taylor, who had worked on several aspects of the implosion system as a consultant in the Theoretical Division, was one of the laboratory's leading experts in explosives phenomena. According to Ralph Carlisle Smith, Taylor "personally predicted the phenomena which occurred at Trinity, including the mushroom [cloud], the heights reached, and the effect of wind on the distribution of particles."[24]

Taylor also made another contribution by encouraging his fellow British scientist, William "Bill" Penney, to join him in Los Alamos. An expert on blast waves, Penney joined Taylor in diagnosing the Trinity test and developed a "brilliantly simple" method for measuring the power of its blast. As Peierls recalled decades later: "He had some wooden boxes prepared with circular holes of various sizes, covered with paper. The blast would puncture the paper covering the larger holes but not the smaller ones, and by noting the size of the largest holes still intact, one could find the strength of the wave."[25] Penney's expertise in blast waves and their effects on structures also made him an ideal candidate to serve on the Target Committee, a group set up by Groves at the urging of General George C. Marshall, chief of staff of the U.S. Army, to select potential Japanese targets for atomic bombing and to develop the mission criteria for the bombing runs.[26] Penney later played a direct role in the success of the combat delivery missions by serving as a consultant on Tinian, the island from which the atomic strikes against Hiroshima and Nagasaki were launched.

The atomic bombs helped bring World War II to an abrupt halt. The scientists of the British Mission had played an important part in building the bombs, and now they would take a lead role in celebrating the laboratory's great accomplishment. A few weeks after the armistice, the British Mission hosted a formal party in celebration of "The Birth of the Atomic Age." The British wives, led by Genia Peierls, planned the party and spared no expense, purchasing the finest whisky, brandy, and, most important, port wine for toasting Churchill, Roosevelt, and

Performance at British party at Los Alamos, 1945. Photo courtesy of Los Alamos National Laboratory Archives.

the Grand Alliance. Mrs. Peierls, Peg Titterton, Else Placzek, Honi Bretscher, and Winifred Moon prepared the meal—soup, steak, kidney pie, and trifle—which was followed by the toasts, offered by Tuck. Tuck also authored a skit tracing the mission's "hazardous journey to the Unknown Desert," which satirized security regulations, housing, and the Trinity test. Not only did the British excel in science and engineering, but in acting as well.[27] The party itself represented the culmination of the British Mission's social contribution to the Los Alamos project. In the confined, primitive community of wartime Los Alamos, Frisch and Titterton's soothing piano melodies, Genia Peierls's parties, and even Fuchs's skill as a ballroom dancer served as pleasant distractions from the serious, unending work of building atomic bombs.

LEGACY OF THE BRITISH CONTRIBUTION
Shortly after the war, approximately half of the British team prepared a memorandum outlining the potential dangers of atomic weapons. They endorsed international cooperation, writing: "if there is to be any hope of avoiding the catastrophe of a war waged with atomic bombs, it is necessary to have 1) International supervision of materials and facilities, and 2) Free movement of scientific information and personnel among all countries."[28] Cooperation among all countries never materialized, and unfortunately the atomic alliance between the United States and United Kingdom quickly collapsed. Hoping to maintain the U.S. monopoly on nuclear weapons, Congress passed the Atomic Energy Act of 1946 (also known as the McMahon Act) that included a provision stating: "That until Congress declares by joint resolution

that effective and enforceable international safeguards against the use of atomic energy for destructive purposes have been established, there shall be no exchange of information with other nations with respect to the use of atomic energy for industrial purposes."[29] Not even the United Kingdom, after all the information and scientific talent it had shared, was exempted.

Another setback in U.S.-UK atomic cooperation would occur as well. In early 1950, Fuchs was arrested in Britain for espionage. According to a U.S. Atomic Energy Commission report, Fuchs, "a highly esteemed scientist," provided detailed information to the Soviet Union on the Trinity device, the gun assembly, and thermonuclear weapons.[30] Right after Fuchs's arrest, his old colleague Peierls went to visit him in prison. When pressed for an explanation of his actions, Fuchs responded: "You must remember what I went through under the Nazis. Besides, it was always my intention, when I had helped the Russians to take over everything, to get up and tell them what is wrong with their system." Peierls recalls: "Shaken by the arrogance and naiveté of this statement, I returned home."[31]

The McMahon Act and the Fuchs affair, as it turns out, were only aberrations in an otherwise cordial and productive relationship. After the war, before the passage of the McMahon Act, a handful of British scientists remained at Los Alamos. Placzek became the leader of the Theoretical Division and, after developing health problems, handed the reins over to the Canadian, Carson Mark. Titterton became a group leader as did Tuck, who, after a temporary return to Britain, became a U.S. citizen and spent the remainder of his career at Los Alamos.

The scientists who returned permanently to Britain found great success as well. Frisch became the first Physics Division leader at the Atomic Energy Research Establishment's Harwell Laboratory, and Penney went on to lead Britain's independent atomic weapons program. Immediately following Britain's first atomic bomb test in 1952, Churchill sent Penney a telegram offering congratulations and informing him of his new title, "Sir William."[32] In 1968 Peierls, the soft-spoken German native who had provided such splendid leadership to the British Mission, was knighted for his contributions to physics.

All too often, the epitaph for the British has been limited to a couple of sentences stripped from the memoir of General Groves: "On the whole, the contribution of the British was helpful but not vital. Their work at Los Alamos was of high quality but their numbers were too small to enable them to play a major role." Taken alone, this statement is misleading. In considering the overall British contribution, which included both technical and political support, Groves is quick to acknowledge that "Prime Minister Churchill was probably the best friend the Manhattan Project ever had"; continuing, he "emerged as our project's most effective and enthusiastic supporter; for that we shall always be in his debt."[33] Churchill's support included providing America with some of the best scientists he had, and it is important to realize that despite the small number of British scientists they still managed to play a significant role. Working with their U.S. counterparts, they set a precedent for nuclear cooperation that would be acknowledged and imitated by scientists half a generation later after the passage of the MDA of 1958. This spirit of partnership, forged during the darkest days of World War II, lives on today as British and U.S. scientists continue to work together.

NOTES

1. Leslie R. Groves, *Now It Can Be Told* (London: Andre Deutsch, 1963), p. 408.
2. Work on bomb designs at Los Alamos started, roughly, in April 1943 and culminated in the Trinity test of July 16, 1945.
3. The Frisch-Peierls memo is reproduced in Ferenc Morton Szasz, *British Scientists and the Manhattan Project* (New York: Saint Martin's, 1992), pp. 141–147.
4. When the Germans invaded Denmark, physicist Niels Bohr (while making his escape to Sweden) telegraphed Frisch: "Tell [Professor J. D.] Cockroft and Maud Ray Kent." Frisch interpreted "Maud Ray Kent" to be some sort of cryptic reference to the nuclear project, thus the name "Maud" was adopted by the committee. In actuality, Maud Ray was a woman who had served as a governess to Bohr's children and was living in the county of Kent. See Margaret Gowing, *Britain and Atomic Energy, 1939–1945* (New York: Saint Martin's, 1964), p. 45.
5. John Baylis, *Anglo-American Defense Relations, 1939–1984: The Special Relationship,* 2nd ed. (New York: Saint Martin's, 1984), p. 5.
6. Maud Committee, *Report by M.A.U.D. Committee on the Use of Uranium for a Bomb* (July 1941), 3 and appendix I, *Nuclear Energy as an Explosive,* section 2 (Los Alamos: Los Alamos National Laboratory Archives).
7. Barton J. Bernstein, "The Uneasy Alliance: Roosevelt, Churchill, and the Atomic Bomb, 1940–1945," *Western Political Quarterly* 29 (1976): pp. 204–205.
8. Ibid., pp. 207–211.

9. Richard G. Hewlett and Oscar E. Anderson Jr., *The New World, 1939/1946,* vol. 1, *A History of the United States Atomic Energy Commission* (University Park: Pennsylvania State University Press, 1962), pp. 275–277.

10. The Quebec Agreement is reproduced in Baylis, *Anglo-American Defense Relations,* pp. 23–24.

11. Szasz, *British Scientists,* p. 12.

12. The project was headquartered in Manhattan, in New York City; hence its name.

13. Dennis Fakley, "The British Mission," *Los Alamos Science* (Winter/Spring 1983): p. 187.

14. An unpublished paper by physicist Cory Coll, "The Participation of Foreign-Born Scientists at Site Y," was particularly helpful in compiling this list.

15. Groves, *Now It Can Be Told,* pp. 143–144. Groves further explains: "Since Fuchs was uncovered, it has often been suggested that I should have investigated each British subject before he was admitted to the project. This would have been most presumptuous and, in fact, impossible without complete infringement of British rights and without the co-operation of the British Government, which we would not have obtained. It was a British responsibility. As partners in the atomic field each nation had to be responsible for its own personnel."

16. Ralph Carlisle Smith, letter to T. O. Jones, September 18, 1945 (Los Alamos: Los Alamos National Laboratory Archives). During the war, Smith enjoyed a unique perspective at Los Alamos as group leader for the laboratory's patent office.

17. Ralph Carlisle Smith, letter to Carroll L. Wilson, July 18, 1949, Los Alamos National Laboratory Archives. Smith writes: "While all the statements are my interpretation of the facts, they have been substantiated in substance by Hans Bethe, consultant, and formerly Theoretical Physics Division Leader at Los Alamos, and by Carson Mark, a former member of the British Mission and present leader of the Theoretical Physics Division of the Laboratory."

18. H. A. Bethe, letter to Carroll L. Wilson, July 18, 1949, Los Alamos National Laboratory Archives.

19. Alison Kerr, letter to Karl Braithwaite, February 8, 1983, Los Alamos National Laboratory Archives.

20. N. E. Bradbury, letter to Carroll L. Wilson, July 18, 1949, Los Alamos National Laboratory Archives. Norris Bradbury succeeded J. Robert Oppenheimer as laboratory director in late 1945.

21. D. A. Baker et al., Obituary for James Leslie Tuck, *Physics Today,* March 1981, p. 87.

22. Smith to Wilson, July 18, 1949.

23. Ralph Carlisle Smith, letter to James L. Tuck, January 29, 1946, Los Alamos National Laboratory Archives.

24. Smith to Wilson, July 18, 1949.

25. Rudolf Peierls, Obituary for William George Penney, *Physics Today,* October 1991, p. 140.

26. Vincent C. Jones, *Manhattan: The Army and the Atomic Bomb* (Washington, D.C.: Center of Military History, United States Army, 1988), pp. 528–530. Minutes of the Target Committee meetings are available on the Los Alamos National Laboratory Web site, http://www.lanl.gov/history/atomicbomb/victory.shtml.

27. Bernice Brode, *Tales of Los Alamos: Life on the Mesa, 1943–1945* (Los Alamos: Los Alamos Historical Society, 1997), pp. 103–107.

28. "Memorandum from British Scientists at the Los Alamos Laboratory, New Mexico," no date, Los Alamos National Laboratory Archives.

29. James D. Nuse, ed., *Legislative History of the Atomic Energy Act of 1946* (Public Law 585, 79th Congress), vol. 1, *Principal Documents* (Washington, D.C.: U.S. Atomic Energy Commission, 1965), p. 13.

30. Atomic Energy Commission, "Memorandum for Information: Evaluation of Fuchs Case by the Committee of Senior Responsible Reviewers," May 8, 1950, annex to appendix, Los Alamos National Laboratory Archives.

31. Rudolf Peierls, *Bird of Passage: Recollections of a Physicist* (Princeton: Princeton University Press, 1985), pp. 223–224.

32. Margaret Gowing, *Independence and Deterrence, Britain and Atomic Energy, 1945–1952,* vol. 2, *Policy Execution* (New York: Saint Martin's, 1974), pp. 494–495.

33. Groves, *Now It Can Be Told,* p. 408.

3

HISTORIC BARRIERS TO ANGLO-AMERICAN NUCLEAR COOPERATION

ANDREW BROWN

Despite being the closest of allies, with shared values and language, attempts by the United Kingdom and the United States to reach accords on nuclear matters generated distrust and resentment but no durable arrangements until the Mutual Defense Agreement of 1958. There were times when the perceived national interests of the two countries were unsynchronized or at odds; periods when political leaders did not see eye to eye or made secret agreements that remained just that; and when espionage, propaganda, and public opinion caused additional tensions.

STATUS IMBALANCE

The Magna Carta of the nuclear age is the two-part Frisch-Peierls memorandum. It was produced by two European émigrés, Otto Frisch and Rudolf Peierls, at Birmingham University in the spring of 1940. Unlike Einstein's famous letter to President Franklin D. Roosevelt, with its vague warning that a powerful new bomb might be constructed from uranium, the Frisch-Peierls memorandum set out detailed technical arguments leading to the conclusion that "a moderate amount of U-235 [highly enriched uranium] would indeed constitute an extremely efficient explosive." Like Einstein, Frisch and Peierls were worried that the Germans might already be working toward an atomic bomb against which there would be no defense. By suggesting "a counter-threat with a similar bomb," they first enunciated the concept of mutual deterrence and recommended "start[ing] production as soon as possible, even if it is not intended to use the bomb as a means of attack."[1] Professor Mark Oliphant from Birmingham convinced the UK authorities that "the whole thing must be taken rather seriously,"[2] and a small group of senior scientists came together as the Maud Committee.

In July 1941 James Chadwick (the physics laureate who had overseen a year of intense research at leading English universities) drafted the Maud report, concisely detailing the necessary steps required to construct a uranium bomb.[3] The report avoided any discussion of the atomic bomb as a deterrent and, perhaps because of the dire military situation, viewed it simply as a new weapon of "decisive possibilities."[4] By September 1941, scientific advisers, Prime Minister Winston Churchill and the chiefs of staff had all accepted the Maud recommendation that work should continue with the highest priority and "on the increasing scale necessary to obtain the weapon in the shortest possible time." Britain was thus the first state to take the decision to acquire an atom bomb.

The Maud report also called for continued collaboration with the United States. Although several U.S. centers had begun research into uranium and the novel element, plutonium, they lacked the urgency and coherence of the British project that was propelled by the immediate Nazi threat. The first reaction from Washington was ambivalent— Vannevar Bush and James Conant (Roosevelt's chief science advisers) thought "the time is ripe for a full examination of whether the whole business should be continued at all."[5] After a further period of digestion came the first big opportunity for Anglo-American cooperation. But feeling that they were ahead in the science and letting imperialism blind them to the economic realities, the British showed no enthusiasm for President Roosevelt's proposal of a joint project. Oliphant, who toured the United States raising awareness of the Maud report, was one of the few who understood the extent of the U.S. prewar atomic program. A year later it had expanded into the Manhattan Project, driven by the unrelenting General Leslie Groves.

By contrast, Tube Alloys, the British atomic weapon project, failed to make any worthwhile progress, and Sir John Anderson, the minister in charge, warned Churchill that the construction necessary for the production of fissile material was out of the question in wartime Britain. Britain was, as Churchill said, "a struggling country beset by deadly foes." One year after the Maud report had optimistically predicted a bomb might be ready by the end of 1943, there was not the steel or the skilled men available to build even a pilot isotope separation plant. Anderson's concern that the pioneering research work done in England was "a dwindling asset"[6] was borne out by the subsequent reluctance on the U.S.'s part to countenance British scientists joining their project. The standoff was not resolved until the Quebec Agreement of August 1943 allowed a pooling of effort: the agreement also stipulated that no information about the project would be communicated to third parties; nor would the weapon be used against an enemy without each other's consent.

The Quebec Agreement set the terms for collaboration on the Manhattan Project through a Combined Policy Committee (CPC), but its sway did not survive the end of the war. As wartime allies, the two nations envisioned their duopoly continuing into the future (after cornering the world uranium supply), but peace brought fresh domestic and international complexities that eclipsed bilateral considerations. A joint declaration from the leaders of the United States, the United Kingdom, and Canada in November 1945 recognized that no national monopoly of atomic power could exist and that atomic weapons more powerful than those used against Japan were possible; it also called for a UN commission on atomic energy to guarantee collective security. In the meantime, there would be continued scientific exchanges between the three countries.[7]

Bernard Baruch, a veteran financier summoned by President Harry S. Truman for diplomatic duty, proposed at the UN his version of the State Department's Acheson-Lilienthal plan, suggesting that all "dangerous" activities like uranium mining and the separation of fissile materials should be controlled by an international atomic development agency; then, after the atomic development agency was successfully established, the United States would scrap the world's only existing nuclear arsenal. While the British would have supported such a plan, the Soviets, for a variety of reasons, resisted it.[8] The spectrum of opinion in the United States ranged from those who believed that the country alone possessed the secret of making atom bombs and should preserve its military advantage at all costs to those who realized there were no scientific secrets, just technical and industrial barriers, and who believed ultimate security would be best served by an effective system of international control.

Aside from the question of international control, Truman was faced with the need for domestic legislation to transfer authority over the

U.S. nuclear program from the secret, U.S. Army–run Manhattan Project to a civilian-led Atomic Energy Commission (AEC) that would report to Congress.[9] The legislation to achieve this transformation was introduced by Senator Brien McMahon (D-Conn.), and it originally offered the prospect of some international exchange of scientific information. By the time Truman signed it into law as the Atomic Energy Act (AEA) in August 1946, the communication of "restricted data" (which included civilian as well as military information) was punishable by death. In the absence of any international agreements, the AEA shaped the U.S. foreign atomic policy.

The British initiated contingency plans for plutonium production as early as September 1945; in January 1947, when there was no international consensus in sight at the UN and the strictures of the AEA supplanted all the wartime agreements from the U.S. point of view, the UK government secretly launched an independent nuclear weapons program. Despite the wartime depredations and the calamitous economic collapse following the sudden termination of Lend-Lease, Britannia was still the world's top cop, and many in Whitehall believed Britain's authority depended on an imperial navy and troops garrisoned across the globe. Not only were the operational costs of this bloated military unsupportable, the opportunity costs in terms of men and materials ensured continuing austerity at home. With the principal economic ministers excluded from the secret January meeting, Foreign Secretary Ernest Bevin carried the day by asserting, "We could not afford to acquiesce in an American monopoly of this new development," and "We've got to have the bloody Union Jack on top of it."[10]

The same month in Congress, the Joint Committee on Atomic Energy (JCAE) began contentious confirmation hearings on Truman's nominations to the civilian AEC. For the first time in the United States there was to be some democratic scrutiny of atomic policy, and the AEC was mandated by the 1946 Atomic Energy Act to keep the JCAE informed. Two awkward skeletons from previous agreements with the British needed to be disclosed: first, the Quebec Agreement required the United States to obtain British "consent" before using the atomic bomb; second, the British were receiving half the uranium shipped from the Congo while the burgeoning U.S. program was critically short of raw material.[11] These concessions sat uneasily with the new Truman doctrine of getting tough with the Soviet Union, especially with those who regarded the atomic bomb as the ultimate guarantee of security.

George Kennan, the diplomat who helped harden Truman's attitude toward the USSR, in August 1947 pronounced the UN atomic negotiations worthless, and the U.S. administration turned back to the CPC as a forum in which to negotiate with Britain and Canada. After months of intense negotiations, a modus vivendi was concluded that erased the wartime Quebec Agreement, boosted the U.S. supply of uranium, and allowed the British to receive technical information on the grounds it would advance "common defense and security."[12] The Pentagon was not convinced that the United Kingdom was a secure site to build atomic plants, and when the CPC was informed (by Donald Maclean from the British embassy) that the United Kingdom was going to build atomic weapons, the extent of technical cooperation, especially regarding plutonium production, and atomic intelligence sharing became controversial.

Internal debate was still going on more than a year later in Washington, when the shocking news that the USSR had exploded a nuclear device increased the tensions. The U.S. monopoly was over, and the United Kingdom now pressed for complete collaboration, including over nuclear weapons. But the United States had achieved its objectives from the modus vivendi, and the exposure of Klaus Fuchs as a spy in February 1950 ended any small prospect of a joint program. There was deep unease in London that U.S. aircraft (potentially to be armed with atomic bombs) had been stationed in the United Kingdom since the 1948 Berlin airlift without any explicit formula governing their deployment. Whereas the Pentagon worried about the security of atomic bombs stored in the United Kingdom, the British began to view those bombs as a potential cause for Soviet retribution against their island that had become a forward U.S. base in the unfolding Cold War. The British were in the dark about the U.S. strategic air plan, which severely limited their capacity to plan any defense measures.

The United Kingdom became the third member of the nuclear club in October 1952 with the detonation of a plutonium device; it came at a time when Britain's conventional defense costs were finally recognized as ruinous and led to renewed hope that the overall defense budget could be cut without detriment to national security.[13] The United States, which now had a formidable stockpile of fission weapons, initiated a super club a month later with a thermonuclear explosion at Eniwetok atoll, and the Soviets followed suit in August 1953. The United Kingdom was increasingly anxious about its position, squeezed between the two superpowers. During the Korean War, there had been a casual reference to the use of atomic weapons by Truman, and after the Eisenhower administration's "New Look" review proposed that security and solvency were achievable through nuclear armaments, Secretary of State John Foster Dulles announced a policy of massive retaliation would be followed.

The United Kingdom, wary of potential U.S. adventurism and fearful about a nuclear exchange with the Soviets vaporizing British cities, felt compelled to develop its own H-bomb. It seemed to offer the only way to restrain one superpower while deterring the other. In recommending the decision in July 1954, Churchill stated that the possession of the most up-to-date nuclear weapons was essential to maintaining influence as a world power and supported the main policy goal of preventing major war.

In the summer of 1956, the U.S. Air Force decided that it would share some of its strategic targeting plans with the Royal Air Force now that the British V-bomber force was at last coming into service, armed with a few fission bombs. There was also tentative agreement to site some Thor missiles in the United Kingdom.[14] Negotiations ceased during the Suez crisis, a period that demonstrated the limitations of both Britain's friendship with the United States (which was completely unsupportive of British and French efforts to topple President Nasser and deny the Egyptians control of the canal) and its independent deterrence (Khrushchev, whose troops were busily invading Hungary, hinted that nuclear retaliation against both the United Kingdom and France over Suez was possible).

Anglo-American relations were at a postwar low, but early in 1957 discussions about strategic coordination resumed both at the chiefs-of-staff level and between Eisenhower and the new prime minister, Harold Macmillan. Macmillan shrewdly built on this rapprochement later in the year, when the U.S. defense establishment suddenly felt vulnerable with the unheralded Sputnik launches. The outcome was the Declaration of Common Purpose that promised to wipe the slate clean and to begin anew Anglo-American collaboration on nuclear policy.[15]

STATESMEN AND THEIR ADVISERS

The international problems that flow from the possession of nuclear weapons are so grave that they demand the personal attention of national leaders. For the early history of the nuclear age, it is rewarding to examine the interactions between the Anglo-American pairings of Churchill-Roosevelt, Attlee-Truman, Churchill-Eisenhower, and Macmillan-Eisenhower to see where collaboration broke down. Although the ultimate responsibility rested at the top, the roles of trusted advisers should not be underestimated, especially in the case of Churchill whose loyalty to Lord Cherwell, the Oxford physicist turned politician, was unbounded. It was Cherwell who warned Churchill, just before the Maud report appeared, that "whoever possesses such a [uranium enrichment] plant should be able to dictate terms to the rest of the world. However much I trust my neighbour, and depend on him, I am very much averse to putting myself completely at his mercy and I would, therefore, not press the Americans to undertake this work."[16]

Once the Anglophobic General Groves took charge of the Manhattan Project, he was able to persuade Roosevelt and his scientific advisers that any exchange of information was to be strictly limited. Curiously neither Cherwell nor Groves interfered with the remarkable wartime attempts of the Danish physicist Niels Bohr to promote a new policy of international openness regarding atomic weapons as a way to avoid a postwar arms race. Although Bohr gained a sympathetic audience from Roosevelt, Churchill reproached Cherwell for bringing Bohr to see him and was able to convince the ailing FDR to dismiss his radical proposals, opting instead for "full collaboration" in military and civilian atomic enterprises to continue after the war "until terminated by joint agreement."[17] This 1944 accord, the Hyde Park aide-mémoire, was never disclosed by Roosevelt to any member of his government and proved to be a dead letter.

Clement Attlee (a man so modest and self-effacing that Churchill quipped, "an empty taxi arrived at 10 Downing St. and out stepped Attlee") proved a quick study in nuclear affairs and developed the most detailed understanding of the implications of any political leader of his time. Within weeks of taking office he wrote to Truman identifying atomic bombs as posing such a threat to the future of mankind that they demanded "a new valuation of what are called national interests."[18] At his behest, the tripartite meeting with Canada was held in Washington in November 1945 that resulted in a declaration urging the UN to set up a commission to oversee the elimination of atomic weapons and the imposition of safeguards so that all could share the peaceful benefits of atomic energy. The declaration was meant to replace the Quebec Agreement but to keep provisions about prior consultation on the use of weapons and the allocation of raw material. Vannevar Bush, General Groves, and Secretary of State James F. Byrnes opposed its terms, and Truman soon abrogated it. Attlee's next trip to Washington came five years later to receive Truman's reassurance that he had not authorized the use of atomic bombs in Korea; Secretary of State Dean Acheson had to restrain the president from pledging to obtain British consent before ordering any such use, and no firm text was forthcoming.[19]

When Churchill returned to office in 1951, he was not sure of the need for an independent bomb program, arguing that the United Kingdom "should have the art rather than the article."[20] Cherwell soon convinced him that the United Kingdom must continue to make its own bombs and not rely exclusively on the United States. Churchill's outlook was obscured by the mists of his wartime relationship with FDR, and he confidently expected that, when he traveled to Washington in January 1952, he would be able to shame the Truman administration into granting the United Kingdom "a reasonable share of what they have made so largely on our initiative and substantial scientific contribution."[21] Even though he achieved no tangible success, the election of Eisenhower rekindled his wartime optimism. Eisenhower was persuaded that the 1946 Atomic Energy Act imposed unreasonable restrictions on America's NATO allies and should be amended; but there were few practical benefits to the United Kingdom, in part because Lewis Strauss (the special assistant to the president on atomic affairs) took a consistently less liberal position than his boss.[22]

The short-lived Eden government collapsed in the wake of Suez, bringing Macmillan, another wartime friend of Ike's, to 10 Downing Street. Macmillan had experienced the frustration of being minister of defence in Churchill's last cabinet, when he reached the conclusion that "there is really no protection against a nuclear attack, certainly in these islands. The only protection is the deterrent of the counter attack."[23] As chancellor of the exchequer under Eden, Macmillan gloomily reflected that expenditure on the United Kingdom's still excessive armed forces had broken the back of the economy without providing any real national security.

When, in the fall of 1957, Eisenhower was reeling from failed disarmament and test ban talks at the UN, the superiority of Soviet missile technology indicated by Sputnik, and deep fears about the vulnerability of the thermonuclear deterrent of the United States, Macmillan showed a velvet touch: "Dear Friend," he wrote, "What are we going to do about these Russians? . . . Has not the time come when we could go further toward pooling our efforts and decide how best to use them for our common good?"[24] Fortuitously Strauss passed through London and was successfully briefed so that Macmillan was soon in Washington to hold wide-ranging talks on NATO and defense policy with Eisenhower, who announced at their conclusion that he would encourage the "close and fruitful collaboration of scientists and engineers of Great Britain, the United States, and other friendly countries."[25] What Macmillan referred to as "the great prize"—the full exchange of nuclear technology and a mutual defense agreement—was at last in reach.

ESPIONAGE, PROPAGANDA, AND PUBLIC OPINION

The three national leaders who met in Washington in November 1945 knew that an extensive network of Soviet spies had been revealed in Canada a few weeks earlier. This sensational news became public in February 1946 at a critical juncture in the passage of the McMahon bill through Congress; it fed the campaign of those in the United States who wished to preserve military security over the nuclear "secrets" and opposed any international exchange of information.[26] The subsequent imprisonment of Alan Nunn May, a British physicist who worked in the wartime Manhattan Project laboratory in Montreal, cast doubts on the political judgment and reliability of his colleagues, such as those in the Federation of American Scientists who had been advocating with some success for international control. May's plea of social responsibility was, on its face, indistinguishable from many opinions expressed in the new Bulletin of the Atomic Scientists. The title of Section 10 in the McMahon bill, "Dissemination of Information," soon became "Control of Information," reflecting more restrictive second thoughts in Washington.

The late 1940s brought heightened anxiety about communism in the United States, primarily owing to the abusive behavior of the Soviets in Europe but dramatized by revelations about U.S. spies like Elizabeth Bentley and the hearings of the House Un-American Activities Committee. The confession of Klaus Fuchs, the head of theoretical physics in the British atomic energy program at Harwell, to passing material (acquired while at Los Alamos) on the subjects of fission and thermonuclear bombs to the Soviets terminated the tentative modus vivendi.

Fuchs's treachery went a long way to explaining why the Soviets had been able to detonate an implosion bomb in 1949. Dean Acheson recorded, "The talks with the British and Canadians returned to square one, where there was a deep freezer from which they did not emerge in my time."[27] When Bruno Pontecorvo, a talented physicist who had worked with May in Canada and Fuchs at Harwell, disappeared to the USSR in October 1950, the British government's inquiry was specifically designed to avoid further damage to nuclear negotiations with the United States.[28] U.S. outrage about the woeful state of British security increased in 1951 with the defection of Donald Maclean, the civil servant at the British embassy in Washington who was in charge of atomic energy affairs from 1944 to 1948. Even the early release of May from prison widened the rift between Washington and London: the U.S. administration thought the original sentence too mild (the Rosenbergs were about to be executed for similar crimes) and that it illustrated a fundamental British "softness" toward communism.[29]

The publicity surrounding the spy cases reinforced the notion that there was a secret that was key to developing nuclear weapons; it was a secret that should be held, as Truman suggested, in "sacred trust" by the United States. Such an idea was in contradiction to what the atomic scientists themselves had been saying publicly since the end of the war. Even after the Soviet thermonuclear detonation 1953, a large element of the U.S. public and polity clung to the hope of an enduring superiority, if no longer a monopoly, in nuclear weapons, but a growing faction of skeptics doubted their aspirations. This was especially true after the H-bomb test at Bikini in 1954, with its excessive fallout suggesting that the new apocalyptic weapons were not under perfect control. The throwaway remark of AEC chairman Strauss (who meant to be reassuring the public after the event) that the H-bomb could be created large enough to take out any city unnerved U.S. citizens and reawakened fears in the United Kingdom.

There was a general revitalization of peace and religious groups, and scientists once again became forceful anti-bomb spokesmen. The Russell-Einstein manifesto of 1955 influenced global public opinion more than any of the preceding international nuclear agreements or declarations. Disarmament movements in the United States and Europe reflected transnational concerns about radioactive fallout and became a significant force in setting the nuclear test ban agenda.[30]

CONCLUSIONS

The tergiversations that characterized UK-U.S. nuclear relations during World War II and its aftermath were the product of both tumultuous times and human judgments and delusions. The story illustrates how changes in U.S. politics can have unforeseen international consequences. In a world of clashing ideologies, an economically strapped United Kingdom engaged in nuclear proliferation, not only in response to a perceived threat from the USSR but because the United Kingdom distrusted the United States and wanted to preserve its status as a great power. International disagreements over nuclear policy may persist for a decade, even when they are being addressed in moderately good faith by wise statesmen who speak approximately the same language.

NOTES

1. L. Arnold, "The History of Nuclear Weapons: The Frisch-Peierls Memorandum on the Possible Construction of Atomic Bombs of February 1940," *Cold War History* 3, no. 3 (2003), pp. 111–126.

2. R. W. Clark, *Tizard* (London: Methuen, 1965). Clark discovered the nontechnical "Memorandum on the Properties of a Radioactive Superbomb" with Oliphant's covering letter in Tizard's papers—the only copy in existence. According to Arnold, Ibid., the technical part "on the construction of a 'super-bomb,' based on a nuclear chain reaction in uranium" was discovered in a cornflake box in a strong room of the UK Atomic Energy Authority in the early 1960s. No copy of the memorandum was made although Cockcroft did disclose its contents to various university groups on a visit to the United States in the fall of 1940.

3. A. P. Brown, *The Neutron and the Bomb* (Oxford: Oxford University Press, 1997), pp. 177–213.

4. M. Gowing, "The Maud Reports," appendix 2, *Britain and Atomic Energy* (London: Macmillan, 1964), pp. 394–436.

5. C. G. Darwin, letter to Lord Hankey, August 2, 1941, quoted in Brown, *The Neutron and the Bomb,* p. 217.

6. Anderson, letter to Churchill, July 30, 1942, quoted in Brown, *The Neutron and the Bomb,* p. 228.

7. Brown, *The Neutron and the Bomb,* p. 310.

8. Ibid., pp. 317–319.

9. R. G. Hewlett and O. E. Anderson, *The New World,* 1939/1946 (University Park: Pennsylvania State University Press, 1962), pp. 482–530.

10. P. Hennessy, *Cabinets and the Bomb* (Oxford: Oxford University Press, 2007), pp. 9 and 57.

11. Brown, *The Neutron and the Bomb,* pp. 312–313.

12. R. G. Hewlett and F. Duncan, *Atomic Shield 1947/1952* (Berkeley: University of California Press, 1990), pp. 261–314.

13. J. Baylis, *Ambiguity and Deterrence* (Oxford: Clarendon Press, 1995), pp. 126–177.

14. Ibid., pp. 234–277.

15. L. Arnold, *Britain and the H-Bomb* (Basingstoke: Palgrave, 2001), pp. 198–199.

16. Brown, *The Neutron and the Bomb,* p. 218.

17. Ibid., p. 269.

18. C. R. Attlee, letter to H. S. Truman, September 25, 1945, quoted in M. Gowing, *Independence and Deterrence* (London: Macmillan, 1974), pp. 78–81.

19. Ibid., pp. 311–314.

20. Ibid., p. 406.

21. Ibid., p. 407.

22. Arnold, *Britain and the H-Bomb,* p. 197.

23. A. Horne, *Macmillan 1894–1956* (London: Macmillan, 1988), p. 389.

24. A. Horne, *Macmillan 1957–1986* (London: Macmillan, 1989), p. 54.

25. R. G. Hewlett and J. Holl, *Atoms for Peace and War, 1953–1961* (Berkeley: University of California Press, 1989), pp. 466–469.

26. R. G. Hewlett and O. E. Anderson, *The New World, 1939/1946,* pp. 500–503.

27. D. Acheson, *Present at the Creation* (New York: Norton, 1969), p. 321.

28. S. Turchetti, "Atomic Secrets and Governmental Lies," *British Journal of the History of Science* 36, no. 4 (2003): pp. 389–415.

29. British Embassy to London Foreign Office, cable, January 3, 1953, file no. KV 2/2218, National Archives, Kew.

30. L. S. Wittner, *Resisting the Bomb* (Stanford: Stanford University Press, 1997).

4

COMPLETING THE TRANSATLANTIC
NUCLEAR BRIDGE: A UK VIEW

BRIAN P. JAMISON

From the perspective of 2008, amending the U.S. Atomic Energy Act of 1954 to permit the signing of the U.S.-UK Mutual Defense Agreement (MDA) in July 1958 seems inevitable, logical, and natural. However, the limited evidence available in the public domain concerning the events surrounding these developments suggests that it was, to use Wellington's comment on the Battle of Waterloo, "a close run thing." Although the placing of Sputnik into orbit in October 1957 generated the public and congressional loss of confidence in U.S. technological prowess, which stimulated the reopening of the U.S.-UK nuclear collaboration after a break of 12 years, the process of legislating on this and, in parallel, determining the scope of the MDA proved to be far from straightforward.

This chapter will therefore examine four distinct sets of activities that were central to facilitating agreement on the MDA and its implementation. It will begin with events leading to the high-level agreement between President Dwight D. Eisenhower and Prime Minister Harold Macmillan in late October 1957 over collaboration on nuclear weapon systems. The chapter will address the initial exchanges in early December 1957 in U.S.-UK committees created to address detailed implementation. It will also cover the congressional debates in the early months of 1958 on the amendments to the 1954 Atomic Energy Act necessary to permit collaboration to occur. These debates generated fears that the high-level commitments would become becalmed in Congress, further delaying their implementation until early 1959 at the earliest. Finally, the decision to separate out some of the issues and postpone dealing with them until the following year, together with the opening exchanges of nuclear weapon information in August and September 1958, will be discussed.

EISENHOWER-MACMILLAN AGREEMENT IN 1957

The United Kingdom had initiated practical work on nuclear weapons in 1940, and through its two Maud reports in 1941 alerted the United States to the possibility that weapon development might take about 24 months. The outcome of this exchange was the creation of the Manhattan Project in mid-1942. In August 1943 the United Kingdom temporarily closed down its own independent nuclear project and moved it to the United States to become part of the U.S. enterprise. However, after World War II, the Atomic Energy Act of 1946, informally known as the McMahon Act, was passed by Congress, barring the British from further collaboration with the United States and the sharing of any nuclear technologies.[1] As Peter Hennessy has noted, the incoming Labour government "protested in vain" but this had no real effect.[2] Work therefore restarted on an independent UK nuclear energy program, and by 1948 Britain was committed to the production of weapon-grade fissile material, the development of a bomb design, and the construction of a stockpile of 200 operational weapons.

Although a number of attempts were made in the late 1940s to restart UK-U.S. collaboration on weapon production, none was successful. Some collaboration occurred on monitoring the USSR's progress with its nuclear program, while the wartime arrangements for monopolizing the global supply of uranium through the Combined Development Trust (CDT) also persisted. The latter resulted in the United Kingdom transferring to the United States its share of world production until the early 1950s. Upon his return to power in October 1951, Prime Minister Winston Churchill was determined to revitalize nuclear collaboration with President Truman[3] on the basis of the United Kingdom only pursuing "the art rather then the article."[4] In his mind, there was "no point in our going into bulk production [of atomic weapons] even if we were able to."[5] However, this approach proved fruitless, and Churchill quickly accepted that Britain would have to develop, manufacture, and deploy its own arsenal of nuclear weapons, including megaton ones.[6] Yet strategically, the overall objective of this British independent effort remained to secure interdependence with the United States.[7] In British minds, collective security was the best, if not the only, viable option for preventing attacks on its small and vulnerable homeland.

By June 1955 the United Kingdom had tested three atomic devices and launched a thermonuclear weapon program,[8] while in November 1955 the Soviet Union exploded a hydrogen device in the megaton range. A year earlier Eisenhower had concluded that the development of nuclear energy programs by a number of countries made a U.S. global initiative on nuclear energy imperative. This led to his "Atoms for Peace" speech in the UN in December 1953 and his request that Congress amend the McMahon Act. The result was the 1954 Atomic Energy Act, which, while specifically forbidding disclosure of information concerning the design and fabrication of U.S. weapons, did allow information on the external characteristics of nuclear weapons and their yields to be shared. It also allowed the administration to negotiate both military and civil agreements for cooperation with other states. Agreements with the United Kingdom were signed on June 15, 1955, but the military agreement offered few immediate possibilities for extending nuclear collaboration other than in the nuclear intelligence field and in the coordination of planning for nuclear attack and defense. The latter was to open the door to bilateral arrangements for UK bombers to deliver U.S. fission bombs in the event of war, which in turn generated pressures for matters such as the storage and safety of nuclear weapons to be shared with the United Kingdom. The civil agreement was comprehensive, but it specifically prohibited any interchange of data that were judged to be of military significance.

Implementation of both agreements ran into difficulties because of the lack of clarity in the legislation over which U.S. government entity was to take decisions. Although legislation appeared to assign ultimate legal and political authority over military nuclear exchanges to the president, it was unclear which U.S. agency was to recommend action to the president. The civil situation was even more confused as the State Department had no clear role in the negotiating process, and the U.S. Atomic Energy Commission (AEC) had to function as both a promotional and regulatory agency. More significantly, the Joint Committee on Atomic Energy (JCAE) believed it had been given a positive policymaking function by the legislation, as it had to approve the AEC actions. Atomic energy thus drifted into a no-man's-land, with a Republican administration and a Democratic-controlled JCAE contesting the right to make policy, and with the AEC sandwiched between them. Eisenhower chose not to intervene personally or exercise his legal authority over military issues, and it was not until 1959 that this source of friction was removed.[9] The situation was further complicated by the U.S. Navy obtaining legal advice that it could exchange information with the United Kingdom on submarine reactors through the civil provisions of the act, and its attempt to do so generated frictions between the U.S. Navy and the JCAE.[10]

Meanwhile, the U.S. Air Force and the Strategic Air Command were increasingly dependent on the United Kingdom for bases from which to pose a nuclear threat to the USSR. Limited cooperation between British and U.S. air services had improved with the activation of Project E, an arrangement under which U.S.-built nuclear weapons or warheads, or both, were to be made available for use on Royal Air Force aircraft and missiles in the event of war. The infighting in Washington effectively prevented further movement toward U.S.-UK nuclear weapon exchanges and collaboration, despite the increasing advantages that many in the Defense Department believed would be gained through such collaboration.[11] It was only when other considerations influenced the situation—including the launch of Sputnik, the vulnerability of air bases to evolving Russian missile technology, and the confirmation of Britain's ability to develop and stockpile its own arsenal of atomic and thermonuclear weapons—that these internal U.S. impediments could be outflanked or overcome.

As Sputnik induced fear and stirred political debate in the United States, it also offered an opportunity for those in both the United Kingdom and the United States who wished to expand Anglo–American nuclear collaboration to overcome opposition to it in Congress and elsewhere. Eisenhower invited Macmillan to Washington on October 23, 1957, to discuss the consequences of the Sputnik launch, and on October 24 convened a meeting of his National Security Council to approve a full interchange of information on military aspects of nuclear energy with Britain. A public commitment to amend the 1954 Atomic Energy Act was inserted—the Declaration of Common Purpose—in the communiqué both leaders issued at the end of their meetings. This document contained reference to Macmillan's personal vision of a future U.S.-UK nuclear relationship combining the capabilities of the two democracies in their common confrontation with the USSR. One key element of this was the notion of "common defense" by which the United Kingdom would accept a major degree of dependence upon the United States to maintain its nuclear weapon arsenals in return for investing the resources released in other military areas important to both countries.

EXCHANGES IN LATE 1957

Among the committees and subcommittees created to implement this declaration was one on nuclear warheads. During its meetings on December 3–5, 1957, Sir Frederick Brundrett, chief scientific adviser in the UK Ministry of Defence (MOD), became convinced that the United States was only "slightly more advanced" than Britain in the scientific aspects of nuclear weapons. The United States, however, was clearly superior in addressing the engineering needed for operational deployment, and "the United Kingdom would have to know about this if it was to save time and avoid duplication" of effort. In his view, restored collaboration was a way of conserving important economic and human resources in the United States and Britain, thus releasing them for other military purposes. Despite the decision to deploy the U.S.-designed and -manufactured Thor intermediate-range ballistic missile (IRBM) in Britain, Brundrett remained convinced that the United Kingdom would have to continue with the development of its Blue Streak medium-range ballistic missile (MRBM) system as the United Kingdom could not "accept the delay in readiness" inherent in arrangements where the warheads for a vital deterrent system would remain in U.S. custody.[12] If the United States were to provide useful warhead information, however, further UK technical efforts to build a warhead for either Thor or Blue Streak could be minimized.[13]

At the time, it was estimated that British resources were sufficient for the further development of only two major nuclear weapon designs simultaneously, the first priority being a lightweight, high-yield, invulnerable weapon for the IRBM. British scientists were concerned that radiation from nuclear explosions (known as the R-1 effect) might immobilize their weapon designs for some time after exposure, and they wanted especially to have access to U.S. information on how to protect against this threat. The United Kingdom was proposing to test a number of nuclear devices in the near future that could fulfill a range of operational requirements, although only one, Blue Danube, a 10-kiloton fission bomb, was in production and operational deployment. These tests were expected to lead to a stockpile of megaton freefall and stand-off-powered bombs for delivery by its V bombers, as well as a megaton warhead for Blue Streak. A tactical bomb for the Canberra jet bomber and naval aircraft (Red Beard) was also planned for production. By the early 1960s, the United Kingdom also hoped to produce a small warhead for surface-to-air antiaircraft missiles and a similar version for the Seaslug naval guided missile.[14] Shortening the development period of this range of weapons and delivery systems and improving political and military preparedness through the standardization of weapons were thus important objectives of the UK negotiators as they assessed the areas for negotiation at the end of 1957. Yet ultimately all depended on the U.S. Congress passing the legislation to revise the 1954 Atomic Energy Act.

DEBATE IN THE UNITED STATES OVER COLLABORATIVE U.S.-UK RELATIONSHIP

The high priority accorded by Eisenhower to revisiting this legislation was underlined by the attention devoted to it in his State of the Union address on January 9, 1958, in which he stressed that is was ". . .wasteful . . . for friendly allies to consume talent and money in solving problems that their friends have already solved."[15] On January 27, bills incorporating the proposed amendments were introduced in both the House and Senate. These were immediately referred to the JCAE Subcommittee on Agreements for Cooperation, which began hearings on them two days later. The amending bills were intended to give the president discretionary authority to sanction four types of activity that had been illegal under the 1954 act. The proposed legislation permitting these exchanges had already been discussed informally at the official level, but these amendments had not yet been approved by Congress.[16]

From the moment that the Eisenhower administration's amending bills were referred to the JCAE, a tug-of-war developed between the U.S. executive branch and the JCAE. Eisenhower and Macmillan were forced to watch this from the sidelines. Apprehensive over the agreement to begin test ban negotiations in Geneva on October 31, 1958, as well as the increasing domestic pressure upon him to abandon testing, Macmillan urged the need for an early start of secret negotiations for the bilateral agreement that would be made possible by the changed U.S. legislation. Eisenhower and his advisers were quick to begin preliminary discussions but were concerned not to offend the JCAE by preempting the legislation it was discussing.[17] By mid-June 1958 the bilateral agreement had been drafted. The legislative process was assisted by the explosion on April 24, 1958, of Britain's first fully success-ful megaton thermonuclear device at the Grapple Y trial. This proved to the scientific community in the United States that, as Edward Teller declared, the laws of physics operated on both sides of the Atlantic.

FORM OF THE U.S.-UK COLLABORATIVE RELATIONSHIP

The detailed arrangements to be contained in the new agreement for cooperation involved four sets of activities. The first was the supply of fissile materials and fusion fuel and was based on the complementary needs of both states for three nuclear weapon materials: uranium 235, tritium, and plutonium.[18] The Royal Navy's aspiration to deploy a fleet of nuclear submarines requiring fissile material for their reactors, as well as the substantial numbers of megaton warheads required by the Royal Air Force, meant that the UK military demand for uranium 235 was likely to exceed the output capacity of the Capenhurst gaseous dif-fusion plant in Cheshire for most of the 1960s.[19] Access to U.S. uranium 235 and tritium, either by purchase or bartering against UK-produced plutonium, would save the United Kingdom the effort and expense of expanding its existing enrichment plant. For the United States, access to UK plutonium would assist in meeting anticipated demands for battlefield nuclear weapons for use by its NATO allies.

The second set of collaborative arrangements resulted from Britain's recognition that its resources in the nuclear-weapon field were limited and that there was no point in reinventing warhead designs that were already in production in the United States. Design information for the physics package of nuclear warheads and non-nuclear components for similar types of nuclear weapons that had been developed indepen-dently by both states would therefore be exchanged.

The third set of activities, providing information to facilitate allied use of U.S. nuclear weapons in wartime, resulted in part from a UK recognition that certain tactical, defensive, or battlefield nuclear weap-ons and their military roles would be dependent on either new NATO arrangements for access to U.S.-owned nuclear weapons or similar UK-U.S. bilateral ones, which were known as Projects E and N.

The fourth set of understandings related to the transfer of a sub-marine reactor and its fuel to Britain on a commercial basis, in return for the transfer of information on the design of the Calder Hall fuel cans.[20]

It was understood that once the agreement had been implemented, the United Kingdom would continue to develop nuclear weapons and carry out research independent of the United States, but both countries would maintain close liaison on similar projects on a need-to-know basis and would continue an exchange in certain component areas.

The bilateral agreement created a fundamentally new relationship between the United States and Britain in the nuclear weapons field. It made possible the sharing of weapons data and designs and radically changed the British weapon program. The other substantive elements in the agreement provided that there could be no transfer of fully assembled atomic weapons between the two states and that any information received under the agreement was to be used exclusively for defense purposes and was not to be communicated to third parties without mutual consent. Although a level of mutual advantage was expected, nowhere in the agreement was reciprocity stated to be the basis for the exchange, unlike the military and civil agreements of 1955.[21]

The 1958 Atomic Energy Act passed through both houses of Congress at the end of June and was signed by the president on July 2. The new agreement was placed before Congress for it to lie there for the statutory 30 days before it came into force. The fissile material and nuclear component elements of the original bill had become entangled in domestic civil nuclear disputes in the JCAE, however, and were deleted to ensure its swift passage. These elements were reincorporated in the amendments agreed by Congress in the spring of 1959. However, discussion between the two countries on warhead design issues commenced at the end of the 30-day period for the raising of congressional objections.

The initial meeting in August 1958, which was kept as small as possible, covered atomic weapons of interest to both parties, described in an unpublished technical annex to the agreement. The U.S. delegation included Dr. William Libby (who succeeded Lewis Strauss as chairman of the AEC), General Herbert B. Loper (assistant to the secretary of defense), Brigadier General Alfred Dodd Starbird (director of military application, AEC), Dr. Norris Bradbury (director of Los Alamos), Dr. Edward Teller (director of Livermore), and Dr. James McCrae (president of the Sandia Corporation). British representatives included Brundrett and Victor Macklen from the Ministry of Defence, as well as William Penney and William Cook from the Atomic Weapons Establishment (AWE) Aldermaston.

What the Americans could disclose depended on further study of what was possible under the new legislation. Both sides also attempted to define a possible basis for both division of research and development effort and further exchanges. Churchill's long-held vision became a reality when, in August 1958, Britain realized the "great prize" of renewed nuclear collaboration with the United States as the Agreement for Co-operation on the Uses of Atomic Energy for Mutual Defence Purposes came into force.

In Washington and Sandia in August and September 1958 the United States and the United Kingdom exchanged drawings, material specifications, and relevant theoretical and experimental information on similar warheads both sides had either produced or were planning to produce.[23] During the first meeting it became obvious to U.S. representatives that the United Kingdom had achieved an advanced state of weapon research and development in both the fission and thermonuclear fields. Both parties discussed in detail neutron sources for initiators, high-explosive specifications, yields, designs, and mechanical and electrical components. British designers had tested radiation implosion and two-stage devices, and they understood the advantages of certain designs. So impressed were the U.S. representatives in the work done in the United Kingdom that they commented that "certain advances made by the United Kingdom would be of benefit to the United States."[24] These exchanges were thus emphatically not a one-way street, and both parties were to accrue significant benefits from them. U.S. nuclear information streamed across the Atlantic rapidly, and the accelerated exchanges formed a sharp contrast with the lingering history of diplomatic trial, error, and mistrust.

This young but intimate working relationship was growing, and it was further strengthened by mutual invitations to attend one another's test series in September and October 1958. British observers were provided with detailed information on test and diagnostic procedures. Detailed meetings at Sandia on September 17–19 went extremely well, the talks being something of a revelation to the weaponeers on both sides of the table who had worked independently in their secret laboratories for more than a decade. British representatives also questioned whether the Polaris submarine and missile system could be made available to the United Kingdom.[25] On October 22–25, British intelligence officials also met with representatives from the Central Intelligence Agency, the Department of Defense, and the AEC to compare their data and interpretations of British and Soviet nuclear weapon capabilities. Their assessments of the nature of Soviet weapon tests were remarkably close, given the fact that they had reached their conclusions independent from one another.

As a result of information obtained in the initial exchanges, the United Kingdom made the decision that it would move ahead and produce in the United Kingdom the Mark 28 bomb, the first mass-produced U.S.-designed thermonuclear weapon.[26] This was driven in part by the inability of the United Kingdom to test a service version of its own thermonuclear weapon design, owing to the October 1958 testing moratorium. To assist in this process, from December 8 to 17, a group of 15 British experts visited major U.S. production facilities, including the Lawrence Livermore National Laboratory in California, with the UK Atomic Energy Authority adding to its shopping list an antimissile warhead and information on warheads of less than one kiloton.[27]

Twelve years of independent history was unraveling during these first few meetings, as a new approach was being put in place. This abridged study of the 1958 MDA can do little more than acknowledge the herculean effort required to establish the United Kingdom's independent nuclear program, and it was on the basis of this effort that effective transatlantic nuclear cooperation and transparency could be reestablished. The resolute yet patient executive leadership and effective, persistent UK diplomacy, supported by demonstrated scientific capability, were the key drivers leading to the MDA. From July 1958 onward, Anglo-American nuclear defense policies became so intertwined by the development of the transformed nuclear relationship that they proved capable of withstanding the vicissitudes of the next 50 years of international history.

NOTES

1. See *Atomic Energy Act of 1946,* Public Law 585, 79th Congress.
2. Peter Hennessy, *Cabinet* (Oxford: Basil Blackwell, 1986), p. 125.
3. Margaret Gowing, *Independence and Deterrence: Britain and Atomic Energy 1945–1952,* vol. 1, *Policy Making* (London: Macmillan, 1974), p. 405.
4. Prime Minister's Personal Minute, serial no. M47c/51, The National Archives (TNA), CAB 21/2281B.
5. Ibid.
6. See Hennessy, *Cabinet,* p. 123.

7. See Lorna Arnold, *A Very Special Relationship: British Atomic Weapon Trials in Australia* (London: Her Majesty's Stationery Office, 1987).

8. Ibid.

9. This situation remained unresolved until 1959 when Eisenhower issued an executive order that delegated his powers to the Department of Defense and the AEC acting jointly and specified that he should be involved only if they disagreed. It also made the secretary of state responsible for the negotiation of agreements of cooperation. See John Simpson, *The Independent Nuclear State: The United States, Britain, and the Military Atom* (New York: St. Martin's Press, 1983), p. 55.

10. For more on this subject see Richard G. Hewlett and Francis Duncan, *Nuclear Navy, 1946–1962* (Chicago: University of Chicago Press, 1974), pp. 225–234.

11. Letter from Sir R. Powell to Minister concerning the Bilateral Agreement, June 6, 1955, TNA, DEFE 13/60.

12. The Thor delivery system stationed in the United Kingdom was to have U.S. nuclear warheads that remained under U.S. custody and control. Blue Streak and its British-produced warheads would be under complete UK control, and thus give Britain the ability to respond to nuclear threats independent of the United States if conditions required this.

13. UK/U.S. Discussions on Scientific and Technical Co-Operation, December 5, 1957, TNA.

14. Nuclear Warheads: Statement of UK position to be read in conjunction with Report of Sub-Committee 'B', n.d., TNA.

15. Simpson, *Independent Nuclear State,* p. 54.

16. Military Bilateral Telegram no. 3597, June 12, 1958, TNA, T225/1024.

17. Jan Melissen, *The Struggle for Nuclear Partnership: Britain, the United States and the Making of an Ambiguous Alliance, 1952–1959* (Groningen: Styx Publications, 1993), p. 48.

18. Simpson, *Independent Nuclear State,* p. 56.

19. Fuel enrichment at Capenhurst dates back to the 1950s and was originally used for defence purposes. The plant was converted in the 1960s for commercial production to supply enriched fuel to civil nuclear power stations.

20. Article III of the MDA specified the terms under which the submarine reactor and a 10-year supply of replacement fuel were to be transferred to Britain. Simpson, *Independent Nuclear State,* p. 150.

21. Ibid., p. 65.

22. Lorna Arnold, *Britain and the H-Bomb* (London: Her Majesty's Stationery Office, 2001), p. 175.

23. This included information applying to the XW-47 warhead, Mark 28, 44, 45, and 48, and an assortment of other designs. The United Kingdom

provided information on its high-yield fission bomb, 2,200-pound ther-monuclear bomb, and various other warheads.

24. Quarterly Progress Report: Oart III—Weapons, July-September 1958, U.S. Department of Energy archives, Box 1444, Folder OTM8, Reports to JCAE, Document number LXXX1-596-184.

25. Future Anglo-U.S. Missile Development, September 18, 1958, TNA, DEFE 13/181.

26. The Macmillan government had also indicated that it wanted to manu-facture some of the other weapons the Americans had shown them in detail.

27. Arnold, *A Very Special Relationship*, p. 253.

5

COMPLETING THE TRANSATLANTIC NUCLEAR BRIDGE: A U.S. VIEW

ERIC RIDGE

At its 50th anniversary, the endurance of America's 1958 Mutual Defense Agreement (MDA) with the United Kingdom epitomizes the
strength of an alliance known simply as the "special relationship." But
collaboration between these two nations has not always been so robust.
Indeed, the uncertainty of the postwar years provided fertile ground
for disagreements between the United States and the United Kingdom
on the issue of nuclear collaboration. Concurrently, debates between
the legislative and executive branches of the U.S. government over
atomic cooperation with the British proved acrimonious as well. As
the post–World War II years dragged on, President Dwight D. Eisenhower inched the United States and United Kingdom closer to cooperation until two Soviet nuclear advances exerted decisive influence on
U.S. policymakers to share nuclear secrets with the British.

First, a successful Soviet thermonuclear test in 1953 inspired a
concerted yet largely ineffective White House–led effort to increase
nuclear collaboration with the United Kingdom, ultimately ending in
an amendment to the Atomic Energy Act. Then, in 1957, the Soviet
Union's Sputnik satellite launch drove the United States and United
Kingdom toward collaboration yet again—this time leading to more
fruitful bilateral discussions that, after considerable debate, eventually
culminated in nuclear cooperation.

The purpose of this chapter is to examine U.S. and British attempts
in the 1950s—before the 1958 MDA—to foster bilateral nuclear collaboration. After examining cases in 1953–1955, and again in 1957, in

which both sides sought to advance atomic collaboration in the wake of Soviet nuclear achievements, this chapter posits that U.S. fear of Soviet progress was the chief motivating factor behind the decision to opt for nuclear collaboration. However, the story of pre-1958 U.S.-UK nuclear collaboration is one of making halting progress more than it is of creating rapid change. In developing a collaborative atomic relationship, the United States and the United Kingdom overcame numerous roadblocks. This chapter chronicles many of the efforts to overcome these obstacles and how some fell short of their goals.

SURPRISE AND DISMAY IN BRITAIN: U.S. REJECTION OF NUCLEAR COLLABORATION IN THE EARLY POST-WAR YEARS

From the smoldering ruins of World War II emerged a global security environment fraught with uncertainties. The issue of how the United States would harness its new atomic technology—and whether it would share nuclear technology with its allies—ranked among the most provocative postwar questions.

In the early and mid-1940s, the United Kingdom had credible reason to hope for strong nuclear collaboration with the United States. During the war, the two nations forged a strong alliance based on similar interests, ideology, and close personal relationships that had developed among the countries' leaders. The two nations soon began cooperating on atomic issues: the United States enlisted scientists from the United Kingdom in the Manhattan Project, and the two nations signed several wartime deals promising continued atomic energy cooperation.[1] It was not always easy, however. One of the first such cooperative agreements, signed at Hyde Park in 1942, quickly came into question the following year when Churchill sent a cable to Roosevelt adviser Harry Hopkins alleging that "the American War Department is asking us to keep them informed of our experiments while refusing altogether any information about theirs."[2] Still dissatisfied, Churchill later warned Roosevelt that Britain had decided to "go it alone" in building an atomic program.[3]

During the next several years, work on the Manhattan Project continued, the United States dropped atomic bombs over Hiroshima and Nagasaki, and ultimately World War II ended. Against this backdrop of change, in April 1946 the British prime minister, Clement Attlee, told the U.S. ambassador to Britain, W. Averell Harriman, that the

British thought the United States should make atomic bombs available to them.[4] However, in August of that year, the U.S. Congress passed the Atomic Energy Act (also known as the McMahon Act for its chief architect, Senator Brien McMahon [D-Conn.]), which prevented the United States from sharing nuclear secrets with other nations, even allies such as the United Kingdom.[5]

Given the U.S. willingness to collaborate during World War II, the Atomic Energy Act represented a surprising reversal in the eyes of the British, who perceived it as isolationist and an affront to British international standing.[6] Atlee argued that the United States was guilty of a breach of faith and spurned British policymakers felt pressure to take action. According to one account, "If Britain was not to get the help to which she believed entitled from the United States, she must undertake the development of atomic energy on her own."[7] Thus the Atlee government decided in January 1947 to begin independent development of nuclear weapons.[8]

In the United States, one of the Atomic Energy Act's chief purposes was to create a structure establishing shared responsibility between U.S. legislative and executive branches over direction and control of the nuclear program. To that end, the law assigned unprecedented powers to an Atomic Energy Commission (AEC) comprising five civilian presidential appointees.[9] As a counterweight, the act also created the Joint Committee on Atomic Energy (JCAE) with 18 members from both the House and Senate, 10 from the majority and 8 from the minority.[10] The two entities were meant to work together closely, as the AEC was charged with keeping the JCAE "fully and currently informed with respect to all of the Commission's activities," thus giving the JCAE "a unique capacity for legislative surveillance."[11] In turn, the JCAE was statutorily required "to make continuing studies of the Atomic Energy Commission and of problems relating to the development, use and control of atomic energy."[12] In short, all legislation pertaining to atomic energy had to go through the JCAE.[13]

This highly anomalous arrangement was met with skepticism from a variety of critics. One account summarized the AEC as "five Atomic Energy Commissioners, whose only tangible link with the American people is their appointment by the President and their confirmation by the Senate, [who] have been empowered to make decisions which not only affect our hopes for material advancement, but may very well determine our national survival."[14] The JCAE also received scrutiny, mostly regarding its wide-ranging authority that included permanent powers of inquiry and a mandate that it be kept "fully and currently informed" of AEC activities, thus leading one observer to conclude that the JCAE was endowed with broader statutory power than Congress had ever concentrated in a joint committee.[15] With both the AEC and JCAE running the atomic program, it was suggested that "the pattern of relations which has evolved between the Congress and the executive branch in atomic energy is almost as unique as the splitting of the atom itself."[16]

A NEW U.S. PRESIDENT AND A SURPRISING SOVIET THERMONUCLEAR TEST: ENOUGH TO SPARK U.S.-UK NUCLEAR COLLABORATION?

During the late 1940s and early 1950s, as Britain developed its own nuclear weapons, that country's leaders maintained hope of collaborating with the United States on nuclear issues. They were encouraged by the U.S. decision to station much of its Strategic Air Command in the United Kingdom during the Berlin crisis.[17] Indeed, nuclear cooperation topped Prime Minister Winston Churchill's agenda when he traveled to Washington in January 1952. In the two leaders' meetings, President Harry S. Truman explained to Churchill that he was constrained by limitations set forth by the legislative branch and was in fact "tied down in atomic matters by a statute."[18] Polite but unyielding, the prime minister requested full U.S. cooperation on atomic energy within the McMahon Act's limitations. Specifically, Prime Minister Churchill suggested engaging in increased discussions between Lord Cherwell (a British nuclear adviser at the Clarendon Laboratory), the Atomic Energy Commission, and the military.[19] Churchill's visit sparked conversation and thoughts but no serious movement toward nuclear cooperation.

Later that year, however, when the British announced a nuclear test in Australia, Senator McMahon issued a statement indicating that he had been unaware of the British contributions to the Manhattan Project when he drafted his legislation. In light of this new information, Senator McMahon in this press release advocated a "rethinking of the entire situation" to likely include increased cooperation between the two nations. President Eisenhower's inauguration in January 1953 further elevated the hopes of nuclear collaboration. A staunch believer in mutual defense, President Eisenhower believed that Europe should become a "third greater power bloc" that was aligned with the United States but strong enough to defend itself.[20] To that end, just six months into office, Eisenhower called the Atomic Energy Act outdated and challenged the United States to develop closer nuclear collaboration with its allies.[21]

The Soviet Union's shocking news in 1953 that it had conducted a thermonuclear test only intensified the president's consternation over nuclear cooperation. In private, he grumbled that the McMahon Act was a "terrible piece of legislation" that significantly undermined the U.S. relationship with its NATO partners.[22] The president's sentiments sparked movement inside the U.S. bureaucracy, especially the executive branch. In December 1953, the White House published NSC 151/2, "Disclosure of Atomic Information to Allied Countries," which called for increased disclosure of atomic energy–related information in order to empower allies to participate more intelligently in military planning, motivate them to act with the United States in times of crisis, assist them in enhancing defense capabilities, encourage their cooperation in U.S. energy programs, and improve their nuclear research and development contributions.[23]

Ten days later, Secretary of Defense Charles E. Wilson told the NATO Council of Ministers in closed session that U.S. decisionmakers were "prepared to seek legislation to permit the United States to share with its NATO allies pertinent information on nuclear and other new weapons."[24] Two months after that, in February 1954, President Eisenhower formally recommended that the JCAE amend the Atomic Energy Act of 1946 to widen cooperation with allies in atomic energy matters and improve procedures for the control and dissemination of atomic energy information.[25] Observing significant changes in the global landscape over the past eight years, including the end of a nuclear monopoly and the increasing capabilities of nuclear weapons, President Eisenhower concluded that "our atomic effectiveness will be increased if certain limited information on the use of atomic weapons can be imparted more readily to nations allied with us in common defense."[26] President Eisenhower garnered support for this view among JCAE members who saw the duplication of efforts among allies in nuclear weapons development as a costly waste of time, money, and brainpower.

The 1954 Atomic Energy Act amended the 1946 version to permit limited transfer of atomic information, but it still forbade the sharing of restricted data on nuclear weapon design and production.[27] Indeed, change was not accomplished quickly or easily. In May 1955, in response to a subcommittee inquiry, Defense Secretary Wilson sent a letter to Senator Henry M. Jackson (D-Wash.) detailing the problems with the 1954 Atomic Energy Act. He wrote, "The Atomic Energy Commission has expressed the opinion that the law does not permit the Commission to exchange Restricted Data pertaining exclusively to reactors concerned primarily with military use," despite strong interest in exchanging such information.[28] Nevertheless, Wilson stated that the DOD "intends to include such information in the bilateral agreements with the United Kingdom and Canada currently being prepared by the Department of Defense."[29] One month later, two agreements pertaining to cooperation with Great Britain were announced: one seeking to foster atomic information exchange to advance mutual defense and the other pertaining to civil uses of atomic energy.[30] President Eisenhower justified to a skeptical Senator Clinton P. Anderson (D-N.Mex.) that the United States would exchange atomic information necessary to the development of defense plans, the training of personnel in the employment of and defense against atomic weapons, and the evaluation of the capabilities of potential enemies in the employment of atomic weapons.[31]

Neither the 1954 Atomic Energy Act nor the 1955 bilateral agreement addressed all the problems associated with nuclear cooperation. Although the legislation was intended to encourage increased cooperation with U.S. allies, it was hamstrung by disputes among the agencies and opposition from congressional policymakers who expressed concerns about promoting proliferation and the possibility of espionage.[32] The latter concern was exacerbated by an FBI investigation of UK atomic facilities that concluded that on-site security was inadequate.[33] Senator Anderson lamented that he was "in favor of helping our British allies in every way possible. But in helping the British," he cautioned, "we should be ever vigilant to protect real security."[34]

Interagency turf disputes between the JCAE and the AEC further delayed or sidetracked agreements.[35] One such case pitted the JCAE chairman, Senator Anderson, against Chairman Lewis Strauss of the AEC over Strauss's refusal to share documents with Anderson regarding a potential DOD agreement with Great Britain. The agreement would provide the United Kingdom with information on the U.S. *Nautilus* submarine as well as research on nuclear propulsion.[36] Anderson felt the refusal to share documents amounted to a breach of the 1954 Atomic Energy Act.

During the next two years, however, the British gained some ground on collaboration. A U.S. visit by the new minister of defence, Duncan Sandys, in January 1957 resulted in President Eisenhower pushing even harder for increased cooperation. Then, at a conference in Bermuda in March of that year, Eisenhower and Prime Minister Harold Macmillan reached agreement on a range of issues including joint intelligence operations, military planning with respect to nuclear materials, and fitting British aircraft to carry nuclear weapons.[37] Bermuda was especially important for both tangible and intangible reasons. The U.S. agreement to provide missiles—including those in the intermediate range of 1,500 miles—marked a practical step toward cooperation and ultimately helped catalyze the eventual revision of the Atomic Energy Act of 1954.[38] Furthermore, it indicated that the U.S.-UK relationship had healed following the Suez Canal crisis of the previous October. As a U.S. government source told the *Los Angeles Times,* the new understanding made it "most unlikely we would split apart again."[39]

SPUTNIK BRINGS U.S.-UK NUCLEAR COLLABORATION ONE STEP CLOSER

The October 4, 1957, Soviet launch of the world's first artificial satellite, Sputnik, sent U.S. policymakers into deep tumult. Sputnik demonstrated not only the USSR's capability to build a powerful booster rocket, but more broadly the strength of the country's missile program, which now clearly placed allied air bases at risk.[40] Eisenhower's science adviser, James Killian, later reflected on the launch:

> Overnight there developed a widespread fear that the country lay at the mercy of the Russian military machine and that our government and its military arm had abruptly lost the power to defend the homeland itself, much less to maintain U.S. prestige and leadership in the international arena.[41]

While the United States assessed the first- and second-order effects of Sputnik, British policymakers identified the launch as a window of opportunity to yet again push the United States toward nuclear collaboration. Seizing the opportunity, the British ambassador to the United States, Harold Caccia, sent a telegram on October 7 from Washington to the Foreign Office pressing for the repeal of the McMahon Act.[42]

Just three days later, as Sandys was privately suggesting to U.S. officials that they "would get a ready response" to a new proposal for greater cooperation, Prime Minister Macmillan wrote to the White House proposing a meeting with President Eisenhower.[43] Within two weeks, Prime Minister Macmillan was on his way to Washington for talks on increased nuclear cooperation, carrying the message that the existing duplication of nuclear efforts was a threat to both countries.[44]

At the conclusion of three days of meetings, President Eisenhower and Prime Minister Macmillan, assisted by Secretary of State John Foster Dulles and Foreign Secretary Selwyn Lloyd, respectively, set forth the "Declaration of Common Purpose," which announced increased interdependence between the two countries and provided notice that President Eisenhower would formally request that the Atomic Energy Act be amended again "as may be necessary and desirable to permit close and fruitful collaboration of scientists and engineers of Great Britain, the United States, and other friendly countries."[45] Roughly one week later, President Eisenhower followed through by requesting the U.S. Congress to amend the act. In so doing, he pointed out that the United States was "getting to the point where we know that a great many of our secrets are known to the enemy, but they are still secret from our friends, which seems rather an anomalous situation."[46]

The sharply divided Congress was thrown into contentious debate, with skeptics on both sides of the aisle. Whereas conservative opposition generally argued on behalf of the U.S. interest in preserving nuclear secrets, liberal opponents feared potential proliferation of nuclear technology. Some members of both parties found common cause in arguing for congressional veto power over any information or material sharing agreement.[47] Eisenhower's request also roiled the highly influential JCAE, which would bear ultimate responsibility for drafting proposed changes to the Atomic Energy Act.[48]

Among supporters of Eisenhower's plan was Montana's Democratic senator and Foreign Relations Committee member, Mike Mansfield, who indicated that the plan would get "sympathetic consideration" from Congress, which was controlled by the Democratic Party.[49] Mansfield also expressed his desire for a NATO scientific group to be established as a liaison between the United States and Euratom, the agency responsible for the supply of European nuclear fuels.[50] Similarly inclined, Florida's Democratic senator, George Smathers, who had publicly voiced concern about Soviet missile advances, said that he strongly supported strengthening NATO and thereby "sharing both the costs and responsibilities of defending the Free World."[51]

Skeptical members of Congress cited the potential for espionage as a reason not to exchange information until it could be verified that the British security system was adequate."[52] Recalling the Los Alamos scientist who passed nuclear secrets to the Soviets, Senator Clinton P. Anderson, influential vice chairman and then former chairman of the JCAE, stated, "I don't want any more Fuchs cases."[53] In addition, the fear of difficulties with other allies—which were not receiving the same level of nuclear sharing—surfaced as another persuasive argument against cooperation. As Senator Anderson noted, "We can't give weapons information to the United Kingdom without giving it to the rest of the NATO communities (or) we make enemies."[54] Finally, some objected on the grounds that the United States would contribute an unequal share in any nuclear-sharing agreement. Articulating this viewpoint, Senator Anderson said, "The British have little or nothing to trade on weapons and the rest of the NATO countries have still less."[55]

After contentious negotiations over these issues and more specific ones such as a plutonium buyback clause that the administration was forced to defer to later debate, groundbreaking legislation was sent forward stipulating that the United States would permit (1) transfer of nuclear weapons design blueprints, (2) fissile material, (3) non-nuclear components such as electronic and mechanical hardware, and (4) nuclear weapon delivery systems.[56] Indeed, it was the cooperation that the United Kingdom and some in the United States had long sought.

CONCLUSION

The foundation of the U.S.-UK Mutual Defense Agreement was built through the bilateral agreements forged in the 1950s. Soviet advances in 1953 and 1957 led to increased interest in atomic collaboration on both sides of the Atlantic but did not always lead to meaningful reforms. The tale of pre-1958 U.S.-UK nuclear collaboration, therefore, is one of making halting progress more than it is of creating rapid change. In developing a collaborative atomic relationship, the United States and the United Kingdom were forced to overcome numerous obstacles. Had they not endured, the "special relationship" would not be as strong as it is today.

NOTES

1. Ritchie Calder, "Cost of Atomic Secrecy: Anglo-U.S. Rivalry," *The Nation,* October 17, 1953, p. 304.

2. Ibid.

3. Ibid., p. 303.

4. Alfred Goldberg, "The Atomic Origins of the British Nuclear Deterrent," *International Affairs* 40, no. 3 (July 1964): p. 413.

5. Anthony Leviero, "Senate Body Votes M'Mahon Atom Bill without Dissent," *New York Times,* April 12, 1946, p. 1.

6. Ken Young, "No Blank Cheque: Anglo-American (Mis)understandings and the Use of the English Airbases," *Journal of Military History* 71 (October 2007): p. 1133.

7. Goldberg, "Atomic Origins," p. 413.

8. John Bayliss, "Exchanging Nuclear Secrets: Laying the Foundations of the Anglo-American Nuclear Relationship," *Diplomatic History* 25, no. 1 (Winter 2005): p. 36.

9. Leviero, "Senate Body Votes M'Mahon Atom Bill," p. 1.

10. Herbert S. Marks, "Congress and the Atom," *Stanford Law Review* 1, no. 1 (November 1948): p. 24.

11. Stephen I. Schwartz, "Congressional Oversight of the [Nuclear] Bomb," in *Atomic Audit: The Costs and Consequences of U.S. Nuclear Weapons since 1940,* ed. Stephen I. Schwartz (Washington, D.C.: Brookings Institution Press, 1998), p. 485.

12. Henry M. Jackson, "Congress and the Atom," *Annals of the American Academy of Political and Social Science* 290 (November 1953): p. 76.

13. Schwartz, "Congressional Oversight," p. 485.

14. Jackson, "Congress and the Atom," p. 76.

15. Marks, "Congress and the Atom," p. 27.

16. Jackson, "Congress and the Atom," p. 76.

17. N. J. Wheeler, "British Nuclear Weapons and Anglo-American Relations 1945–54," *International Affairs* 62, no. 1 (Winter 1985–1986): pp. 71–86.

18. "Meeting of the President with Prime Minister Churchill, In the Cabinet Room of the White House," White House Meeting Notes, January 7, 1952, p. 3, available at the Digital National Security Archive, http://nsarchive. chadwyck.com.

19. Ibid., p. 5.

20. Bayliss, "Exchanging Nuclear Secrets," p. 36.

21. "President Would Give Public More Atom Data, Help Allies," *New York Times,* July 9, 1953, p. 1.

22. Bayliss, "Exchanging Nuclear Secrets," p. 36.

23. "NSC 151/2: A Statement of Policy by the National Security Council on Disclosure of Atomic Information to Allied Countries," National Security Council, p. 1, available at the Digital National Security Archive, http://nsarchive.chadwyck.com.

24. Kenneth Miller, "U.S. Offers Atomic Data, Weapons to 13 Allies," *Washington Post,* December 16, 1953, p. 1.

25. John D. Morris, "President to Ask Power This Week to Give Atom Data," *New York Times,* February 14, 1954, p. 1.

26. Ibid.

27. William M. Blair, "President Lauds New Atom Pacts," *New York Times,* June 21, 1955, p. 17.

28. Charles Wilson, "Memo to Senator Jackson," May 10, 1955, available at the Digital National Security Archive, http://nsarchive.chadwyck.com.

29. Ibid.

30. "Proposed Agreement for Cooperation between the Government of the United States of America and the Government of the United Kingdom of Great Britain and Northern Ireland for the Cooperation on the Uses of Atomic Energy and Mutual Defense Purposes," Report no. 2299, U.S. House of Representatives, 85th Cong., 2nd Session, June 20, 1955, p. 2.

31. William M. Blair, "President Lauds New Atom Pacts," *New York Times,* June 21, 1955, p. 17.

32. Bayliss, "Exchanging Nuclear Secrets," p. 37.

33. Warren Unna, "No Title," *Washington Post and Times Herald,* July 24, 1956, p. 8.

34. Ibid.

35. Bayliss, "Exchanging Nuclear Secrets," p. 39.

36. Unna, "No Title," p. 8.

37. Bayliss, "Exchanging Nuclear Secrets," p. 40.

38. Jack Raymond, "Dulles Says U.S. May Supply NATO with Atom Arms," *New York Times,* July 17, 1957, p. 1.

39. Robert Hartmann, "U.S. Will Arm Britain with Guided Missiles," *Los Angeles Times,* March 25, 1957, p. 1.

40. Walter LaFeber, *America, Russia, and the Cold War, 1945–2002,* 9th ed. (New York: McGraw-Hill, 2002), p. 203.

41. J. R. Killian, *Sputnik, Scientists, and Eisenhower: A Memoir of the First Special Assistant to the President for Science and Technology* (Cambridge: MIT Press, 1982), p. 7.

42. Bayliss, "Exchanging Nuclear Secrets," p. 42.

43. Ibid.

44. Drew Middleton, "Britain Seeking U.S. Science Ties," *New York Times,* October 18, 1957, p. 5.

45. Dwight D. Eisenhower and Harold Macmillan, "Declaration of Common Purpose between the President of the United States and the Prime Minister of the United Kingdom," Washington, D.C., October 25, 2957.

46. Warren Unna, "Sharing A-Secrets: Anderson Warns Special Protections Are Needed," *Washington Post and Times Herald,* November 9, 1957, p. A13.

47. "Wash-4/NYK," memorandum from Washington Steele to Jessup, Roosenburg, May 8, 1958, available at the Digital National Security Archive, http://nsarchive.chadwyck.com.

48. Stephen I. Schwartz, "A Brief History of Congressional Oversight of Nuclear Weapons" (presentation at Carnegie Endowment International Nonproliferation Conference, Washington, D.C., November 8, 2005), http://www.carnegieendowment.org/static/npp/2005conference/presentations/Schwartz.pdf.

49. "Hill Support Growing for Secrets Pool," *Washington Post,* November 2, 1957.

50. Ibid.

51. Ibid.

52. Unna, "Sharing A-Secrets."

53. Ibid.

54. Ibid.

55. Ibid.

56. Warren Unna, "A Secrets for Allies: Main Stumbling Bloc Apparently Removed," *Washington Post and Times Herald,* March 13, 1958, p. A13.

6

BRITAIN'S DUAL NATURE IN U.S.-RUSSIAN NUCLEAR ARMS CONTROL

RICHARD WEITZ

Even before the signing of the U.S.-UK Mutual Defense Agreement (MDA) in 1958, Britain's role as a nuclear weapon state allied closely with the United States has often placed the country in a complex position in the context of Washington-Moscow nuclear disarmament and arms control negotiations. On the one hand, British policymakers have often served as a catalyst prodding the superpowers to overcome their differences and pursue arms control measures beneficial to the entire international community. On the other hand, London's own development of a robust nuclear arsenal has complicated bilateral arms control negotiations between Washington and Moscow.

Although the size and capabilities of the United Kingdom's nuclear arsenal have varied markedly over time, London has always made these force-sizing decisions unilaterally. The only arms control agreements that have directly affected the evolution of the UK nuclear forces have been the prohibitions against nuclear testing and the limits on nuclear sharing contained in the Nuclear Non-Proliferation Treaty (NPT). Since Soviet times, Moscow has attempted to include British (and French) nuclear weapons in the numbers to be permitted in arms control treaties, while London and Washington have resisted such proposals. This pattern is likely to persist.

ERA OF FAILED DISARMAMENT
During World War II, an important issue confronting the British and U.S. governments as they labored to manufacture the first atomic

bomb was whether to divulge information about their joint nuclear development program to third countries, especially their formal but distrusted ally, the Soviet Union. In Britain, Prime Minister Winston Churchill opposed sharing atomic secrets with Moscow. He sought to forge an enduring defense alliance with the United States in which nuclear weapons would help defend Europe from possible Soviet aggression.[1] The provisions of the 1943 Quebec Agreement that governed Anglo-American wartime nuclear cooperation prohibited the sharing of information related to nuclear weapons with third parties without the other's consent.[2]

The Labour government that assumed power after the war actively participated in international deliberations on how to establish an effective multilateral regime to control nuclear weapons. On November 15, 1945, Churchill's successor as prime minister, Clement Attlee, President Harry Truman, and Prime Minister William Lyon Mackenzie King of Canada issued a trilateral declaration in Washington calling for the establishment of a commission under the auspices of the United Nations to assess how to avert "the spreading of the specialized information regarding the practical application of atomic energy" before "safeguards acceptable to all nations were devised."[3] British defense experts and academics engaged with their U.S. colleagues to develop new theories and concepts (for example, means of verification) that helped shape the strategic arms control debate for decades to come.[4]

One of the first major transatlantic disagreements on nuclear arms control issues occurred during the deliberations concerning the Baruch Plan in 1946. The U.S. proposal to the UN Atomic Energy Commission in June 1946 outlined a mechanism that included widespread sharing of basic scientific knowledge regarding the peaceful uses of nuclear energy, elimination of existing atomic bombs, an agreement to refrain from building new ones, and the establishment of an extensive multinational verification system—which would include international control of all nuclear materials and facilities engaged in manufacturing fissile products—in order to ensure that nuclear energy would be used only for peaceful purposes.

The Soviet government, which would not develop a working atomic bomb until 1949, insisted that the United States had to eliminate all its existing nuclear weapons and cease producing new ones before the world community could establish a multilateral control regime. London also opposed the U.S. plan. British officials argued that allowing many countries to research and develop civilian nuclear power posed risks, given the prospects for establishing an effective supranational verification authority. British leaders also considered atomic bombs as possibly necessary to help defend their country against future aggression, a concern stimulated by Washington's initial failure to commit to European security.[5]

The subsequent formation of the North Atlantic Treaty Organization (NATO) in 1949, which committed U.S. military assistance to Western Europe under Article 5 (and whose credibility increased after the United States intervened on behalf of South Korea in the face of Communist aggression the following year) reassured the United Kingdom about its transatlantic security ties. Despite London's decision to conduct the first British nuclear weapons test in Australia in October 1952 and to develop an operational nuclear capability in following years, the British delegation submitted various nuclear arms control proposals that were sufficiently similar to those presented by the French and Soviet governments as to raise hopes that some agreement might prove possible. But the new Eisenhower administration, which saw nuclear weapons as an essential element of its New Look strategic policy, declined to endorse ambitious nuclear disarmament proposals, while the British were uninterested in less comprehensive measures that might constrain their own nuclear weapons development program.[6]

LONDON PUSHES FOR LIMITS ON NUCLEAR TESTING

By the time that the MDA was signed, the international disarmament community had redirected its efforts from eliminating existing arsenals to limiting their possible use. British and U.S. scientists publicized the detrimental effects of radioactive fallout to human health generated by the frequent testing of ever-larger hydrogen bombs. These revelations increasingly engendered support for the UK-based Campaign for Nuclear Disarmament and the multinational Pugwash transnational peace movement, which had a large British component. These and other groups mobilized mass popular pressures on Western governments to curb nuclear weapons testing.[7]

Although verification and other difficulties prevented the United Kingdom, the United States, and the Soviet Union from adopting a comprehensive prohibition on nuclear testing in 1961, the three governments did agree in 1963 to a trilateral Partial or Limited Test Ban

Treaty (LTBT), which banned nuclear tests or other nuclear explosions in the atmosphere, in outer space, or under water (but not underground). Anglo-American security ties helped the United States and the United Kingdom accept the LTBT. On the one hand, British pressure helped induce their more skeptical U.S. colleagues into agreeing to the LTBT by helping to develop the seismic monitoring technologies that reassured Washington that they could detect any militarily significant atmospheric test.[8]

On the other hand, Washington's commitment to continue UK-U.S. nuclear weapon collaboration helped reassure London about accepting a ban on above-ground testing.[9] Britain gained access to the U.S. underground test site in Nevada beginning in 1962, to U.S. warhead designs and some non-nuclear components for British warheads, and to the same U.S.-manufactured submarine-launched ballistic missiles deployed on U.S. strategic nuclear submarines (SSBNs).[10] Without such reassurances, the British might have felt the need to continue testing to catch up with the more advanced research and development programs of the United States and the Soviet Union.[11]

More controversially, British representatives sometimes played the role of go-between and honest broker between the Soviet Union and the United States. For example, in November 1958 Prime Minister Harold Macmillan traveled to Moscow on his own initiative to propose the idea of establishing an agreed quota of annual on-site inspections. His efforts to continue negotiations at the May 1960 Paris summit, even after the downing of a U.S. U-2 reconnaissance aircraft over Russia, notably antagonized Eisenhower, but the Macmillan government soon developed good, if not conflict free, security ties with the John F. Kennedy administration that assumed office in early 1961.[12]

The British government of Harold Wilson saw the 1968 NPT as important for reducing Soviet-NATO tensions as well as for affirming Britain's leading international role as a responsible nuclear weapons power.[13] London shared Moscow's concern about foreclosing West Germany's possible acquisition of an independent nuclear deterrent.[14] The British government assisted in securing the support of the non-nuclear states to the NPT by helping bridge differences between Moscow and Washington regarding "negative security assurances,"[15] which involve a nuclear weapon state agreeing not to employ nuclear weapons against non-nuclear states except under certain limited conditions.[16]

Some analysts believe that there is a conflict of interest between the MDA and Articles I and II of the NPT relating to the prohibition of transfer of nuclear weapons or control over such weapons. They also perceive tensions between the MDA and Article VI, which calls for the parties to pursue nuclear disarmament.[17] Others argue that, because the MDA provides for the transfer of technology and information and not whole weapons, it does not compromise Articles I and II of the NPT.[18] They also consider Article VI a long-term objective requiring a favorable transformation in the international security environment.

The British government served as both a catalyst and an impediment to the realization of a Comprehensive Nuclear Test-Ban Treaty (CTBT), which became an object of intense discussion between Washington and Moscow in the late 1970s. The Labour government of James Callaghan saw the negotiations as an opportunity to exercise leadership in nuclear arms control—as well as bolster its image as international peacemaker among the British electorate—after London had been largely excluded from the formal deliberations over the 1974 Threshold Test Ban Treaty and the 1976 Peaceful Nuclear Explosions Treaty. Yet, members of the British defense establishment, like their U.S. counterparts, opposed further limits on Britain's ability to test nuclear weapon designs. UK officials feared that such measures might impede development of technologies deemed essential for ensuring that Britain's submarine-launched strategic systems could penetrate the improving Soviet ballistic missile defense (BMD) architecture.[19]

ARMS CONTROL AND THE THIRD-COUNTRY PROBLEM

During the late 1960s and 1970s, the Soviet-U.S. policy of mutual détente entailed direct bilateral negotiations on limiting the scale of their nuclear buildups through formal treaties. Under the terms of the 1972 Strategic Arms Limitation Talks (SALT I), Moscow and Washington essentially agreed to freeze the number of long-range offensive ballistic missiles in their active arsenals. The 1972 Anti-Ballistic Missile (ABM) Treaty, amended in 1974, severely constrained the BMD systems either side could deploy. Finally, the 1979 SALT II accord imposed comprehensive limitations on the development of both countries' strategic arsenals.

At first, the Soviets were satisfied to have their status as a nuclear superpower coequal with the United States, as was confirmed by the bilateral exclusivity of the SALT negotiations. As the talks progressed, however, Soviet negotiators began seeking compensation from Washington for the British (and French) nuclear weapon systems, which Moscow argued would likely reinforce the U.S. nuclear arsenal in any major war between NATO and the Warsaw Pact. For example, the Soviets issued a unilateral statement affirming their right to increase the size of their strategic submarine fleet in accordance with any increase in the size of the British and French nuclear arsenals, a position the U.S. government refused to accept.[20] Soviet negotiators likewise unsuccessfully demanded compensation for the British and French nuclear forces during the subsequent Strategic Arms Reduction Talks (START) of the 1990s.[21]

European governments were worried that the SALT process would weaken Washington's extended nuclear guarantee to its NATO allies by codifying a Soviet-U.S. nuclear balance in which America's loss of nuclear superiority would make U.S. policymakers more reluctant to wage a major war, even to defend Western Europe.[22] The bilateral structure of the SALT and START agreements also meant that the framework might not optimally address certain Soviet capabilities, especially the USSR's intermediate-range nuclear forces, which threatened West European countries but not the United States.[23]

Owing to their tight nuclear ties with the United States, the British had a specific concern about how SALT's "non-circumvention" provisions might inhibit Anglo-American nuclear cooperation, such as Britain's right to acquire U.S.-manufactured delivery systems for use in launching its own nuclear warheads. Soviet and subsequently Russian strategic arms control experts have long sought to prevent the United States from exploiting its defense ties with the United Kingdom, whose nuclear forces were not constrained under SALT or START, to test by proxy technologies and operational concepts that the Pentagon could then adopt for its own use. For example, in 1998 Moscow claimed that the United States was circumventing START I by allowing the British to test a U.S.-made Trident missile with more than the eight warheads permitted the U.S. Navy under START.

U.S. administrations have consistently objected to attempts to extend SALT or START constraints to impede the unique "existing pattern of cooperation" between U.S. and British strategic forces.[24] The British government has sought to reduce Moscow's concerns by affirming that the United Kingdom would only seek a "minimum" strategic force "in no way comparable to the nuclear forces of the Soviet Union and the

U.S." In July 1991, the Soviet government indicated it would acquiesce to the arrangements, but warned it might withdraw from START "if the United States were to alter its existing pattern of cooperation with the United Kingdom on strategic offensive arms in such a way that the terms and purposes of the START Treaty would be circumvented and the strategic balance altered."[25]

The British and U.S. governments worked closely, through NATO and bilaterally, to parry this Soviet campaign.[26] Henry Kissinger relates that, during the late 1960s and 1970s, "the British played a seminal part in certain American bilateral negotiations with the Soviet Union—indeed, they helped draft the key document. In my White House incarnation then, I kept the British Foreign Office better informed and more closely engaged than I did the American State Department."[27]

Through such collaboration, British officials managed to avoid SALT II terms that would have prevented the United Kingdom from deploying air-launched cruise missiles on British aircraft.[28] Although some compromises in the final texts of the various SALT and START agreements appear to reflect at least a tacit linkage between the U.S. and British forces under the rubric of achieving "strategic equivalence," the outcome generally favored London by allowing continued Anglo-American nuclear weapons cooperation.[29] Less directly, the constraints on the growth of the USSR's strategic offensive and especially strategic defensive capabilities helped keep the British deterrent viable despite its limited size and effectiveness.[30]

In the end, the fact that the total number of warheads possessed by Britain, China, and France amounted to at most 10 percent of the superpower total during the Cold War meant that Soviet strategic planners were willing to overlook the potential effects of these "second tier" countries.

During the late 1970s and early 1980s, the United Kingdom became even more involved in the so-called Euro-missile crisis. The British government, as a full participant in NATO's Special Consultative Group, assumed an important role in shaping and implementing the alliance's 1979 decision to base improved U.S. ground-launched cruise missiles (GLCM) and intermediate-range Pershing ballistic missiles on West European soil in an effort to induce the Soviets to negotiate limits on their ongoing deployments of SS-20 intermediate-range ballistic missiles.

The British government encountered severe domestic opposition as it sought to carry out this dual-track policy, which many critics considered excessively provocative. Mass protests arose against the basing of U.S. GLCMs in Britain. The deployment's opponents tended to blame the Reagan administration, which they considered hostile to arms control, for the deadlock in the Soviet-U.S. negotiations.[31]

During this period, Soviet negotiators argued that all Britain's nuclear weapons, and not just the U.S. intermediate-range missiles deployed in the United Kingdom, should be included in any calculation of the strategic balance in Europe.[32] Shortly before the U.S. missiles arrived on British soil in late 1982, Soviet officials proposed to limit their own SS-20s based in Eastern Europe to the total number of nuclear launchers of Britain and France. The Conservative government of Margaret Thatcher rejected the Soviet proposal to include the United Kingdom's submarine-based force in the intermediate-range nuclear arms control negotiations, arguing that their function was that of basic, if last resort, deterrence against Moscow rather than a bargaining instrument, which was how NATO governments often characterized the GLCMs and Pershing missiles. The French, U.S., and German governments also rejected the Soviet offer, which would have "de-coupled" the U.S.-Soviet strategic balance, governed by SALT, from the European strategic balance. They feared that such separation would imply that Washington might not automatically commit its strategic nuclear deterrent against Moscow in case of a nuclear war in Europe.[33]

Nevertheless, leading members of the opposition Labour, Liberal, and Social Democratic Party supported various proposals to constrain Britain's Polaris submarine-based deterrent, which London had always committed to NATO's defense against a possible Soviet attack.[34] Many British experts also evinced little enthusiasm for the Reagan Strategic Defense Initiative which, if emulated by the Soviets, could have led to the demise of the ABM Treaty and potentially undermined the capability of the smaller British nuclear deterrent to penetrate Soviet missile defenses.[35] Prime Minister Thatcher also told the Soviets after the 1986 Reykjavik summit—where Presidents Reagan and Gorbachev almost agreed to eliminate many of their nuclear forces—that Britain planned to remain a nuclear weapon state indefinitely.[36]

Following the failure of Moscow's confrontational tactics to prevent the deployment of U.S. missiles, the new Soviet leadership under Mikhail Gorbachev yielded and agreed to adopt a "zero-option" for Soviet and U.S. mid-range (500 to 5,500 kilometers) ballistic missiles throughout the world under the terms of the 1987 Intermediate Nuclear Forces (INF) Treaty. The elimination of the INF systems in turn stimulated interest among the Western arms control community in reducing shorter-range nuclear systems, which have a range of less than 500 kilometers, commonly referred to as tactical nuclear weapons (TNW).[37]

During the Soviet period, Britain's TNWs did not become a major arms control issue. British policymakers were unwilling to abandon these systems, given the Soviet military's overwhelming qualitative and quantitative superiority in such weapons as well as the USSR's massive conventional and chemical weapons arsenals in the European theater.[38] British strategists also thought these weapons could help compensate for the end of clear U.S. nuclear superiority over the Soviet Union that the United States enjoyed during the early Cold War period. Owing to the buildup of Soviet nuclear forces during the 1960s and 1970s, U.S. negotiators had to settle for strategic arms control agreements such as SALT that enshrined U.S.-Russian nuclear equivalence. Some British leaders saw their nuclear forces, strategic as well as tactical, as usefully reinforcing the U.S. deterrent by requiring Soviet planners to confront "a second centre for decision making" regarding the possible use of nuclear weapons in NATO's defense. In the words of Defence Minister Francis Pym, from the view of Soviet leaders, Britain's nuclear weapons "doubles their uncertainty, complicates their planning and increases their risks. It is in this way that our strategic and theatre nuclear forces contribute so much to the collective deterrence of the Alliance."[39]

As the Cold War ended, the presidents of the Soviet Union and Russia joined with the U.S. president in a process of parallel unilateral reductions and constraints on these shorter-range systems. In accordance with the Presidential Nuclear Initiatives (PNI) of 1991–1992, Russia and the United States eliminated many of their TNWs and removed other TNW systems from operational deployment, transferring the warheads to separate secure storage.[40]

Although the British government did not formally participate in these reciprocal reductions, London decided to eliminate unilaterally its TNW arsenal. In 1991, the British government halved its stockpile of WE177 nuclear gravity bombs. In 1992, the Ministry of Defence announced it would remove all TNW from its surface warships and fighter aircraft, including warplanes on aircraft carriers or based on shore, leaving only the nuclear warheads on Britain's strategic submarines and some WE177s (retired a few years later) on its fleet of Tornado bombers.[41] At present, Britain's entire nuclear deterrent consists of a single launch platform, a single missile, and a single warhead type.[42]

After the disintegration of the USSR, the British, U.S., and Russian governments renewed their interest in extending the LTBT—which permitted underground nuclear testing—into a CTBT. The means of verification needed to underpin a complete ban on nuclear testing had improved since the 1970s, and the three countries had entered into an unofficial moratorium on nuclear testing since the early 1990s. During the negotiations from 1994 to 1996 at the Geneva-based Conference on Disarmament, the UK Atomic Weapons Establishment helped develop the treaty's verification provisions, whose International Monitoring System involves hundreds of networked monitoring stations distributed throughout the world. On April 6, 1998, the United Kingdom and France became the first nuclear weapon states to ratify the CTBT,[43] followed by Russia in June 2000. The United States and China have signed but not ratified the treaty.

BRITAIN AND THE FUTURE OF ARMS CONTROL

After a brief lapse during the 1990s, the issue of how to integrate British nuclear capabilities into previously bilateral Russian-U.S. arms control processes has again become an issue for Moscow. Even before the recent NATO-Russian dispute arose regarding U.S. plans to deploy ballistic missile defense assets in Poland and the Czech Republic, President Vladimir Putin and other Russian leaders suggested that Russia might have to withdraw from the INF Treaty because the accord uniquely discriminates against Russia. They argued that, since 1987, a number of new countries located on Russia's periphery have developed intermediate-range missiles. Moscow and Washington recently agreed to try to induce other countries to join the INF Treaty—and Britain could play an important role in this regard.

The Russian government has begun advocating multilateralizing other bilateral Russian-U.S. arms control processes. At his year-in-review news conference in January 2008, Foreign Minister Sergey Lavrov observed, "Objectively the time has come to open the framework of relations in the area of strategic stability for other states, primarily European, in order to ensure common security."[44] In his address at the February 2008 session of the Munich Security Conference, First Deputy Prime Minister Sergey Ivanov likewise argued, "Sooner or later, we will have to start working in a multilateral format."[45]

Attempts to negotiate official limitations on TNW, a perennial concern of analysts worried about nuclear terrorism because these munitions appear less secure than Russia's strategic weapons, could prove the most contentious nuclear arms control issue that might involve Moscow, Washington, and London. The Russian government has already indicated that it would insist on challenging conditions for any formal TNW arms control agreement, which could affect the U.S. Air Force nuclear bombs thought to be stored in the United Kingdom. On September 3, 2007, Colonel General Vladimir Verkhovtsev, head of the Russia's Defense Ministry's 12th Main Directorate, which is responsible for Russia's nuclear weapons, told reporters that Russia would require that other countries—"above all France and Britain"—join with Moscow and Washington in any future TNW arms control talks.[46] The current U.S. administration has not expressed interest in discussions on TNW.

Russian strategists seem to include Britain's Trident system within the TNW category. Since 1998, when Trident became the United Kingdom's only nuclear weapons system, British government representatives have attributed a "sub-strategic role" for its warheads in addition to their strategic deterrent missions. Although British spokespersons no longer use the term formally, analysts believe it refers to using a Trident missile to launch a single, low-yield nuclear warhead, but for strategic purposes (for example, as a "warning shot") instead of to influence the outcome of a particular battle.[47]

The Russian and U.S. governments will soon need to negotiate a successor agreement to START and the Strategic Offensive Reductions Treaty (SORT), which was signed in 2002 in Moscow. The latter stipulates that both sides must reduce their nuclear arsenals to between 1,700 and 2,200 "operationally deployed strategic warheads" by December 31, 2012. Russian negotiators might again seek to limit the size, operations, or information sharing with the nuclear forces of Britain and France. Britain's transition to a Trident submarine fleet whose most advanced missiles are theoretically capable of attacking targets in Russia with superior accuracy means that Russian planners likely consider the counterforce potential of these systems in assessing the vulnerability of Russia's strategic arsenal to a NATO preemptive attack.

Alternately, Moscow may focus on the argument that a future Russian-U.S. strategic arms control agreement must take into account the British and French systems to preserve nuclear parity between Russia and the United States—raising again, as with INF, the issue of how to transform a traditionally bilateral arms control process into a multilateral structure.

The U.S. plan to incorporate British-based sites into its evolving European-based BMD architecture, which has elicited intense Russian opposition, is also arousing controversy in the United Kingdom. British governments generally opposed national missile defenses during the Cold War. No technically and financially feasible system could have protected Britain from the enormous Soviet missile arsenal. Even a modestly effective Soviet BMD system, such as the one the Soviets were building around Moscow, threatened to negate the ability of the British deterrent to inflict considerable destruction on vital Soviet targets.[48]

With the end of the Cold War, however, British military planners, like their U.S. colleagues, see BMD as potentially helping defeat and thereby deter the limited long-range ballistic missile arsenals of Iran and other states of proliferation concern. According to the British media, Prime Minister Tony Blair personally engaged in a months-long campaign to persuade the Bush administration to deploy BMD interceptor missiles on British soil.[49]

Although the successor Labour government of Gordon Brown has apparently dropped that idea, it appears to share the concerns of its predecessor and that of the current U.S. administration that countries of proliferation concern will soon threaten Europe with ballistic missile strikes and that emerging BMD technologies might help counter this danger. Defence Secretary Des Browne said that plans to allow the U.S. military to use the Royal Air Force base at Menwith Hill for BMD purposes "continues the tradition of cooperation in support of UK, US and allied interests."[50] An opposition leader, Liberal Democrat Nick Clegg, complained that "committing this country to using our facilities in Yorkshire as a sort of advance listening post for the missile defence system has provoked [a] terrible reaction from the Russians."[51]

London and Washington are also jointly resisting operational arms control measures, such as legally binding reductions in the alert status of their nuclear weapons or limits on the permissible patrol paths for their strategic submarines, that aim to reduce risks of preemptive attacks; these proposals have some support in Moscow.[52] Several members of Parliament have attributed the recent deterioration in British-Russian relations to London's close security ties with Washington.[53]

Less controversially, Britain has worked with the United States on multilateral efforts to enhance the safety and security of the former Soviet Union's nuclear legacy. Both countries are leading contributors to the "Global Partnership against the Spread of Weapons and Materials of Mass Destruction," launched at the June 2002 Group of Eight summit in Canada. Britain has assumed a prominent role in eliminating Russia's stockpile of chemical weapons, while U.S. aid has focused on destroying and securing Russia's nuclear weapons and related material.

As Russia and the United States propose various multilateral nuclear fuel cycle initiatives and advance the new Global Initiative against Nuclear Terrorism, Britain might also have a special role. Some governments might prefer to deal with Britain, at least initially or in partnership with the United States, rather than with Washington alone. For example, the British government served as a bridge between Tripoli and Washington in a successful campaign to induce Libya to renounce its nuclear weapons program.[54]

How the members of the British defense community, like their U.S. and Russian counterparts, resolve their fundamental ambivalence regarding nuclear weapons has always presented a serious problem for the nuclear nonproliferation regime. Although British policymakers are eager to curb further proliferation of nuclear weapons to third countries, their recent actions and declarations, including the 2006 Defence White Paper, make clear they are unwilling, under present conditions, to abolish their own strategic arsenal.

The Labour government of Gordon Brown has sought to deal with these tensions by stressing the linkage between arms control and disarmament. Prime Minister Brown and other British leaders have argued that, by promoting such arms control measures as the CTBT and a Fissile Material Cutoff Treaty and by offering to host a technical conference of P5 nuclear laboratories on the verification of nuclear disarmament before the 2010 NPT Review Conference, London can play an important role in creating a more favorable environment for the long-term realization of the NPT goal of eliminating nuclear weapons.

Although the Russian and U.S. administrations in early 2008 seem less responsive to such concerns, the new governments that will soon take power in both countries might be more open to these new initiatives, allowing London once again to resume its catalytic role in Russian-U.S. arms control.

NOTES

1. Barton J. Bernstein, "The Uneasy Alliance: Roosevelt, Churchill, and the Atomic Bomb, 1940–1945," *Western Political Quarterly* 29, no. 2 (June 1976): pp. 202–230.

2. J. P. G. Freeman, *Britain's Nuclear Arms Control Policy in the Context of Anglo-American Relations, 1957–68* (New York: St. Martin's Press, 1986), p. 9.

3. Cited in William Epstein, *The Last Chance: Nuclear Proliferation and Arms Control* (New York: Free Press, 1976), p. 7.

4. Margaret Gowing (with Lorna Arnold), *Independence and Deterrence: Britain and Atomic Energy 1945–52,* vol. 1, *Policy Making* (London: Macmillan Press, 1974), p. 72.

5. Freeman, *Britain's Nuclear Arms Control Policy,* pp. 13–14.

6. Ibid., pp. 19–20.

7. Ibid., p. 33.

8. Ibid., pp. 40–81.

9. Ritchie Ovendale, *British Defence Policy since 1945: Documents in Contemporary History* (Manchester: Manchester University Press, 1994), p. 129. The United Kingdom has not conducted a nuclear test, in Nevada or elsewhere, since 1991.

10. Michael Quinlan, "The Future of United Kingdom Nuclear Weapons: Shaping the Debate," *International Affairs* 82, no. 4 (2006): p. 628.

11. Lorna Arnold and Mark Smith, *Britain, Australia and the Bomb* (New York: Palgrave Macmillan, 2006), p. 83.

12. Ian Clark, *Nuclear Diplomacy and the Special Relationship: Britain's Deterrent and America, 1957–1962* (London: Oxford University Press, 1994).

13. Nicholas J. Wheeler, "The Dual Imperative of Britain's Nuclear Deterrent: The Soviet Threat, Alliance Politics and Arms Control," in *UK Arms Control in the 1990s,* ed. Mark Hoffman (Manchester: Manchester University Press, 1990), p. 37.

14. Peter Malone, *The British Nuclear Deterrent* (London: Croom Helm, 1984), p. 33.

15. Epstein, *The Last Chance,* 138.

16. "U.S. 'Negative Security Assurances' at a Glance," Arms Control Association, January 2008, http://www.armscontrol.org/factsheets/negsec.asp.

17. "US-UK Mutual Defence Agreement Renewal and the NPT, Early Day Motion 1407 in the UK Parliament," June 24, 2004, http://www.acronym.org.uk/docs/0406/doc14.htm.

18. "UK-US Mutual Defence Agreement," June 22, 2004, *Daily Hansard*, http://www.publications.parliament.uk/pa/ld200304/ldhansrd/vo040622/text/40622-02text/40622-02.htm#40622-02_head()

19. Dan Keohane, "Britain's Performance in Implementing Article VI of the NPT," in *The Nuclear Non-Proliferation Treaty*, ed. Ian Bellany, Coit D. Blacker, and Joseph Gallacher (London: Routledge, 1985), pp. 38–39. In an interview, a former U.S. government official cited the joint opposition of the British and U.S. nuclear weapons communities as a major obstacle to achieving a CTBT at this time.

20. Malone, *British Nuclear Deterrent*, pp. 183–184.

21. Kerry M. Kartchner, *Negotiating START: Strategic Arms Reduction Talks and the Quest for Strategic Stability* (New Brunswick: Transaction Publishing, 1992), pp. 70, 110.

22. Samuel Payne Jr., *The Soviet Union and SALT* (Cambridge: MIT Press, 1980), pp. 79–81.

23. Richard E. Hays, "The Inherent Inadequacies of SALT: The Inapplicability of a Bipolar Solution to a Multilateral Problem," *Western Political Quarterly* 112, no. 2 (Summer 1997): pp. 631–648.

24. "U.S. Statement on Non-Circumvention of the START Treaty," July 29, 1991, http://www.fas.org/nuke/control/start1/text/declsts.htm.

25. "Soviet Statement on Non-Circumvention of the Start Treaty," July 29, 1991, http://www.fas.org/nuke/control/start1/text/declsts.htm.

26. Ovendale, *British Defense Policy since 1945,* 156.

27. Henry A. Kissinger, "Reflections on a Partnership: British and American Attitudes to Postwar Foreign Policy," *International Affairs* 58, no. 4 (1982), p. 577.

28. Laurence Freedman, *Britain and Nuclear Weapons* (London: Macmillan, 1980), pp. 96–100.

29. Wallace Irwin Jr., ed., *SALT II: Toward Security or Danger* (Washington, D.C.: Foreign Policy Association, 1979), p. 30.

30. David S. Yost, *European Security and the SALT Process* (Beverly Hills: Sage Publications, 1981), pp. 30–31.

31. Malone, *British Nuclear Deterrent*, p. 41.

32. Ibid., p. 93.

33. Malone, *British Nuclear Deterrent*, pp. 182–184; see also Werner Field, *Arms Control and the Atlantic Community* (New York: Praeger, 1987), pp. 40–41.

34. Keohane, "Britain's Performance," pp. 40–41.

35. Keith B. Payne, "From The Dilemmas of Deterrence, Defense, and Disarmament," *Strategic Arms Control after SALT,* ed. Stephen J. Cimbala (Wilmington, Del.: SR Books, 1989), p. 125.

36. Ken Booth and John Baylis, *Britain, NATO, and Nuclear Weapons: Alternative Defence versus Alliance Reform* (New York: St. Martin's Press, 1989), p. 161.

37. Mbow Amphas-Mampoua, *The United States, Russia, and European Security* (Pittsburgh: Dorrance Publishing Co., 2004), p. 32.

38. Martin Holmes et al., *British Security Policy and the Atlantic Alliance: Prospects for the 1990s* (Cambridge: Pergamon-Brassey's International Defense Publishers, 1987), pp. 26–27.

39. Cited in Timothy Garden, *Can Deterrence Last? Peace through a Nuclear Strategy* (London: Buchan & Enright, 1984), http://www.tgarden.demon.co.uk/writings/candet/cdl4.html.

40. Courtney Keefe, "The Presidential Nuclear Initiatives (PNIs) on Tactical Nuclear Weapons At a Glance," Arms Control Association, March 2006, http://www.armscontrol.org/factsheets/pniglance.asp.

41. William E. Schmidt, "British Are Planning to Remove A-Arms from Ships and Aircraft," *New York Times,* June 16, 1992, http://query.nytimes.com/gst/fullpage.html?res=9E0CE2DB163FF935A25755C0A964958260.

42. Des Browne, "A Disarming Proposal," February 5, 2008, http://comment-isfree.guardian.co.uk/des_browne/2008/02/a_disarming_proposal.html.

43. "Britain and France Ratify Nuclear Test Ban," UK Foreign & Commonwealth Office Daily Bulletin, April 6, 1998, Disarmament Diplomacy, no. 25 (April 1998), http://www.acronym.org.uk/dd/dd25/25france.htm.

44. "Transcript of Remarks and Replies to Questions by Russian Minister of Foreign Affairs Sergey Lavrov at a Press Conference on the Foreign Policy Outcomes of 2007, Russian MFA Press Center," Ministry of Foreign Affairs of the Russian Federation, January 23, 2008, http://www.mid.ru/brp_4.nsf/e78a48070f128a7b43256999005bcbb3/f18f960c1aa32c6dc32573da003fc60f?OpenDocument.

45. Cited in Mark John, "Ivanov Says Russia and U.S. Must Take Lead on New Arms Regime," Reuters, February 10, 2008, http://uk.reuters.com/article/worldNews/idUKL1030195520080210?feedType=RSS&feedName=worldNews.

46. Cited in "Russian Official Signals Firm Stance on Missiles and Kosovo," *International Herald Tribune* (Associated Press), September 3, 2007, http://www.iht.com/articles/2007/09/03/asia/russia.php.

47. Jeremy Stocker, *The United Kingdom and Nuclear Deterrence* (London: Routledge, 2006), pp. 10, 25–26; and Quinlan, "The Future of United Kingdom Nuclear Weapons," pp. 628–629.

48. Jeremy Stocker, *Britain and Ballistic Missile Defence: 1942–2002* (London: Frank Cass, 2004).

49. "Bombs Bursting in Air," *The Economist,* February 23, 2007, http://www.economist.com/opinion/displaystory.cfm?story_id=8744629; and Stephen Fidler, Christopher Adams, and Daniel Dombey, "Blair Seeks British Role in US Missile Defence," Financial Times, February 24, 2007.

50. Cited in "Long History of UK-US Defence Ties," BBC News, November 26, 2007, http://news.bbc.co.uk/1/hi/uk/7113062.stm.

51. "MP to Alert NATO to Missile Fears," BBC News, November 27, 2007, http://news.bbc.co.uk/2/hi/uk_news/england/north_yorkshire/7114392.stm.

52. Edith M. Lederer, "UN Panel OKs Resolution on Nuclear Alert," ABC News (Associated Press), November 1, 2007, http://abcnews.go.com/International/wireStory?id=3809332.

53. Sophie Walker, "British-U.S. Link Seen Hurting Ties with Russia," Reuters, November 25, 2007, http://uk.reuters.com/article/topNews/idUKL235139120071125?feedType= RSS&feedName=topNews.

54. Wyn Q. Bowen, *Libya and Nuclear Proliferation* (London: Routledge, 2006), pp. 59–65.

7

THE SPECIAL NUCLEAR RELATIONSHIP AND THE 1980 TRIDENT DECISION

KRISTAN STODDART

Much has been written on the "special relationship" Britain has with the United States. Much less has been written on their "special nuclear relationship" created by the signing of the Mutual Defense Agreement (MDA) in 1958 and its 1959 amendments.[1] These agreements on warhead and materials exchanges were supplemented in 1963 by the Polaris Sales Agreement (PSA), a deal concluded following the cancellation of the U.S. Skybolt air-delivered nuclear missile to be supplied to the United Kingdom. The PSA extended arrangements existing under the MDA to assist the United Kingdom in procuring the latest U.S. means of strategic nuclear delivery. Both agreements were essential to negotiations in 1979 and 1980 for the sale of the U.S. Trident submarine-launched ballistic missile (SLBM) system to Britain.

Speculation that the UK's Polaris force was likely to be replaced with either cruise missiles or with a new generation of multiple independently targetable reentry vehicle (MIRV) intercontinental ballistic missiles (ICBMs) had been around both Whitehall and wider defense circles since at least 1977.[2] In December 1979 the UK government signed a five-year extension to the 1958 MDA.[3] This was pivotal to future negotiations with the Americans. Without it the British government was unable to request any new information from the United States regarding its MIRV warheads. The PSA provided an established mechanism for negotiations regarding both the missile and associated reentry system.[4] Both agreements were the fundamental mechanisms for the continuation of the existing special nuclear relationship and the procurement of the Trident missile system that now serves as the cornerstone of the UK's nuclear deterrent.[5]

THE DUFF-MASON REPORT

Between 1977 and 1979 the Labour government under Prime Minister James Callaghan engaged in planning work for the replacement of the existing Polaris system. It recognized that a decision would soon be required to build a replacement system for deployment in the mid-1990s, when Britain's four Polaris submarines would be coming to the end of their operational lives, given that the lead time to bring replacements into service would be about 15 years.[6] In the summer of 1977 the Ministry of Defence (MOD) began to examine the Polaris replacement issue in detail, and in parallel the prime minister organized a subcommittee of the Ministerial Committee on Nuclear Policy (MCNP) to address all the issues involved. Owing to the Labour Party's 1974 commitment not to seek to replace Polaris, Callaghan and his colleagues had to tread carefully.[7]

This small MCNP subcommittee comprised Prime Minister Callaghan, Foreign and Commonwealth Secretary David Owen, Chancellor of the Exchequer Denis Healey, and Secretary of State for Defence Fred Mulley. They were advised that by the end of the 1970s the issue of replacement would become acute, given the anticipated lead times. By the beginning of 1978, consideration was being given in the MOD to a number of options regarding successor systems, including cruise missiles, Trident, or developing an indigenous SLBM that, unlike the Chevaline upgrade for Britain's Polaris force, would be MIRVed.[8]

Two working parties were formed to advise this four-man committee. One working party was set up under Professor Sir Ronald Mason, chief scientific adviser to the MOD, with the remit to examine the technical options regarding possible replacements for Polaris. The second was chaired by Sir Anthony Duff, deputy under-secretary (DUS) at the Foreign and Commonwealth Office. His committee was charged with a far-reaching study of the wider international implications of the alternative replacement systems. Together they produced the comprehensive Duff-Mason Report, submitted to the MCNP subcommittee in December 1978.[9] The report recommended that the submarine-based arsenal be retained if it was affordable, and that a replacement missile system should deploy continuously and have a greater number of warheads than Chevaline, the British government's largely indigenous method for improving Polaris against Soviet antiballistic missile (ABM) defenses.

This latter requirement could be accomplished either through a MIRVed ballistic missile capability or through sea-launched cruise missiles, given that Soviet defenses, especially Soviet antiballistic missile defenses around Moscow, were expected to improve significantly from the early 1980s onward. Air-launched and ground-launched missile systems were discounted on grounds of vulnerability and because they were not capable of the global reach of Trident, which had a projected range of more than 4,000 nautical miles. As Britain was not prepared to devote the financial resources needed for an autonomous nuclear weapons capability, and because cooperation with the United States was the cornerstone of its foreign and defense policy, further collaboration with the Americans was the preferred option.

Part II of the Duff-Mason Report dealt with the operation of future strategic systems. This indicated the terms of reference for "independence." This was defined as "true [operational] independence of the capability, maintainable for at least one year if the support of a collaborative partner were withdrawn."[10] The report recommended exploration of the option to acquire the Trident C-4 missile with "elements of 'UK uniqueness'" in a submarine platform.[11] This meant more technical discussions were required regarding the number of warheads to be used if a MIRVed configuration was chosen. This had long been favored as the preferred option by the MOD on technical and strategic grounds, as it was seen to provide the only assurance of "future proofing" the UK deterrent against improvements in Soviet ABM defenses over the 20–30 year life span of a successor system.[12]

Exploration of this option had to be discussed within the context of the 1958 MDA and the 1963 PSA. Nuclear technology transfer would be enabled through the intergovernment mechanisms established by the MDA, such as the joint working group (JOWOG) system of technical exchanges, where UK nuclear warhead technology could be discussed with the Americans to *mutual* advantage. These exchanges covered not only information on nuclear warheads but also data on nuclear effects, vulnerability, and theoretical physics. It was not the case that the United States simply passed nuclear warhead and weapons information to the British without an appropriate amount of information being sent in return. Nor was it the case that after the early 1960s the Atomic Weapons Research Establishment (AWRE) copied

U.S. weapons designs. Rather, the United Kingdom made its own initial designs to meet national requirements and then discussed them with its U.S. counterparts to shared benefit.

In 1979 it was believed that there was little value in Britain seeking to design a Polaris successor system with the French "unless the US were to offer us an inadequate successor system, or one so hedged with restrictions that it was no longer truly independent."[13] However, the Trident option would make significant additional demands upon UK fissile material supplies and warhead manufacturing capabilities. It was estimated that the Trident C-4 option would require 576 warheads, production of which would need to begin in 1988.[14] This number was based on deploying 16 missiles, each armed with eight warheads aboard four submarines, with sufficient spares to guard against reliability failures.[15] The exact figures are not in the public domain.

The MCNP subcommittee that met either side of the New Year failed, however, to formally agree on the choice of Trident as a successor system,[16] although Callaghan personally saw it as the best option.[17] Despite the doubts held by the other members of the subcommittee, it was decided at its January 1979 meeting that Callaghan should make an informal request to President Carter for Trident when they met at their upcoming summit meeting. This request would be on a personal basis and without an official government commitment.

The approach was made during the four-power summit at Guadeloupe on January 4–6, 1979, and it was greeted favorably.[18] Subsequently, Sir Ronald Mason, the chief scientific adviser in the MOD, and Sir Clive Rose, a deputy secretary in the Cabinet Office, were sent to Washington in the middle of February 1979 for "exploratory talks" with their opposite numbers. They were joined by cabinet officials from both countries: Fred Mulley, UK secretary of state for defence, and Harold Brown, U.S. secretary of defense.[19]

However, a decision on a replacement system was now halted. Time had now run out for James Callaghan's Labour government, and this decision would pass to the incoming administration of Margaret Thatcher following Conservative victory in the May 1979 general election. To assist with the deliberations regarding a successor system, Callaghan broke with government convention that information from an outgoing government was not made available to an incoming opposition party, and he supplied Margaret Thatcher with a summary of his recent meeting with Jimmy Carter and his Polaris replacement file.[20]

MARGARET THATCHER AND THE
PURCHASE OF TRIDENT

Unlike her Labour predecessors, Margaret Thatcher and her new Conservative government were fully committed politically to maintaining a British nuclear deterrent. In opposition Thatcher had been critical of Labour's policies on the nuclear issue. In office she was to be a strident advocate of both the deterrent itself and strengthening the bonds between Britain and the United States in foreign and defense policy.[21]

Domestic concerns regarding nuclear weapons were increasingly apparent at the time of Thatcher's election victory, with the issue of the modernization of NATO's long-range theater nuclear forces (LRTNF) high on the political agenda. The replacement of the USSR's SS-4 and SS-5 missiles with the SS-20 had heightened existing tensions.[22] NATO responded to the Soviet SS-20 with a commitment to deploy its own mobile missile, the U.S. Pershing II, and ground-launched cruise missiles (GLCMs) as part of the "dual track" decision of December 1979, which had been agreed to by the Callaghan government prior to leaving office. The heightened concerns over the LRTNF situation made any decision regarding the replacement of Polaris with Trident controversial.

Soon after Margaret Thatcher arrived in government, contacts with the Americans were renewed by the new secretary of state for defence, Francis Pym, with President Carter reaffirming his previous commitment by continuing the discussions begun with Callaghan at the beginning of 1979.[23] Furthermore the government "had received firm assurances" that the second Strategic Arms Limitation Treaty (SALT II), signed in June 1979, would not have an adverse bearing on the U.S. commitment to supply the system.[24] However, the Thatcher government favored rapid negotiation on the proposed sale of Trident lest the issue run afoul of the difficult process of ratification of the treaty through the U.S. Senate.[25]

Importantly, 1980 was an election year in the United States. In the past, the most significant policy decisions had frequently been left for an incoming administration to take; an administration that would not be in place until January 1981. This placed greater pressure on the British government to successfully complete negotiations before the end of 1980.[26] Moreover, the Soviets were again pushing for the inclusion of both British and French forces in the ongoing bilateral superpower Strategic Arms Limitation Talks.[27]

Understandably, the British did not want to see their arsenal includ-ed in these discussions, but as they were dependent on U.S. technology their leverage was limited. The government had, however, received as-surances from the Carter administration that any "no transfer" clause proposed by the Soviets would be rejected, and that this was a non-negotiable matter.[28] The fact that the previous Labour government had engaged in an abortive discussion to include UK strategic forces in SALT II—if they could be a party to discussions—added to Margaret Thatcher's resolve to rapidly conclude the purchase of Trident.[29]

Using the Duff-Mason Report as a basis for a decision regarding a successor system, Thatcher formed her own cabinet subcommit-tee, MISC 7, in order to debate the points more fully and to formulate a strategy. To aid MISC 7, the chief of the defence staff, Sir Terence Lewin, and the group of senior civil servants who had supervised the Duff-Mason investigations were reconstituted, and by October 1979 the secretary of defence publicly announced:

> We will go on improving the Polaris force so that it will remain an ultimate deterrent to aggression in the 1990s. Furthermore consid-eration is already being given to the action that will be necessary to continue our strategic deterrent capability for as long as is necessary thereafter.[30]

At this point most of the informed opinion in Whitehall had already been canvassed and the Chiefs of Staff, chaired by Admiral Lewin, came out resoundingly in favor of a follow-on force. Their only reservations were associated with the cost and its impact on conventional forces at a time of flux in NATO.[31]

On December 6, 1979, a formal decision was made by the MISC 7 committee for the government to try to procure the Trident C-4 sys-tem, minus the warheads and submarines, both of which would be built in Britain. This decision was later brought to the attention of the full cabinet and came six months after SALT II had been agreed be-tween the United States and Soviet Union. Detailed discussions led to two requests from the Carter administration.

The first request was to develop a base on the British-owned island of Diego Garcia in the Indian Ocean. Second, the United States want-ed the British to pay for the staffing of the Rapier air defense system, which the Americans were intending to purchase for the air bases they operated in the United Kingdom.[32] Thatcher's government agreed to both of these requests, and the Americans in turn agreed to forgo the substantial research and development costs of Trident, substituting instead a fixed 5 percent levy.[33] This package was agreed by Prime Minister Thatcher and U.S. Secretary of Defense Harold Brown on June 2, 1980.

On July 15, 1980, the cabinet was informed that the sale of Trident had been agreed by the United States.[34] Prior to the formal signing, President Carter stated the U.S. desire to see the bipartisan nuclear relationship extended as the "United States attaches significant importance to the nuclear deterrent capability of the United Kingdom and to close cooperation between our two Governments in maintaining and modernising that capability."[35] This point was echoed by Harold Brown to his opposite number, Francis Pym, who noted that the Trident purchase represented "an important contribution to our continued close defence cooperation, which enhances the security not only of the United States and the United Kingdom, but of our allies and the world generally."[36]

The formal sales agreement was signed by an exchange of notes between Sir Nicholas Henderson, the British ambassador to the United States, and Warren Christopher, the U.S. secretary of state on September 30, 1980.[37] Although congressional approval was a prerequisite for the confirmation of the Trident agreement, with the president granting wide-ranging authority in defense and foreign policy, this was not expected to present any problems.[38]

Shortly thereafter an exchange of notes was published. It stated publicly why Trident was being made available to the British. In a press briefing that followed, it was maintained:

> Strategic cooperation is . . . an important component of the close cooperative relationship between the United States and Great Britain. This is a relationship that encompasses close cooperation in foreign policy and defence policy across the board, whether it be bases in England, deployment of ground-launch cruise missiles in Great Britain, collaboration in the foreign policy area . . . [or] joint use of facilities in Diego Garcia.[39]

The deal also held open the possibility of the British purchase of the Trident D-5 version, which had a longer range and greater payload capacity, although this was still in development in the United States.[40]

British experience of operating Polaris, which was supported by the United States, and developing Chevaline generated a great deal of political momentum to continue cooperation on a successor system. These arrangements were only made possible by the 1958 MDA and the 1963 PSA. The costs of going it alone in an age of increasingly sophisticated and expensive nuclear warhead technology and delivery systems were too much for the United Kingdom to bear without major cuts in conventional defense expenditure. Operating Polaris as both a survivable and credible nuclear deterrent alongside their U.S. allies came to heavily influence the available options when it came to the replacement question. During the same period, the British continued to test their nuclear designs using concepts and principles that could benefit the U.S. weapons program under the 1958 MDA.

The MDA, along with the 1963 PSA, provided established mechanisms for the transfer of nuclear technology and thereby facilitated rapid negotiations on Trident. In this endeavor the UK government was influenced strongly by the lessons learned through the development of the largely indigenous and costly Chevaline program.[41] These experiences strongly indicated to the British that keeping in step with U.S. developments of Trident should be a guiding principle of UK-U.S. nuclear weapons cooperation. If this path was followed, there was every chance of avoiding a need for a unique midlife upgrade of the British Trident force such as that necessitated by the Chevaline modification for Polaris.[42]

CONCLUSION

While operationally independent, the UK Trident force remains to this day highly dependent on the United States. This was indicated in a report prepared for public use by the MOD for the House of Commons Defence Committee in October 1980. The report revealed that Trident, like Polaris before it, requires ongoing U.S. support for spares, training, and range facilities for missile tests, along with technical information and services in support of the weapon system.[43] The existing infrastructure already in place, including shore facilities and missile and submarine support, coupled with the experience of running Polaris have always made renewal or replacement of the SSBN platform the most likely choice for the government over other options.[44]

This was only possible with continuing support and political agreement from the United States. Purchasing Trident off-the-shelf from the

Americans was preferred by the British government, given its experience with Chevaline, which had proven very costly. This was only made possible, however, by the continuation of the 1958 MDA and the ongoing exchanges of nuclear warhead design information in relation to Trident MIRVed warheads. The PSA facilitated the supply of missiles and the associated reentry systems technology.

Moreover, the Trident decision demonstrates that the British government was no longer prepared to go it alone in the nuclear age (as France had attempted).[45] Since the time of Winston Churchill, British prime ministers and senior members of the cabinet have realized that bipartisan sharing of nuclear weapons technology with the United States is not only cost-effective for the country but also serves wider defense and foreign policy goals.

The replacement of the Polaris missile with the U.S. Trident system enhanced and extended the strategic credibility of the British strategic nuclear deterrent into the twenty-first century and, in the process, avoided many of the pitfalls experienced with Chevaline. Equally important, the retention of a credible nuclear capability allowed the British, along with the French, to maintain the "second center of decision" role in the Euro-Atlantic area.[46] The debates that took place in Britain during 2006 and 2007 replayed many of the debates of 1979 and 1980 and, although the nuclear threat has changed radically, many of the core arguments retained a cogency that would have been familiar to the policymakers of the second Cold War during the 1980s.

NOTES

1. All references prefaced by TNA are taken from The National Archives, Kew, in the United Kingdom. Any omissions, errors of fact or interpretation in this article are the author's own. On the MDA see John Simpson, *The Independent Nuclear State: The United States, Britain and the Military Atom*, 2nd ed. (Basingstoke: Macmillan, 1986), pp. 142–157.

2. Ian Smart, "British Foreign Policy to 1985: The Future of the British Nuclear Deterrent: Technical, Economic and Strategic Issues," *Royal Institute of International Affairs* (1977).

3. *The Times*, December 14, 1979.

4. Nicola Butler, "US-UK Mutual Defence Agreement," *Disarmament Diplomacy*, no. 77 (May–June 2004): pp. 56–62.

5. They also remained central to the 2007 Trident renewal decision.

6. The increasingly long lead times were due to the increasingly sophisticated levels of technology. "Britain's Strategic Nuclear Forces: The Choice of a System to Replace Polaris," TNA, DEFE 25/325, July 1980.

7. The Labour Party manifestos can be found at "British Government and Elections since 1945," Political Science Resources, http://www.psr.keele. ac.uk/area/uk/uktable.htm.

8. On the development of Chevaline, see John Baylis and Kristan Stoddart, "Chevaline: The Hidden Programme, 1967–1982," *Journal of Strategic Studies* 26, no. 3 (December 2003): pp. 124–155.

9. "Terms of Reference for a Study of Factors Relating to Further Consideration of the Future of the United Kingdom Nuclear Deterrent," TNA, DEFE 25/325, undated 1978; see also James Callaghan, *Time and Chance* (London: Collins, 1987), p. 553.

10. "The Future of the UK Nuclear Deterrent," TNA, DEFE 25/335, August 13, 1979. It was felt at the working level that the Polaris force with the Chevaline front end could continue for four or five years without further U.S. help and Trident for up to seven years. Confidential correspondence, April 6, 2006.

11. "The Future of the UK Nuclear Deterrent."

12. Ibid.

13. Ibid.

14. Ibid.

15. The Conservative government of John Major (1990–1997) announced a ceiling of 96 warheads per submarine; the 1998 Strategic Defence Review (SDR) conducted by Tony Blair's Labour government reduced this number to 48. If evenly spread among 16 missiles, the maximum complement of Britain's four Trident submarines, this gives a figure of six warheads per missile until the 1998 SDR, with three from 1998 onward. "CMND 3999—The Strategic Defence Review 1998" (London: Her Majesty's Stationery Office, 1998). However, Trident can use inert reentry vehicles, in which nuclear warheads are placed, alongside penetration aids (if needed) in the space vacated by a reduced number of warheads. These could ensure the penetrability of a reduced capacity UK Trident force even against sophisticated missile defenses.

16. Callaghan, *Time and Chance*, p. 556.

17. Peter Hennessy, *Muddling Through: Power, Politics and the Quality of Government in Postwar Britain* (London: Gollancz, 1996), p. 126.

18. Callaghan, *Time and Chance*, p. 556.

19. Ibid., p. 556–557.

20. Hennessy, *Muddling Through*, pp. 126–127; Lord Owen, correspondence with author, March 2006.

21. Sir William Jackson and Lord Bramall, *The Chiefs: The Story of the United Kingdom Chiefs of Staff* (London: Brassey's, 1992), pp. 386–400.

22. Pavel Podvig, ed., *Russian Strategic Nuclear Forces* (Cambridge: MIT Press, 2001), pp. 17, 132, 134, 224–226.

23. Sir Michael Quinlan, interview with author, August 3, 2006.

24. Margaret Thatcher, *The Downing Street Years* (New York: Harper Collins, 1993), pp. 244–245.

25. Simpson, *Independent Nuclear State*, pp. 173–174, 196.

26. Thatcher, *Downing Street Years,* pp. 244–245.

27. This had been attempted throughout the SALT process. Kristan Stoddart, "Losing an Empire and Finding a Role," in vol. 3, *October 1964–June 1970,* of *Nuclear Weapons and International Security since 1945,* ed. John Simpson (Basingstoke: Palgrave, forthcoming).

28. Sir Michael Quinlan, interview with author, August 3, 2006.

29. Denis Healey, *The Time of My Life* (London: Penguin, 1990), p. 313.

30. Francis Pym (speech to Conservative university students, Nottingham, October 26, 1979; quoted in Lawrence Freedman, *Britain and Nuclear Weapons* (Basingstoke: Macmillan, 1980), p. 63.

31. Freedman, *Britain and Nuclear Weapons,* p. 63.

32. Thatcher, *Downing Street Years,* p. 246.

33. According to U.S. law, compensation must be made for the research and development involved in developing a system sold to a foreign country.

34. Peter Hennessy, *Cabinet* (London: Blackwell, 1986), p. 155.

35. "CMND 7979, The British Strategic Nuclear Force Texts of Letters exchanged between the Prime Minister and the President of the United States and between the Secretary of State for Defence and the United States Secretary of Defense, July 1980" (London: Her Majesty's Stationery Office, 1980).

36. Ibid.

37. "Sir Nicholas Henderson to Department of State Washington," TNA, FO 93/8/460, September 30, 1980.

38. "COMMGEN FCO London to MODUK," TNA, DEFE 25/325, September 9, 1980.

39. "(TEXT) U.S. Sale of Trident One Missiles to U.K. (Background Briefing)," TNA, DEFE 25/325, July 15, 1980.

40. "Britain's Strategic Nuclear Forces: The Choice of a System to Replace Polaris," TNA, DEFE 25/325, July 1980.

41. Peter Malone, *The British Nuclear Deterrent* (London: Croom Helm, 1984), p. 114.

42. See Kristan Stoddart, "Maintaining the 'Moscow Criterion': British Strategic Nuclear Targeting, 1974–1979," *Journal of Strategic Studies,* 2008 (forthcoming).

43. "M E Quinlan DUS(P) to PS to Secretary of State ANNEX A," TNA, DEFE 25/325, October 3, 1980.

44. Malone, *British Nuclear Deterrent,* pp. 106–125.

45. Richard Ullman, "The Covert French Connection," *Foreign Policy,* no. 75 (Summer 1989), pp. 3–33; and Kristan Stoddart, "Nuclear Weapons in Britain's Policy towards France, 1960–1974," *Diplomacy and Statecraft* 18, no. 4 (December 2007): pp. 719–744.

46. The second center of decision role in NATO was formally recognized by the Ottawa Declaration of June 19, 1974; see "Declarations on Atlantic Relations issued by the North Atlantic Council ("The Ottawa Declaration"), http://www.nato.int/docu/basictxt/b740619a.htm.

8

NUCLEAR WEAPON ACCIDENT RESPONSE

MICHAEL J. WEAVER

The United States and the United Kingdom share a special relationship in the area of nuclear weapon accident response, with important political, technical, and operational aspects, although it was not always so. In fact, it was mainly disagreements between the United Kingdom and the United States during a tabletop exercise (TTX) that led to technical exchanges between the two countries on responses to a U.S. nuclear weapon accident or incident in the United Kingdom.

These disagreements centered on the response roles and responsibilities during a possible U.S. nuclear weapon accident in the United Kingdom, which was in charge and had the authority to authorize operations at the accident site. This, coupled with the restrictions on the release of U.S. restricted data design information of nuclear weapons, made communications a challenge, to say the least.

ESTABLISHMENT AND EARLY WORK OF JOWOG 41
On October 17, 1985, the stocktake leadership meeting established Joint Working Group 41 (JOWOG 41) as a forum for cooperation in the scientific, engineering, safety, and environmental fields associated with effects and potential hazards of an accident or mishap involving nuclear warheads. JOWOG 41 covered technical information related to means of responding to and dealing with such events. JOWOG 41 was also to identify mutually agreed techniques and procedures for responding to nuclear weapon accidents or significant incidents. This charter remains essentially unchanged for more than 20 years.

Stocktake leadership comprised senior-level decisionmakers from the UK Ministry of Defence (MOD), the U.S. Department of Defense (DOD), and the U.S. Department of Energy (DOE). They met at roughly 18-month intervals to determine the strategic road map for areas of cooperation under the 1958 Mutual Defense Agreement (MDA).

In the early days of JOWOG 41, the exchanges devoted a significant amount of time to understanding the differences in terminology, emergency response philosophy, and roles and responsibilities. Identifying differences in terminology was critical to ensuring that communication was open and functional. JOWOG 41 developed and published a glossary of terms and acronyms, containing more than 200 unclassified terms that listed both UK and U.S. definitions. For example, differences in terminology, such as "render safe" and "stabilization," could lead to gross misunderstandings.

For U.S. emergency responders, one of their first actions after securing the accident site is to execute "render safe" procedures. These procedures are typically non-energetic procedures that would prevent the weapon from producing nuclear yield. Render safe is a concept that UK responders do not usually associate with a weapon accident. The concept of render safe to the UK responders is one of using energetic means to disrupt a device. UK responders would use the term "stabilization" to refer to what the U.S. responders call render safe. The consequences of these misunderstandings could be disastrous in a real event by delaying or preventing a successful response to a nuclear weapon accident.

U.S.-UK COOPERATION FOR EMERGENCY RESPONSE

As the communication barriers were removed, JOWOG 41 was able to devote more time to exchanging information in the areas of weapon recovery, health and safety, and other aspects of emergency response. The cooperation in these areas was unfettered by the professional competition that was prevalent in the weapon programs of the day. This was demonstrated in several tangible ways, such as the codevelopment of nondestructive evaluation capabilities to assess the condition of the weapon involved in an accident. Several improvements in imaging, radiation detection, modeling, and assessment resulted in greatly increased and improved capabilities for both the UK and U.S. emergency response teams.

In a U.S. nuclear weapon accident or an incident in the United Kingdom, the U.S. DOE Accident Response Group (ARG) would serve in an advisory-support role to the U.S. military. The mission of the ARG is to provide technical expertise and specialized capabilities to assist the DOD in recovering from an accident or a significant incident involving nuclear weapons.

The U.S. DOE National Nuclear Security Administration (NNSA) maintains the ARG, which comprises technical experts and emergency response personnel. Among the ARG personnel are senior scientific advisers, weapons engineers and technicians, experts in nuclear safety and high-explosive safety, health physicists, radiation control technicians, industrial hygienists, physical scientists, packaging and transportation specialists, and other specialists from the DOE and NNSA weapons complex.

ARG team members assess the condition of a weapon involved in an accident and provide technical advice to the DOD explosive ordnance disposal teams to develop joint plans for recovery of a damaged weapon. Team members also assist in the plans for packaging, transporting, and disposing of the weapon. To ensure safety, the DOE-NNSA nuclear explosive safety experts are part of an independent team that reviews all such plans.

The health and safety of the public, the environment, and emergency responders is the top priority of the ARG. The ARG health physics, industrial hygiene, and safety personnel evaluate the potential hazards to personnel from exposure to radioactive, toxic, and other hazardous materials and environments. In addition, they prescribe the appropriate personal protective equipment for working safely with the identified hazards. They also provide initial radiological data and protective action recommendations to local and state officials. Their expertise has been gained from evaluating the hostile environments associated with the testing of nuclear devices and from laboratory research and development with special nuclear materials and high explosives.

A provision under the 1958 MDA provided for the United States to conduct nuclear weapon accident exercises in the United Kingdom on a regular basis. This joint exercise program between the United Kingdom and the United States has been instrumental in identifying areas of cooperation, providing a catalyst for change, and providing a means for evaluating the effectiveness of proposed solutions.

RESULTS OF JOINT EXERCISES

In 1985 the first joint exercise, Elite Storm, was a TTX in which a limited number of participants from the United Kingdom and the United States gathered to discuss a fictitious scenario of a U.S. nuclear weapon accident in the United Kingdom. The major goals of Elite Storm were to test the notification procedures; evaluate the U.S. concept of operations for responding to a nuclear weapon accident in the United Kingdom; evaluate the UK-U.S. interface; and test the command, control, and communications of the integrated response forces.

During Elite Storm, the UK participants were limited to a simulation cell, meaning that a small number of UK participants simulated the entire UK response capability. The United States had a slightly larger number of exercise participants as they sought to exercise their notification and response procedures.

Elite Storm uncovered many opportunities for increased cooperation between the United Kingdom and the United States:

- The initial notification and alerting procedures failed to notify all the relevant response organizations;

- The roles and responsibilities relating to the interfaces between the UK and U.S. responders were not clearly defined, and this led to confusion and conflicts; and

- Classified communications were very slow in getting established, and this greatly impeded an effective response.

To address the issue of failure to notify all the appropriate response organizations, JOWOG 41 compiled a comprehensive procedure for initial notification and callout. This procedure is reviewed and updated as contact information changes. In addition, as technology improves, the alerting procedures and method of notification are revised to take advantage of the technical advances.

The lack of clearly defined roles and responsibilities for the UK and U.S. responders was the most complex and challenging of the lessons learned. This issue had implications in every aspect of the weapon accident response, from the command and control elements to the weapon recovery, the health and safety, and public affairs and media interactions. At the core of these issues was: "Who is in charge and what is the procedure for authorizing actions during the weapon accident response?"

The U.S. philosophy for command and control during a weapon accident response is to delegate authority to the responders at the accident site. For the U.S. weapons in the custody of the DOD, this is the DOD on-scene commander (OSC) of the emergency response force.

The UK approach is to establish a command and control system consisting of levels of authority—Gold, Silver, and Bronze—with regard to actions that could be authorized on a weapon involved in an accident. Another significant difference in the UK command and control structure is that the decision authority is shared between military and civilian officials, with the civilian representative being the greater of the two authorities.

Gold command contains the most senior UK personnel and represents the ultimate decisionmaking authority in a UK emergency response. In this respect, the Gold command is similar in authority to the U.S. DOD OSC. While the U.S. DOD OSC would be located at or near the accident site, the UK Gold command would usually be located in the county seat of the geographical area where the accident had occurred, which could be several miles from the accident site.

The UK Silver command is located in close proximity to the accident site (less than five miles, if possible) but intentionally not at the site. Silver command's senior-level personnel and decisionmakers have limited authority to authorize actions at the emergency site, but they keep Gold command well informed of the status of operations. Bronze command develops and submits proposed courses of action up the chain and executes operations approved by Gold and Silver commands.

In the U.S. model, the functions of Gold, Silver, and Bronze are all colocated at the accident site in the joint operations center, under the control of the U.S. DOD OSC. Following the first TTX, the United States adopted the strategy of Gold, Silver, and Bronze commands for responding to a U.S. nuclear weapon accident in the United Kingdom. This required significant changes to U.S. operational procedures.

With regard to communications, both sides noted that having redundant capabilities was vital, as invariably one or more systems suffered periods of inoperability. In addition, there were some incompatibilities between the UK and U.S. communication gear.

In May 1989, a few hundred participants from the United Kingdom and United States conducted a five-day command post exercise (CPX), Proper Watch. The overall goal of Proper Watch was to exercise and evaluate the joint operational procedures for a combined response. The major objectives were to exercise and evaluate:

- Alert and notification procedures for a U.S. nuclear weapon accident in the United Kingdom;

- Procedures and interfaces between the UK and the U.S. response forces on a combined response; and

- Integrated UK-U.S. command, control, and communications structure.

Although progress had been made since TTX in 1985, the list of lessons learned from Proper Watch looked very similar: notification, communication, and roles and responsibilities topped the list. The notification process held room for improvement. Communications were improved, but there were still resource shortages, hardware failures, and incompatibilities between UK and U.S. equipment.

Defining roles, responsibilities, and authorities required the most work. A written concept of operations was produced for areas such as weapon recovery, health and safety, and public affairs, but this concept of operations was not exercised until Proper Watch.

Considerable differences persisted between the United States and the United Kingdom in the approach to weapon recovery. The UK approach is to do as many operations at the accident site as possible, including performing full disassembly of the weapon at the accident site. This allows the United Kingdom to package individual components separately and transport them to final disposition. By separating the high-explosive material from the nuclear material, the United Kingdom had absolutely precluded any possibility of nuclear yield and greatly reduced any other potential hazards associated with radioactive material dispersal from a follow-on action during transportation and disposal.

The U.S. approach to weapon recovery is to minimize operations in the field. The U.S. strategy is to assess the condition of the nuclear weapon and perform immediate render safe procedures (RSP) to preclude the weapon from producing nuclear yield. Standard U.S. initial RSP is to ensure that the weapon is electrically safe and mechanically stable at the accident site.

When the initial RSP is complete, more deliberate actions to assess the condition of the nuclear weapon would occur. A portable linear

Damaged weapon made safe to ship.
Photo courtesy of Los Alamos
National Laboratory Archives.

accelerator is used to take high-energy radiographs (X-rays) of the nuclear weapon, to evaluate its internal condition. This information is critical to the development of the follow-on actions, which include continuation of RSP, packaging, and transportation plans. The goal of the follow-on actions is to make the weapon safe to ship and remove it from the accident site as soon as possible. It would be transported to a secure, fixed facility, where the damaged weapon could be completely dismantled and safely disposed.

In response to requests from the weapon safety experts of the Atomic Weapons Establishment (AWE), a fruitful area of exchange began. They requested the technical specifications and operational procedures for the equipment that the United States deployed to an accident site. This equipment included hand-held radios, radiation detectors, air samplers, a portable linear accelerator, and real-time radiography imager. They requested this information so that they could perform safety assessments on the potential use of the equipment in the close proximity of a damaged nuclear weapon. The AWE experts wanted to evaluate the equipment and associated procedures before the accident occurred, so that during the emergency they could focus on the damaged weapon and specifics of the situation. Although the United States had much of this information available, it was not always well organized or complete. The U.S. approach to ensuring that equipment is safe to use during a nuclear weapon accident is to evaluate the equipment, procedure, and specific situation while on scene at the accident site.

SAFETY EVALUATIONS

This UK request, perhaps inadvertently, prompted the United States to rethink the field approach to safety evaluations. The request provided the incentive for the United States to develop a process that came to be known as the Nuclear Explosive Safety Evaluation (NESE), modeled after the Nuclear Explosive Safety Studies that are performed on all nuclear operations in the U.S. nuclear weapons complex.

The purpose of the NESE was to establish a methodology for pre-certifying the equipment and procedures identified for potential use at a nuclear weapon accident site. Equipment that could be identified for potential use under a broad range of special circumstances was precertified through a NESE process. The approved equipment and specific procedures for its use served to constitute an ARG Master Equipment List (AMEL). The AMEL was then used as the basis for an in-field weapon recovery evaluation of the equipment needed in the specific situation. Because the actual field circumstance could not be predicted, the results of a NESE did not constitute blanket approval for use of the equipment in the field. Likewise, the absence of an AMEL listing did not preclude the use of an item of equipment certified at the site.

The NESE and AMEL process served as a primary means for sharing technical information and formed a firm foundation for discussing approaches to weapon recovery and safety evaluations. For the United States, the NESE and AMEL process brought a degree of formality and preparation that had been missing in its accident response. It also improved the efficiency of U.S. field operations.

A standard format for NESE documentation was jointly developed under JOWOG 41 to ensure consistency and completeness of the technical information. The U.S. NESE documents and AMEL are provided to AWE on an annual basis or whenever significant updates occur. AWE reviews these documents and provides their assessments to the ARG. This gives the AWE responders a chance to assess the U.S. equipment and evaluate the safety with regard to UK environmental and health regulations, prior to any time pressures associated with an accident response. On several occasions, AWE provided feedback to the ARG that prompted the ARG to change the operating procedures or modify the equipment to comply with UK safety standards, or both. The peer review supplied by AWE was valuable for improving the ARG capabilities.

The portable linear accelerator (LINAC) is an example of the United States changing response equipment and procedures based on AWE evaluations of the AMEL. The LINAC is one of the primary U.S. diagnostic tools, and U.S. response teams rely heavily on it to develop the render safe, packaging, transportation, and disposition plans. UK

LINAC warning system and shutoff switch.
Photo courtesy of Los Alamos National
Laboratory Archives.

safety regulations required that all linear accelerators have audible and visual alarms prior to and during operation. In addition, an emergency shutoff switch needed to be integrated into the operating system of the LINAC. The U.S. ARG designed and fabricated a warning system with an emergency shutoff switch that has become an integral part of the LINAC.

This NESE-AMEL process helped pave the way for integrating the UK and U.S. responders in a way that more clearly defined the roles and responsibilities associated with weapon recovery and met the expectations of both countries.

Just as the NESE was performed by ARG and AWE experts on equipment and procedures prior to deployment, a similar safety evaluation was performed in real time at an accident site. This was called the weapon recovery safety evaluation (WRSE). The WRSE team is to provide an independent safety assessment of proposed operations at the accident site to ensure nuclear and other safety considerations are met. It was a natural extension of the NESE-AMEL process to integrate UK and U.S. experts on the WRSE team, although there are still some classification barriers. This proved to be effective.

Similar to the NESE, a standard format for weapon recovery plans was jointly developed to facilitate the WRSE in the field. The weapon recovery plan had signature lines for U.S. and UK responders, which greatly clarified roles and responsibilities.

The standards and methodology associated with health and safety posed another significant area of challenge to JOWOG 41. Mundane units of measurement led to countless discussions regarding which system of units to use. The United States used the Imperial system of measurement units, first defined in the British Weights and Measurements Act of 1824, and the United Kingdom utilized the System International (SI). Thus, the majority of the instruments used for contamination monitoring were not capable of changing from one system of units to the other. The issue became further complicated when it faced issues such as how to interpret data, develop integrated data sets, and report the data in a consistent fashion. These topics led to the creation of the health and safety (H&S) working group in JOWOG 41.

The H&S working group developed the methodology for standardizing the calibration of radiation detection instruments and the format for reporting the instrument readings so that data could be shared between the U.S. and UK responders. This also led to a joint effort to develop an automated way to assemble, collate, process, and display large amounts of radiation detection data. Prior to this, the data had been tabulated and displayed by hand, which was very time-consuming and subject to human error.

This collaborative effort led to an electronic system that could be programmed to receive radiation detection data from a variety of different instruments (UK and U.S. origin) and to assemble, collate, and display the data in an integrated table and on a map. This electronic system was capable of acquiring and displaying data from instruments, regardless of whether they were SI or Imperial system units. As new information was collected by field teams, it could be downloaded into the electronic system and a real-time update could be displayed. This capability greatly improved the ability of the health and safety advisers to provide technical advice in a timely fashion to local authorities and other decisionmakers regarding the protection of the public and the environment.

ADDITIONAL BENEFITS OF COLLABORATION
Although the United Kingdom and United States each maintains separate hazard modeling capabilities today, these tools have improved greatly as a result of the countries' collaboration. In addition, the protocol for modeling hazard conditions and releasing information is reviewed on a regular basis in JOWOG 41 to ensure that there is a common understanding and agreement. Today, there are agreed operational procedures in place that specify how the dispersion models are used and the information is made available, thus avoiding the confusion of having differing results.

JOWOG 41 was not limited to an exchange of technical information about U.S. capabilities. The AWE response team had unique and distinct capabilities from the U.S. ARG. One such capability was dubbed

Temporary lightning protection pole test.
Photo courtesy of Los Alamos National
Laboratory Archives.

the lightning pole. Given the preponderance for rain in the United Kingdom, AWE felt it prudent to have a mobile temporary lightning protection pole (TLPP) that could be erected at the accident site to shield a damaged weapon from any lightning strikes that might occur in the area. The United States had no such capability. The TLPP became the topic of intense technical debate: Would the TLPP shield a damaged weapon from a potential lightning strike or would it draw lightning to the damaged weapon? After much debate, a joint test program was proposed and agreed to. Testing was conducted at a lightning test facility in the United States by a joint team of UK and U.S. electrical safety experts. The results of the tests were inconclusive, but the joint test program led to a greater understanding by both sides on the potential hazards and advantages.

The first field training exercise (FTX), named Diver Mist, was to be the first ever full FTX. It was scheduled to be held in the spring of 1992, although it did not take place until April 1994, owing to the Balkan conflict. In an FTX, the actual procedures are executed by participants, unlike in a TTX and a CPX where the procedures are "notionally" performed. The role of JOWOG 41 in sorting out the roles, responsibilities, and procedures was critical.

Diver Mist involved more than 1,200 participants from the United Kingdom and United States and lasted five days. The exercise was designed to be as realistic as possible, requiring the exercise participants to actually execute the tasks, while play continued 24 hours a day. The exercise began with a blast and large fire engulfing a large aircraft

Diver Mist accident scene. Photo courtesy of Los Alamos National Laboratory Archives.

fuselage. High-fidelity training aids and props were carefully placed around the exercise site to add to the realism. In addition, a corps of volunteers was recruited to play the roles of the personnel involved in the simulated aircraft crash.

The overall objectives for Diver Mist remained the same as in the previous exercises. The level of integration between the UK and U.S. responding forces was better than had been anticipated by both sides. At the end of the day, both nations believed that, if an accident were to occur tomorrow, the UK and U.S. response forces could effectively integrate and work together to resolve the accident.

Diver Mist became the springboard to a fruitful joint training and exercise program. Small-scale technical drills and training events were developed to address specific lessons learned in Diver Mist. Since Diver Mist, the United Kingdom and the United States have conducted more than 10 of these small-scale events in addition to exchanging observers on numerous other events. Two large-scale, national-level nuclear weapon exercises have also been held since Diver Mist. The last FTX, Dimming Sun, was held in June 2004.

It can be argued that as the nuclear weapon inventories have been decreasing, so has the probability of a nuclear weapon accident. Although it has been more than 25 years since the United States has had a nuclear weapon accident, the consequences of such an event remain unchanged. The last accident involving U.S. nuclear weapons was the 1980 Titan explosion. In 1986 the Soviet Union lost its Yankee, with 16 submarine-launched ballistic missiles (presumably with warheads), and in 1989 it lost a Mike-class nuclear attack submarine assumed to carry nuclear-armed torpedoes. Information on accidents in other countries is difficult to find or not available.

Although some may feel that the exchanges between the United Kingdom and the United States have been one-sided, in the area of nuclear weapon accident response both nations have significantly improved their capabilities. The technical and operational capabilities that have been developed and improved as part of the JOWOG 41 exchange are also applicable to other radiological and nuclear threats. While the probability of a nuclear weapon accident may have decreased, the challenge to contain nuclear proliferation and to counter the threat of nuclear terrorism has increased. This nuclear challenge requires the close cooperation and integration of the best technical and operational minds that the two nations have to offer. JOWOG 41 has established and maintained that type of cooperation for more than two decades.

NUCLEAR DELIVERY SYSTEMS RESULTING FROM THE MDA

GLEN M. SEGELL

The Polaris Sales Agreement of 1963 between the United States and the United Kingdom is well known. It was the first agreement between two states for a nuclear missile weapon delivery system launched from a nuclear-propelled submarine. The agreement demonstrated the trust and fidelity that existed between the two states. The rationale for the agreement was the unified defense policy of both states based upon a nuclear deterrent. This deterrence policy arose from the recognition that it was not possible, in the age of aircraft and missiles, to defend any location. An enemy could strike deep behind the battle lines at civilian, military, and industrial targets. So it was conceived that nuclear weapons, with a credible means of delivering them globally and the intent to do so, would deter an adversary from attacking. Adversaries would be deterred from an offensive as it would result in retaliation by nuclear weapons. This assumption was the basis of the Cold War, where battle did not take place directly between states possessing nuclear weapons.

Less well known are the airborne nuclear weapon systems serving the same deterrent policy. The procurement debate over these systems indicates that it was not a foregone conclusion that the United Kingdom would necessarily procure the nuclear delivery system from the United States or that it would necessarily be submarine based.[1] The options debated at the time highlighted the competition among the armed services (about the optimal operational viability and credibility), the political echelons (about the benefits of collaboration versus independence), and the Treasury (about cost). The United Kingdom had options to collaborate with other European allied countries, especially those within the North Atlantic Treaty Organization (NATO) or to be independent. This demonstrated the political apprehensions of reliance on the United States, especially given the United Kingdom's refusal to commit to the Vietnam campaign. Indeed, it was well into the 1990s that the United Kingdom retained an airborne nuclear delivery capability (in addition to the submarine-launched Polaris missile) in the form of the type WE-177 free-fall nuclear bombs deliverable by aircraft such as the Tornado.

It is the purpose of this chapter to show that the Mutual Defense Agreement (MDA) of 1958 was more important than realized at the time. It was instrumental as the basis for technical collaboration and political and military partnership in developing airborne nuclear delivery capability, including the F-111 aircraft (and its diminutive version, the Tornado), the F-4 Phantom aircraft, and the Harrier jump-jet aircraft. These aircraft comprised the United Kingdom's airborne nuclear delivery capability. The Tornado highlighted how Anglo-American collaboration could be extended to other allies, as it was manufactured collaboratively by the United Kingdom, West Germany, and Italy through a NATO consortium infrastructure and was based on U.S. technology. These projects represented a two-way street of cooperation. The Harrier was a UK design, and the F-4 was a U.S. design. The F-111 was a U.S. design, but its diminutive version, the Tornado, was a NATO project. Such collaboration, the basis for this chapter's topic, is in accordance with Article II A.4 of MDA that stipulates, "Each Party will communicate to or exchange with the other Party such classified information, sensitive nuclear technology, and controlled nuclear information as is jointly determined to be necessary to the development of delivery systems compatible with the atomic weapons which they carry."[2]

It is important to note that the UK-U.S. procurement policy on nuclear delivery systems evolved along cooperative lines in spite of issues that could have prevented it.[3] These issues include the escalation of the Cold War and the rise in dominance of the United States and the USSR as superpowers in a bipolar system, which, along with decolonization, resulted in a diminished role in the world for Britain, corresponding shifts in potential areas of military operation, technological developments that affected specific weapons systems along with the inability of Britain to financially afford developing and procuring such systems, relations between branches of the armed services after the abolishment of conscription, a subsequent new central organization of defense in the United Kingdom, and a change in government in 1964 to the Labour Party's Harold Wilson (October 1964–June 1970) after the previous Conservative Party had been in power since October 1951.[4] The MDA was instrumental as a basis for the continued UK-U.S. cooperation on both the airborne and submarine nuclear delivery systems.[5]

AIRBORNE INSURANCE POLICY

By the mid-1950s a nuclear deterrence was perceived to be the best means of defense for the United Kingdom. Defense against an adversary would be achieved by making the adversary aware that the costs of aggression would be devastatingly high through nuclear retaliation. Holding the line on the Rhine River with air and land forces while maintaining a nuclear deterrent to strengthen negotiations on a cessation of hostilities was the central military philosophy against the most probable enemy: the USSR and its allies in the Warsaw Pact alliance. The initial thinking was that the deterrent would be airborne via the Valiant, Victor, and Vulcan (V-bombers) long-range bombers armed with free-fall nuclear bombs.[6] After the Suez crisis of 1956 this was reconsidered owing to the facts that the airfields were clearly vulnerable, aircraft could be brought down before they reached their target, and the United States and Soviet Union were clearly forging ahead with high-altitude, supersonic long-range bombers and were developing missile capabilities comprising aircraft-, land-, and submarine-launched systems.[7]

A rethink on the delivery was manifest in the 1957 Defense White Paper.[8] It took into account the successful testing of long-range, land-based missiles (Atlas missiles) by the United States, the potential introduction of the H-bomb into the United Kingdom's weapon arsenal, and the advent of nuclear propulsion, notably for naval submarine vessels.[9] The white paper also noted that long-range bombing, reconnaissance, and the projection of military credibility could be combined in one aircraft as a platform with different systems to suit many purposes. Thus, all manned aircraft projects, bar Royal Air Force (RAF) Operational Requirement 339 (the TSR.2 aircraft), would be canceled.

Between 1957 and 1962 a protracted debate ensued on the nuclear weapon delivery systems. This debate involved technological developments in vertical take-off and landing (VTOL) aircraft, multirole combat aircraft, the pros and cons of long-range bombers on long runways with hardened shelters compared with dispersed airfields closer to the target, the availability of airfields worldwide, integrated weapon systems as opposed to mere platforms, and the options of land- or sea-based missiles.[10] Because of cost considerations and the expected duration of service of the V-bombers, the debate in 1959 tended toward an airborne delivery system with manned aircraft that could deliver free-fall nuclear bombs. By 1960 the thinking favored standoff air-launched missiles such as the U.S.-developed Skybolt, owing to the vulnerability of aircraft to surface-to-air missile defenses.[11]

In addition to the debate on runways and bases for air power, there was a debate over the availability of naval bases around the world. By 1961 the MDA was instrumental in securing an understanding from the United States to acquire nuclear propulsion for submarines.[12] The system to procure was influenced by the 1958 Middle East crises in Jordan and Lebanon and the 1961 Berlin crisis that highlighted the political necessity of signaling intentions to an adversary and recalling forces at the last minute without engaging militarily.[13]

TURNABOUT OF 1962–1964

The October 1962 Cuban missile crises served as a catalyst for the United Kingdom to strengthen ties with both the United States and other countries in Europe. On November 29, 1962, France and the United Kingdom signed the Anglo-French civil supersonic transport Concorde agreement, which was deposited at the UN as an international agreement. France saw the engine technology offered as essential for the development of its own military nuclear deterrent (*force de frappe*). The Bristol Siddeley Olympus 593 engine for the Concorde was also being developed for the TSR.2 aircraft.[14] The United Kingdom was offering this technology as an incentive for President Charles de Gaulle of France to agree to UK entry into the European Economic Community (EEC).[15] On December 14, 1962, the engine failed on a test bed. The United Kingdom did not inform France of this immediately, under the assumption that further development would eventually result in a successful engine for both the TSR.2 as well as the Concorde aircraft.

Following increasing costs and a number of test failures during early flight testing, on December 19, 1962, President John F. Kennedy informed Prime Minister Harold Macmillan that he had canceled the Skybolt project. The U.S. military was ready to deploy several other reliable land-, sea-, and aircraft-based nuclear weapon systems, and the Skybolt was thought to be too expensive and too complicated to perform well. Coincidentally, the decision to cancel the Skybolt was taken on the same day as its first successful test, following five previous test failures.[16] Owing to these circumstances, Prime Minister Macmillan met with President Kennedy on the Caribbean island of Bermuda for a summit conference. It was at that summit in December 1962 that Kennedy offered Macmillan the submarine-launched Polaris system so that the United Kingdom would have submarine-based nuclear weapons.

Secretary of Defense Robert McNamara also suggested that the United Kingdom procure a pet project of his, the variable-geometry technology F-111 fighter-bomber that was being developed with both a naval and a land variant and that was capable of delivering a nuclear weapon.[17] The F-111 complemented the United Kingdom's Canberra aircraft design that flew in the U.S. Air Force as the B-57. The F-111 offer was militarily appealing, essentially because of the failure of the TSR.2 engine and the possibility that eventually the United Kingdom would not be able to afford Polaris or that the Polaris would also be canceled by the United States.[18]

As a policy of "insurance," which was the procurement policy of the day, Prime Minister Macmillan decided to proceed along the Polaris and F-111 options from the United States while also seeking to develop the TSR.2 indigenously. This would offer three options for the replacement of the V-bomber nuclear delivery aircraft. This would also satisfy having the Concorde engine as the entry ticket for the EEC negotiations with France. However, in mid-January 1963 President de Gaulle became aware of these Anglo-American agreements and of the December 1962 failure of the TSR.2 engine on the test bed. Subsequently, on January 31, 1963, he vetoed the UK application for entry into the EEC.[19]

The military and the political echelons, along with the Treasury, entertained a protracted and well-informed debate regarding which of the three options would be the best way forward for the nuclear deterrent should all three become available at acceptable cost, in the required time frame, and in meeting the defense and foreign policy agenda.[20] There was consensus that nuclear deterrence was the best form of defense. Essentially it was understood that an airborne nuclear deterrent, though cheaper, would be more vulnerable than a submarine nuclear deterrent, given that airfields and runways might be destroyed before aircraft could take off.[21] In fact, suggestions of having an airborne deterrent continuously airborne, with aircraft in rotation, were squashed because of the possibility of such aircraft crashing, the subsequent radiation, or not having a runway available in the event of a recall before delivery of the nuclear bombs. Submarines under water would be hard to detect, could remain stationed for prolonged periods, and posed minimal radiation risks to the civilian population.[22]

The question of whether there should be an airborne nuclear deterrent in addition to a submarine-based nuclear deterrent was thus addressed. Evaluations by the armed services of their requirements, in addition to the nuclear delivery option, were instrumental in deciding that an airborne delivery option would be retained, even though Polaris would be the primary system.[23] The political echelons were keen for this debate, given the onset of the Vietnam War in which they did not wish to participate, the ongoing military situations in the residual colonies, and the UK involvement in the confrontation between Malaysia and Indonesia. Clearly the military was of the opinion that it was possible for an aircraft to be a platform suitable and adaptable for many purposes.

Following decolonization and the changing role of Britain in the world, there was a rapidly decreasing availability of bases and runways. Several alternatives were considered: long, hardened runways with hardened underground shelters in the United Kingdom and perhaps Western Europe; overseas runways (that is, bases with shorter runways for shorter-range aircraft to strike at the same targets as the long-range bombers); dispersed runways, roads, or flat fields very near the potential battle zones with possibly extended logistical lines; and sea-based platforms (such as aircraft carriers that could provide an alternative to both long and hardened runways in the United Kingdom and overseas). In the end, a diversity of options was considered ideal.[24]

Thus, the RAF Operational Requirement 345 was approved for a vertical take-off and landing/short take-off and vertical landing (VTOL/STOVL) aircraft that would be within the framework of MDA.[25] Viability of the design was a major consideration, and two Hawker Siddeley Company prototypes (P.1127, subsonic; and P.1154, supersonic) were offered with different range, weight, and payload capabilities. Both designs provided enormous benefits, notably the ability to fly off roads, forest clearings, small carriers, and ships without the need for a long, hard surface runway that would be easy to destroy. They also allowed the aircraft to operate close behind the lines. A trial squadron of the subsonic version (P.1127) Kestrel aircraft was commissioned and was jointly tested by the RAF, U.S. Marines, and West German Luftwaffe.[26] This aircraft would be produced as the Harrier and would see successful service during the Falklands conflict (1982) and Gulf War (1991) for both the United Kingdom and United States, albeit in a tactical rather than a nuclear delivery role.

WATERSHED OF 1964

Following his victory in the 1964 elections, Prime Minister Harold Wilson set in motion a review of weapons procurement. He found that there had been a lack of overall coordination in planning and policy. Too many projects were procured as insurance, and none had entered service, resulting in a costly overlap. The separate armed services were adamant that if any projects were to be canceled it could effectively make a branch of the armed forces redundant as well as produce a devastating effect on industry and employment.[27]

With swift and decisive leadership, Wilson scrapped the TSR.2 aircraft—the only manned aircraft to be spared the 1957 cuts of RAF Operational Requirement 339. The Hawker Siddeley Company Type 681 transport aircraft and the Hawker Siddeley Company Type P.1154 supersonic aircraft were also scrapped. This was not because they were not needed to meet defense policy, but because they were too costly for their solely British market. The government, however, authorized the continued development of the TSR.2's engine for the Concorde civil supersonic aircraft.

Weapons procurement within the context of British defense and foreign policy, as decided by the new government, would be collaborative with allies to enhance the alliances.[28] Collaboration would also result in the reduction of costs through longer production runs and smaller per unit costs. Such collaboration was consistent with the 1957 defense posture that forward defense would be maintained through collective arrangements such as NATO and through special bilateral agreements such as the MDA.[29] Hence, agreement was reached to procure from the United States the F-4 Phantom and the C-130 Hercules in the place of the P.1154 and HS.681. They would have the same operational roles, with substantial production under license in the United Kingdom, which would take into account industrial and employment concerns. The F-4 Phantom was a nuclear delivery–capable aircraft and thus provided an intermediate insurance for the aging V-bombers before Polaris entered service.[30]

The United Kingdom once again attempted accession to the EEC, using technology as the entry ticket and to further the policy of allied collaboration. An Anglo-French agreement was reached on five projects;[31] these projects comprised the Puma, Lynx, and Gazelle helicopters, the Jaguar aircraft, and the Anglo-French variable-geometry aircraft (AFVGA). All of these made use of U.S. technology.

The AFVGA was to meet a joint Anglo-French specification that included, inter alia, the delivery of nuclear free-fall bombs.[32] The AFVGA was based on the F-111 design with shared technology of variable-geometry wings. The development of the F-111 itself had substantial delays and setbacks and was never procured by the United Kingdom, even though the U.S. Air Force stationed them in Great Britain and eventually used them in the strike against Libya in 1986. France later withdrew from the AFVGA project, which for a short while continued as the United Kingdom variable-geometry aircraft. Eventually, in 1968, the United Kingdom collaborated with Italy and West Germany in the Panavia consortia to manufacture the design as the multirole combat aircraft known as the Tornado.[33] The aircraft saw combat in the Gulf War (1991) and in Iraq (2003) and was also sold to Saudi Arabia. The Tornado remained the main airborne nuclear delivery platform for the Type WE-177 free-fall nuclear bomb until the bombs were withdrawn from service in the 1990s.

Given these decisions on aircraft for the immediate and medium-term threat environment that included options for nuclear delivery in a cost-effective manner, the necessity of a submarine-based nuclear deterrence was by no means certain.[34] It could also be possible to have a land-based ballistic missile for nuclear deterrence purposes, as both the United States and the USSR were demonstrating. So the new prime minister initiated a debate over the necessity of Polaris. Factors taken into account to justify a nuclear-propelled, submarine-based ballistic nuclear missile system included its longevity of service beyond that of any aircraft, the ability to be on station 24 hours a day in an almost absolute secret location (which would alleviate the concern inherent to an airborne-based deterrent dependent on a runway that could be destroyed), and the difficulty for a potential adversary to detect and destroy the submarine before it could be effective (which might be the case for a land-based ballistic missile system).

These three considerations meant that the actual number of nuclear warheads and missiles could be kept to a minimum. Minimal damage would occur should an accident take place involving a submarine because the accident would be below the seas and away from any populated area. Should an adversary strike a UK land-based site (for example, an air base or ballistic-missile site), the fallout would be extremely harmful given the small size of the British Isles. Further, there were political and technological advantages of cooperation with the United States. All of these factors thus favored a submarine-based nuclear deterrence over the other alternatives. The inhibiting factor would be the financial cost. To resolve this, agreement was reached with the United States on a package deal and a loan scheme that would offset the cost and enable payment over a period of many years.[35] Prime Minister Harold Wilson thus authorized the submarine-based Polaris force to be Britain's nuclear deterrent.[36]

It would not be surprising that such a decision would be repeated by Prime Minister Margaret Thatcher when the time came to replace the Polaris system. It was decided to adhere to MDA and procure from the United States the Trident nuclear submarine system. It would also not be surprising that such factors would remain germane when deciding on the replacement of Trident in the early 2000s. By that time the submarine-based nuclear deterrent was the sole deterrent delivery system, as the RAF's WE-177 bombs had been phased out.

CONCLUSION

To be sure, MDA provided a baseline agreement that set the scene for the debate, culminating in the decisions of 1964 that provided the United Kingdom with a defense and deterrent policy posture for the duration of the Cold War and beyond and a doctrine that would include Anglo-American and Anglo-European political, military, and industrial collaboration. The combination of nuclear-propelled submarines with nuclear ballistic missiles (Polaris), a naval fleet based on a commando carrier group structure with VTOL/STOVL aircraft (Harrier), and the land-based F-4 Phantom and Tornado aircraft with Type WE-177 nuclear free-fall bombs was not only a formidable nuclear deterrent through the 1970s, 1980s, and 1990s but was also seen as sufficient to wield political influence in Washington, Paris, Moscow, and, indeed, the UN Security Council.

To collaborate on such projects on a two-way street with the United States, the United Kingdom aimed to situate itself firmly in the "special relations" context in a Cold War bipolar system where it also enjoyed having "nuclear umbrella protection" from the United States.[37] Enjoying the technology spin-off, the United Kingdom was also able to collaborate with other European NATO member countries such as France, Italy, West Germany, and later Spain to achieve economies of scale and to cement the self-perceived role as an Atlantic bridge between America and Europe.[38] Such a posture adhered to the 1957 white paper's pronouncement that the "forward defense of the UK would be maintained through collective arrangements and special bilateral agreements."[39] These respective arrangements are represented by the United Kingdom's relationship with NATO and the United States. Clearly MDA has stood the test of time, not only in principle but also in practice.

NOTES

1. Sir Frank Cooper, head of the Air Staff Secretariat (1955–1960) and permanent under-secretary of state, Ministry of Defence (1976–1982), interview with author, December 11, 1991.

2. "1958 US-UK Mutual Defence Agreement," signed July 3, 1958, amended May 23, 1994, British-American Security Information Council Web site, http://www.basicint.org/nuclear/1958MDA.htm.

3. William Stewart, aircraft desk at British embassy in the United States (1955), director of Anglo-French combat trainer programme (1966–1970), and director general of the Tornado program (1970–1973), interview with author, April 28, 1992.

4. Tony Benn, minister of technology (1966–1970), interview with author, July 2, 1991.

5. "U.S.A.F. liaison with Air Ministry: works project," file no. AIR 20/10691, National Archives, London.

6. "V bomber force: future policy," file no. AIR 2/14699, National Archives, London.

7. "Note on American ballistic missile programme 1958," file no. AVIA 6/17322, National Archives, London.

8. "Future Defence Policy," House of Commons Paper 124, Session 1957–1958, vol. 23.

9. "Visit of Minister of Supply to US discussions on possible integration of U.K./U.S. research and development," file no. AVIA 54/1907, National Archives, London.

10. "Visit of Minister of Defence to U.S.A. to request assistance on research and development," file no. AVIA 54/1909, National Archives, London.

11. "Strategic air-to-surface missile interdependence with the USA," file no. AIR 2/15261, National Archives, London.

12. "Long-term naval programme presentation to Minister of Defence," file no. ADM 205/192, National Archives, London.

13. "Chief of Staff Committee: Secretary Standard files, 1958–1961," file no. DEFE 32/6, National Archives, London.

14. "Anglo-French collaboration on supersonic transport aircraft," file no. AVIA 63/20, National Archives, London.

15. Basil Blackwell, deputy chief engineer at Bristol Siddeley Engines (1959–1962) and sales director at Bristol Siddeley Engines (1963–1969), interview with author, July 2, 1991.

16. "Skybolt negotiation of Anglo-American agreement," file no. AIR 2/15603, National Archives, London.

17. "U.S.A./U.K. relationship in aeronautical R&D," file no. AVIA 65/14, National Archives, London.

18. "U.K./U.S.A. coordination offensive bomber operations," file no. AIR 8/2201, National Archives, London.

19. "Supersonic passenger aircraft and research into supersonic aircraft design," file no. AIR 8/2296, National Archives, London.

20. "Agreements with U.S.A. on standardisation of equipment and exchange of information on inventions and patents," file no. T 225/101, National Archives, London.

21. Julian Amery, secretary of state for air (1960–1962) and minister of aviation (1962–1964), interview with author, June 24, 1992.

22. Lord Nelson of Stafford, chairman of English Electric Company (1962–1983), member of Government Advisory Council on Scientific Policy (1955–1958), member of Advisory Council to Ministry of Technology (1964–1970), interview with author, April 2, 1992.

23. "Chief of Staff Committee Minutes of Meetings, 5th meeting COS (62)6," file no. DEFE 4/142, National Archives, London.

24. "Future aircraft: policy," file no. AIR 20/7395, National Archives, London.

25. "OR.345: V/STOL ground attack fighter aircraft," file no. AIR 2/17376, National Archives, London.

26. "P.1127 tripartite evaluation," file no. AIR 2/15879, National Archives, London.

27. *Report to the Plowden Committee* (London: Society of British Aerospace Companies, 1965).

28. "Anglo-American cooperation material and correspondence," file no. AVIA 46/92, National Archives, London.

29. "Cooperation with Royal Navy and within NATO on future aircraft requirements," file no. AIR 20/10567, National Archives, London.

30. "RAF/USAF collaboration," file no. AIR 20/6727, National Archives, London.

31. "Interdependence: Anglo-French groups and committees on aircraft research and development and production," file no. AIR 2/16736, National Archives, London.

32. "Anglo-French Staff talks," file no. DEFE 6/79, 38, National Archives, London.

33. Ivan Yates, chief projects engineer of Electric English Company (1959–1965), projects manager at British Aircraft Corporation (1966–1970), director at Preston BAC Division (1970–1973), director at SEPECAT (1973–1976), and director at Panavia (1977–1983), interview with author, March 30, 1992.

34. "The position of the United Kingdom in world affairs," CAB 130/153, National Archives, London.

35. "North American supply documents: extracts collected by official historians," file no. AVIA 46/149, National Archives, London.

36. "Strategy after 1970," file no. DEFE 6/80, National Archives, London.

37. "Procurement of equipment by U.S.A. policy and procedure," file no. DEFE 7/239, National Archives, London.

38. "NATO aircraft equipment government to government," file no. DEFE 7/241, National Archives, London.

39. "Future Defence Policy," House of Commons Paper 124.

10

UK INDEPENDENCE OR DEPENDENCE?

TARA CALLAHAN AND MARK JANSSON

The 2006 Defence White Paper concerning the future of the British nuclear weapons program made the case for the United Kingdom to maintain its nuclear arsenal as an ultimate protector from states hostile to the United Kingdom and its allies. In his foreword to the Defence White Paper, Prime Minister Tony Blair asserted that an "independent British nuclear deterrent is an essential part of [the United Kingdom's] insurance against the uncertainties and risks of the future."[1] In addition to Blair's statement, the oft-used term "independent" throughout the white paper—as well as in other literature on the subject—raises questions about the United Kingdom's nuclear ties to the United States and the implications of those ties.

The debate over the independence of the United Kingdom's nuclear weapons program is largely due to the fact that the United Kingdom no longer deploys nuclear-armed aircraft as it did during the Cold War, but instead retains just one nuclear delivery option, the Trident submarine-launched ballistic missile (SLBM) system, which requires substantial U.S. cooperation for its preservation and maintenance. The current fleet came into service in 1994 and has an operational service life of 25 years. Because the design and construction of new submarines will take approximately 17 years to complete, high priority has been placed on initiating this process so that the UK SLBM system can retain its deterrent viability without interruption in the 2020s.

Some critics of the United Kingdom's recent push for an updated nuclear program question the benefit of a nuclear deterrent that is tied to U.S. technology and, by extension, U.S. interests. Sir Rodric Braithwaite, former chairman of the British Joint Intelligence Committee and ambassador to Moscow, posits that British reliance on the United States for Trident D5 missiles and other system components severely undermines the United Kingdom's ability to act independently on behalf of its interests.[2] A perceived lack of autonomy on the United Kingdom's part could limit the ability of its nuclear force to deter adversaries, which is perhaps why such care is taken to articulate the independence of the United Kingdom's nuclear force.

As policymakers in the United Kingdom contemplate the future direction of the British nuclear program, it is important to look beyond superficial assessments of the United Kingdom's independent nuclear capability to establish a more complete view of its nuclear force composition, structure, and operation. Because the UK and U.S. nuclear programs are closely linked, it is worth considering the degree to which the UK nuclear program is integrated with the U.S. program and how this relationship may affect the United Kingdom's nuclear strategy. How do strategic relationships, defense spending, and policy affect the United Kingdom's nuclear strategy and, more specifically, the decision to upgrade its nuclear program?

According to Sir Michael Quinlan, former permanent under-secretary in the Ministry of Defence (MOD), there are two forms of nuclear independence: operational independence (the ability to launch nuclear strikes regardless of the wishes of others) and technical independence (the ability to produce nuclear weapons and their delivery systems in isolation).[3] As stated in a report to the Defence Committee of the House of Commons, "Decision-making and use of the system remains entirely sovereign to the UK. Only the Prime Minister can authorize the use of the UK's nuclear deterrent . . . [and] all the command and control procedures are totally independent."[4] However, the technical aspects of the British nuclear program also factor into the United Kingdom's ability to possess a truly independent deterrent, and this has implications on the decision to extend the Trident system.

This chapter will provide an analysis of the British "independent nuclear deterrent" from both technical and operational standpoints and will also address several economic and strategic considerations—not captured in a strict operational-technical analysis—that bear heavily on UK decisionmaking on nuclear issues. Building on this analysis, the chapter will conclude with a brief discussion of the relevance of the United Kingdom's nuclear weapons arsenal to British deterrence strategy, to NATO, and to the role of British nuclear weapons in international affairs.

CURRENT CAPABILITIES

As the United Kingdom considers the future of its nuclear program, it must consider how questions regarding its technical autonomy and the current terms of its "special relationship" with the United States impact its strategic decisionmaking calculus. There are four components of a technically independent nuclear program—a platform, a delivery system, a warhead, and the possession of fissile materials—components that depend to varying degrees on cooperation with the United States.

The current UK nuclear force structure is composed of four British-produced and -operated Vanguard-class submarines equipped with Trident D5 missiles acquired from the United States. Despite service-extending maintenance, the life of these current submarines will end in the early 2020s. The extended period of time required to design and manufacture new submarines has imposed considerable pressure on the United Kingdom to make a decision about the future of its nuclear forces. The British Parliament, aware of these time constraints, demanded a parliamentary vote on Trident's renewal. Prime Minister Tony Blair responded by promising a "proper debate" on the issue and subsequently delivered a white paper detailing the government's case: that the timely initiation of the replacement process was vital to the United Kingdom's ability to maintain a credible nuclear deterrent without interruption.[5]

DELIVERY SYSTEM: TRIDENT II (D5) BALLISTIC MISSILES

The Trident II (D5) SLBM is currently the United Kingdom's sole nuclear warhead delivery system. The D5 missiles, with an estimated range of roughly 7,400 kilometers and accuracy to within a few meters, are leased from the United States. Under current arrangements, Britain has a contract with the United States to acquire 58 missiles from a larger pool produced by Lockheed Martin for the U.S. Navy and stored at Kings Bay, Georgia.[6] Of these, eight were expended in tests at the eastern test range off the coast of Florida before they crossed the Atlantic, leaving the British with title to 50 missiles. The actual missiles belonging to the United Kingdom are not segregated at Kings Bay, and this allows the British to benefit from performance data on the entire

D5 population. British boats pick up their load of D5s at Kings Bay, and the UK-manufactured Trident warheads are later mated to on-board missiles at the Royal Naval Armament Depot at Coulport. This is a unique arrangement among nuclear weapons states. Ultimately, according to Vice Admiral George ("Pete") Nanos, former director of Strategic System Programs for the U.S. Navy, "in the Trident system there's no such thing as a purely U.S. or UK missile."[7] Former Labour defence secretary Denis Healey offered a more disapproving view when he stated that Trident was merely a "rent-a-rocket" enterprise.[8]

Nonetheless, it is likely that the Trident SLBM is the United Kingdom's most effective, efficient, and reliable option for nuclear delivery owing to its invulnerability to attack, its range, and its manageable cost. On this last point, the Defence White Paper also noted that the Trident missile would be the United Kingdom's most cost-effective option even if adapted in the future for a silo-, air-, or surface ship-based delivery platform.[9]

AUTONOMY OF PLATFORM: TRIDENT SUBMARINES

The Trident fleet at present consists of four Vanguard-class SSBNs: HMS *Vanguard,* HMS *Victorious,* HMS *Vigilant,* and HMS *Vengeance.* As a matter of UK policy, at least one SSBN is on constant patrol to maintain a continuous at-sea deterrence posture. Stationed in western Scotland at the Clyde Submarine Base, the submarines each carry 16 Trident missiles equipped with three nuclear warheads that are kept in a detargeted state.[10] The UK submarine industrial base, which constructs the Vanguard submarines and products solely for the United Kingdom, comprises BAE Systems at Barrow-in-Furness, Rolls-Royce's Marine Power at Derby, and Devonport Management Limited.[11]

In contrast with the United Kingdom's dependence on the United States for missiles, the British independently manufacture their nuclear-armed submarines, and it appears that this will continue to be the case for the foreseeable future: the 2005 defence industrial strategy stipulates that the United Kingdom will retain the ability "to deliver, operate and maintain these platforms, without significant reliance on unpredictable offshore expertise."[12] The strategy allows for some submarine components to be acquired offshore but only under specific arrangements needed to guarantee supply or involve purchasing components from a broad supplier base.[13] Progress on consolidating the United Kingdom's submarine industrial base has been difficult, but the

MOD has reported improving communication and movement toward the establishment of a long-term cooperation agreement among industry leaders to further increase efficiency and performance in submarine production.[14] To that end, in October of 2007, BAE Systems assumed deputy leadership of an integrated project team—created by the MOD to develop the concept design for the successor submarine to the Vanguard class—comprising British personnel from the Ministry of Defence, BAE Systems, Rolls-Royce, and Babcock Marine.[15]

To ensure compatibility of the new class of British submarines with future U.S. SLBM designs, Prime Minister Tony Blair wrote to President George W. Bush in December of 2006 seeking assurance that any successor would be "compatible with, or is capable of being made compatible with" the D5 missile system the United Kingdom was installing on its new SSBNs.[16] In a carefully worded response, Bush affirmed the future compatibility of U.S. and UK systems and went on to guarantee that the United States would see to it that the United Kingdom would retain its ability to deploy an effective nuclear delivery system throughout the service life of its new submarine force.[17] As long as the United States honors this commitment, the United Kingdom should have everything it needs to maintain a high level of independence in its submarine production.[18]

AUTONOMY OF WARHEAD DESIGN AND FABRICATION

The United Kingdom's Trident warheads are designed by the Atomic Weapons Establishment (AWE) at Aldermaston and assembled at Aldermaston and Burghfield. The first batch of UK Trident warheads was completed in September 1992, and it is estimated that the United Kingdom currently holds 185 that are "operationally available."[19] These warheads undergo maintenance and refurbishment at AWE and are reputed to be capable of selective yield ranging from less than one kiloton to one hundred kilotons.[20]

Despite the fact that British nuclear warheads are developed and manufactured in the United Kingdom, the British rely on the United States to supply several nonnuclear warhead components and materials, including neutron generators and the tritium gas used to manipulate yield.[21] Reliance on U.S. missiles is important because the United Kingdom's warheads must fit the specifications of the D5 missile. The design of the British warhead sharply resembles the W76 warhead that the United States manufactures and mates to most of its Trident missiles.[22] In fact, a declassified U.S. Department of Energy (DOE) stockpile stewardship update directly links these designs; the DOE work plan to address W76 needs between 1999 and 2001 included the engineering, design, and evaluation schedule of the UK warhead.[23]

FISSILE MATERIALS

Although it is suspected that there are indigenous uranium resources in southwest England, all domestic exploration activities were halted in 1983.[24] Instead the United Kingdom imports uranium oxide from Australia, Canada, Russia, Namibia, South Africa, and the United States.[25] The lack of an indigenous uranium supply has virtually no impact on the independence of the United Kingdom's nuclear weapons production ability, however, as the United Kingdom already possesses 21.7 metric tons of highly enriched uranium (HEU). Although the United Kingdom announced that it has ceased separating plutonium for military purposes, it still holds 3.2 metric tons of plutonium designated for military use.[26] This is enough fissile material to produce hundreds of additional warheads, far more than the United Kingdom would need in the foreseeable future given the long half-life of these materials, not to mention the fact that the United Kingdom is currently seeking to further reduce the size of its nuclear stockpile.

The 1958 Mutual Defense Agreement helped open up U.S.-UK nuclear trade to provide the British with uranium 235, tritium, and lithium in exchange for British plutonium.[27] Should the United Kingdom decide that it needs to produce more HEU in the future, it could obtain raw materials from another trading partner in the Nuclear Suppliers Group and subsequently enrich and reprocess without U.S. assistance.[28] British Nuclear Fuels plc (BNFL), wholly owned by the British government, provides for all of the United Kingdom's nuclear fuel cycle needs, including enrichment, fabrication, reprocessing, and waste management.[29] This is likely to remain a moot point, however, in terms of nuclear weapons development for the foreseeable future.

Thus, the United Kingdom relies on the United States for its supply of D5 missiles, which in turn impact submarine and warhead design and create a degree of British dependence in three of the four main technical areas discussed above. This begs the question as to why the United Kingdom would allow its nuclear force—a pillar of its national security for decades—to become dependent on another country, even a close ally such as the United States.

NUCLEAR ECONOMICS

A UK nuclear force developed in concert with the United States costs much less than an entirely autonomous program—and this is crucial for the United Kingdom, given the size of its defense budget and its past experience with cost overruns incurred while independently developing its Chevaline program in the 1970s. Despite its high cost and questionable necessity, Chevaline was considered an overall success within the UK weapons establishment.[30] Nonetheless, the MOD conceded that the "experience of the Chevaline system shows just how expensive the resolution of problems in this field by programmes unique to the United Kingdom can be."[31]

In the late 1970s, after the British determined the need for a long-term replacement for Chevaline, Margaret Thatcher wrote in a letter to President Jimmy Carter that "the objective of the United Kingdom Government is to take advantage of the economies made possible by the cooperation of the United States in making the Trident I missile system available in order to reinforce its efforts to upgrade its conventional forces."[32] Today, after years of reliance on Trident, the cost of developing an indigenous missile construction capability would require a long period of advance planning and put an intense strain on an already overstretched British defense budget.

The total acquisition costs of the current Trident program were £12.57 billion at 1996–1997 prices, and the annual cost of the program is estimated at around £200 million per year over 20 years of service.[33] The United Kingdom produced both Polaris and Trident SSBN programs on time and within budget, owing primarily to the commonality of the U.S. and UK programs, which share the same missiles and have similar warhead designs.[34] Historically, through information sharing, technology transfers, and nuclear materials exchange, U.S.-UK cooperation has helped limit the financial burden of the British nuclear program. In fact, the British secretary of state for defence, Des Browne, stated that in the unlikely event of a withdrawal of U.S. technical support for Trident, "the main impact on the UK would be in terms of the cost of maintaining the system rather than on its operational effectiveness."[35]

History has also shown that, although cooperation with the United States reduces costs, parting ways can significantly increase them. When the U.S. Navy phased out its Polaris system in the 1970s, for example, the United Kingdom was forced, at great cost, to open production lines to deal with a first-stage rocket motor problem on Polaris. Continued cooperation is perhaps even more important today, as the United Kingdom and United States have partnered in a low rate production continuity strategy to ensure that an adequate demand exists to keep critical missile components supply lines open. The interruption of production caused by a 1998 cut in U.S. funding for missile components required restarting costs of 144 million dollars.[36] In effect, while shared production minimizes costs, it also binds the United Kingdom to the production regimen and modernization decisions of the United States.

Finally, even though the Trident program costs less than a completely independent nuclear program, it still takes up a substantial portion of the defense budget that might otherwise be allocated to conventional forces. Treasury proposals are currently being discussed that would cut £4.5 billion from the defense budget over the next three years.[37] There are expensive delays in development of the Nimrod reconnaissance aircraft, Astute submarines, and Type 45 destroyer program, which are already estimated to cost £2 billion more than originally forecast.[38] With an already strained defense budget, it will be difficult to include another £15–20 billion to renew the Trident submarine fleet.[39] Defense officials have estimated that the lifetime costs of Britain's new Trident nuclear program could also amount to twice the estimated initial building cost.[40]

In the absence of assistance from the United States it may prove difficult for the Labour government to justify the high cost of extending the Trident fleet. Parliament voted strongly (a 409–161 vote) in favor of Prime Minister Blair's plan to renew Trident, but the issue has been divisive and could become increasingly unpopular with increasing costs. Member of Parliament Chris Huhne has gone as far as suggesting that British soldiers in Afghanistan are the ones paying the price for Trident renewal, stating that "you cannot properly equip [British] soldiers in Iraq and Afghanistan and spend twenty billion pounds on replacing Trident."[41]

Others have objected to Trident renewal on the grounds that increased investment in conventional forces and intelligence capabilities, rather than nuclear weapons, would in fact make the United Kingdom a stronger U.S. partner, not a weaker one. Former UK defence secretary Michael Portillo contends that "if the UK diverts billions of pounds from its future defense budgets into nuclear weapons that will never be used, it will have less money to spend on useful things such as air-craft carriers and submarines that fire cruise missiles." He also stated that the United Kingdom would be a better ally for the United States if it did not "waste money" renewing Trident. Portillo's argument may one day gain more traction. Although Parliament stood solidly behind Trident during the vote on renewal, it is possible that given the current state of the British defense budget and the controversy inside and outside government, significant cost increases could erode this base of support.

IMPLICATIONS OF INDEPENDENCE
Beyond cost, serious questions remain to be answered about the strategic usefulness of a nuclear weapons program so closely linked to the much larger U.S. force. Although the United Kingdom relies on U.S. technology for Trident missiles and their associated launch, fire control, and navigation systems, it retains operational independence, meaning that it does not require U.S. approval to launch a nuclear strike. Withdrawal of U.S. support could adversely affect the ability of the United Kingdom to maintain its nuclear capability over the long term, as it would require the British to either develop an indigenous missile system production capability or find a new production partner. Commodore Tim Hare, former director of nuclear policy in the MOD, acknowledged that "it would be difficult if the United States withdrew its design authority and logistics support for the missiles, fire control launcher and navigational sub-systems [and] eventually it would cause some difficulty" but "it would take quite a long time."[42]

The long-term complications created by a U.S. withdrawal of support do not, in fact, preclude the United Kingdom from firing a nuclear missile at an adversary during a moment of peril. Accordingly, the 2006 Defence White Paper stressed that the "UK's nuclear forces must remain fully operationally independent if they are to be a credible deterrent."[43] In establishing the United Kingdom's operational independence, the white paper further noted that only the prime minister can authorize the firing of UK nuclear missiles via directions given through a secure communication system.[44]

The operational independence of the United Kingdom dates back to the Cold War. The British goal was to have a nuclear deterrent that was independent of the United States and would appear to Moscow to be independent of the United States. Therefore, for the British to be wholly coalesced with U.S. strategy would have, in a sense, undermined the independence of Britain's nuclear deterrent, which was the driving motivation for its creation.[45] On the U.S. side, President Eisenhower saw nuclear collaboration with the British and other allies as a means of making the NATO alliance a more formidable bulwark against the Soviets.[46] Although the same nuclear-sharing strategy was not extended to other European countries, the United States has remained an ardent supporter of a strong, independent UK deterrent capability since the 1958 agreement.

The United States and United Kingdom retain nuclear weapons in part as a security guarantee to NATO allies. Indeed, the Defence White Paper posited that the United Kingdom's independence in nuclear strike decisionmaking "enhances the overall deterrent effect" of allied forces.[47] The British nuclear force therefore not only makes an attack on its homeland less likely but also reassures NATO allies that the United Kingdom can provide a nuclear backup in the event of U.S. hesitance with respect to its Article 5 commitments under the North Atlantic Treaty to defend NATO members.[48] It is important to note, however, that the use of UK nuclear forces remains strictly a British prerogative, as NATO commanders have no authority to impose their views on the British government regarding UK-owned nuclear weapons or their use.[49] This further reinforces the Defence White Paper's implicit argument that the United Kingdom's complete command and control over the weapons makes its technical dependence on the United States for missiles and other components of the Trident system a nonissue for the purposes of formulating deterrence and broader defense strategies.

At the beginning of the Cold War, it was difficult at times to justify the creation of a British nuclear deterrent to counter the Soviet threat, given the nuclear security guarantee to Europe already issued by the United States.[50] Now that the Soviet threat is gone, the United Kingdom has had to restate its case for possessing nuclear weapons. The central argument embraced by the government is that, although the strategic threat from the Soviet Union has subsided, nuclear disarmament would be "imprudent" so long as the United Kingdom could not rule out the possibility that a new or resurgent global power might seek to threaten British interests.[51]

The prudence argument is familiar. What is interesting, particularly with respect to the U.S.-UK relationship, is that the white paper also continues to endorse the traditional British concern with the possibility that an adversary may "miscalculate" the U.S. willingness to respond to an attack on the United Kingdom, hence the need for Britain to retain its own nuclear strike capability as a means of deterrence. This is not a new concern but a continuation of the traditional British policy that led to the Cold War emphasis on a "second center of decision-making." Sir Michael Quinlan has noted that by ". . .December 1962, serious thinkers both within and outside the government had come to recognize that the fundamental case for UK capability, and indicators for its character and scale, must be sought in hypotheses of independent action from which the United States stood aside."[52]

Although the United Kingdom's independent nuclear capability may, as noted above, serve to strengthen the collective power of the NATO alliance, its stated position on the need to retain its own arsenal also brings the notion of "extended deterrence" into question: If an adversary may underestimate the willingness of the United States to respond in defense of an intimately close ally such as the United Kingdom, then it is certainly possible to make a similar "miscalculation" when contemplating an attack on other NATO members. It is plausible to argue that the United Kingdom provides nonnuclear NATO members with a second option to seek retaliation on their behalf, but an alternative, proliferation-encouraging lesson that may be drawn from this scenario is, as the Defence White Paper also states, that "conventional forces cannot deliver the same deterrent effect."[53]

Of course, this determination will not necessarily lead to proliferation. As the totality of the British experience demonstrates, developing and maintaining a nuclear arsenal is not easy. It requires enormous commitments of time, money, and industrial capacity—enough in fact to present significant challenges to a rich and scientifically advanced state such as the United Kingdom. Furthermore, the fact that the United Kingdom, already with the smallest stockpile size of any nuclear weapons state recognized under the Nuclear Non-Proliferation Treaty (NPT), has pledged to reduce its stockpile size even further signals that the amount of prestige a country garners on the world stage is not simply a function of how many nuclear weapons it holds. The new British government under Gordon Brown has in fact called for a world free of nuclear weapons and progress on Article VI obligations laid out in the NPT.

Although the phrase "independent nuclear deterrent" may never have been accurate from a technical standpoint when applied to the United Kingdom, it still rings true from an operational perspective. Despite plausible arguments that the United Kingdom is somewhat constrained in its foreign policy making by its degree of technical dependence on the United States, the British can be confident that their operational independence is sufficient to address their national security needs. For the British, and also for the Americans, the diplomatic, economic, and strategic benefits of maintaining the nuclear relationship outweigh the costs, especially given the congruence of the two allies' foreign policy objectives. The United States, therefore, has an important role to play in supporting the British as it seeks to protect its interests and to set the standard for de-emphasizing the salience of nuclear weapons in international relations; and the two longtime allies may do well to think of these as mutually reinforcing priorities that will frame the future of their relationship.

NOTES

1. Secretary of State for Defence and Secretary of State for Foreign and Commonwealth Affairs, "The Future of the United Kingdom's Nuclear Deterrent, December 2006," Report no. CM 6994 (London: Her Majesty's Stationery Office, 2006), p. 5.

2. Sir Rodric Braithwaite, "End of the Affair," *Prospect,* no. 86 (May 2003). See also Ian Davis, "U.S.-UK Nuclear Cooperation and the Future of the UK Trident System" (presentation at meeting of the All-Party Parliamentary Group on Global Security and Non-Proliferation, Westminster, London, February 5, 2002).

3. Michael Quinlan, "The Future of United Kingdom Nuclear Weapons: Shaping the Debate," *International Affairs* 82, no. 4 (2006): pp. 630–632.

4. House of Commons Defence Committee, *The Future of the UK's Strategic Deterrent: The Strategic Context: Government Response to the Committee's Eighth Report of Session 2005–2006* (London: Stationery Office Limited, July 26, 2006), p. 5, http://www.publications.parliament.uk/pa/cm200506/cmselect/cmdfence/1558/1558.pdf.

5. See also Walter C. Ladwig III, "The Future of the British Nuclear Deterrent: An Assessment of Decision Factors," *Strategic Insights* 4, no. 1 (January, 2007), http://www.ccc.nps.navy.mil/si/2007/Jan/ladwigJan07.asp.

6. Rebecca Johnson, Nicola Butler, and Stephen Pullinger, *Worse Than Irrelevant? British Nuclear Weapons in the 21st Century* (London: Acronym Institute for Disarmament Diplomacy, 2006), p. 20, http://www.acronym.org.uk/uk/Worse_than_Irrelevant.pdf. Trident missiles are also stored in

the United States in Bangor, Washington, but these missiles play no role in the British program.

7. Vice Admiral George P. Nanos, interview, Project on Nuclear Issues, Center for Strategic and International Studies, Washington, D.C., January 17, 2008, Section IV of this volume.

8. Dan Plesch, "We've Been Conned Again," *New Statesman,* March 27, 2006.

9. Des Browne and Margaret Beckett, "The Future of the UK's Strategic Deterrent" (presentation to Parliament, London, England, December 5, 2006, p. 24).

10. Quinlan, "The Future of United Kingdom Nuclear Weapons," p. 637.

11. Keith Hartley, "The Economics of UK Nuclear Weapons Policy," *International Affairs* 82, no. 4 (July 2006): pp. 675–684.

12. John Reid, "Defence Industrial Strategy White Paper" (presentation to Parliament, London, England, December 2005, p. 71).

13. Ibid.

14. House of Commons Defence Committee, "The Defence Industrial Strategy Update: Government Response to the Committee's Sixth Report of Session 2006–07" (London, Stationery Office Limited, April 27, 2007), p. 3, http://www.publications.parliament.uk/pa/cm200607/cmselect/cmdfence/481/481.pdf.

15. BAE Systems, "Future Submarines Integrated Project Team Office Officially Opens," press release, October 12, 2007.

16. Prime Minister Tony Blair, letter to President George Bush, December 7, 2006; see "US to Discuss UK Trident Lifespan," BBC News, December 20, 2006, http://news.bbc.co.uk/2/hi/uk_news/politics/6197711.stm.

17. President George W. Bush, Reply to letter from Prime Minister Tony Blair, December 7, 2006.

18. A recently issued U.S. Navy invitation for bids on a new underwater-launched missile system test-bed capable of supporting missiles larger than the D5 raised some concern in the United Kingdom that the United States may not follow through on Bush's assurance to Blair (see Rob Edwards, "Oops! American Missile to Replace Trident Is Too Big for British Submarines," *Sunday Herald,* April 9, 2008). However, the specificity of the communication between Bush and Blair, not to mention the importance of the United Kingdom in maintaining a continuous supply line of components for D5 life extension, makes it highly unlikely that the United States will fail to honor Bush's guarantee.

19. "Table of British Nuclear Forces, 2002," Natural Resources Defense Council, http://www.nrdc.org/nuclear/nudb/datab18.asp.

20. "Britain's Nuclear Weapons: The Current British Arsenal," Nuclear Weapon Archive, April 30, 2001, http://nuclearweaponarchive.org/Uk/UKArsenalRecent.html.

21. Rebecca Johnson, "End of a Nuclear Weapons Era: Can Britain Make History?" *Arms Control Today* (Arms Control Association), April 2006, http://www.armscontrol.org/act/2006_04/coverstoryUKnuclear.asp.

22. Johnson, Butler, and Pullinger, *Worse Than Irrelevant?*

23. *Stockpile Stewardship Plan: Second Annual Update—Systems Engineering and Nonnuclear Component Design Evaluation* (Washington, D.C.: U.S. Department of Energy, Office of Defense Programs, April 1998), chap. 5, Fig. 5-5.

24. *Uranium 2003: Resources, Production, and Demand* (Paris: OECD Nuclear Energy Agency; Vienna: International Atomic Energy Agency, 2004), p. 231, http://www.neutron.kth.se/courses/reactor_physics/NEA-redbook2003.pdf.

25. *Country Nuclear Fuel Cycle Profiles,* Technical Reports Series no. 404 (Vienna: International Atomic Energy Agency, 2001), http://www-pub.iaea.org/MTCD/publications/PDF/TRS404_scr.pdf.

26. *Global Fissile Material Report 2007* (Princeton, N.J.: International Panel on Fissile Materials, 2007), pp. 10–21. http://www.fissilematerials.org/ipfm/site_down/gfmr07.pdf.

27. John Baylis, "Exchanging Nuclear Secrets: Laying the Foundation of the Anglo-American Nuclear Relationship," *Diplomatic History* 25, no. 1 (Winter 2001): p. 41.

28. Ibid., p. 54.

29. Ibid., p. 24.

30. Graham Spinardi, "Aldermaston and British Nuclear Weapons Development: Testing the 'Zuckerman Thesis,'" *Social Studies of Science* 27, no. 4 (August 1997): p. 566.

31. "The British Strategic Nuclear Force: Text of Letters Exchanged between the Prime Minister and the President of the United States and between the Secretary of State for Defence and the U.S. Secretary of Defense," Cmnd 8517, March 11, 1982. See also "US-UK Nuclear Weapons Cooperation up for Renewal," Disarmament Diplomacy 76 (March/April 2004), http://www.acronym.org.uk/dd/dd76/76news04.htm.

32. Lawrence Freedman, "Britain: The First Ex-Nuclear Power?" *International Security* 6, no. 2 (Autumn 1981): p. 87.

33. Frank Boulton and Liz Waterston, "Should the UK Replace Trident?" Medact briefing, August 8, 2005, http://www.comeclean.org.uk/articles.php?articleID=116.

34. Michael Quinlan, "The Future of United Kingdom Nuclear Weapons: Shaping the Debate," *International Affairs* 82, no. 4 (2006): p. 628.

35. "Nuclear Weapons," House of Commons Daily Debates Hansard, Parliament Publications and Records, May 22, 2006, http://www.publications.parliament.uk/pa/cm200506/cmhansrd/vo060522/text/60522w0014.htm#06052325002271.

36. Ibid.

37. David Hencke and Richard Norton-Taylor, "RAF and Navy Hardest Hit by £4.5 Billion MoD Cuts," *The Guardian,* February 18, 2008.

38. Richard Norton-Taylor," MPs Warn of Spending Cuts for Hard-Pressed Forces," *The Guardian,* January 28, 2008.

39. "Call to 'Invest' Trident Funding," BBC News, January 26, 2008, http://news.bbc.co.uk/1/hi/scotland/glasgow_and_west/7210540.stm.

40. Richard Norton-Taylor, "Trident Questions Must Be Answered, Say MPs," *The Guardian,* March 7, 2007.

41. "Trident Divides Huhne and Clegg," BBC News, October 31, 2007, http://news.bbc.co.uk/2/hi/uk_news/politics/7071066.stm.

42. Peter Walker, "How to Buy a Nuclear Deterrent," *The Guardian,* June 22, 2006.

43. Secretary of State for Defence and Secretary of State for Foreign and Commonwealth Affairs, "The Future of the United Kingdom's Nuclear Deterrent, December 2006," p. 22

44. Ibid., p. 23.

45. James Schlesinger, interview, Project on Nuclear Issues, Center for Strategic and International Studies, Washington, D.C., January 9, 2008, Section IV of this volume.

46. Jon Baylis, "Exchanging Nuclear Secrets: Laying the Foundations of the Anglo-American Nuclear Partnership," *Diplomatic History* 25, no. 1 (Winter 2001): p. 57.

47. Secretary of State for Defence and Secretary of State for Foreign and Commonwealth Affairs, "The Future of the United Kingdom's Nuclear Deterrent, December 2006," p. 18.

48. North Atlantic Treaty, April 4, 1949, North Atlantic Treaty Organization Online Library, http://www.nato.int/docu/basictxt/treaty.htm. Article 5 of the North Atlantic Treaty stipulates that any attack against a NATO member shall be considered an attack against the alliance.

49. Quinlan, "Future of United Kingdom Nuclear Weapons," pp. 627–637.

50. Lawrence Freedman, "Britain: The First Ex-Nuclear Power?" p. 91.

51. Secretary of State for Defence and Secretary of State for Foreign and Commonwealth Affairs, "The Future of the United Kingdom's Nuclear Deterrent, December 2006," p. 6.

52. Michael Quinlan, "The British Experience," in *Getting MAD: Nuclear Mutual Assured Destruction, Its Origins and Practice,* ed. Henry S. Sokolski (Carlisle, Pa.: U.S. Army War College, Strategic Studies Institute, 2004), 261, http://www.strategicstudiesinstitute.army.mil/pdffiles/PUB585.pdf.

53. Secretary of State for Defence and Secretary of State for Foreign and Commonwealth Affairs, "The Future of the United Kingdom's Nuclear Deterrent, December 2006," p. 20.

11

UK-U.S. AIR FORCE COLLABORATION

JEFFERY H. RICHARDSON

The U.S.-UK Mutual Defense Agreement (MDA) of 1958 ushered in a prolonged period of cooperation between the two countries with respect to strategic nuclear deterrence. During the past several decades, that cooperation has been dominated by two processes: (1) programmatic exchanges between the U.S. Department of Defense (DOD) and the UK Ministry of Defence (MOD) that have tended to focus almost exclusively on submarine-launched ballistic missile (SLBM) systems through the Polaris Sales Agreement (PSA) and subsequent arrangements and (2) nonprogrammatic technical exchanges between the Department of Energy (DOE) and the Atomic Weapons Establishment (AWE). With respect to nuclear information, the substantial operational database represented by U.S. Air Force systems (historical lessons from retired systems, current operations of largely Cold War legacy systems, and perspectives of potential future systems) has not been widely shared. One clear indication of this recent lack of communication with respect to nuclear information is the relative lack of statutory determinations pertinent to Air Force operational nuclear weapon systems.

POST–COLD WAR NUCLEAR POLICY

The United States, along with the four other nuclear weapon states (the United Kingdom, France, China, and Russia), is in the process of developing and implementing nuclear policy for the post-Cold War. An early manifestation of this review is the evolution of the new triad along with the current public debate regarding the reliable replacement warhead (RRW).[1] The natural technological lifetime associated with nuclear warheads and delivery systems necessitates an analysis of alternative options with respect to the entire nuclear weapons complex, including not only the weapon delivery systems and the warheads, but also the supporting acquisition, facility, and technological infrastructure. The United Kingdom is undergoing a similar review and published in 2006 a strategic white paper, "The Future of the United Kingdom's Nuclear Deterrent."[2]

The agreement reached between President George W. Bush and Prime Minister Tony Blair in December 2006 to enhance collaboration between the United States and the United Kingdom has provided a timely incentive for both sides to seek synergistic cooperation and leverage technical and resource investments.[3] The Air Force's analysis of future strategies, being developed in its nuclear enterprise road map, gives a notional timeline for the future component and system decisions it faces. The UK's white paper provides a similar timeline for future UK main decision points with respect to both warhead and delivery systems. Thus, the U.S. Air Force is taking advantage of these parallel timelines by exploring options with respect to nonnuclear components and technology relevant to weapon and delivery systems. The benefit to the U.S. Air Force will be access to new technology, resources, and data possessed by the United Kingdom. Similarly, the United Kingdom will validate new simulation codes with historical data and share in the evaluation of new technology and operational, functional system architectures pertinent to future systems. Where appropriate, this collaboration also includes participation of the U.S. Navy, which has a longer and more extensive history of technical interactions with the United Kingdom through the PSA and its subsequent amendments.[4]

The Joint Atomic Information Exchange Group was established by the DOD and DOE to control the transfer of classified atomic information between the United States and foreign governments. Before the exchange of letters between President Bush and Prime Minister Blair, much of the technical research and development cooperation under the MDA had been conducted via the joint working group (JOWOG) process. JOWOGs have been established to cover a wide range of technologies pertinent to the development and maintenance of nuclear weapons (for example, nuclear materials, computational technology, warhead electrical components, manufacturing practices, and nuclear warhead physics).[5] JOWOGs are a convenient venue for information exchange and for coordinating joint work of mutual interest that does not have an immediate programmatic impact and is not driven by schedules, milestones, or budgetary considerations. The primary participants in the JOWOG process are the U.S. DOE national laboratories, particularly the National Nuclear Security Administration (NNSA) laboratories (Lawrence Livermore National Laboratory, Los Alamos National Laboratory, and Sandia National Laboratories), and the AWE in the United Kingdom.

ENHANCED COLLABORATION BETWEEN THE UNITED STATES AND THE UNITED KINGDOM

One of the purposes of the enhanced collaboration made possible by the agreement between President Bush and Prime Minister Blair was to move beyond interactions in JOWOGs. Enhanced collaboration enables more focused joint efforts that should result in concrete deliverables that meet the constraints of schedules, milestones, and budget considerations. Although DOD organizations have been less active than the DOE laboratories in the JOWOG process (with the major exception of the U.S. Navy and the Trident channel), the enhanced collaboration has provided an opportunity for greater DOD participation. It has enabled a more defined management structure in order to facilitate deepened collaboration across the full spectrum of the U.S. and UK nuclear weapons complex. A number of nuclear weapon areas are being developed into enhanced collaboration projects, primarily along the traditional NNSA technical areas such as nuclear weapons physics. The first DOD effort under this enhanced collaboration is the next generation fuze (NGF) project, initiated by the U.S. Air Force and the United Kingdom with active U.S. Navy participation.

The programmatic motivation from the U.S. side is the continual aging of the stockpile. The Air Force has the greatest diversity of systems in the stockpile as well as some of the oldest. It also has the greatest diversity of delivery platforms. Consequently, the Air Force has the greatest technical challenge with respect to maintaining and certifying its portion of the U.S. stockpile. It is exploring various options for maintaining the stockpile, either through warhead refurbishments, replacements (for example, through the ICBM long-range planning group and nuclear enterprise road map), or both. Warhead refurbishments might be conducted at varying levels of complexity and completeness over a prescribed time period (from replacement of limited life components in the field to complete warhead lifetime extension programs). The RRW, currently under intensive scrutiny and in part awaiting a new nuclear posture review, is one approach to the replacement of weapon systems.

NEXT GENERATION FUZE PROJECT

Regardless of the path forward, the fuze system in some of the Air Force missile systems will need some level of refurbishment in the next decade. The level of feasibility of an integrated arming, fuzing, and firing (AF&F) system will be evaluated. The Nuclear Weapons Council in the United States has specifically requested this evaluation. The Ministry of Defence in the United Kingdom has also identified fuze development as one of the key technologies to be evaluated for its phased assessment and decision process concerning its future nuclear deterrent. Although the United Kingdom has not committed to any specific path forward with respect to the warhead system, prudent decisionmakers wish to explore the technical, budgetary, and schedule limitations of various potential options. Because the fuzing system interacts with the overall weapons electrical system, this project leverages existing traditional JOWOG collaboration with new enhanced collaboration projects that are evaluating common adaptable electrical system architectures. The programmatic advantages of overall cost savings, reduced development time, reduced redundancy, and improved performance drive the exploration of commonality and adaptability.

Thus, the NGF enhanced collaboration project was established to identify and evaluate the adaptability and commonality achievable in a replacement fuzing system. This evaluation will occur at both the system and component level, so that issues of commonality and adaptability can also be evaluated at the modular level. Because the project is a collaborative effort between the United States and United Kingdom, it will promote synergy and leverage in technical development efforts for modern fuzing. One of the primary deliverables is an evaluation of technology readiness levels for a variety of future fuzing options.[6] Identification of levels of commonality and adaptability will result in several programmatic advantages, including flexibility, redundancy, and overall life-cycle cost savings as well as ease in future maintenance and sustainment.

Although the Air Force as a whole has extensive history in international collaboration, the part of the Air Force responsible for the intercontinental ballistic missile (ICBM) component of the nuclear triad does not have an extensive history of international cooperation.[7] The genesis of the NGF project included reciprocal visits. First, a delegation of U.S. Air Force personnel from Headquarters, Space Command (program and operational responsibility), and Hill Air Force Base (maintenance and logistic responsibility) visited or discussed UK facilities and capabilities at AWE, Lockheed INSYS, and Thales in December 2006. A subsequent visit from U.K. representatives of MOD, AWE, and Thales visited Hill AFB, Lockheed Martin Valley Forge, and Headquarters Air Force at the Pentagon June 2007. This June meeting represented the first time a UK delegation had been to Hill AFB to observe aspects of the Air Force programs for maintenance and refurbishment of the Minuteman III ICBM missile system.

The UK delegation and Air Force personnel discussed Air Force plans for refurbishment and upgrades to different elements of the ICBM system as well as examples of adapting warheads to different delivery systems. A proposal for future joint work, which included participation of the U.S. Navy, on fuzing systems was developed and approved in October 2007 at the Enhanced Collaboration Government-to-Government Second Level meeting at AWE.

The NGF project consists of a series of tasks that are partially constrained by limitations to the exchange of legacy information (caused by the absence of appropriate statutory determinations that explicitly permit transmission). These tasks are also constrained by the different levels of maturity and complexity that each participant—U.S. Air Force, U.S. Navy, and United Kingdom—is addressing with respect to requirements for its next generation fuze. The U.S. Navy is the most mature and least complex, with one delivery system and one or two potential warhead systems; the U.S. Air Force has the most complexity and fluidity with respect to future development; and the United Kingdom is the most undefined and least mature but has a relatively straight decision process. Consequently, the exchange of information is rich and helps to broaden the perspectives of all participants.

The NGF project consists of each participant first characterizing its technical challenge, that is, the desired attributes in a future fuze. Examples of these attributes include operational constraints and requirements (temperature ranges, radiation, and shock environments), electrical power budgets, memory options, and electrical systems. These attributes can later be developed into technical requirements that can be evaluated for commonality at the system and component level. Because current Air Force fuzing systems are based on technology from the 1970s and 1980s, it is critical to evaluate and then prioritize current technology options to provide the desired attributes. From the UK perspective, it is important to evaluate the relative level of maturity of the various technology options in order to minimize costs and risks, as the United Kingdom is facing significant decisions with respect to supporting nuclear weapons complex infrastructure. To that end, all three participants will be evaluating potential joint demonstration projects that can mitigate risk by prioritizing, developing, and validating potential technology solutions prior to implementing their respective decisions. Sharing test facilities and computer simulation codes helps to minimize development costs; decrease the budget, schedule, technical, and operational risks; and optimize performance.

The three participants in the NGF project have different cultures with regard to contracting work. The U.S. Navy primarily uses government contractors (Sandia, a NNSA laboratory) for its fuze development work. The U.S. Air Force primarily relies on private contractors (Northrop Grumman and Lockheed Martin Valley Forge) for its fuze development work. The United Kingdom is considering a mix of government and private contractors (AWE and Thales) as it considers how to reinvigorate its nuclear weapons infrastructure. Working out the details for sharing classified and proprietary information among such a diverse set of interacting participants will present organizational challenges to enhanced collaboration.

The U.S. Air Force may reap considerable benefit from the NGF project. Participants can leverage the previous, current, and future investments of the others—for example, past flight test data, various environmental test facilities, different computer codes, and manufacturing practices. In addition, the investment in establishing collaboration with the United Kingdom offers benefits for the Air Force beyond the NGF project. A second programmatic area of high interest for both the Air Force and Navy is aero shells and reentry vehicles. Although not an immediate issue for either service, the fact is that both materials and manufacturing processes used to develop the current inventory are no longer available. Complementary Air Force and Navy programs are involved in evaluating alternative materials, alternative manufacturing processes, and available test facilities. The Navy and the United Kingdom currently share some reentry body information under the Trident channel through the Joint Reentry Steering Working Group. The United Kingdom also faces a series of decisions with respect to the reentry vehicle for its future strategic deterrent, making this a ripe area for expanded future U.S. Air Force–UK collaboration.

Before the current NGF project, the most recent Air Force–UK collaboration involved ballistic missile defense.[8] This collaboration is an outgrowth of cooperation in strategic defense dating back to the U.S. Strategic Defense Initiative.[9] There has been little recent collaboration specifically focused on the nuclear enterprise, particularly because of the long-standing UK focus on an SLBM deterrent. It is expected that the involvement of the U.S. Air Force with the UK strategic complex will be greatly enhanced over the next decade compared with the past several decades. This enhancement is to the benefit of both countries with respect to direct technical cooperation and to supporting each country's respective strategic decision and evaluation process, and it generally helps to promote mutual defense as well as greater cooperation on matters of international security.

NOTES

I would like to thank my United States Air Force colleagues for pursuing this novel pathway of enhanced collaboration for helping to meet Air Force mission requirements: Major Lance Adkins, Brad Elwell, Eric Hoffman, Les Lyon, Bill Mullins, and Doug Weiss. I would also like to thank our British embassy touchstone, Iain Dawson, who has been invaluable in helping structure the effort from the UK side. Finally, without the enthusiastic cooperation from our technical counterparts at AWE, this collaboration would not be possible.

1. Jonathan Medalia, *The Reliable Replacement Warhead Program: Background and Current Developments,* Report no. RL32929 (Washington, D.C.: Congressional Research Service, December 18, 2007).

2. Secretary of State for Defence and Secretary of State for Foreign and Commonwealth Affairs, "The Future of the United Kingdom's Nuclear Deterrent, December 2006," Report no. CM 6994 (London: Her Majesty's Stationery Office, 2006).

3. House of Commons Defence Committee, "Annex 2: Exchange of Letters between the Prime Minister and the President of the United States of America," in *The Future of UK's Strategic Nuclear Deterrent: The White Paper,* vol. 1 (London: The Stationery Office Limited, March 7, 2007), http://www.publications.parliament.uk/pa/cm200607/cmselect/cmdfence/225/225i.pdf.

4. "Facts: Polaris-Poseidon-Trident: The British Strategic Systems Programs," U.S. Navy Web site, n.d., http://www.ssp.navy.mil/about/history_facts_5.shtml.

5. "List of Joint Working Groups (JOWOGs)," Los Alamos National Laboratory Web site, April 1, 2005, http://badge.lanl.gov/jowogs.shtml.

6. John C. Mankins, "Technology Readiness Levels: A White Paper," Advanced Concepts Office, Office of Space Access and Technology, NASA, April 6, 1995, http://www.hq.nasa.gov/office/codeq/trl/trl.pdf.

7. For more information about the organization of U.S. Air Force ICBM units, see the Web site of the Air Force Space Command, http://www.afspc.af.mil/.

8. Statutory Determination: Minuteman III and Peacekeeper Inter-Continental Ballistic Missile Systems (2005); "Global Ballistic Missile Defense: A Layered Integrated Defense," 4th ed. (Washington, D.C.: Department of Defense, Missile Defense Agency, April 4, 2006), http://www.mda.mil/mdalink/pdf/bmdsbook.pdf.

9. "Britain and Missile Defence," Web site of Campaign for Nuclear Disarmament, June 2003, http://www.cnduk.org/pages/binfo/mdrole.html; Leyla Kattan and Nigel Chamberlain, "The Missile Defence Debate Gap in Britain: As Wide as Ever in 2004," British American Security Information Council, February 24, 2005, http://www.basicint.org/pubs/Notes/BN050224.htm.

Part Three

REFLECTIONS AND FUTURE PROSPECTS

THE FUTURE OF THE 1958 MUTUAL DEFENSE AGREEMENT

LINTON F. BROOKS

In 1946, at Westminster College in the small midwestern city of Fulton, Missouri, Winston Churchill, then seven months out of office, delivered a sobering assessment of world affairs. His speech has become famous for the first use of the term "Iron Curtain." It also contains the first high-level use of the term "special relationship" to describe the bond between the United States and the United Kingdom. As Churchill described it, the special relationship "requires not only the growing friendship and mutual understanding between our two . . . systems of society, but the continuance of the intimate relationship between our military advisers. . . ."[1]

Although the iron curtain is gone, the special relationship has endured and flourished as a symbol of an alliance of equal partners with common commitments to international security, to democracy, and to cooperation. For 50 years, a unique and important aspect of this relationship has been the extensive nuclear cooperation enabled and symbolized by the 1958 Mutual Defense Agreement. One observer noted:

> The special relationship as related to nuclear weapon systems has had a long and enviable history. Indeed, *there exists no other program where the United States has worked so intimately with another country for such an extended period of time on the gravest matters of national security.*[2]

Other essays in this volume document the accomplishments of the past. This chapter examines the prospects for continued close nuclear

cooperation in the future. There is no inherent reason why cooperation must continue, no matter how close it has been in the past. After all, the world of 2008 is very different from the world foreseen by
Churchill at the start of the Cold War. The growing ethnic diversity in
both countries has weakened the assumed common cultural approach
of which Churchill spoke in 1946. The monolithic enemy of 1946 is
gone, replaced with a diverse set of international challenges. The inter-
vening decades have shown that the interests of the two states are not
always the same. Can this unique and intimate relationship endure in
this quite different world?

LESSONS OF THE PAST

One reason for optimism about the future of nuclear cooperation
is the historical record. The special relationship has survived differences over British actions in the Suez and U.S. actions in Vietnam.
It has survived dramatic changes in the world, including the end of
the British Empire and the rise of an integrated Europe as a force in
world politics. It has survived the end of the Cold War and the rise of
new international threats. The nuclear component of that relationship
has survived the U.S. 1963 cancellation of Skybolt, periods of atrophy
in the British nuclear program in the late 1970s, significant strategic
disagreement over the value of the Strategic Defense Initiative in the
1980s, and the attempt by some in the United States to "delegitimize"
nuclear weapons in the 1990s. Yet none of these events came anywhere near to ending—or even truncating—cooperation under the
1958 agreement.

This should not be surprising. Underneath the changes lie enduring fundamentals. Both the United States and United Kingdom remain
committed to democracy, human rights, and the rule of law. Both have
global interests, and both recognize that it is sometimes necessary to
act far from home to ensure the stability of the international system
and the security of their respective countries. As a result, as their close
cooperation in Iraq and in the broader war on terrorism shows, the
special relationship remains firm. The nuclear component of that relationship is probably as strong as or stronger than it has ever been, as
witnessed by the breadth and depth of ongoing cooperation (some of it
documented elsewhere in this volume) and by the smooth manner in
which the two countries worked together to support the recent British
decision to replace Trident.

Even considering the persistence of the special relationship, nuclear cooperation under the 1958 agreement has been remarkably impervious to challenge. None of the flurry of reexaminations of U.S. nuclear policy conducted over the past year has mentioned it, let alone questioned its wisdom. Senior statesmen now advocating that the United States take the lead in moving the world toward the elimination of nuclear weapons have set forth a series of practical steps to reduce reliance on nuclear weapons in national security. U.S.–UK cooperation was not mentioned.[3] The same congressional critics who saw U.S. proposals for a reliable replacement warhead (RRW) as threatening the international nonproliferation regime were silent on continued Anglo-American nuclear cooperation. In the United States, nuclear cooperation with the United Kingdom, like the broader strategic relationship, has become an accepted part of the national security landscape, often unnoticed and inevitably unquestioned.

In the United Kingdom, the situation is somewhat different. In the past, some have argued (erroneously) that the 1958 agreement was inconsistent with the Nuclear Non-Proliferation Treaty.[4] This argument, which has no basis in fact, does not appear to have widespread appeal. It is not clear how much relevance it had during the recent debate on a replacement for Trident,[5] although opponents used Britain's dependence on the United States as an argument that the British nuclear deterrent was not truly independent. It appears that, as in the United States, the 1958 agreement is and will remain generally accepted except, perhaps, by those opposed to the United Kingdom remaining a nuclear power.

One reason why relations under the 1958 agreement have been particularly successful and are seldom challenged is that they take place almost entirely at the technical level and are thus insulated both from policy fluctuations in relations between the two countries and, at least in the United States, from broader policy debates. In the United States, the Department of Energy's National Nuclear Security Administration and the Office of the Assistant to the Secretary of Defense for Nuclear, Chemical, and Biological matters jointly manage the interaction. It is important to note that both these U.S. organizations have a technical rather than a policy focus. Further, except for the high-level reviews (stocktakes) conducted at roughly 18-month intervals with the chief scientific adviser of the British Ministry of Defence, the program largely operates at the working level, primarily in interactions between the U.S. weapons laboratories and the Atomic Weapons Establishment at Aldermaston in the United Kingdom. These interactions, normally conducted in joint working groups (JOWOGs), deal with specific areas of physics, engineering, or material science. There are frequent informal contacts between senior officials on both sides, but because the cooperation is so well established and smooth these contacts rarely involve details of the 1958 agreement.[6]

This structure isolates efforts conducted under the 1958 agreement from the broader policy process. Officials from the State Department and the Foreign Office do not participate in the periodic stocktake meetings. Their involvement is relegated to the periodic routine amendments extending transfer provisions, most recently the ten-year extension of these provisions agreed to in 2004. The policy organization within the Department of Defense is involved only infrequently, when the secretaries of defense and energy submit to the president recommendations for revising the parameters of the cooperation. These presidential "statutory determinations" (so called because they are mandated by Section 91c of the Atomic Energy Act) are broad, infrequent, and enduring.[7]

During the past 50 years, extensive cooperation with the United Kingdom has become an accepted practice within the U.S. nuclear weapons community. The details and intensity of that cooperation have varied, but it is inconceivable to most nuclear professionals that cooperation could end altogether. In the same way, the special relationship in some form has become a permanent aspect of U.S. security policy. Although with international relations—as with the stock market—past performance is no assurance of future potential, this decades-long record of success bodes well for the future.

PROSPECTS FOR ONGOING COOPERATION

There are better reasons than simple historical inertia for assuming that nuclear cooperation will continue. The same reasons that have made cooperation valuable in the past will make it equally valuable in coming years. What may change is that the effort will become more of a two-way street. In the past, because of the huge disparity in size between the two programs, the United Kingdom often derived more technical benefit than the United States, although the United States derived major geostrategic benefits from having a close and capable ally competent across the full spectrum of warfare.

The disparity in program size will, of course, continue. The United States retains a far larger stockpile, maintains a greater number of warhead types, and has made significantly greater investment in complex research tools such as the National Ignition Facility, microengineering facilities, dynamic radiography machines, and supercomputers. But overall pressures on the national security budget in the coming years coupled with the need for recapitalization of the aging U.S. nuclear weapons complex will inevitably put pressure on the scientific portion of the U.S. weapons budget. As a result, the United States may derive greater technical benefits from collaboration in the future. Peer review, always important, will become even more so as the experience of nuclear testing recedes into the past. Fiscal pressures will make shared experiments more and more attractive. The major revitalization conducted in recent years at the Atomic Weapons Establishment, Aldermaston, will improve British technical capability and thus the technical value of ongoing exchanges. These trends suggest future cooperation will be even more collaborative and in even greater depth than in the past.

The value of cooperation may increase as both sides seek to deploy replacement warheads that offer greater reliability over time and incorporate modern safety and security features. In the United States, the RRW program, although not funded by Congress in fiscal year 2008, will probably continue in some form. The United Kingdom has not yet announced whether it will reuse existing Trident warheads on the successor system or develop a replacement warhead. Press accounts, however, have suggested that a so-called high surety warhead, with goals very similar to those of the U.S. RRW, will be developed.[8] Similar scientific challenges in areas important to the continued effectiveness of respective nuclear deterrents in the United States and the United Kingdom could prove an important spur for intensified technical collaboration.

Finally, as important as the 1958 agreement is, it is only a subset and a symbol of the broad and deep cooperation and dialogue between the two countries on nuclear issues. This dialogue benefits both parties. For example, as the United States continues to search for consensus on the function of nuclear weapons in the twenty-first century, it can benefit from considering the British approach to harmonizing nuclear policy decisions with nonproliferation objectives. The 1958 agreement is not a prerequisite for quiet, candid discussions on nuclear policy, but the channels it establishes and the personal relations it fosters make such discussions easier and more fruitful.

NEW AND EXPANDED AREAS

Not only will traditional areas of technical cooperation remain important, but new, post–Cold war areas of cooperation are likely to intensify in coming years. During the Cold War, there was only limited interest in the problems of nuclear terrorism in either country. Today such terrorism is arguably the most important threat facing each. The current extensive cooperation on nuclear terrorism will certainly continue and is likely to expand. One clear area for technical cooperation is in understanding the construction, detection, and neutralization of improvised nuclear devices. A second area might be developing common approaches to dealing with the discovery of such devices in states lacking nuclear weapons expertise. Other opportunities for technical cooperation in countering nuclear terrorism will probably emerge as well.

One of the important early results of the 1958 agreement was to assist the United Kingdom in developing nuclear propulsion for its submarines. Under the agreement, the United States transferred information, technology, and a complete submarine power plant to the United Kingdom. During the past 50 years, cooperation in propulsion plant technology has been robust and has covered lessons learned on individual technical issues of interest to both countries. As the United Kingdom moves toward a new class of strategic ballistic-missile submarines to replace its current Vanguard class, opportunities for expanded cooperation will likely emerge. Such cooperation will surely benefit the strategic interests of the United States by ensuring the continued effectiveness of the British independent deterrent.

Additional opportunities for cooperation, opportunities presently unforeseen, may well emerge in the coming years. One of the strengths of the 1958 agreement is its adaptability, which will make it easier to respond to new challenges and new opportunities.

WILD CARD

The analysis above suggests that the nuclear component of the special relationship will remain strong. The only obvious development that could change that assessment would be a future decision by Britain to cease being a nuclear power and to eliminate its nuclear deterrent.

Unlike the other recognized nuclear weapon states under the Nuclear Non-Proliferation Treaty, the United Kingdom has, in the past, taken serious internal looks at nuclear disarmament. A decision to move to unilateral disarmament sometime in the future would make the 1958 Mutual Defense Agreement and the nuclear relationship it embodies irrelevant.[9]

Such a step, however, appears unlikely. The recent decision to replace Trident puts the United Kingdom on the path to retain a nuclear deterrent for the next half century. It is significant that a Labour government took this major decision, for the Labour Party has been the traditional home of the British movement for unilateral nuclear disarmament. Based on traditional attitudes, a future Conservative government would be virtually certain to sustain the current government's decision on Trident replacement. There are objective reasons why this is so. As Prime Minister Tony Blair wrote in explaining the decision to replace Trident:

> Those who question this decision need to explain why disarmament by the UK would help our security. They would need to prove that such a gesture would change the minds of hardliners and extremists in countries which are developing these nuclear capabilities. They would need to show that terrorists would be less likely to conspire against us with hostile governments because we had given up our nuclear weapons. They would need to argue that the UK would be safer by giving up the deterrent and that our capacity to act would not be constrained by nuclear blackmail by others. The Government believes that now, as in the Cold War, such an argument is misguided.[10]

Both the politics of the United Kingdom and the power of the prime minister's analysis suggest that the United Kingdom will remain a nuclear power. If so, cooperation under the 1958 agreement will continue to be vital.

CONCLUSION

States make and keep international agreements because it is in their national security interest to do so. As long as the United States and the United Kingdom find it necessary to maintain a nuclear deterrent, they will find close technical cooperation to be in their interest. The closeness of the nuclear relationship, like that of the broader strategic partnership within which it is embedded, may wax and wane with changes in the international situation, but the basic relationship will remain strong. Insulated by structure and custom from policy fluctuations, technical cooperation under the 1958 agreement will remain robust. It is not possible to foresee the specific details of that cooperation in the coming years, but it is as sure as anything in international relations can be that it will be extensive and will continue to be founded on technical candor, shared expertise, and mutual respect.

As usual, Winston Churchill expressed it best. In the same Fulton, Missouri, speech that discussed the iron curtain and the special relationship, he said that if the United States and the United Kingdom worked together "with all that such cooperation implies . . . in science and in industry . . . there will be an overwhelming assurance of security."[11] For 50 years, the 1958 agreement has been one of the strands forging the special relationship. There is every reason to believe this situation will continue in the coming decades.

NOTES

1. Winston S. Churchill, ed., *Winston Churchill's Speeches: Never Give In!* (London: Pimlico, 2006), p. 418.

2. Leo Michel, "Observations on the Special Relationship in Security and Defense Matters" (emphasis added), in *U.S.-UK Relations at the Start of the 21st Century,* ed. Jeffrey D. McCausland and Douglas T. Stuart (Carlisle, Pa.: U.S. Army War College, Institute of Strategic Studies, January 2006), p. 161, http://www.ndu.edu/inss/Repository/Outside_Publications/Michel/Michel_US-UK_Relations_January2006.pdf.

3. George P. Shultz, William J. Perry, Henry A. Kissinger, and Sam Nunn, "A World Free of Nuclear Weapons," *Wall Street Journal,* January 4, 2007. See also the same authors in "Toward a Nuclear-Free World," *Wall Street Journal,* January 15, 2008.

4. "The US-UK Mutual Defence Agreement: Contributing to Vertical Proliferation?" British American Security Information Council, March 5, 2005, http://www.basicint.org/nuclear/NPT/2005rc/brief05.htm. The argument was made in the context of the 2005 review conference for the Nuclear Non-Proliferation Treaty.

5. For example, a Chatham House summary of the British nuclear debate never explicitly mentions the 1958 agreement; see *International Affairs* 82, no. 4 (July 2006). Similarly, the exhaustive and thoughtful House of Commons Defence Committee report, "The Future of the UK's Strategic Nuclear Deterrent: the Strategic Context," HC 986, June 30, 2006, is silent on the subject, as are the extensive memorandums submitted to that committee, many of which oppose Trident replacement explicitly on

grounds that weapons modernization is inconsistent with the obligations of the Nuclear Non-Proliferation Treaty.

6. In the four and one-half years I served as administrator of the National Nuclear Security Administration (and thus as the senior U.S. official responsible for cooperation under the 1958 agreement) I can recall no instance in which it was necessary for either side to raise any issues at senior levels about the details of the cooperation.

7. There is one exception to this pattern of infrequent, broad presidential guidance. British nuclear tests conducted at the U.S. test site in Nevada were approved by the president on a test-by-test basis; see Troy Wade, "UK Testing at the Nevada Test Site, 1962–1991," in this volume.

8. Ian Bruce, "Britain in Top-Secret Work on New Atomic Warhead," *The Herald* (London), September 4, 2007.

9. A global decision to eliminate nuclear weapons in the next few decades would also make nuclear weapons cooperation irrelevant, but such a decision is almost certainly politically and technically infeasible. The dissolution of NATO would require finding a new mechanism to meet the requirements of Section 91c of the Atomic Energy Act that limits nuclear weapons cooperation to states that are "participating with the United States pursuant to an international arrangement by substantial and material contributions to the mutual defense and security," but this should not be difficult to do.

10. "Foreword to the White Paper by the Prime Minister," in "The Future of the United Kingdom Nuclear Deterrent," prepared by Secretary of State for Defence and Secretary of State for Foreign and Commonwealth Affairs (London: Her Majesty's Stationery Office, December 2006), p. 5, http://www.mod.uk/NR/rdonlyres/AC00DD79-76D6-4FE3-91A1-6-A56B03C092F/0/DefenceWhitePaper2006_Cm6994.pdf.

11. Churchill, ed., *Winston Churchill's Speeches,* pp. 423–424.

13

THE PATH AHEAD FOR
NUCLEAR COOPERATION

MICHAEL QUINLAN

Half a century of U.S.-UK nuclear collaboration has yielded more ef-fective, timely, and economical outcomes than would otherwise have been achieved in several aspects of equipment, technical understand-ing, and force deployment. But collaboration between the two coun-tries has often been no less productive in shared outlook across a broad range of policy matters in NATO and elsewhere. Although the respon-sibilities and direct interests of the United States are wider than Brit-ain's, Britain has customarily judged it right to address the full ambit of challenges in managing a nuclear world rather than just those of UK-specific concern. There is still in prospect a wide span of issues for action-oriented dialogue.

Both countries face questions about future warheads and the in-frastructure to underpin them. Debate in Britain has not developed as it has in the United States about the reliable replacement warhead (RRW), but there lies in wait a decision about what warhead should equip the new submarine force to which the government and Parlia-ment have committed Britain in principle.[1] This will have to be faced at around the same time as the main decision, perhaps five years hence, on the submarine production order. The boats themselves will pose design questions. The Trident D5 missile is a settled given,[2] but four boats or three? Sixteen missile tubes or fewer? Just possibly, a shift to LEU (low enriched uranium) fuel for propulsion (perhaps a long-term question also for U.S. warships)?

All this constitutes a significant agenda, but the policy agenda is weightier still. It embraces proliferation, nuclear terrorism, nuclear energy for civil use, disarmament, deterrence doctrine, force design, and the contested aspiration eventually to abolish all nuclear armories. On these themes U.S. policies need to carry a wider constituency than just Britain, but U.S.-UK dialogue and cooperation offer dividends to both.

Preventing any further proliferation of nuclear weapon ownership must rank high among shared priorities. Though the nuclear nonproliferation regime centered on the 1968 Nuclear Non-Proliferation Treaty (NPT) is not globally precarious, it risks being weakened in several ways. One is that North Korea or Iran might escape from the regime—and, worse, might not pay a heavy price. North Korea, even if its evasive negotiating record continues, is the less worrying since its environment is less beset by tension and repercussive dangers. Iran is more important in size, resources, and regional influence and is far from being a status-quo-accepting international player. The U.S. intelligence assessment of December 2007 that Iran had no current nuclear weapons program was not a certificate of innocence. It conveyed that Iran had earlier had such a program, in flagrant contravention of NPT commitments, and that there was no assurance against its resumption. There had been other treaty-breaching concealments from the International Atomic Energy Agency (IAEA) and secret dealings with the A. Q. Khan network. Iran continued to evade key IAEA questions and reject UN Security Council requirements about its activities.

It is not easy to judge the long-term intentions of a government in which there are probably differences and unsettled opinions within an environment not skilled in strategic analysis. The right asserted to full independence in generating nuclear energy is not debarred by the NPT. But even if that were genuinely all that Iranian leaders want, it would carry Iran to a threshold capability from which an operational nuclear weapon armory could be developed swiftly. It would both damage the nonproliferation regime globally and risk provoking emulation by others in an unsettled region where Iranian attitudes already prompt widespread disquiet.

The U.S. intelligence judgment helpfully weakened arguments for preemptive military action that could have conferred no more than temporary benefit, at the cost of grave wider and longer-lasting repercussions (perhaps including even UK dissociation). But the imperative

remained both to find internationally agreed ways—preferably induce-
ments, or else prospective penalties, or a combination—of persuading
Iran to change course and to consider how best to confine the damage
if Iran did go ahead. This surely needs a broad U.S.-involving dialogue
with Iran to weaken the regime's more extreme apprehensions and to
challenge its unwillingness to weigh the legitimate concerns of others.

A wider long-term danger to the nonproliferation regime is that
general weaknesses within its working will continue unremedied.
These weaknesses relate to shortcomings in the coverage and verification of its safeguards, to the ease and freedom from penalty with which
parties can withdraw from the treaty, and to the absence of arrangements reconciling entitlement to nuclear energy for civil purposes with
avoiding the risks of clandestine or threshold weapons capability.

Assurance that the purposes of the regime are being respected requires comprehensive constraints and guarantees that these are being
complied with. Full-scope treaty safeguards apply the verification tools
of the IAEA to all fissile material within a state, but discoveries in 1991
about Iraq's activities highlighted the need to tighten the system. The
IAEA formulated an additional protocol to reduce the risk that future
contraventions might go undetected. This gained widespread support,
but acceptance and implementation are far from universal. Rectify-
ing this should be an important aim (and would need enhanced IAEA
resources).

Article X of the NPT allows parties to withdraw on giving six months'
notice. Such a provision has many parallels in other treaties. It is questionable, however, whether a penalty-free let-out remains acceptable
in a field where the purpose of a globally accepted treaty has become a
major norm of the international system and where withdrawal by one
party may crucially affect whether the treaty's benefits continue to accrue to other parties. It is unrealistic to envisage amending the treaty
to remove the right of withdrawal, but it would be desirable to devise
an evident package of disagreeable consequences that any withdrawing
state must expect to undergo.

A third problem is that nothing in the treaty directly debars non-
nuclear parties from developing capability for nuclear energy generation and use in ways—whether or not so intended—from which they
could swiftly move to the construction of nuclear weapons, through
having capability to enrich uranium or reprocess weapons-usable plutonium from spent fuel. The significance of this is widened by the like-

lihood that the global importance of nuclear energy will be enhanced and its spread accelerated because of pressure on oil and gas resources, concerns about energy security, and demands that fossil-fuel use be cut back on climate-change account. A surge of countries coming to a threshold nuclear weapons capability would imperil confidence in the nonproliferation regime. Yet nonnuclear weapon states (NNWSs) will justifiably look for dependable and nondiscriminatory arrangements to ensure, on economically reasonable terms, the permanent access to nuclear energy that Article IV of the treaty promises.

All these issues will come to the fore at the 2010 review conference of NPT parties. The 2005 conference was a failure. It must be common ground between the United States and the United Kingdom (whether on its own or working as a member of the European Union) that a repetition would be not only an opportunity missed but a serious setback to the nonproliferation regime. The review conference is not a forum for agreeing on precise solutions to all problems, but it will shape the political context and atmosphere within which they can be tackled.

That context and atmosphere may bear also upon a recurrent weakness external to the regime. Key states have often been unwilling to attach priority, as against other national interests, to enforcing the regime's obligations. The international handling of North Korea and Iran illustrates the difficulties of sustaining comprehensive international pressure. So too does the saga of dealing with Iraq over weapons of mass destruction (WMD) in the mid-1990s. Greater willingness then by China, France, and Russia to match the readiness of the United States and the United Kingdom to enforce strictly the Security Council's 1991 resolutions might have weakened—if not destroyed—the case later made for the action taken in 2003 with such damaging consequences. A successful NPT review conference in 2010 could make it more difficult politically for key countries to sidestep their enforcement responsibilities.

There is then the question of nuclear proliferation to terrorists. Everything reasonably possible should clearly be done to keep the risk, whether thought large or small, to a minimum. There is still much to be done to fulfill the mandatory provisions of UN Security Council Resolution 1540 in 2004 requiring all member states to establish, operate, and report on their arrangements to prevent the acquisition or movement of WMD-related matériel by nonstate actors. Collective political pressure to fulfill the resolution's requirements needs to be maintained and perhaps even intensified. If some states have difficulty with the task, others such as the United States and the United Kingdom should be ready to help.

In two further technical respects U.S. and UK cooperation in leading wider international action could help to reduce fears of nuclear terrorism. The first is to compile a comprehensive data bank about fissile material to heighten the likelihood that material used in a terrorist attack could be traced to the state from which—whether deliberately or through negligence—it had come. This could reinforce deterrence and stimulate effort on security arrangements. The second possibility concerns the fact that some nonnuclear states may lack the technical expertise needed to minimize the effects of a nuclear attack. Proliferation risks make it impossible to provide comprehensive information beforehand, but nuclear weapon states (NWSs) could make advance arrangements for rendering prompt expert assistance.

The United States and Britain have often shown some divergence of view, at least in emphasis, on how close and important the link is or should be between nonproliferation and continued disarmament by the NWSs. Both countries rightly reject portrayals of the NPT as primarily a bargain about disarmament. Such a bargain is only one, and the least specific, of the three enshrined in the treaty. (The others are the central bargain, especially among the NNWSs themselves, not to add to the number of NWSs and also the Article IV undertaking about access to nuclear energy.) Nevertheless, both Article VI and subsequent political undertakings make it impossible to separate nonproliferation from disarmament, and any attempt to insist on that would be widely damaging.

The working and tightening of the nonproliferation regime will continue to impose substantial burdens and constraints on the NNWSs. Their willingness to accept this cannot be insulated from what the NWSs do to reduce the size and salience of their armories and to lessen any risks in retaining them. Four of these five states have already done a great deal in this direction and might with advantage seek to make the facts more widely understood.[3] The exception may be understandable in the near term, given China's modest inventory (publicly claimed[4] to be the smallest among the five) and its lack of allies, as well as its uncertainty—related to misgivings over, for example, U.S. ballistic missile defense (BMD) programs—about whether the United States accepts a relationship of mutual deterrence.

Ideas of ultraminimal or virtual armories would be more likely to erode than enhance confidence in stable security even if the difficulties of negotiating their complexity could be surmounted. But there remains considerable scope to do more in disarmament and arms control. This will be all the more necessary to the extent that the nuclear powers decide—however legitimately in their own terms—to undertake continuance projects such as UK construction of new strategic nuclear submarines and the U.S. RRW program.

The Comprehensive Nuclear Test-Ban Treaty and the projected Fissile Material Cutoff Treaty are high-profile projects that the great majority of NPT parties desire and expect to see brought to fruition. Even those who (like this writer) doubt whether in cold strategic logic they carry all the weight that enthusiasts ascribe to them must recognize that they have acquired a global political importance that has force in its own right. Their future inescapably bears upon whether NWSs are seen as serious about reducing the risks and salience of their armories and, therefore, upon the willingness of NNWSs to continue meeting their own responsibilities. Even if difficulties continue to impede the two treaty projects, there may be valuable scope meanwhile to exploit further the possibilities for beginning to realize their aims through strengthened moratoriums and similar political undertakings.

Most reductions in nuclear armories since the Cold War have been made unilaterally. That remains the speediest and simplest path, but there is still a role for international agreements. They may have particular value in persuading Russia—conscious of uncertainty and unrest around its enormous borders and also of nuclear weapons as a special factor in its international standing—to accept additional limitation. It is to be hoped that a more lasting and rigorous successor to the 2002 Moscow treaty could be negotiated.[5] Exploratory discussion between the United States and Russia has begun.

The Moscow treaty envisaged a level of 1,700–2,200 for each country's *operational stock* of *strategic weapons*. It said nothing about nondeployed reserve stocks or systems classed as nonstrategic. Constraint upon reserve stocks may be hard to achieve for some time yet, but further reduction in operational strategic holdings, possibly to a limit somewhere in the order of 1,000–1,200, might be a proper objective. It is hard to believe that such a level would not give both countries stable and credible deterrence.

It would be very desirable also to bring nonstrategic systems into account. Russia is generally believed to have several times the U.S. holding of these. It may be difficult, however, to agree on reductions to transparent and equal levels while Russia remains concerned about the continued holding of U.S. nuclear weapons in Europe for NATO and the planned U.S. BMD deployment in central Europe.

NATO has no need to apologize for U.S. warheads in Europe. But it is difficult now to see any compelling case for their retention. Aside from the diminution of threat since the Cold War, the United States has delivery systems that could swiftly bring nuclear weapons to bear anywhere in the world without using forces and equipment stationed in Europe. The political case for the deployment—the desire to underscore U.S. commitment to its European allies and the merit of involving those allies in the responsibilities of nuclear deterrence—no longer has great force. The warhead holding is currently believed to be below 500, with perhaps one-third earmarked for non-U.S. delivery systems under dual-key arrangements. Withdrawal would relieve European allies still participating in those arrangements of awkward decisions ahead about replacing the aircraft assigned to the role within hard-pressed budgets and amid pressure for better contribution to European defense effort in other ways. It need do no harm to alliance cohesion and confidence provided that its presentation maintained three key principles:

- The full military capability of the United States remains unequivocally committed to the defense of all NATO allies and to the agreed NATO strategic concept (whether the present or any new one);

- Allies for their part maintain their acceptance of the concept, including its nuclear aspects; and

- There is no question of declaring any part of alliance territory a nuclear weapons–free zone into which weapons could never be reintroduced at need for security and deterrence.

There seems no reason why affirming any of these principles should be difficult.

There may well be underlying differences of judgment between Britain (not directly involved) and the United States about plans for a

BMD system in central Europe. General skepticism about the strategic value and technical effectiveness of BMD is not absent from U.S. commentaries, but it has usually been more evident in Britain. Transatlantic opinions may well diverge, therefore, about how high a price abandonment or modification of the BMD plan would be. At the least, however, candid discussion could be salutary. Russian objection may reflect general resentment at new western military deployments in areas once part of Russia's own protective glacis. More concretely, it has rested upon suspicion that, while the plans have been explained as motivated by concerns about potential Iranian capability, their effect if not indeed their hidden intent might be to lay a foundation for eroding Russia's own deterrent power. That suspicion, however unreal or exaggerated, must be likely to impair Russian willingness to constrain its offensive holdings. Even if Iran does acquire significant operational nuclear weapon capability—an eventuality, at worst, not in early prospect—massive western deterrent power would still bear down on its wielding (especially in the directions relevant to the BMD plans). Shelving the plans—or staging them in some way dependent on Iranian developments or accepting a cooperative U.S.-Russia BMD arrangement less than ideal in U.S. operational terms—would not seem a large sacrifice, especially if it could be coupled with deeper Russian commitment to posing severe penalties for Iranian continuance along the nuclear path. Not all U.S. opinion will regard more comprehensive constraint upon Russian nuclear weapon holdings as important enough to warrant making policy shifts like those sketched above. It would, however, contribute valuably to international perceptions of disarmament impetus, and such shifts do not seem likely to be strongly opposed by the European members of NATO to whose security they primarily relate.

Another aspect of behavior by the NWSs that sometimes attracts censure is that public information about their armories is more limited than critics would like. Transparency is not always an automatic good. Uncertainty or ambiguity may help deterrent stability for small or not-yet-matured armories, where the absence of precise knowledge may healthily dispose adversaries to overestimate capability, or where full disclosure might be thought to heighten preemption risk. The loss of secrecy might drive states with armories of small size or limited quality to expand their capabilities or adopt higher readiness states. Nevertheless, in most situations transparency aids stability and confidence across the nonproliferation scene. It might be helpful if France and the United Kingdom were voluntarily to commit themselves, alongside the extensive statements already made about their force levels,[6] to not exceeding those levels and to accepting international verification in line with whatever arrangements may be agreed in a new bargain between the United States and Russia.

Another field for U.S.-UK dialogue concerns the concepts for which, and the arrangements under which, nuclear armories continue to be maintained. One example is the matter of first use. New promises of no-first-use would have no merit; it is unreal to imagine that in a situation so desperate as to bring nuclear action into contemplation a state would feel bound by a peacetime promise. But the NWSs could usefully declare that they now regard it as highly unlikely that they would have to contemplate first use, and that they would seek so to shape their policies, postures, and doctrines as to keep the eventuality as securely excluded as possible. Some collective declaration on these lines (perhaps alongside explicit repudiation of caricatures that pretend that NATO has a policy of first use or even one of preemptive first strike) could feature in the next updating of the alliance's strategic concept.

NWSs could also explicitly abandon any remaining arrangements for keeping nuclear weapon systems on short-notice alert and for any concept of launch on warning or launch under attack. The real risk of mistaken launch under such arrangements is remote, but the circumstances in which they would come into play are now so improbable as not to warrant their political and presentational costs. The priority as between evident availability for prompt nuclear use and evident assurance against precipitate or mistaken use can surely be shifted in favor of the latter.

Over the span of the nuclear age there has been a progressive narrowing of the extent to which nuclear weapons might be thought necessary to compensate for shortcomings in what conventional weapons can do. The United States has a formidably weighty, varied, and far-reaching array of conventional capabilities for identifying major targets and striking them effectively. It is hard to believe that maintaining nuclear weapons for any purely military purpose remains necessary. The refusal of the U.S. Congress to approve expenditure for new bunker-buster capabilities points away from such ideas. The politico-strategic judgment thus implied—which this writer would share—is that the range of circumstances in which, and of purposes for which, the availability of this specialized potential would be crucial for either use or deterrence is too narrow and improbable to justify the political costs of developing new capabilities when the international community is looking for further reduction in the salience of nuclear weapons.

Formal renunciation of options might be neither credible nor desirable. There is a case, however, that deterrence concepts, operational doctrine, and force provision should be geared essentially to sending a final political warning to discourage an offending regime from continuing aggression, and thereafter—in the very last resort—to rendering it unable or very unlikely to reoffend. That ultimate stage might well include military assets among those to be targeted, but the aim would not be classical military victory or preemptive disarming. Such a reorientation—moving still further away from interpretations of mutual assured destruction as the virtual demolition of societies and regarding as a crucial consideration keeping the collateral loss of innocent life to the minimum possible—might have implications not only for reducing future armories but also for modifying explosive yield.

Beyond all this there looms the aspiration eventually to abolish all nuclear armories. This has been voiced, over the years, in international political declarations in which the United States and Britain have joined. It was given renewed prominence in 2007 by distinguished former U.S. public servants.[7] UK ministers have both supported independent study[8] and proposed that scientific experts from the NWS governments should discuss verification issues.[9] The U.S. administration has been more reticent. But even amid differences of emphasis or expectation, it was possible to recognize the merits of examining the abolitionist idea thoroughly:

- To clarify what might have to change in the world's political conditions to induce current possessors of nuclear weapons to regard the abolitionist goal as desirable;

- To consider what might be needed, for example, in enhancing methods of resolving or managing disputes for the world to dispense with the contribution that nuclear weapons are reasonably believed to have made to the remarkable absence, for more than 60 years, of major war between advanced states; and

- To explore concretely what abolition would have to mean and which verification and enforcement systems would be needed.

This is a massive study agenda. The case for pursuing it, so as to anchor policy debate in deeper understanding, can be acknowledged by those who expect it to demonstrate that abolition is genuinely feasible as well as those who predict the contrary.

There will be challenges and opportunities not foreseen in this essay, perhaps including scope for French involvement if President Nicolas Sarkozy ends his country's artificial semidetachment from NATO. But the central theme of sympathetic yet independent-minded dialogue will continue to merit British governmental effort to engage in the full range of nuclear issues and U.S. governmental attention while that effort is sustained.

NOTES

1. Secretary of State for Defence and Secretary of State for Foreign and Commonwealth Affairs, "The Future of the United Kingdom Nuclear Deterrent" (London: Her Majesty's Stationery Office, December 2006), http://www.mod.uk/NR/rdonlyres/AC00DD79-76D6-4FE3-91A1-6A56B03C092F/0/DefenceWhitePaper2006_Cm6994.pdf; and House of Commons Official Report, March 14, 2007, cols. 298–398.

2. See exchange of letters on December 7, 2006, between Prime Minister Tony Blair and President George W. Bush.

3. For a summary of what the United States has done, see Dr. Christopher Ford (U.S. special representative for nuclear non-proliferation), "Procedure and Substance in the NPT Review Cycle: The Example of Nuclear Disarmament," Press release, United States Mission to the United Nations in Geneva, March 17, 2007, http://geneva.usmission.gov/Press2007/0317Annecy.html.

4. Jeffrey Lewis, "The Ambiguous Arsenal," *Bulletin of the Atomic Scientists* 61, no. 3 (May-June 2005), pp. 52-55, cites a statement by the Chinese Foreign Ministry in April 2004 that "among the nuclear weapon states China possesses the smallest nuclear arsenal."

5. Treaty between the United States of America and the Russian Federation on Strategic Offensive Reductions, May 24, 2002, http://www.state.gov/t/ac/trt/18016.htm.

6. The United Kingdom has published much information, most recently when announcing further stockpile reductions in December 2006. On March 21, 2008, President Nicolas Sarkozy also announced further reductions and declared the size of France's warhead holding.

7. "A World Free of Nuclear Weapons," *Wall Street Journal,* January 4, 2007, and also public statement of January 15, 2008.

8. On June 25, 2007, Foreign and Commonwealth Secretary Margaret Beckett announced support for a study by the International Institute for Strategic Studies on the abolition of nuclear armories.

9. See Des Browne, "Laying the Foundations for Multilateral Disarmament" (speech to UN Conference on Disarmament, Geneva, February 5, 2008), http://www.mod.uk/defenceinternet/aboutdefence/people/speeches/sofs /20080205layingthefoundationsformultilateraldisarmament.htm.

14

CREATING A BILATERAL NUCLEAR POLICY FRAMEWORK

FRANKLIN C. MILLER

In the spring of 1984, the Mutual Defense Agreement (MDA) was almost 26 years old and the Polaris Sales Agreement (PSA) had been in existence for 21 years. Under their combined auspices, robust technical cooperation between the U.S. and British governments was occurring on a regular basis. It is striking, though, that this situation did not carry over into the field of nuclear deterrence policy. To be sure, the two governments interacted in the area of NATO nuclear policy, as the alliance's two nuclear powers Washington and London had always assumed a leadership role in NATO's nuclear debates. U.S. and UK nuclear forces were assigned to NATO's strategic retaliatory strike plan,[1] and discussions about the preparation and coordination of that plan occurred between American and British officers at Supreme Headquarters Allied Powers Europe (SHAPE). But the two nations' national deterrent plans—and the policy assumptions upon which they were based—remained largely off limits.

The fact that the two Western powers, both of whose nuclear forces were designed to deter aggression by a common enemy, never discussed the premises of the deterrent process, or the best way to ensure effective deterrence of the Soviet leadership, or the optimum employment of a common military system (the submarine-launched ballistic missile [SLBM]) was simply accepted. Whether this stemmed from a concern on the part of British officials that mere mention of the UK "national plan" to U.S. counterparts might be perceived by some as undercutting its independent nature, or whether U.S. military officials refused to discuss the single integrated operational plan (SIOP) owing to concerns about classification levels, or simply because policymakers on both sides failed to recognize the synergy and value in such interaction is unclear; the simple fact was that the subject was never broached. All of this was about to change, thanks, oddly enough, to nuclear arms control.

When the United Kingdom negotiated with the U.S. government the purchase of the Trident II (D5) missile in the spring of 1982, Her Majesty's government (HMG) made clear that its national requirements would cause it to use all 12 of the warhead carriage positions on the missile. By 1984, as the U.S. planners began to consider optimal loadings of the D5 for SIOP purposes, they came to the conclusion that a maximum of eight warheads would likely be sufficient for the United States. With this input, members of the U.S. arms control community, busily constructing what would become the warhead-counting and attribution rules of the Strategic Arms Reduction Treaty (START), proposed configuring the D5 missile so that it could never carry more than eight reentry vehicles. Because I was a member of the U.S. team that had negotiated the D5 sale to the United Kingdom, it became my task to confer with British counterparts to determine whether this would cause London concern; the answer was yes, that eight positions were insufficient and would not meet UK national requirements.

The requirements themselves were not explained (neither did the U.S. government comprehend them), nor in the practical terms of the issue at hand did they need to be: the United Kingdom had contracted to buy a missile in a certain configuration, and the United States was obliged to make the missile available in the configuration that had been agreed upon. Ultimately, this assertion of the British position, and the fact that the United Kingdom was not to be limited by START, was sufficient to prompt the arms control community to count the U.S. D5 as carrying only eight warheads despite the fact that it could in fact carry twelve. More fundamentally, however, the blinding reality that we were basically ignorant of how the British government thought about nuclear deterrence (and that Britons were similarly ignorant of our approach) was unsettling. To be effective, a deterrent needed to rest on our best understanding of what the Soviet leadership valued and our ability to make clear to that leadership that we would hold those valued assets "at risk." A series of questions arose; some were:

- How did London assess the Soviet leadership's value structure?

- Was this different from our own assessment? If so, how and why?

- Given debates that were occurring within the Defense Department at that time about our own methods of calculating damage, how did the United Kingdom measure the effectiveness of its strike plans?

The time had clearly arrived for proposing a discreet dialogue. The first step was to obtain approval for this from the U.S. side. Given the strength of the case on its merits and the strong relationship between the Reagan and Thatcher administrations, I was able to obtain support from Secretary of Defense Caspar Weinberger easily. Tapping into the British system proved a more difficult task. After a series of false starts with London, I discovered that the key actually lay much closer to home. Under the PSA, the Royal Navy seconded a captain to the U.S. Navy's Strategic Systems Project office in Crystal City, Virginia. The incumbent captain (later Rear Admiral) Richard Irwin was an individual with whom I had dealt as the United States and United Kingdom negotiated the details of storing spare Trident IIs earmarked for the United Kingdom at the U.S. Naval Base at Kings Bay, Georgia.

On one occasion in early 1986 I expressed to Captain Irwin the U.S. interest in opening a dialogue on nuclear deterrence and my inability to find the right individual in London. Irwin was struck by the idea and reported it to the Ministry of Defence's assistant chief of defence staff for policy and nuclear, Rear Admiral (later Admiral) Jock Slater.[2] Slater and I explored the initiative shortly thereafter during a visit to the Pentagon. After consultations with his chain of command, he sent word through Captain Irwin that the United Kingdom, without making further commitment, would be prepared to entertain a "home and home" series of two meetings to test the value of the proposition. All topics, to include the premises underlying the national plan and the SIOP and the gross morphology of those plans themselves, were on the table.

The first "nuclear staff talks" occurred in the fall of 1986. The U.S. team consisted of myself, a member of my staff, and an officer from the Joint Staff; the British team, equally small, was headed by an individual who was essentially my UK counterpart, Air Commodore (later Air Vice Marshal) Peter Harding. The initial meetings confirmed that there was much to discuss.[3] The talks initially were restricted to discussions of strategic deterrence and strategic weapons systems; by the late 1980s their ambit increased to cover questions related to nuclear deterrent systems of all ranges and to the deterrence of rogue states seeking or armed with nuclear weapons. Later, in the 1990s, the agenda expanded again to include missile defenses and their impact on deterrence. Similarly, the composition of the teams expanded as representatives of U.S. Strategic Command, the Department of Energy's National Nuclear Security Administration, and the U.S. Navy's Strategic Systems Project office were added to the U.S. team and appropriate British counterparts joined the UK team.

The great value of the talks can be broken down into two areas: direct and indirect.

First, the talks fulfilled their initial obligation: they provided a forum for an exchange of views on a bilateral basis on a wide range of subjects related to nuclear deterrence.

As it turned out, the U.S. and British views of the Soviet leadership's value systems were indeed different; the UK side's understanding of what was important to the Soviet leadership proceeded from assumptions different from our own. In this regard, however, neither team sought to convince the other it was correct; instead, the value lay in enriching the tapestry of shared knowledge that the sides had created. Each team, however, took away points to consider, and frequent exchanges of views occurred in writing between the plenaries held every six months. Some of these found their way into changes in operational planning.

The United Kingdom had a much deeper technical understanding of the effects of fire damage that occur subsequent to nuclear detonations; the United States had traditionally focused narrowly only on blast damage. The technical discussions proved useful to clarifying for the U.S. side the use of a broader set of metrics.

The UK side also had considerable experience in using penetration aids because of the United Kingdom's deployment of the Chevaline system[4] on the UK Polaris missile. The insights the United Kingdom provided in this area were of significant interest to U.S. officials involved in research on ballistic missile defenses. Indeed, the United Kingdom offered in the talks to present a highly classified video of the deployment of the Chevaline penetration aid in space to the U.S. team, an offer that was not only accepted but that led to the video being shown to Secretary Weinberger in a meeting with his British counterpart.

For its part, the U.S. side was able to provide extensive background and information on the complexities associated with targeting a system of multiple independently targetable reentry vehicles (MIRVs): the Polaris A3TK/Chevaline that the United Kingdom deployed was a relatively simple system that carried a small number of warheads, none of which was independently targeted. As discussed above, the United Kingdom was transitioning to a highly MIRVed Trident II/D5, which carried up to 12 independently targeted warheads. The techniques for employing this much more sophisticated weapons system were significantly more complicated than those used with Polaris, and the "deconfliction" problem of ensuring that the reentry vehicles deployed in a manner that would not result in "fratricide" was not a trivial problem. U.S. team members were able to provide their British counterparts with the insights and techniques the United States had developed in its more than two decades worth of experience in operating highly MIRVed SLBMs.

The United States briefed the UK team contemporaneously about the lessons it was learning from the major overhaul of the nuclear planning process and the SIOP carried out by the Department of Defense in 1989–1991 and how these altered the view of U.S. authorities with respect to implementing deterrence policy.

Second, the talks established an enduring web of relationships among key nuclear policy officials (and their successors) on both sides, which has proved to be of immense value. As the initial participants became more senior and were promoted to positions of greater responsibility, the relationships previously created became a direct channel to senior players on both sides of the Atlantic who could address or solve nuclear-deterrent and related issues (and indeed sometimes unrelated issues) as they arose.[5]

Prominent among these issues were the manner in which the UK independent deterrent was to be dealt with in START (wherein the United States used mutually agreed language to make clear that U.S. support to the United Kingdom's maintenance of a strategic deterrent was a relationship that existed before the treaty, was not limited to the sale of any specific weapons system, was not constrained by the treaty in any way, and neither was the independent deterrent covered by the treaty).

A second important topic that was addressed through these channels was U.S.-UK coordination on potential substantial changes in

NATO's theater nuclear force posture, which was later proposed by NATO's High Level Group (HLG) and subsequently approved by the alliance's defense ministers at Taromina, Sicily, in the fall of 1991. Later—throughout the 1990s—these relationships were critical to ensuring U.S.-UK coordination on a wide variety of issues dealing with NATO nuclear policy that were being considered by the HLG and by ministers. A complete accounting of other major topics discussed and resolved successfully through the relationships created by the nuclear talks is not possible in this chapter, but these included the sale of Tomahawk cruise missiles to the United Kingdom, access to Royal Air Force bases for U.S. Air Force heavy bombers, and HF/VHF communications.

An additional indirect outcome of the talks was the establishment of a new channel of cooperation on the operational level. As noted earlier, British officers were assigned to the SHAPE nuclear targeting center in Mons. In the late 1980s, owing largely to a drawdown in staff caused by reductions in allied manning contributions, SHAPE decided to close the targeting center. Discussions in the U.S.-UK nuclear policy channel led to the recommendation by Washington and London to SHAPE that the center be reestablished at the Joint Strategic Target Planning Staff (now part of U.S. STRATCOM) at Omaha, Nebraska, and that British officers be assigned to the center to represent SHAPE. Once accepted by SHAPE and staffed by the United Kingdom, this created yet another leg to the special relationship established by the MDA. Where initially the only cooperation between the United States and the United Kingdom on nuclear matters was through the technical channels in the atomic weapons domain and then, additionally, through the PSA, now there existed both a senior-level policy channel and an operational linkage between target planners.

This strong four-element relationship will prove to be of great significance in the decades ahead. Challenges face the U.S. and British nuclear communities in all of these areas. The modernization of the U.S. and British nuclear weapons stockpiles in an era of no nuclear testing requires consultations among experts who come at the problem from different backgrounds and in different ways; the MDA will see to this. The challenge of building a new generation of ballistic missile submarines featuring many shared components (and, different from the previous Polaris and Trident programs, one in which the United Kingdom will be building its submarines before the U.S. Navy builds the first follow-ons to the Ohio-class boats) will require an extraordinary degree of cooperation and integration. The PSA will allow for this.

The policy communities will necessarily need to be involved in watching over these two technical efforts and will undoubtedly have to intervene from time to time to resolve lower-level disputes that, if allowed to linger, might imperil achieving politically important objectives in a timely manner. The same policy communities will need to consult on the evolution of deterrent concepts and policies in the changing world of the twenty-first century. Finally, as both nations' arsenals shrink, and as the political need for targeting flexibility becomes ever more important, the interaction between the planning communities—of great value today—will become even more important in the future. The foundations of the past 50 years will continue to serve both nations well as they manage the next 50 together.

NOTES

1. In fact, although a portion of U.S. strategic and theater-tactical nuclear forces was assigned to NATO (while the majority of those forces, particularly the strategic forces, was reserved for the unilateral U.S. deterrent or single integrated operational plan [SIOP]) in accordance with the December 1962 Nassau Agreement between President John F. Kennedy and Prime Minister Harold Macmillan, the principal justification for the UK strategic deterrent was to support NATO. As the Nassau joint statement put it: "The Prime Minister made it clear that except where H.M.G. may decide that supreme national interests are at stake, these British forces will be used for the purposes of international defense of the Western alliance in all circumstances."

2. Slater was an extraordinary officer who later rose to become vice chief of the defence staff and then first sea lord.

3. The value of the proposition was then, and remains today, strong. The talks, which rapidly moved to a semiannual meeting alternating between capitals, are now in their 22nd year.

4. In the 1970s the United States sought to partially counter the Soviet antiballistic missile system around Moscow by replacing Polaris with the Poseidon system, capable of carrying ten independently targeted warheads. The British elected not to purchase Poseidon but rather to develop Chevaline, a sophisticated system of penetration aids for their Polaris missile. Chevaline reduced the (not independently targetable) warheads on the British Polaris from three to two.

5. Indeed, the senior policy channel was used from time to time to resolve in the MDA or PSA context some of the more technical issues that had become bottled up in the respective bureaucracies.

15

REFLECTIONS ON THE STRENGTH OF THE 1958 AGREEMENT

KEITH O'NIONS, ROY M. ANDERSON, AND ROBIN PITMAN

From the vantage point of our personal experiences during the past ten years we reflect in this chapter on the strength of the 1958 Mutual Defense Agreement (MDA) and its success in enabling UK-U.S. collaboration on the nuclear deterrent; on the performance, safety, and security of nuclear weapons; and, more generally, on the safety and security of radiological materials.[1] Against a background of a changing international environment, we explore more fully the extraordinary scientific and technical challenges that have been addressed during the past decade, often with very great urgency, by the UK and U.S. communities. A confident and trusting relationship established between these communities through years of collaboration under the umbrella of the 1958 agreement has certainly paid dividends.

OVERVIEW

In 1958, when the MDA was signed, only the United States, the Soviet Union, and the United Kingdom had a nuclear weapons capability, and collaboration at that time was driven by an urgency imposed by the Cold War. Shortly after the agreement was signed these states entered into a moratorium on atmospheric testing of weapons; this became formalized in the Partial Test Ban Treaty of 1963. During the following decades of geopolitical change, concepts and policies of deterrence were developed and introduced. Furthermore, France and China also

---

became nuclear weapon states, options for nuclear warhead delivery systems multiplied, and at the same time several other nations began nuclear weapons programs.

By 1996 when the Comprehensive Nuclear Test-Ban Treaty (CTBT) opened for signature, the five nuclear weapon states faced the new challenge of sustaining stockpiles of nuclear warheads without underground testing: the era of science-based stockpile stewardship had commenced. This new regime of stockpile stewardship, introduced after the moratorium on underground testing in 1992, has been truly transformational with a new and much greater level of reliance on science-based methods. Fortunately, throughout the 1970s and 1980s the United Kingdom had already made a strong commitment to science-based methodologies for the design and certification of warheads, with its validation depending on both laboratory experiments and underground tests. This approach provided a sound foundation on which the new science-based stewardship regime could be built and the justification for the necessary major investments in technical facilities. In turn the new challenges presented by the CTBT served to reinvigorate collaboration under the 1958 agreement.

The welcome end to the Cold War brought about new uncertainties and dangers. The potential availability of nuclear warheads, nuclear materials, and nuclear expertise from the former Soviet Union gave rise to new concerns regarding proliferation and the possibilities for nuclear terrorism. The events of September 11, 2001, and the possibility of terrorists producing dirty bombs or improvised nuclear devices focused minds further on nuclear materials security around the world. These new challenges have called yet again on the 1958 agreement and the depth and agility of U.S.-UK collaboration permitted under it. Nowhere has this been more important than for the safety and security of nuclear and radiological materials and their denial to terrorists.

Global events are now forcing simultaneous debates on the desirability of civil nuclear power—as a future source of non-carbon-based energy—and on the future of nuclear weapons themselves. At the same time, although pressure mounts on the existing five nuclear weapon states recognized by the Nuclear Non-Proliferation Treaty (NPT) to reduce warhead stockpiles and progress on the signature and ratification of the CTBT, the prospect of additional states acquiring nuclear weapons in the coming decade is very real. Looking further into the future, we can see that international attention is focusing on the possibility of a world without nuclear weapons, a vision fully endorsed recently by the British government.[2] Just how and when this might be achieved remains highly uncertain, but major technical and political challenges will have to be overcome if such a state is to be achieved.

END OF UNDERGROUND TESTS:
THE SCIENCE-BASED PROGRAM

The MDA brought to an end the completely separate existence of the U.S. and UK nuclear weapon programs and rekindled a collaboration that had its origins in the Manhattan Project. Crucially for the United Kingdom, it provided immediate access to the Nevada Test Site and U.S. experience: a total of 19 underground test firings of UK warheads were carried out in Nevada up to the moratorium in 1992. For both partners it triggered enduring scientific collaborations in a diverse range of fields, as relevant today as they were in 1958. Because the United Kingdom carried out a constrained and relatively small number of underground tests, these tests tended to be highly instrumented and supported by extensive above-ground laboratory experiments. Icecap, the planned firing of a UK warhead, was probably the most highly instrumented of the underground tests. In the end the announcement of a test moratorium in 1992 intervened, and this joint UK-U.S. test firing was canceled. During that period the United Kingdom had progressively developed an integrated approach to warhead design and certification whereby science-based design models of the warhead were calibrated and validated using the results from underground nuclear tests and laboratory experiments.

By the end of the 1970s a strong laboratory-based component to the design and validation of UK warheads was firmly established and had become an essential adjunct to the limited program of UK underground tests. This included hydrodynamics experiments, the use of lasers for high-energy-density physics experiments, and computational modeling following the advent of sufficiently fast computers and codes.

The warhead for the WE177 (a free-fall bomb that existed in a number of variants), the Chevaline submarine-launched ballistic missile (SLBM), and the UK Trident warhead that is deployed in the present-day Trident strategic deterrent were all developed under this regime with collaboration with U.S. scientists and engineers and access to U.S. facilities. It is an essential feature of the certification of these warheads—hence, the credibility of the present deterrent—that the assurance of their safety and performance is firmly referenced to underground nuclear tests carried out at the Nevada Test Site.

Since the UK signature and ratification of the CTBT in 1996 and 1998, respectively, the certification of safety and performance of the Trident deterrent has been provided through a warhead science program[3] analogous in its aims to that of the U.S. science-based stockpile stewardship (SBSS) program.[4] The aim of both of these was to offset the potential increase in risk and uncertainty that would inevitably accrue with the passage of time after the end of underground testing.

The SBSS includes the provision of major new facilities such as the National Ignition Facility (NIF), a 600 terawatt (10^{12} watt) laser currently in the final stages of commissioning at the Lawrence Livermore National Laboratory, and the Dual Axis Hydrodynamic Radiographic Test (DAHRT) facility at the Los Alamos National Laboratory. A major investment has been made during the past decade in the Advanced Simulation and Computing program to drive the development of advanced computing capabilities and to exploit the orders of magnitude increases in computing power that have become available as a result. This program expects to have petaflop capability (10^{15} floating point operations per second) available by 2009.

In each of these areas there has been a continuing and effective collaboration between the United States and United Kingdom. Given the very different scales of the U.S. and UK programs, however, the United Kingdom has sought wherever possible to develop capabilities that are complementary to those of the U.S. program. For example, the United Kingdom has always placed great emphasis on hydrodynamic experiments. These allow the deformation of a warhead primary constructed of simulant materials to be studied in response to explosively driven shocks up to the point where a real weapon would become nuclear critical. A number of facilities at the Atomic Weapons Establishment (AWE), Aldermaston, are suitable for such firings, and during recent years joint hydrodynamic experiments with similar aims have been carried out in collaboration with the U.S. weapon laboratories at the Ula underground facility in Nevada. These are termed "subcritical" experiments as they are configured so that they cannot possibly reach nuclear criticality. The most recent of these was the Krakatau experiment fired in February 2006 that provided data of direct benefit to both the U.S. and UK warhead certification efforts.

For the calculation of the nuclear phase of a warhead's operation, knowledge of the behavior of warhead materials up to the extreme temperatures and pressures accompanying the nuclear processes of fission and fusion is essential. Such conditions are difficult to create experimentally in the laboratory, but lasers can be used to create plasmas that reach relevant temperatures and pressures. Since the mid-1970s the United Kingdom and United States have had complementary experimental programs to reach these conditions and to develop techniques and measurement tools to investigate the behavior of relevant materials under these conditions. Results from these laser physics experiments have been used to obtain equation of state and opacity data important for the validation of nuclear weapon design codes. The techniques will be of increased value when the NIF is fully operational in 2010 as much higher temperatures and pressures will become accessible and experiments with thermonuclear fusion will be possible.

The Orion laser currently under construction at AWE is an excellent illustration of the complementary nature of the UK and U.S. programs. Orion, which is expected to commence operations in 2010, is a smaller and lower-cost facility than the NIF. It uses two pulses, rather than the one distinct pulse that will initially be available on the NIF. One of these comprises ten beams with a total power of 10 terawatts (10^{12} watt) combined into a relatively long 1 nanosecond (10^{-9} sec) pulse, which is used to compress the target material. The second, much shorter pulse has about 1,000 times the power of the first and is used to raise the compressed material to very high temperatures. NIF and Orion will be able to access different parts of the temperature and pressure space relevant to the operation of nuclear warheads and, like the earlier generation UK and U.S. laser physics collaboration, will allow experiments designed for one laser to be investigated further on a second laser. The benefits to the United Kingdom and United States of this dual capability and approach are likely to be substantial.

As indicated above, in the CTBT era, continued assurance of nuclear warhead safety and performance will rely more and more on high-fidelity computer-based modeling and simulation. It will be necessary, for example, to develop much-improved models and algorithms for the physics of turbulent mixing, particle transport, and material properties. Furthermore, accurate simulation of warheads will require greater three-dimensional engineering detail in the models than is currently achieved; in turn this will drive the requirement for further increase in computational power. It will be essential for these models to remain firmly referenced to previous underground test data, however, and be further validated through increasingly sophisticated laboratory experiments that will include hydrodynamics, high-energy-density physics, and subcritical tests of simulated warhead components.

Development and verification of the methodologies that now underwrite the assessments of safety and performance of nuclear warheads in the CTBT era has been a major area for cooperation under the 1958 agreement. Each nation maintains its own independent nuclear weapon design capability and its own methodology to underwrite the safety and performance of its warhead designs. It is this that has enabled reciprocal U.S.-UK peer review of the results of the science-based approach. This in turn has created an element of challenge to the computational models and their predictions for both collaborators.

IMPERATIVES AFTER SEPTEMBER 11, 2001

The most recent phase of collaboration under the MDA was both unexpected and urgent: it followed immediately from the events of September 11, 2001. By 2001 the number of nuclear weapons–capable nations had risen to eight, and other countries had declared programs or were suspected of having them. Some of the activities of the A. Q. Khan network were understood, but their full extent was unknown. In addition, there were considerable concerns about the security of nuclear materials around the world, particularly following the breakup of the Soviet Union.

The combination of these factors brought into focus the potential for terrorist groups to acquire nuclear materials and develop dirty bombs or improvised nuclear devices. This presented the United States and the United Kingdom and their nuclear weapon communities with an urgent need to be able to identify and track nuclear materials around the world and understand the potential for their use in improvised nuclear devices. How to detect and defeat such materials became a new focus of urgent effort under the 1958 agreement.

Little can be said of these activities, but collaborative programs have been put in place to enable the detection and tracking of nuclear materials, the analysis of such materials, and the defeat of an improvised nuclear device, be it a nuclear warhead in the real sense or a radiological dispersion device. Such work is done in very close cooperation with, and with the support of, agencies in both the United Kingdom and the

United States. The MDA has enabled the nuclear weapon communities to support these undertakings from the development of highly capable sensors for future deployment to the provision of active support to operations against terrorist activities.

Collaborative work is under way to develop further joint capabilities to analyze intercepted material with the ultimate objective of being able—with the close cooperation of intelligence and law enforcement organizations—to identify the source of materials, be they from isolated interceptions, from a captured improvised device, or from the results of a nuclear or radiological dispersal detonation.

The difficulty of such operations was brought into sharp relief in November 2006 with the poisoning of Alexander Litvinenko with polonium-210. A major operation was conducted by the UK authorities with extensive support from AWE in the detection and analysis of the polonium. U.S. colleagues under the provisions of the 1958 agreement supported AWE in these endeavors. Lessons learned from this exercise will be important to the future establishment of robust analytical, forensic, and operational procedures.

TOWARD A WORLD WITHOUT NUCLEAR WEAPONS

In December 2006 Prime Minister Tony Blair introduced in Parliament a white paper entitled "The Future of the United Kingdom's Nuclear Deterrent,"[5] setting out the decision to maintain the deterrent system beyond the life of the current Vanguard submarines with a new generation of ballistic missile–carrying submarines and to extend the life of the Trident D5 missiles. The white paper also explained that a number of further decisions will need to be taken over the coming years, principally in respect to the warhead and delivery system.

The existing nuclear warhead design is likely to last into the 2020s although we do not yet have sufficient information to judge precisely how long we can retain it in service. Decisions on whether and how we may need to refurbish or replace this warhead are likely to be necessary in the next Parliament. The UK government's decision to maintain a nuclear deterrent capability, which was endorsed by the House of Commons on March 14, 2007, was made in the context of a policy to work toward a world without nuclear weapons, while recognizing the relevance of nuclear weapons to UK deterrence for the foreseeable future. The white paper was supported by an exchange of letters between the prime minister and the president of the United States,[6] in which assurances were exchanged regarding future cooperation between the two states in the areas of submarines, nuclear propulsion, missiles, and nuclear warheads, thus setting the groundwork for continuing strong collaboration under the existing agreement in the future.

The notion of moving toward a world without nuclear weapons, as called for by the new prime minister, Gordon Brown, presents a series of enormous challenges—some of which would require close involvement and collaboration of the world's nuclear weapon communities. Of the questions that need to be addressed, some are political, some organizational, and some technical. Is it possible or practical to have a world without nuclear weapons? If it were, how would such a situation be verified? How would any breakout be detected? How would progress toward the end state be monitored and verified? The nuclear weapon laboratories of the United States and United Kingdom would play a key role in any such deliberations and the technical work that would be necessary to support it. This initial work—some of which has been under way for some time—is enabled by the 1958 agreement.

50 YEARS ON AND ENDURING

In the world of international diplomacy, 50 years for the survival of any single agreement is unusual. Successful international collaboration in a sensitive area over such a period of time is exceptional. Given the unpredictable nature of the threats we have faced during the past five decades and those we are likely to face in the coming 50 years, there is a real sense today in both the United States and the United Kingdom that the 1958 MDA is as essential for our future security as it was in 1958.

What has enabled the MDA to endure for such a long period and to remain so highly valued by both partners? Opinions may differ, but from our standpoint the following points would appear relevant.

The original agreement was drawn up in a political era very different from today's, with a very different set of imperatives linked to the single threat posed by the Soviet Union. Yet it has subsequently been sustained through 50 years of considerable global political change. A great strength was the simplicity of drafting, which provided in a straightforward way the framework for a collaborative arrangement unencumbered by detailed political prescriptions that might have expired long since.

The agreement has facilitated collaboration at many levels and in various areas. These include laboratory scientists and engineers, laboratory managers, operators in the U.S. and UK militaries, civil servants, and politicians. It is the active and long-term engagement at all these levels that has built mutual trust and confidence that have become critical components of the relationship between the two countries. At times it has been the exceptional personal relationships developed over the years that have come to the rescue in difficult times and eased us into a new phase. This has been particularly true for the scientists and engineers who have found stimulation and friendship among the very few colleagues with whom they can discuss research in highly classified areas.

The UK dependence on laboratory experimentation (as opposed to frequent underground tests) from the 1970s onward resulted in different techniques and methodologies being used by the United States and the United Kingdom. The complementary approaches, which arose through the independent nature of programs, proved to be an enduring strength of the agreement. The opportunity for exceptionally talented scientists and engineers to test and challenge one another has been invaluable to both sides. In the post-9/11 world this confident intellectual and experimental challenge has paid dividends yet again.

This difference of approach has underpinned the independence of the UK warhead program from that of the much larger U.S. program. The United Kingdom's ability to develop independent theoretical and computational models of its nuclear warheads and validate them through testing and laboratory experimentation has been a crucial element, as has its final ability to engineer and deploy a warhead. This has provided a basis for challenge in methodologies and understanding between the two nations. It has proved to be just as important in terms of the safety of warhead stockpiles as well as the assurance of performance and reliability. Today, in the absence of testing, this aspect of the relationship, namely peer review, has taken on an even greater significance.

FUTURE FOR THE 1958 AGREEMENT

After 50 years it might reasonably be expected that it is time to produce a different sort of agreement between the United States and the United Kingdom to reflect new realities and new challenges.

These challenges are indeed very different from those of 50 years ago. The United Kingdom has committed to the continuing maintenance of its nuclear deterrent. This will require us to continue to assure the safety and performance of our stockpile through a warhead science program without underground testing. The United Kingdom is also committed to working toward a nuclear weapons–free world. At the same time nuclear proliferation and international terrorism remain live issues.

It is not only the formal agreement that is important. It is also the deep trust and confident relationship that has been built up during 50 years and passed from one generation to the next by those engaged in the many different fields involved in developing, maintaining, and ensuring the performance and safety of the components of a nuclear deterrent and the underlying capabilities. We have every confidence that this combination will prove to be robust in the face of the difficult issues that we will inevitably confront in the years ahead.

In our view, in all respects, the 1958 MDA remains fit for purpose in the light of future challenges.

NOTES

1. For the purposes of this article we have concentrated on nuclear warhead matters and have set aside the equally important area of naval nuclear propulsion, which is covered in another chapter in this book.

2. Des Browne, "Laying the Foundations for Multilateral Disarmament" (speech to UN Conference on Disarmament, Geneva, February 5, 2008), http://www.mod.uk/defenceinternet/aboutdefence/people/speeches/sofs/20080205layingthefoundationsformultilateraldisarmament.htm.

3. Keith O'Nions, Robin Pitman, and Clive Marsh, "Science of Nuclear Warheads," *Nature* 415 (2002): pp. 853-857.

4. Raymond Jeanloz, "Science-Based Stockpile Stewardship," *Physics Today* 53, no. 12 (December 2000): pp. 44–50, http://www.physicstoday.org/vol-56/iss-5/pdf/vol53no12p44-50.pdf.

5. Secretary of State for Defence and Secretary of State for Foreign and Commonwealth Affairs, "The Future of the United Kingdom's Nuclear Deterrent" (London: Her Majesty's Stationery Office, December 2006), http://www.mod.uk/NR/rdonlyres/AC00DD79-76D6-4FE3-91A1-6A56B03C092F/0/DefenceWhitePaper2006_Cm6994.pdf.

6. George W. Bush (letter to Prime Minister Tony Blair, December 7, 2006), http://www.pm.gov.uk/files/pdf/letter_Blair.pdf; and Tony Blair (letter to President George W. Bush, December 7, 2006), http://www.pm.gov.uk/files/pdf/letter_Bush.pdf.

16

THE MDA: A PRACTITIONER'S VIEW

TIM HARE

It is right that 50 years of cooperation on nuclear matters between the United Kingdom and the United States is given quiet recognition. The U.S.-UK nuclear relationship—enshrined in two formal agreements, the Mutual Defense Agreement (MDA) of 1958 and the related Polaris Sales Agreement (PSA) signed in 1963—has underpinned the United Kingdom's ability to deploy a nuclear deterrent capability during the latter half of the twentieth century. Opposing views regarding this symbol of military and political power will continue to fuel a national debate; however, what cannot be denied is that the United Kingdom's membership of the nuclear club in the post–World War II era has defined much of our foreign and security policy and has reflected Britain's perception of its role in the world.

I shall address the history and practice of these two key agreements from the perspective of an operator on the ground. For it is here that I have some experience to offer, first flirting with the agreements in the 1970s as a young military officer engaged in the support of the United Kingdom's Polaris capability, later as an executive in the Trident acquisition project and modest policy positions within the UK Ministry of Defence (MOD). I should also emphasize that these are my personal views based on my experience up to 2002 and should not be read as a formal MOD or UK government position either then or now.

THE TWO AGREEMENTS

The MDA and the PSA are complementary. Put simply, the MDA opens and controls a number of channels for information exchanges and for technical and scientific engagement, including transfer of materials, on nuclear reactor and weapon technologies. The agreement also requires that the United States and United Kingdom do not share any bilateral discussion data or joint information on nuclear matters with a third party unless both sides agree to such sharing. This codicil was reflective of the initial nervousness in the United States, after a number of spy scandals, that sensitive nuclear information might leak to parties not in sympathy with U.S. foreign policy or nuclear objectives. The PSA (now modified for Trident) allows the United Kingdom to acquire, support, and operate the U.S. Trident strategic weapon system that embraces the launcher, fire control, and navigation subsystems housed in the four Vanguard-class strategic nuclear submarines (SSBNs), together with the missiles themselves "pooled" with the United States. The PSA also allows for support, training, and operational testing of the system utilizing U.S. facilities. To understand their working-level operation it is necessary first to comprehend both the nature and context of the relationship.

U.S.-UK BUSINESS RELATIONSHIP

At its heart, the U.S.-UK nuclear relationship is political and geo-strategic and built on trust. Although there is much sentimental talk about the "special relationship" and the United Kingdom being a "bridge between the United States and Europe," neither of these fully reflects the truth. Indeed, even the wiser talk of "common values" is fragile when put under scrutiny except at the very highest level, where there is indeed a common belief in the fundamentals of free-dom, justice, and democracy. Beneath this veneer however, differ-ences are apparent in constitution, culture, religion, behavior, and (yes!) language.

What is a truth is that the United Kingdom has long been (and re-mains) a very strong political and military ally of the United States in world affairs. The corresponding key to the nuclear relationship is the core belief that it is reflective of that status and that there is mu-tual political advantage in sustaining a UK nuclear capability alongside that of the mightier United States. For the United Kingdom there is the additional core advantage of the ability to deploy an operationally independent nuclear deterrent at an affordable price, which underpins the nation's wish to remain an active participant in international affairs and a member of the first order of world powers. For the United States the arrangement underscores the United Kingdom as a dependent global ally and allows for an alternative nuclear decisionmaking center to complement its own. A further advantage is in securing a close ally in the wider arena of such international institutions as NATO and the Nuclear Non-Proliferation Treaty (NPT) and thus being able to project a joint approach to nuclear issues and have better sway with the international community.

Although the United Kingdom continues to seek close cooperation with the United States on nuclear issues, there is clear direction that this must be constrained to ensure retention of the United Kingdom's "operational independence" as a nuclear weapon state. The relationship acknowledges that in areas of technology exchange, acquisition, and long-term support, there will be some clear dependence on the United States. Such key issues as operational control, warhead design and manufacture, and safety must, however, remain sovereign to the United Kingdom to preserve its independent status. Although the antinuclear movement in the United Kingdom remains a minority view, this could change dramatically if independence were truly compromised (or seen to be compromised) or if the capability crossed a threshold that made it unaffordable.

If this describes the broad nature of the relationship, what of the context? For the UK official, military officer, or diplomat new to the business, the key is to understand the U.S. government machine and how it works. First to note is that the U.S. bureaucracy is large, complex, and tricky to manage. Second is that the U.S.-UK nuclear relationship is tied up with the much wider military relationship. Third, that, although the United Kingdom is trusted and respected, the United States is very much the senior partner.

The methodology by which the nuclear relationship works consists of a number of separate channels embracing policy, technology, acquisition, support, and intelligence. The status of these information channels is reflective of the wider health of the relationship. If the relationship is in a healthy state, then all channels are open and information flows freely. However, should the relationship sour in any area, then a channel might close or be constrained. What is sometimes difficult for the UK official is that the constrained channel is sometimes evident in an area totally divorced from the center of any dispute! For example, a worry about reactor technology transfer might manifest itself in the sudden constraining of an operational channel. This is demonstrative of the sophisticated and interwoven (and sometimes plain baffling!) nature of the U.S. machine, and it requires some skill and experience to manage it effectively.

Personalities too play a strong part. At the highest level, the relationship between president and prime minister sets the tone for the other government echelons and the related exchanges. This aligns with close ties between officials and military officers from both sides and at all levels forged over many years as individual career paths have crossed.

For the UK official new to the business, it is this complex nature of the U.S. government machine that can be confusing. For the sake of our current discussion on the nuclear relationship, this may be divided as follows: First are the DOD U.S. civil servants. These are generally wise men and women with huge experience in the U.S. government and industrial machine and expert knowledge of nuclear matters. They have a global approach, are generally easy to engage with, and have much in common with their UK counterparts. More unpredictable are the complementary (often senior) administration appointees, who change with the president and who are often in strong positions to direct the nature of the relationship.

The second grouping comprises the U.S. scientists and engineers—some employed as civil servants, others as contractors—who, unlike their UK counterparts, are often in post for a very long time, thereby generating extraordinary levels of continuity and expertise. The two countries' scientific communities are very close, with a relationship based on mutual respect and a common desire for the pursuit of nuclear science. In managing specific programs, such as the strategic weapon system, the U.S. military (in this case the U.S. Navy) often has primacy; however, these officers are supported by a very strong cadre of civilian engineers made up of career civil servants and contractors. Indeed the chief engineer (normally a senior-level presidential appointee) is a very powerful figure and pivotal in the U.S.-UK decisionmaking process over design and transfer issues. The major participation of U.S. contractors at all levels reflects an industrial base much more closely aligned with the U.S. government machine than in the United Kingdom.

Finally there is the U.S. Navy: although there is a very strong operational bond between the U.S. Navy and the Royal Navy (nowhere more so than in the domain of submarine operations), it would be wrong to assume that the two navies are the same. In the United States, the U.S. Navy is a major force in the land, well integrated (at the more senior level) into the political and industrial establishment. U.S. Navy officers are by nature very conservative and hierarchical, and they adopt a very serious approach to their work with little margin for the nonestablishment view.

In the United Kingdom, governance of nuclear issues across Whitehall is primarily managed by civil servants—administrators, diplomats, scientists, and engineers—with rather less direct industry representation. Military officers are evident in the MOD chain with Royal Navy officers in particular providing expertise in the operational and technical areas of program management, nuclear reactor technology, system acquisition, and support.

This then is the cast of players that must manage the relationship through very different government machines. How do the two bureaucracies interact to effect the nuclear relationship on the ground? I shall explore three core areas of mutual interest: nuclear policy; nuclear operations; and nuclear technology, which includes nuclear warheads, reactors, and submarine construction.

NUCLEAR POLICY

Fundamental to the U.S.-UK nuclear relationship is trust. This is reflected through broad agreement on policy coupled with a clear understanding of the subtleties implicit in the differing status of our two nations (the United States being the world's superpower, with the United Kingdom a medium-sized European state), the relative scales of nuclear arsenals, and our respective approaches to disarmament. Bilateral policy exchanges are held regularly and at varying levels alongside corresponding work with NATO. Trust in ensuring the security of sometimes highly sensitive information underpins the very open, transparent dialogue at varying levels of detail, which is the mark of these engagements. Policy staff talks embrace a wide range of issues, from addressing core conceptual questions, such as what nuclear weapons are for and what the nature of deterrence is, to working on more specific issues such as threat analysis, targeting strategy, declaratory

policy, capability developments, arms control, approaches to proliferation, and global disarmament.

At the highest level there is clear, broad agreement that in today's
security environment there remains a role for nuclear weapons in
deterring aggression and the prevention of war, particularly while
global proliferation remains active and the wider security environment is so very unstable. Also there is agreement that maintaining
a credible capability must be juxtaposed with a positive but realistic
approach to global disarmament, the NPT, related treaties, and arms
control. In addition, there is unwritten acknowledgement that maintenance of a bilateral policy dialogue is helpful to both nations in
providing a platform for the airing of views while assessing options
for approaches to nuclear-related issues that are so fundamental to
world security.

Immediately below this level, recognition of the huge difference in
scale in terms of overall nuclear capability generates some differences
in policy execution. Whereas the United States maintains a triad of
land-based, air-launched, and sea-launched missiles with an overall
warhead count in thousands, the United Kingdom's minimum capability is vested in a single submarine-launched system with only 160
operationally available warheads. This has immediate implications for
issues such as targeting strategy, declaratory policy, and readiness levels. Take targeting strategy as an example: against the threat of a major
nuclear power, the United Kingdom is constrained by the size of its
capability to essentially a countervalue strategy, whereas the United
States has the flexibility to embrace both counterforce and countervalue approaches. In the tetchy area of so-called tactical or substrategic
weapons, again the United States has enormous flexibility, whereas the
United Kingdom's policy is one of deploying its capability in a deterrence role only, with no margin for tactical use.

Indeed, it is interesting to note that the recent UK white paper has
deleted reference to the much-debated substrategic capability, which
was poorly understood in the United Kingdom although the rationale
for such a role in the deterrent context—that is, the deterrence effect
of a low-yield option against smaller nuclear threats—remains sound.
Furthermore, the United Kingdom does not acknowledge any potential
use for nuclear weapons in a war-fighting role to achieve purely military aims. Finally, with capability vested in only four UK submarines
against fourteen in the U.S. arsenal (and that alongside land-based

and air systems), the United Kingdom's readiness and alert-status constraints are much more acute.

Approaches to arms control and the NPT remain the subject of continuous discussion. The United States, as the major nuclear power, is in
a more difficult position than the United Kingdom, sitting in the forefront of negotiations and often the target of criticism from some NPT
members. Although there has been some margin for both to reduce
their nuclear arsenals since the Cold War, the United States has to lead
and face the other major world nuclear powers head on. Furthermore,
the United States has to manage the complex superpower bilateral relationship with Russia, which has a strong nuclear dimension.

The impetus of arms control activity is, of course, reflective of the
government or administration in power. In the United Kingdom, the
Labour government has a strong disarmament lobby and has to balance
the maintenance of a minimum nuclear capability with an active arms
control agenda focused on the NPT. Indeed the recent UK initiative
for a disarmament verification conference is demonstrative of this.[1] In
the recent past the United Kingdom adopted a range of disarmament
measures, from ratification of the Comprehensive Nuclear Test-Ban
Treaty and detargeting of its missiles to a reduction in warhead numbers and reduced alert status of its nuclear force. In the United States,
the George W. Bush administration has been rather quieter on arms
control, with a focus on other international issues and a changing relationship with Russia. There are signs, however, of a renewed impetus
with such recent disarmament initiatives led by former secretary of
state George P. Shultz and former senator Sam Nunn, with perhaps
more significant change in the future should the Democrats win the
2008 U.S. presidential election.

U.S.-UK nuclear weapons policy has a strong NATO dimension and
is a further subject of bilateral exchange. The United States chairs the
major governing body—the High Level Group (HLG)—which drafts
nuclear policy issues for NATO ministers to endorse. Managing this
group brings with it its own set of political issues—for example, the
absolute agreement among member states on the wording of NATO
nuclear doctrine—and is complicated by the sensitive nature of nuclear weapons in a number of member states and the French dimension (France is not a member of the HLG but of course has a view on
NATO nuclear policy). Providing leadership and forging a joint approach from the two nuclear weapon states committed to NATO is

helpful, and the subset of bilateral exchanges on NATO issues supports this process.

We have only scratched at the wide spectrum of policy issues discussed at these series of exchanges, but their importance cannot be overemphasized. In agreeing core policy principles and acknowledging differences in detail, the tone is set to allow the other exchange channels to be conducted in an atmosphere of cooperation, progress, and understanding.

NUCLEAR OPERATIONS

In the conduct of nuclear operations, again there is a wide-ranging set of exchanges in place, primarily between the two uniformed services, the Royal Navy and U.S. Navy. With common objectives forged through NATO, there has been a long and very close engagement between the two submarine forces. That this operational relationship has penetrated some of the most sensitive areas of national capability and technology development is reflective of the strength of the wider relationship and reaps major advantages of cooperative engagement for both nations. Understanding of such operational issues as targeting methodology, intelligence, antisubmarine warfare tactics, water space management, and other issues core to the effectiveness of a submarine-based deterrent force has had huge benefits. A key example is the extraordinary engineering and procedural disciplines inherent in maintaining an effective nuclear capability that, over the years, has transformed the United Kingdom's approach to engineering management, training methodology, and procedural application in submarines.

NUCLEAR TECHNOLOGY

Although both policy and operational issues are the subjects of regular exchanges, it is the technology area that is the most dynamic. Technology exchanges embrace three main areas: nuclear warheads, nuclear reactors, and submarine construction. Nuclear warhead design engages scientists from both sides of the Atlantic and is managed through a series of joint working groups. Warhead technology is a very special science. Although warhead design has made enormous progress during the past 60 years, much of the science remains theoretical or even unknown. The requirement to design warheads able to deliver the required yield but at the same time be deployed safely on a missile with no nuclear testing allowed by treaty remains an enormous challenge, taxing the intellect and knowledge of the very best the science establishment can muster. The relationship between Atomic Weapons Establishment, Aldermaston, and the corresponding U.S. laboratories (Livermore, Sandia, and Los Alamos) is very close and based on a history of strong personal relationships between both sets of scientists.

The second key technology area underpinning the relationship is the use of nuclear reactor power for submarine propulsion. Here the working relationship is somewhat different. Put simply, Admiral Hyman Rickover of the U.S. Navy, widely acknowledged as the "father" of the nuclear navy, believed that submarine nuclear reactor design and construction were the crown jewels of U.S. technology and should be safeguarded at all costs.

After political agreement with the United Kingdom in the early 1960s, Rickover championed the transfer of a U.S. reactor design and its systems to the United Kingdom, and this was duly fitted in the first UK nuclear submarine, HMS *Dreadnought.* Rickover felt strongly that to be a credible and responsible operator of nuclear reactor plants, the United Kingdom must stand on its own feet, develop a sovereign design and engineering capability, and fund it accordingly. The U.S. program was based on engineering excellence and absolute quality; Rickover considered that a similar approach should be followed by the United Kingdom. Accordingly Rolls-Royce was selected to lead a group of UK engineering companies to establish the industrial base, and it remains today the UK technical authority for all nuclear reactors in UK submarines.

As a consequence of Rickover's views, the information exchange in this channel was intentionally constrained in the early days as a means of encouraging UK independence. Although the design evolution of the two naval nuclear programs has resulted in detailed engineering differences in the reactor plant, both countries continue to use the same basic technology, and improvements in key areas such as reactor core life are similar.

The United Kingdom is the only nation with which the United States conducts any exchange of nuclear propulsion technology, and there exists a robust program that underpins both the in-service reactor plant and future development. This close cooperation on nuclear propulsion is enabled through transfer of officers and regular, open exchanges between engineers from both nations. This enduring relationship is due to a number of reasons: the political importance to the United States in ensuring that the United Kingdom remains in the nuclear submarine business; the need for both sides to share the cost burden of design, development, and production; the opportunity to share sensitive and often highly classified information with like-minded but essentially independent experts; and because both sides have something of genuine interest to share with each other.

One clear example of this is evident in the construction of nuclear submarines, where a healthy exchange between the U.S. primary shipyard (Electric Boat Corporation) and the UK submarine build facility at Barrow in Furness owned by BAE Systems is now in place. During the recent Astute program, U.S. assistance in areas such as computer-aided design has been invaluable, and the exchange of shared experience in the design and build of these hugely complex nuclear submarines has been beneficial to both as affordability becomes the critical factor.

THE FUTURE

Where do we go from here? The recent decision by the United Kingdom to procure new submarine platforms with the aim of continuing with its minimum deterrent capability for the foreseeable future has galvanized both nations into more aggressive exchange activity. For, in program terms, we now find ourselves in new territory, in that the UK program is "ahead" of the United States. The United States has effectively underwritten its Trident system and the Ohio-class SSBNs to the early 2040s, thus decisions on replacements—submarines, missiles systems, and warheads—do not have to be made for some time. The United Kingdom, however, must make some early choices, particularly in its submarine design, to ensure that it can accommodate not only the current Trident system but possibly a next-generation missile also. There is also recognition in the United Kingdom that a new design warhead will probably be required for the 2020s. There will thus be a need for vigorous discussion with the United States to understand current thinking and where any future designs might go.

Coupled with this is the requirement to maintain current capabilities and manage policy development on a variety of issues. These include the evolving role of nuclear weapons in a volatile security environment, the relative approaches to the forthcoming NPT review, and response to new initiatives on arms control (for example, the recent Shultz-Nunn proposals), all in an era of major change in the U.S. government resulting from the November 2008 presidential election.

At the same time, there is a joint concern over the affordability of the nuclear submarine and weapons programs, neither of which comes cheap. The salience of nuclear submarines has reduced since the Cold War, and there is internal pressure from both sides of the Atlantic to reduce the increasing costs associated with nuclear infrastructure and related safety regimes. It is this latter issue that probably necessitates, more than most, the continuing need for open dialogue under the MDA, in particular in the technology areas for nuclear reactors and warheads. Enhanced exchange can only bring benefit to both nations through the pooling of intellectual effort and research, which will contribute to the sustainment of credible, effective, and affordable deterrent capabilities on both sides of the Atlantic.

CONCLUSION

The MDA has served as a powerful vehicle for communication between two close allies in the highly sensitive area of nuclear capability. The relationship is close, respectful, and based on deep trust. Although nuclear weapons continue to reflect the ultimate achievement of military and political power and acquisition of a nuclear capability remains the desire of a number of potential adversaries, the long-term threat of nuclear blackmail sadly remains. It is vital therefore that both countries maintain the ultimate guarantor of our respective nation's security vested in our nuclear capabilities. Although it is fundamental that the United Kingdom retains its operational "independence," the MDA will continue to facilitate the necessary dialogue to ensure the technology base required to design, procure, and support the UK capability. For the United States, technology transfer the "other way" across the Atlantic, some alternative thinking, and joint approaches to nuclear weapon issues with a close ally can only bring benefit in the longer term. This will underpin the common twin objective of maintaining peace through the sustenance of a credible, affordable, nuclear capability while pursuing multilateral and bilateral policies to reduce the global nuclear weapons threat at the same time.

NOTE

1. Des Browne, "Laying the Foundations for Multilateral Disarmament" (speech to UN Conference on Disarmament, Geneva, February 5, 2008), http://www.mod.uk/defenceinternet/aboutdefence/people/speeches/sofs/20080205layingthefoundationsformultilateraldisarmament.htm.

17

NUCLEAR TESTING: A U.S. PERSPECTIVE

TROY E. WADE II

The path that led the United Kingdom to the Nevada Test Site (NTS) in 1962 was a long one. It began in 1952 near Monte Bello Island off the Northwest Coast of Australia. From that beginning, the UK atmospheric nuclear test requirements took UK scientists to Woomera, Australia, to Maralinga, Australia, back to Monte Bello, back again to Maralinga, and then to Malden Island and Christmas Islands in the Pacific Ocean.

The road to the NTS narrowed a bit when the Mutual Defense Agreement (MDA) was signed on July 3, 1958. Although this agreement did not specifically reference the UK underground nuclear testing in Nevada, it did provide broad definitions, resulting in the November 3, 1961, letter from Prime Minister Harold Macmillan to President John F. Kennedy requesting permission for the United Kingdom to conduct underground nuclear tests at the NTS. Prior to this request, the question of the United Kingdom using the NTS was raised by Sir Roger Makins at a meeting with Chairman Glenn T. Seaborg of the Atomic Energy Commission (AEC), William Penney, and various UK personnel. The letter was received one day prior to President Kennedy's announcement that ended U.S. atmospheric testing. The MDA and the letter from Prime Minister Macmillan clearly laid the groundwork for cooperation at the NTS, beginning in 1962 and continuing today, although there has been no nuclear testing at NTS since the testing moratorium of 1992, prior to the Comprehensive Nuclear Test-Ban Treaty (CTBT) of 1996.

On February 8, 1962, Chairman Seaborg of the AEC announced that there would be a nuclear test at the NTS, conducted by the United Kingdom, "within the next few weeks." In his announcement, Seaborg also referenced the 1958 MDA.

Although the two countries had cooperated in nuclear mutual defense activities dating back to the Manhattan Project and had conducted joint nuclear tests at Christmas Island, the decision to test at the NTS came with new and unexpected complications. Seeing the competitive spirit between the Los Alamos (LANL) and Lawrence Livermore (LLNL) national laboratories, the United Kingdom drew an analogy with Ford and General Motors conducting a research and test program at the same location.

The first joint working group (JOWOG) set up to consider UK testing concluded that one or the other of the two U.S. nuclear weapons laboratories would take the lead for assuring that UK test objectives were met. Test safety and containment requirements remained under U.S. federal oversight. From there it was determined that, while the United Kingdom would provide the test device and diagnostic hardware specific to that device, everything else would be of U.S. design. This included the canister and the data cables leading from the UK diagnostics to the U.S. trailers outfitted with the U.S. recording equipment. As one can imagine, there were interface issues.

Other experiment differences came to the surface as well. The United Kingdom had to learn to adapt to the different schedule for dry runs of necessary signals employed by the two U.S. laboratories. In addition, there were different philosophies related to the number of and requirements for tests of the electrical and mechanical systems prior to the conduct of the experiment. These tests were known as dry runs, and the specific differences between U.S. laboratory procedures required complicated differences in the UK design.

The biggest and most interesting difference between the two laboratories that was facing the British scientists dealt with how a canister, containing the test device, was lowered to the bottom of the hole. LANL chose to use wire rope harnesses as the method of suspending and lowering the tremendous weight of the test package. This meant that an enormous crane was used for the lowering, or emplacement. The LLNL chose to use a crane, but used a drill pipe for the emplacement.

Another major difference was the design of the canister used for the test. LANL used a single canister that contained both the test device and the diagnostics. LLNL used two canisters, one for the test device and one for the diagnostics. This difference significantly affected the hardware provided by Atomic Weapons Research Establishment (AWRE). Both methods resulted in different engineering requirements for AWRE test personnel. In the very early stages of the test program, LANL was the sponsoring partner, so the real eccentricities and differences in individual methods did not present a problem until 1974.

The United States resumed nuclear testing in 1961 after the 1958 moratorium. It used that year to improve the U.S. nuclear deterrent and to develop the skills needed to conduct and record nuclear underground tests in measurements of nanoseconds or less. These time measurements were necessary to assess the success or failure of that test. With E. R. Drake Seager as the designated trial superintendent for the UK AWRE and Bob Campbell the test director for LANL, the first UK test, code-named Pampas, was conducted on March 1, 1962, at NTS. That test was followed by Tendrac on December 7, 1962. These first two tests of the WE177 warhead design were in vertical holes drilled in the desert. They presented the AWRE test personnel with the enormous engineering challenge of matching their test needs with the uncertainties of a new testing technique. Those two tests helped the AWRE begin the sophistication of their nuclear stockpile.

The next four tests conducted jointly by the AWRE and LANL at the NTS were conducted to better understand the safety requirements associated with the handling, storage, and transportation of nuclear weapons containing plutonium. In a letter written to Dr. Glenn Seaborg, Dr. Gerald Johnson, assistant to the secretary of defense for atomic energy, referred to discussions with AWRE and Sir Solly Zuckerman about safety that required resolution. The tests (Double Tracks, May 15, 1963; Clean Slate 1, May 25, 1963; Clean Slate 2, May 31, 1963; and Clean Slate 3, June 9, 1963) resulted in an agreement to resolve the differences by conducting experiments that would deliberately disperse the plutonium in the weapons into the environment. The four safety tests demonstrated that the AWRE safety calculations were correct, and the United States undertook the necessary actions to place U.S. safety concerns in concert with those of the AWRE.

On August 5, 1963, the Limited Test Ban Treaty, banning nuclear testing in space, in the atmosphere, and underwater, was signed in Moscow by Secretary of State Dean Rusk, Foreign Minister Sir Alec Douglas-Home, and Foreign Minister Andrei Gromyko.

The next three tests conducted by the AWRE at the NTS (Cormorant, July 17, 1964; Courser, September 25, 1964; and Charcoal, September 10, 1965) were part of the AWRE program to adapt the WE177 warhead design to the Polaris submarine-fired missile. This was in accordance with an agreement that the United States would sell the UK Polaris missiles. These three tests were conducted by AWRE working with LANL in vertical holes.

The Charcoal test produced the largest yield of any AWRE test fired until then, in the range of 20–200 kilotons. During these 1964 and 1965 tests, the AWRE teams and the LANL teams worked out many of the difficult interface problems that had plagued them. The LANL team was headed by an individual known as the test director, and the AWRE team was headed by a scientist designated the trial superintendent.

In the testing jargon of the United States, the test director was the designated laboratory individual who had the responsibility for preparing for and conducting the proposed nuclear test safely and securely and for assuring that all test objectives were accomplished. The UK trial superintendent had precisely the same responsibilities for AWRE but had to look to the U.S. test director for the final decision. Rarely did an impasse present itself, but on those rare occasions a compromise was reached. Both the test director and the trial superintendent were jointly responsible for compliance with the provisions of the MDA. At the time of the test, a U.S. federal official, designated the test manager or test controller, had the overall responsibility for the safe and secure conduct of the test and for compliance with federal regulations and presidential approvals regarding the test.

As the experiences of working together developed, almost every principal experimenter on the U.S. side had an AWRE counterpart. Details were resolved so that AWRE test device parts and hardware, including the nuclear material, were flown from the United Kingdom by Royal Air Force airplanes, which landed at Nellis Air Force Base in Las Vegas, Nevada, or, on rare occasions, at Indian Springs Air Force Auxiliary Field closer to the NTS. By this time, the AWRE teams, which had grown to several tens of people, had also established themselves as proper residents of Mercury, Nevada, the company town at the entrance to the NTS, but much more importantly at the NTS Steak House, the center of all social activities at the NTS.

UK policy was designed to protect AWRE presence at NTS by keeping the presence of AWRE personnel at the NTS secret. Thus, while conducting the first AWRE tests in 1962 and 1963, AWRE personnel were badged as LANL employees, but the NTS radio transmissions and the British accents heard at the mess halls at the NTS did not hide the AWRE presence very well. Nonetheless, both organizations endeavored to protect AWRE presence at NTS until after the completion of each test, a practice that continued until the last AWRE test in 1991. AWRE faces became well known to most of the NTS support personnel, from cooks, to teamsters, to ironworkers, to electricians. It was a great example of international cooperation toward a common national defense goal.

An LANL employee recalled that a few of the first AWRE personnel to come to NTS in this first test series had flown from United Kingdom to Nellis and then were transported directly though Las Vegas, Nevada, to the NTS. The next day they saw the herd of cattle that the AEC was raising on the NTS and concluded that the combination of the sights of Las Vegas and the cows on the test range were quite different from the Wild West they had seen in the movies and the pictures of the NTS that they had conjured up in their minds. Over time, the AWRE personnel came to know the NTS almost as well as they knew AWRE, and they were considered by all as equal players at the NTS.

During this time, AWRE and the U.S. counterparts also managed to establish the necessary approval system for conducting nuclear tests. The director of AWRE would make a request to the chairman of the AEC, who would then make a recommendation to the president through the secretary of state and the secretary of defense. The policy up until the end of the test program in 1992 required that each test had to be approved by the National Security Council and the president of the United States.

From 1965 until 1974 no underground nuclear tests were conducted by the United Kingdom at the NTS. This was a decision taken by the UK government based on the Science and Technology Act passed in 1965 that permitted the United Kingdom Atomic Energy Authority to undertake "scientific research in such matters not connected with atomic energy." The focus of AWRE shifted from weapons research to those avenues of research that could be applied to other programs and problems such as supporting the Concorde aircraft development program and supporting UK medical and biomedical research. This policy continued in effect until concerns about the warhead on the AWRE Polaris system required additional testing.

The UK underground nuclear test program resumed on July 17, 1974, with a test code-named Fallon, the first in the series of tests of the Chevaline warhead design. Fallon was conducted with LLNL as the lead U.S. laboratory, the first time that the AWRE and LLNL teams worked together on a test. It also meant that the AWRE team had to deal with many techniques that were different from what they became used to as they worked with LANL.

By the time of this series of three tests, the U.S. laboratories and AWRE test teams were working well together. Don Collyer was the trial superintendent for most of the AWRE tests, alternating with Harry Powell. Ken Johnston was the AWRE engineer with principal responsibility for the Chevaline tests. U.S. test directors included Joe Behne (LLNL) and Walt Wolff and Ron Cosimi (LANL). All these tests were conducted in vertical holes, and the AWRE team participated in the design and development of the containment system for the tests. Each underground test had to be designed and built in a way that assured that no radioactive gases or debris would escape from the test hole, an activity called containment in which there was almost as much prayer as there was science. The AWRE participants helped in the understanding of pressures and temperatures that were generated by the test and in so doing became experts themselves in containment.

In 1976, both the U.S. laboratories and the AWRE were affected by the adaptation of the limits prescribed in the Threshold Test Ban Treaty (TTBT) that limited yields of weapons to be tested to 150 kilotons. This treaty was drafted in 1976; was signed by the United States, the United Kingdom, and the Soviet Union in 1978; and entered into force on December 11, 1990. Both the United States and the Soviet Union had announced in 1976 their intent to abide by the provisions of the TTBT until the companion treaty, the Peaceful Nuclear Explosions (PNE), was successfully negotiated, allowing both the TTBT and the PNE to enter into force at the same time.

The yield limitation of 150 kilotons specified by the TTBT required redesign of test requirements by both the U.S. design labs and the AWRE. The implementation procedures associated with TTBT requirements also added an "independent" review of the design laboratories' yield calculations, complicating the AWRE program for proceeding toward an underground test.

The AWRE team continued its underground nuclear tests at the NTS throughout the remainder of the 1970s. Banon (August 26, 1976),

Fondutta (April 11, 1978), Quargel (November 18, 1978), Nessel (August 29, 1979), and Colwick (April 26, 1980) were conducted in partnership with LLNL, which was the designer of the warhead for the Poseidon missile.

Dutchess, an underground nuclear test conducted on October 24, 1980, with a yield of less than 20 kilotons, was part of the AWRE series designed to upgrade the UK submarine warhead to the equivalent of the U.S. Trident system. After carrying out six underground nuclear tests with LLNL as a partner, the AWRE team participating in Dutchess moved back to a partnership with LANL. Although the reasons for making the change in U.S. labs is not public knowledge, the change required the AWRE team to redesign emplacement hardware consistent with the methods used by LANL, which were quite different from those used by LLNL. After an agreement reached in 1978 between the United States and the United Kingdom, data concerning the effects of nuclear weapons on military systems began to be exchanged, influencing the AWRE warhead design teams for the next decade.

Another major challenge was presented to the AWRE scientists and engineers with the move to Pahute Mesa holes for most of the tests beginning with Fondutta. The Pahute Mesa test area, in the extreme northwest corner of the NTS, was added to the NTS in late 1963 to provide a location where tests of higher yields could be conducted with minimum seismic impact on populated areas such as Las Vegas. The increase in elevation from Yucca Flat to the test areas on Pahute Mesa meant that the more extreme winter weather could affect access as well as comfort. Tests sited in areas 19 and 20 on Pahute Mesa also meant traveling as far as 60 miles from the base camp in Mercury, Nevada. All test procedures used on the Pahute Mesa were the same as those used in Yucca Flat, the only difference being the extra miles added to the already long days needed to conduct a test.

In 1980, as the United Kingdom was moving toward its decision to acquire the Trident missile system with an AWRE warhead, the AWRE designed an experiment to be executed in an event code-named Serpa, the first in a series of developmental tests under the leadership of AWRE director, Peter Jones.

Working with LANL on November 12, 1981, AWRE conducted the Rousane test in area 4. On April 25, 1982, the AWRE test, Gibne, was conducted in area 20 on Pahute Mesa, with LLNL as the participating partner. Once again working with LLNL, AWRE in 1983 conducted the test, Armada, in area 9 with a stated yield of "less than 20 kilotons." The NTS became a familiar place to the two AWRE trial superintendents, Don Collyer and Harry Powell, and to senior AWRE personnel Ken Johnston, Ron Siddens, and Clive Marsh. Working with LANL on May 1, 1984, AWRE conducted a test code-named Mundo in area 7 of NTS.

In December of 1984, a test code-named Egmont was to be conducted in a vertical hole on Pahute Mesa, with LLNL as the participating U.S. laboratory. After a series of successful activities involving the installation of the AWRE device to be tested and the diagnostic system in the canister, the canister was sealed and a routine emplacement began. This required lifting the 200-ton canister system to enable the movement and lowering the tower assembly gear and the careful "feeding" of all of the signal cables. As the assembly approached the bottom of the hole, the weight on the end of the drill string suddenly decreased, indicating that there was water in the hole. By the time the lowering operations stopped, it was clear that some significant portion of the test canister was submerged. Test Director Joe Behne of the United States made the decision to "come back out of the hole" with the entire assembly. Trial Superintendent Don Collyer of the United Kingdom notified AWRE that the device might be wet and that the device team should return immediately to the NTS. After the two days it took to bring the assembly back up from the hole that was 2,000 feet deep, it was determined that the lower half of the test canister, containing instrumentation, had indeed been submerged, but that the top of the canister, containing the device to be tested, had not been submerged.

It took a few days for Don Collyer and his team to determine that the device was not harmed and to replace the instrumentation that had become wet. In the meantime, Joe Behne confirmed that the water had been pumped out of the hole, and the emplacement operations started again. Egmont was detonated successfully on December 9, 1984, among many comments about what might or might not be an appropriate test for a submarine-launched missile warhead.

On November 12, 1985, during the preparations for going "downhole" in area 3 with an AWRE test device for the test Kinibito, the rack containing all the diagnostics accidentally dropped two to three feet and sustained a little damage to the bottom of the canister. All operations were halted by the U.S. test director, Walt Wolff, and tests were

Test code-named Houston, at U19az, in 1990. Photo courtesy National Security Technologies (NSTec).

conducted to assure the integrity of the electrical systems as well as to allow the diagnostic physicists to ensure that alignment of the detector lines of sight inside the canister was not damaged. After much discussion, it was collectively determined that all systems appeared to be intact and in alignment and that the preparations for the test should proceed. The test was conducted successfully on December 5, 1985.

Don Collyer, who had spent so much time at the NTS, was once asked about the differences between working at the NTS and working in Australia at the Maralinga test site. He explained that to travel from the NTS site to the next town, Las Vegas, was only 100 miles, but the travel from the Australian site to the nearest town was 1,000 miles. Second, he said that at the NTS no insects bothered you, but in Australia all test personnel wore netting to protect themselves from being covered by flies. Test Director Joe Behne of LLNL talked about one of his visits to the United Kingdom, when he was taken to a small pub in a small town near Aldermaston. Because the old pub burned down in 1583, he was taken to the new pub, built in 1597. Such experiences made the partnership more meaningful.

As this series of AWRE development tests was coming to a close, a test code-named Darwin was conducted on June 25, 1986, on Pahute Mesa, with LLNL as the test partner. This was followed by the test, Midland, conducted July 16, 1987, in collaboration with LANL in area 7 of the NTS. In late 1987 AWRE became the Atomic Weapons Establishment (AWE). The change in name was consistent with the combination of two nuclear facilities under a single management organization. There were no AWE tests in Nevada in 1988, although

AWE/LLNL team, at test code-named Bristol, at U4av, in 1991. Photo courtesy Lawrence Livermore National Laboratory (LLNL).

discussions about weapons effects continued in some detail in more than one JOWOG meeting. A partnership with LLNL resulted in the test code-named Barnwell conducted on December 8, 1989. This was followed on November 14, 1990, by a test code-named Houston conducted on Pahute Mesa, with LANL as the technical partner.

Although it was not originally planned as the final test, on November 26, 1991, an AWE test code-named Bristol was conducted in a hole in area 19 with LANL as the participating laboratory. The yield of less than 20 kilotons indicated it might have been a system test or a component test.

A familiar and famous NTS visitor stop these days is the location of a proposed AWE test code-named Icecap. The planned test was in the final stages of preparation and was scheduled to be conducted in late 1992. The decision by President George H. W. Bush to observe a testing moratorium and to create the right political atmosphere for negotiations on the CTBT caught both the U.S. NTS people and the AWE by surprise. Although significant AWE funds had been expended toward the Icecap test, the test could not proceed. The Icecap tower stands today in area 3 at NTS as a monument to what had been done as well as a component of what could be done if nuclear testing is ever required again.

The cooperative agreement between the United States and the United Kingdom that enabled 24 UK underground nuclear tests to be conducted continues today. In compliance with the CTBT, however, continued cooperative testing is done with high-explosive and nuclear materials that do not result in a fission reaction. The AWE and the U.S.

laboratories still collaborate and conduct subcritical tests that help define both nations' requirement to keep the nuclear stockpile safe and secure without nuclear testing. It is a great testimony to the original 1958 MDA that joint experiments involving the United States and the United Kingdom continue after 50 years.

In the past few years, for example, two major underground subcritical tests have been conducted at the NTS, supported by LANL: Etna in February of 2002 and Krakatau (after the famous volcanic explosions near Java) in February of 2006. Both were complicated experiments involving materials science measurements that support current requirements for stockpile confidence.

An interesting sidelight of these experiments is that the United Kingdom's reluctance to reveal the presence of UK citizens at NTS, which began in 1962, continued through the conduct of these two subcritical tests. For the purpose of those experiments, the AWRE personnel were identified locally as Texans, which made the distinction even easier. Nonetheless, the LANL scientists and the AWRE scientists gathered on most Tuesday nights for what was known as "choir practice," just another example of the cooperation between the scientific communities of the two countries.

There are three spin-offs from the cooperation between the United Kingdom and the United States in full-scale nuclear testing that are worthy of merit. The first has to do with the establishment of the cooperative mechanisms known as joint working groups, or JOWOGs. These groups were established in the late 1950s as forums for exchanging weapons research and design information.

The second has to do with JOWOGs that were established to provide guidance regarding responses to accidents involving nuclear weapons in the United States or United Kingdom. The participation of the United States in a UK nuclear weapons accident exercise, conducted by AWRE and MOD in Norwich in the mid-1970s, led directly to the successful incorporation of a U.S. environmental impact statement that allowed the dispersion of live radioactive isotopes while conducting these kinds of exercises at the NTS. Several joint exercises have been conducted in recent years.

The third, and perhaps most important in today's world, has to do with JOWOGs dealing with incidents involving nuclear material, whether in response to an incident at a nuclear power plant or an incident involving illegal or inappropriate use of nuclear material, such as might be used in an act of terror against either the United States or the United Kingdom. AWE contributed a lot to solving the technical problems associated with a terrorist act, and AWE was particularly helpful in establishing radiation standards that have prevailed through the years.

The 50 years of cooperation in the exchange of nuclear weapons information and nuclear testing information has made an indelible impact on both nations. Both can be proud of the nuclear deterrent that they cooperatively and jointly developed and of the continuing cooperation in matters necessary to protect that deterrent. The efforts of the United Kingdom and the United States resulted in experiments at the NTS that made significant contributions to the science and the defense of both nations.

NOTE
The writer is indebted to Joe Behne and Maxine Trost (Lawrence Livermore National Laboratory); Walt Wolff, Tom Scolman, and Chuck Costa (Los Alamos National Laboratory); Cheryl Oar, Jeff Gordon, and Martha Demarre (National Security Technologies); and Darwin Morgan, Hilda Hernandez, and Linda Cohn (National Nuclear Security Administration).

18

COLLABORATION ON COUNTERPROLIFERATION: THE LIBYAN CASE

ROBERT G. JOSEPH

Today in Tripoli, the leader of Libya, Colonel Moammar al-Ghadafi, publicly confirmed his commitment to disclose and dismantle all weapons of mass destruction programs in his country. . . . The United States and our allies are applying a broad and active strategy to address the challenges of proliferation, through diplomacy and through the decisive actions that are sometimes needed. We've enhanced our intelligence capabilities in order to trace dangerous weapons activities. We've organized a proliferation security initiative to interdict dangerous materials and technologies in transit. We've insisted on multilateral approaches like that in North Korea to confront threats. . . .

Our understanding with Libya came about through quiet diplomacy. It is a result, however, of policies and principles declared to all. Over the last two years, a great coalition of nations has come together to oppose terror and to oppose the spread of weapons of mass destruction. We've been clear in our purposes. We have shown resolve. In word and in action, we have clarified the choices left to potential adversaries.

—President George W. Bush
December 19, 2003

This chapter is adapted from a forthcoming case study on the motivations behind, and lessons learned from, Libya's decision to abandon its weapons of mass destruction and long-range missile programs.

This evening Colonel Gaddafi has confirmed that Libya has in the past sought to develop WMD capabilities, as well as longer range missiles. Libya came to us in March following successful negotiations on Lockerbie to see if it could resolve its WMD issue in a similarly cooperative manner. Nine months of work followed with experts from the United States and the United Kingdom, during which the Libyans discussed their programmes with us. As a result, Libya has now declared its intention to dismantle its weapons of mass destruction completely and to limit the range of Libyan missiles to no greater than 300 kilometres, in accordance with the parameters set by the Missile Technology Control Regime.

The UK, U.S. and our partners are determined to stop the threat of WMD. We have played a leading role in the IAEA, with our closest allies, on the issue of Iran and nuclear weapons. We strongly support the Six Party talks on North Korea. We have enforced Security Council resolutions relating to Iraq. We have played a leading role in the Proliferation Security Initiative designed to interdict the passage of cargoes which could be used in WMD programmes. These actions show that we are serious about effective multilateral action against WMD. . . .

—Prime Minister Tony Blair
December 19, 2003

The near simultaneous announcements by President Bush and Prime Minister Blair of Libya's decision to abandon its nuclear and chemical weapons programs, and to allow their complete dismantlement and removal, reflected the culmination of a close and effective partnership on counterproliferation. This partnership included joint operations in the intelligence field aimed at penetrating and unraveling the A. Q. Khan nuclear proliferation network that served as Libya's central supply line, and joint political coordination at the highest level in the interactions with Libya that resulted in perhaps the greatest nonproliferation success in decades.

Underlying this success was the recognition that traditional nonproliferation policies and approaches, although essential, were insufficient to meet modern proliferation challenges. President Bush understood from the start of his first term that protecting against contemporary weapons of mass destruction (WMD) threats would require a fundamental change in how the United States and other countries perceive the proliferation threat and respond to it. Within the U.S. government, this meant that it would no longer be sufficient to react to proliferation after the fact with political condemnations and economic sanctions. Instead, proactive measures would be taken to prevent and roll back proliferation. And, equally important, there was a requirement for new concepts of deterrence, dissuasion, and defense as well as new capabilities to deal with the full range of WMD threats.

President Bush set forth the U.S. approach to defeating modern WMD threats at the beginning of his administration. In May 2001 at the National Defense University, in his first major address on national security affairs as president, he announced:

> . . .this is still a dangerous world, a less certain, a less predictable one. More nations have nuclear weapons and still more have nuclear aspirations. Many have chemical and biological weapons. Some already have developed the ballistic missile technology that would allow them to deliver weapons of mass destruction at long distances and incredible speeds. And a number of these countries are spreading these technologies around the world.

In this same speech, President Bush called for a "new policy, a broad strategy of active nonproliferation, counterproliferation and defenses." And he emphasized the need for friends and allies to work together to prevent and protect against their common threats, including from ballistic missiles. In what would become a clear multilateral approach, and despite the caricature to the contrary, the president emphasized the indivisibility of U.S. interests and security with those of its allies. As a first step, he stressed the need to take the "N" out of "NMD" (national missile defense) to ensure that not only the United States but U.S. partners as well were protected from rogue states like North Korea and Iran. He dispatched high-level delegations to major capitals around the globe, starting with London, to discuss this new approach to security.

Consistent with this view of emerging threats, President Bush also began to establish a new framework for action, putting in place a comprehensive strategy involving proactive diplomacy, actions to counter WMD proliferation directly, and better means for organizing and equipping ourselves and our friends and allies to respond to the use of such weapons. The message was clear to all: the United States and its international partners must be serious in their determination to prevent and protect against WMD threats, and willing to use all tools—

diplomatic, economic, scientific and technological, and military—to achieve this goal.

In December 2002, the Bush administration published the "National Strategy to Combat Weapons of Mass Destruction." The document identified three major pillars:

- Protection, or counterproliferation; including interdiction, deterrence, and defense;

- Prevention, or nonproliferation; including support for regimes such as the Nuclear Non-Proliferation Treaty (NPT) and the chemical and biological weapons conventions, increased cooperative threat reduction efforts, greater controls on nuclear materials, export controls, and sanctions; and

- Response, or consequence management; including capabilities to mitigate the effects of WMD use.

To integrate the pillars, the strategy called for improvements in several key enabling functions, including intelligence collection and analysis, research and development, international cooperation, and tailored strategies against state and nonstate proliferators.

Promulgated publicly at the time the United States and the United Kingdom were leading the international effort within and outside of the UN Security Council to compel Iraq to account for its WMD programs and activities, the national strategy received substantial attention in the world press. Although the coverage differed from country to country, one theme was constant: the continued proliferation of WMD and missiles by hostile states would no longer go unopposed. Libyan leaders could not have missed the message.

PROMOTING EFFECTIVE INTERNATIONAL INITIATIVES

To implement the new strategy, the president initiated a highly visible diplomatic campaign to encourage other states to join the effort to prevent and protect against WMD proliferation. The United Kingdom played an early and important role in each component of the campaign. In the Group of Eight, the United States successfully proposed in 2002 the establishment of the Global Partnership, with the goal of providing $20 billion over ten years for threat reduction and nonproliferation projects. In May 2003, the president announced a second initiative that drew worldwide attention. Made public at a press conference in Poland, the Proliferation Security Initiative (PSI) would create an impressive coalition of the willing to stop the trade in proliferation materials and equipment through proactive enforcement of national and international authorities. Great Britain was to play a leading role in the PSI core group that developed the statement of principles, articulating the objectives and commitments for those willing to participate.

In the counterproliferation field, a number of initiatives to develop improved capabilities for deterrence and defense against WMD threats also received wide attention in the international press. Following the September 11, 2001, attacks and the subsequent anthrax crimes, several steps were taken in the biodefense field, including Biowatch and Bioshield, and the expansion of vaccinations of U.S. forces against anthrax. Missile defense was another key priority to bolster deterrence and protection against states like North Korea and Iran. The U.S. withdrawal from the Anti-Ballistic Missile Treaty and the president's public announcement that the United States would deploy a defense of all 50 states against a North Korean–type of ballistic missile attack made headlines around the globe.

Another much publicized priority was adapting U.S. nuclear forces to the new security environment, reflected in the administration's Nuclear Posture Review (NPR). The NPR specifically updated U.S. strategic planning to help address the new threats posed by proliferation. Administration briefings and unauthorized leaks of the findings and recommendations of the review were covered extensively in the foreign media. A May 2003 report in the Libyan press noted that in its nuclear posture review of 2001 the U.S. administration urged development of a wide range of new nuclear capabilities; it went on to say that the United States might in some circumstances use nuclear weapons against countries that did not have them, for example, Syria, Libya, Iran and Iraq. Despite its inaccuracies, this and other reports in the Libyan press undoubtedly registered with the Libyan leadership.

As with the public articulation of a comprehensive strategy to combat proliferation, putting in place effective multilateral initiatives such as PSI and acquiring new capabilities to deter and defend against WMD showed the seriousness with which the Bush administration pursued the goal of combating WMD and missile proliferation. The president was direct in stating publicly his commitment to developing the counterproliferation capabilities needed to deter and defend against WMD threats. In this way, while increasing national efforts to prevent proliferation in the first instance, the president added a new dimension to combat WMD and their means of delivery. Interdiction would block proliferation directly and produce incontrovertible evidence of its attempt. The threat of the use of force to defend U.S. and allied security meant that those who illicitly pursue these weapons must consider carefully the risks inherent in their actions. Both of these factors would play directly on the Libyan decision to abandon WMD and longer-range missiles.

DISRUPTING AND DEFEATING WMD THREATS

The initial Libyan request to meet with U.S. and UK officials to "clear the air" about WMD programs in Libya came only days before the invasion of Iraq in March 2003. That invasion followed more than six months of intense diplomatic maneuvering at the UN in New York and in the Middle East and Gulf region. President Bush and Prime Minister Blair had been the leading forces behind the effort to compel Saddam Hussein to account for the chemical, biological, and nuclear materials that remained obscured by more than a decade of Iraqi denial and deception. All agreed that Iraq's actions constituted material breach of numerous Security Council resolutions going back more than a decade. The United States and the United Kingdom emphasized their determination to enforce these resolutions and hold Iraq accountable on WMD, even if force was required. Their joint position was straightforward: Saddam needed to make a strategic choice. He could choose to cooperate fully with international inspectors and provide a complete and accurate accounting of Iraq's programs, or he would be removed from power.

The buildup of hundreds of thousands of U.S., UK, and other coalition troops sent a tough message not only to Baghdad but also to others who sought WMD, especially in the region. The message was clear—those who seek such weapons will put their security at risk—and was backed by action. Libya, which had long possessed chemical weapons and had embarked on a large-scale clandestine effort to enrich uranium for nuclear weapons, received the message. The immediate concern of the Libyan leadership was that, after Iraq, it would be the next target for military action. This concern may well have been aggravated in the fall of 2002 by stories in the international press, sourced to Prime Minister Ariel Sharon of Israel, that Iraq had sent a number of its nuclear physicists to Libya to work on a joint weapons program.

Early 2003 saw a convergence of additional factors that may have aggravated Tripoli's concern that, after Iraq, Libya would be next. One was Washington's stepped-up campaign in January to deny Libya the chairmanship of the UN Commission on Human Rights. Another may have been press stories based on unclassified Central Intelligence Agency reports and testimony that U.S. intelligence believed Libya, described as a state sponsor of terror, was expanding its nuclear infrastructure and pursuing chemical and biological weapons capabilities. Together, these and other actions taken by the United States in the region suggested to the Libyan leadership that the United States would seek regime change in Libya. Although the Bush administration had not formally adopted regime change in Libya as an active policy goal, the concern was perceived as real and served as a motivation to reach out to the United States.

In reaching out in early 2003, Colonel Qadhafi sought accommodation on two key issues of central importance. First, in a January interview with *Newsweek,* he stressed that support in the Arab world for Osama bin Laden was a threat not just to the United States but also to his own rule. Noting that he had been a target of an Al Qaeda assassination attempt, he indicated that Libyan intelligence would cooperate to "wipe out" this threat through the exchange of information with the United States and Great Britain. Second, in March, Qadhafi embarked on a secret WMD initiative: he directed his son, Saif al-Islam, to approach the United States through British contacts for a dialogue on WMD.

Although intimating that "everything would be on the table" and that Libya would be willing to renounce WMD, Qadhafi's son did not include in the Libyan request any commitment to abandon programs that Tripoli publicly continued to deny existed. For example, Libya formally continued to reject claims by U.S. intelligence that it was seeking WMD. In January 2003, the Libyan Foreign Ministry spokesperson, Hassouna al-Shawesh, emphasizing that Libya was a signatory of the NPT, dismissed a U.S. charge that it was building its nuclear infrastructure: "These are allegations the CIA habitually puts out to serve interests hostile to the peoples" of other states, he said. Given this posture, the March 2003 request to "clear the air" was perceived at the time as a Libyan attempt to hedge against what was most likely a potential liability to the regime more than it was thought to be a signal of Libya's intent to abandon WMD programs.

TIMELINE

On December 19, 2003, Colonel Qadhafi announced that Libya had voluntarily decided to give up its nuclear and chemical weapons programs and missiles beyond the 300-kilometer range, making clear that he now believed that these weapons programs no longer added to Libya's security or well-being. In March 2004, the ship, *Industrial Challenger,* arrived in the United States with more than 500 metric tons of cargo—including everything from centrifuges to Libya's 800-kilometer-range SCUD C force. This marked an end to Tripoli's nuclear weapons program and its possession of longer-range missiles. It can be argued that this is one of the most significant nonproliferation achievements to date.

A number of key events provide the essential background for understanding the reasons behind Libya's strategic decision to abandon its WMD and longer-range missile programs. These events began in March 2003.

March 2003: Saif al-Islam approached British intelligence with the offer of talks with the United States and United Kingdom to "clear the air" regarding WMD programs in Libya. At this same time, on the eve of the coalition invasion of Iraq, Colonel Qadhafi was quoted in the French press as stating: "Once Bush has finished with Iraq, we will very soon be targeted."

April 2003: The first meeting of U.S., UK, and Libyan intelligence personnel was held, during which there was discussion of the need for a technical visit to Libya by U.S. and UK experts, but no agreements were reached. The chief of Libyan intelligence was the principal point of contact for Libya and would continue to act as such through the remainder of the process.

August 2003: Agreement was reached within intelligence channels to meet with Colonel Qadhafi to discuss prospects for technical visits.

September 2003: A meeting was held in Tripoli with Colonel Qadhafi, during which he agreed in principle to allow the technical visits, but he deferred to his senior leadership to work out the details. No date was agreed during the follow-on discussions.

October 3, 2003: The ship, BBC *China,* was interdicted en route to Libya, its destination. Five large shipping containers were off-loaded in an Italian port and were determined to contain thousands of centrifuge parts manufactured in Malaysia by the Khan nuclear proliferation network.

October 7, 2003: Evidence of the program was presented to the Libyans; Libya immediately agreed on dates for a visit of a U.S.-UK technical team.

October 2003: The first technical team on-site visit occurred.

November 2003: Following the completion of the first technical visit, the Libyans were presented with additional intelligence concerning their nuclear program. Arrangements were agreed for the second technical visit.

December 2003: The second U.S.-UK technical team on-site visit occurred.

During the first visit of the technical team, much was learned about Libya's WMD and missile programs. By the end of the second visit, the Libyans:

- Admitted having a nuclear weapons program and buying uranium hexafluoride feed material for gas centrifuge enrichment;

- Acknowledged making about 25 tons of sulfur mustard chemical warfare agent, aerial bombs for the mustard, and small amounts of nerve agent;

- Agreed to inspections by the International Atomic Energy Agency (IAEA) and the Organization for the Prohibition of Chemical Weapons (OPCW) and to abide by the range limitations of the Missile Technology Control Regime (MTCR).

Perhaps most encouraging as well as most disturbing, the Libyans at the end of the second visit delivered nuclear weapons design materials acquired from A. Q. Khan. These materials were described as possessing an alarming level of detail, identifying everything Libya would need to make a nuclear bomb.

Although a number of questions remained even after the return of the experts in December, UK and U.S. intelligence assessments concluded that Tripoli was in fact coming clean about its WMD and missile activities. Both services believed that the best means of addressing outstanding issues was to deepen the engagement with Libya (through U.S. and UK experts as well as through the OPCW and IAEA) and allow for further access to Libyan personnel and facilities. On this basis, the decision was made to hold secret policy discussions.

December 16, 2003: The first U.S.-UK policy discussion was held with the Libyans. All required measures were taken to keep the talks secret. The initial opening statement by the Libyan side, emphasizing the need to remove sanctions, moved backward from commitments made earlier in the month. U.S. and UK representatives emphasized that the purpose of the meeting was not to negotiate specific steps or responses to Libyan actions on the part of the United States and United Kingdom. At the same time, U.S. and UK participants made clear that, if Libya did move forward with its commitment to end its WMD and longer-range missile programs, one major barrier to improved relations would be removed.

Almost six hours of tense discussions focused primarily on the draft text for a public Libyan statement. Libyan participants initially resisted any explicit mention of the existence of Libya's WMD programs or a commitment to eliminate the programs. U.S.-UK representatives insisted that such references be included.

Discussion of the Libyan statement was followed by an even more frank discussion of specific actions Libya would need to take to eliminate its WMD and longer-range missile programs. The U.S. representative raised the requirement for a formal commitment from the Libyan delegation to eliminate WMD and missile programs and emphasized the need for an explicit agreement at the table from the Libyan representatives to the following commitments:

Nuclear: (1) Remove all materials and equipment related to the nuclear weapons programs: all centrifuges and all parts and associated equipment, all uranium hexafluoride and other nuclear materials, all uranium conversion equipment, all documentation, and (2) sign and implement the additional protocol.

Chemical: (1) Eliminate and destroy all chemical agents, munitions, and equipment, and (2) complete accession to the Chemical Weapons Convention.

Biological: (1) Allow monitoring of facilities in an atmosphere of complete openness, and (2) commit to not pursue biological warfare capabilities.

Missiles: (1) Remove all ballistic missiles with a range greater than 300 kilometers (SCUD Cs) as well as all associated equipment, (2) pledge to not develop or deploy ballistic missiles with a range greater than 300 kilometers, and (3) abide by the parameters of the MTCR.

U.S. and UK representatives made clear that Libyan agreement to these precise commitments was essential if there was to be a successful outcome. Although initially reluctant, the Libyan participants agreed at that meeting to each point and to the explicit requirement for monitoring and international inspections in all WMD and missile areas.

Although all of these commitments were important, two were unique and precedent setting. The first was the removal of all components of the nuclear program. This was essential to avoid a future problem if the Libyans were to argue later that equipment acquired for activities such as uranium conversion or even enrichment could be retained for a so-called peaceful nuclear program. The Iran case, in which Iran cynically manipulated the provisions of the NPT to acquire sensitive technologies for weapons purposes under the guise of a peaceful program, was very much present in the minds of the U.S. and UK participants. Confirming that this was a real possibility, Saif al-Islam stated publicly on December 20, one day after the announcement of the Libyan decision, that "of course, this program could be used for peaceful purposes." By this time, however, the commitment to remove all such equipment had been agreed and announced. The second unique and precedent-setting commitment was the elimination of missile capabilities beyond the MTCR parameter of the 300-kilometer range, to which Libya had no legal obligations.

For their part, the Libyan participants emphasized the importance of characterizing their decision to abandon WMD and longer-range missiles as "voluntary" and in Libya's self-interest. U.S. and UK representatives were quick to agree that this was accurate and should be done.

December 18, 2003: When the meeting on December 16 ended, it was unclear how Colonel Qadhafi would react to the draft statement hammered out around the table. To encourage Libyan acceptance of the statement and to get final buy-in from Qadhafi, Prime Minister Blair reached out to the Libyan leader. During what was the first direct conversation between these two men, Colonel Qadhafi reportedly expressed concern about the appearance of the Libyan decision being portrayed as caving in to pressure as well as the vulnerability of Libya to attack now that it had revealed its WMD programs to the United States and United Kingdom. According to press reports, the prime minister gave assurances that a Libyan statement—if clear on possession and elimination—would be met with positive statements by the prime minister and president.

December 19, 2003: Through the UK channel in Tripoli, Washington and London provided reactions to the draft Libyan announcement. The next version came close to what was required. A final brief exchange produced agreement on what all three sides could accept, including references to centrifuge and chemical weapons programs, and an explicit obligation for immediate international inspections, including the monitoring of Libya's missile force, to meet its elimination commitments.

For the next several hours, U.S. and UK officials were in constant contact awaiting confirmation of the Libyan statements. During this time, the Libyans sent word to Washington and London that Qadhafi's statement would be released as a written statement. Although this was a last-minute change from what had been expected to be an in-person announcement, this was accepted as a necessary face-saving step.

The wait continued well into the afternoon Washington time, late evening in London. Finally, confirmation was received that the Libyan statements had been made. The statement made by the Libyan foreign minister conformed to the agreed text. The statement released in the name of Colonel Qadhafi was sufficient to meet the requirements. Once confirmed, Prime Minister Blair and President Bush made their separate but coordinated announcements.

19

NUCLEAR TESTING: A UK PERSPECTIVE

PART 1. THE UK VIEW*

CLIVE MARSH, PETER ROBERTS, AND KEN JOHNSTON

The 1958 moratorium on nuclear testing was broken by the Soviet Union with a massive series of tests starting in 1961. The 1958 Mutual Defense Agreement between the United States and United Kingdom then facilitated access to the Christmas Island test facilities by the United States and to the underground test facilities at the Nevada Test Site (NTS) by the United Kingdom. Access to NTS was required by the United Kingdom when it became necessary to test designs for what were to become Polaris and the free-fall bombs for the Royal Air Force although, for a time, joint use of Christmas Island was considered.

Radiochemical analysis of the postshot debris was a key technique for measuring the nuclear yield of devices tested in the atmosphere, but testing underground posed new problems. Airburst debris collected by sampling aircraft was relatively pure (containing only the condensed particulate from the vaporized device), but fission products from a contained underground event would be dissolved in a lot of molten rock. In fact a 10-kiloton event would melt about 5,000 tons of the surrounding rock, which would subsequently cool to produce a material like black volcanic glass, containing the dissolved bomb debris.

It was the radiochemists' job on these tests to add a unique radiochemical indicator to the device just before it was lowered "downhole" (this was a readily detectable nuclide not present in the surrounding soil; it was added to indicate what fraction of the postshot debris had been recovered) and then to supervise the postshot

---

drill-back and sampling. After several areas were sampled, a roughly calibrated gamma monitor was used to verify that an "ample sample" had been obtained.

Speed was of the essence. Short-lived fission product nuclides would decay rapidly, and radiochemists waiting at Atomic Weapons Research Establishment (AWRE) needed measurable amounts for their analyses. The samples were loaded into lead pots for rapid transport to the United Kingdom. The hard work of analysis could then begin.

With the warhead designs for Polaris and the air-delivered strategic systems completed and proved in underground tests in Nevada, by the mid-1960s the United Kingdom had entered a self-imposed moratorium on further design and testing that was to last for nearly a decade. AWRE was busy building the stockpile for entry into service, but otherwise the late 1960s and early 1970s were relatively quiet times, certainly by comparison with the 1950s. It was, however, important to find ways of retaining and recruiting scientists and engineers for the future. A new recruit to the Design Mathematics Division, for example, would have found a surprisingly academic environment, with work under way on astrophysics and fast reactor safety among the varied topics studied. There was relatively little emphasis on next-generation design requirements, with weapon-related studies mainly addressing some long-standing issues and paper studies on what might be possible.

INTERACTION WITH THE UNITED STATES

From the UK perspective, interaction with the United States therefore was fairly intimidating, with little new and of real substance to offer. Still, regular meetings were held, with the United States showing at least polite interest. The United Kingdom was a very junior partner, while the United States mainly focused on its active weapon development and nuclear test program. In general there was no "need to know" the details of the U.S. experiments but, where relevant, helpful comments were made on UK studies.

By 1974 the need to resume nuclear testing became essential to support the Chevaline program that upgraded Polaris to sustain deterrence through countering emergent Soviet antiballistic missile systems. For the first test there was heavy reliance on the United States, especially in terms of fielding the device. With only about one test annually, the value of comprehensive prompt diagnostics to complement radiochemistry was appreciated from the outset.

One such diagnostic, for example, measured the temperature history within the exploding device but required complex calculations to design the experiment and interpret the data. Keen to gain full advantage of these data, the United Kingdom requested from the United States a numerical program, or computer code, that could simulate the physics. The code duly arrived and, after a period of configuring to run on the AWRE computers, completed the test problem with impressive speed and efficiency. Unfortunately that was the only problem we could ever get it to calculate, and although the source code was available it was particularly impenetrable, having thousands of lines of Fortran and no subroutines. Doubtless our U.S. colleagues would have come to our aid, but we determined instead to write our own comparable code as part of the road to capability recovery. Apart from being able to progress the diagnostic design and interpretation, this now enabled truly independent assessments. This was of great value to both countries and became an area of increasing collaboration as various codes at AWRE were enhanced or rewritten.

The availability of experimental data not only stimulated the cycle of model prediction, to compare with results and then to model improvement; it also stimulated collaboration and the inclusion of relevant U.S. data. Because of the value of such data, methods were explored to gain further value from the limited UK test program. It was realized that the environment of a nuclear explosion could be used to explore various aspects of weapon physics, from materials property data to inertial fusion ignition and burn studies. Here again collaboration was stimulated through the engagement with such parallel U.S. programs as Halite-Centurion.

It took roughly a decade of testing by the United Kingdom to recover its independent nuclear design and fielding capability although, of course, all tests were undertaken collaboratively with the United States at the NTS. First impressions on arriving at the NTS were set by the presence of armed security provided by the Wackenhut guard force. Physics designers arriving for a test were probably regarded as tourists by the diagnostics and fielding teams who usually stayed at NTS for several months preparing and checking equipment. Various briefings were held in the days leading up to a test, and for the designers the main focus would be on the maximum credible yield (MCY) calculations and the expected diagnostic levels, which would determine the experimental settings.

All such calculations were undertaken by both UK and U.S. scientists. MCY calculations were very conservatively assessed and a more than adequate depth of burial thus determined to ensure full containment of the nuclear test. Similarly, both parties calculated nuclear performance details so that diagnostic ranges could be set to capture as much data as possible. On the day of the test, activity centered on the building known as CP (control point)—the heart of which resembled a space rocket launch control. As the countdown proceeded, various stations reported in on wind direction, confirmed that no staff were in the area and that miners had been evacuated, and assured that appropriate warnings had been given to operators of high-rise buildings in Las Vegas. Direct lines were opened to U.S. and UK governments to ensure immediate communication. On one occasion the countdown was halted with only minutes remaining when four protestors suddenly appeared at ground zero, literally standing directly above the nuclear device buried deep beneath them. The response by the U.S. authorities was swift, assured, and impressive. A helicopter appeared on the scene in no time, engulfing the protestors in clouds of dust. When the dust cleared the protestors had gone and the countdown resumed.

The final seconds of the countdown were inevitably anxious, with everyone involved mentally reviewing the work for which they were responsible. Then, when the countdown reached zero, one tried to detect the seismic shock as a first indication of success. Relief, especially for the designers, was the immediate, palpable emotion. Tensions remained a little longer for the diagnosticians as they then went on to learn the relative success of their data collection. But confirmation was always obtained quite quickly, and the phone lines would immediately be humming. For those directly involved in the test—UK and U.S. staff—attention naturally then turned to the detail of the diagnostic results, a process that could involve an agonizing wait of several hours.

Toward the end of the test program, the United Kingdom fielded a design novel to both countries. This added additional stress because confidence had to be derived solely from computer modeling and supporting nonnuclear experimental data. On this occasion some diagnostic teams set their trigger thresholds as low as possible to cover a potential failure. In the end the complex device performed at the top end of prediction, and the United Kingdom had established itself with a demonstrated independent capability, a valued peer alongside the United States.

The safety of our nuclear warheads has always been of paramount importance to the United Kingdom, and a proposal to secure modern benchmark safety data for the future found strong support on both sides of the Atlantic. It is significant that our final nuclear data from underground testing was safety related and derived from a collaborative undertaking with the United States.

Although the cessation of testing caught both U.S. and UK scientists somewhat by surprise, throughout its strategic-deterrent history the United Kingdom has been ever conscious that a ban on nuclear testing might be just around the corner, either in the form of a dramatic reduction in the allowable nuclear yield of the test or, indeed, a complete ban. Our preparation in designing devices for tests was always thorough and painstaking, involving numerous calculations and nonnuclear experiments to achieve safety and give best prospects of success. But we have also continued to push at the frontiers of experiment techniques to gain better and more relevant data from laboratory experiments lest the day arrived when the safety and performance assurances for our stockpile warheads have to be underwritten without recourse to further nuclear tests.

AWE's HELEN laser and applications of world-leading pulsed radiography were just two examples of advanced research preparing for the eventuality of a Comprehensive Nuclear Test-Ban Treaty (CTBT). During the 1970s and 1980s, the United Kingdom and United States exchanged ideas and technologies, but it was not until the 1990s that both countries focused on developing nuclear design capability in the context of the CTBT in order to underwrite their stockpiles and to be able to certify and manufacture new designs should they be required.

In late 1992 the U.S. Congress enacted the Energy and Water Development Appropriations Act 1993 (Public Law 102-377). Section 507 of that act directed the ending of all U.S. (and therefore British) nuclear testing after September 1996 and severely restricted both the number and the purpose of tests conducted in the interim. After an internal review in early 1993, however, the incoming Clinton administration elected to end testing immediately, with no phaseout. The decision was based on technical and strategic considerations and on concerns that Congress would not support the limited number of tests allowed by the recently passed appropriations act.

Since the end of the testing era, the new approach inevitably has involved the improvement of computational simulation, the validation against the nuclear test archive, and the acquisition of new experimental data and advanced nonnuclear hydrodynamics and plasma dynamics facilities in the United Kingdom and United States. Collaboration in all these activities, coupled with a robust peer-review process, is now at the heart of the special relationship as we move forward into the next 50 years of the 1958 Mutual Defense Agreement between our nations.

PART 2. A PERSONAL PERSPECTIVE*

PETER SANKEY

My deep sleep is rudely broken by a door slamming nearby. Where on earth am I? Footsteps sound in the corridor followed by the automatic closing of the exit door. Slowly I remember, Room 120 of the Los Alamos National Laboratory (LANL) green dormitory block at the Nevada Test Site (NTS). Last year it was the blue Lawrence Livermore National Laboratory (LLNL), but no, definitely Los Alamos this year. Cannot believe I am awake this early. A glance at the red, garish light-emitting diodes on the clock informs me it is 2:45 a.m. As the alarm goes off I remember the note pinned to my door when I finally returned to my room at almost 11:00 last night: DON'T FORGET THE WEATHER BRIEFING AT CP AT 03:30 a.m.! The signature is of Harry Powell, my boss, the UK underground trials director.

This particular stint at NTS began just over three months ago, in September, when the Digits, Anals, Fibre Optimists, and I flew from London experiencing an Indian summer, via Washington, to a very hot Las Vegas, just like the proverbial oven when we stepped from the McCarran Airport terminal. The airport shuttle deposited us at our "weekend home" for the next three months, the infamous Somerset House Motel, just off the Las Vegas strip at Convention Center Drive. Friendly faces welcome us at reception. As always, I hope I am not given the room over the bins; the refuse always seemed to be collected at some unearthly hour on a Sunday morning.

We are all exhausted after the flights but manage the short walk over the road to the Somerset Bar where we are welcomed by "the Limeys

---

are here to let off another nuke!" So much for the fact that conducting a UK test at NTS was classified secret until the shot was fired! A quick drink and then off to bed.

Monday morning starts with a short drive to the Department of Energy Nevada Operations Office to collect badges for the test site and vouchers for safety shoes to be exchanged at the local store. The journey continues on Interstate 15 and U.S. Route 95 to NTS. About an hour and a quarter later (we remember to stick to the speed limit at Indian Springs), the dreaded sign "MERCURY" appears on the right side, off the slipway, past the usual group of protestors, and we drive through gate 100 before arriving at the Blue Box trailer that is the Mercury UK headquarters, complete with the picture of the Queen! After exchanging the smart Avis cars for battered white range cars, I collect the accommodation block and room keys for my "weeknight home," a vast improvement on the "bachelor officer quarters" of previous years!

The next day the regular daily commute begins, and I drive the 60-odd miles to area 20. The trailer park and ground zero at U20az has been leveled and graded. There is activity around the 2,500-foot-deep shot hole, and the UK trailers are in place, 600 feet back from the hole, having survived the road journey from the EG&G facility, North Las Vegas.

The time comes to seek out the important contacts on the U.S. side. Good news: Ron Cosimi is test director, big John McMullen is the J6 boss, Dave Gardiner is looking after the cables, Frank Cverna and Nick King the PINEX (pinhole imaging neutron experiment) principals, with Rolf Peterson and Jim Armstrong my immediate counterparts. While I am doing this the trailer crews check the trailers, which were configured in Las Vegas back in the early summer. The Analogue trailers 984 and 9129 house the high-bandwidth traveling-wave tube oscilloscopes. Trailer 984 is recording the primary and secondary reaction history gammas and neutrons of the device under test; the copper cables are relatively long for this shot so we are aiming for an overall bandwidth, including the optimum equalizers, approaching 400 megahertz. Trailer 9129 is taking signals from the new measurement techniques, utilizing transmission along optical fibers to attempt improved fidelity of the primary boost region of the device. One such measurement is fiber optics alpha measurement (FOAM), whereby high-energy gamma output from the device primary is incident upon single mode optical fibers creating Cerenkov radiation (a characteristic blue light) in the core of the optical fiber. The light is converted by a detector in the trailer to volts, which are then recorded on fast, high-bandwidth oscilloscopes.

Digital trailer 9124 houses one of the crown jewels of UK expertise, the unique-in-the-world digital alpha recording equipment. AWE developed this technique, which samples the amplitude of the approximately exponential primary gamma signal at fixed exponential levels to determine the corresponding time measurement when the rising signal passes through each level. This system is much envied by the United States, which evaluates its fidelity on a couple of their own shots.[1] Trailer 9124 houses similar electronics that provide a first off indication of the primary boost curve. Trailer 946 is fully utilized, covering high-explosive supercharge, primary and secondary gamma and neutron timing measurements, together with the recording of the PINEX experimental technique capturing images of the neutron burn of the device primary. In addition, we are also evaluating the effectiveness of new-on-the-market Hewlett-Packard and LeCroy digitizers that, unlike the digital alpha system in 9124, digitize the signal amplitude at fixed time intervals. Overspill recording of the signals from other device experiments are housed in three U.S. trailers.

A UK shot is always a complex, interesting set of experiments. The physics designers are keen to cover the outputs of the device to the highest degree. Accordingly, although we agree on a priority coding of A, B, and C for experiments, it inevitably transpires that all experiments are ranked A, with a few A+! The first weeks on the site are occupied with building the final configuration of the recording equipment, including calculation and installation of the required delay elements. Another important task is to configure the array of electronic equipment to simulate the amplitude and timing characteristics of the signals from the device under test.

Days turn into weeks, the euphoric feeling of being engaged on a momentous experiment slowly subsides, and, ever more, thoughts turn to loved ones—my wife Alexandra and our daughters Elisabeth and Rebecca—five-and-a-half-thousand miles away. Everyone really looks forward to the "unofficial" weekly five-minute phone call home! Despite this feeling, most people settle down to the task making the most of it. Cruel to say, those who cannot, for whatever reason, are unfortunately flown back to the United Kingdom.

The tedious tasks of focusing the scopes and positioning the signal pulse in 984 and 9189 take several weeks, checked by hundreds and hundreds of Polaroid film shots of the simulated signals. Although the amplitude and time axes are calibrated for every scope, it is important to position the pulse in the central area of the face as the scopes are notoriously nonlinear.

"Simultaneity" is another lengthy process. The aim here is to ensure that the time characteristics of every pulse to be recorded are known to a high order of accuracy from known incident fiducials, that is, the load ring pulse timing that fires the high-explosive supercharge. Although each trailer undertakes this task, the execution is very different. In the analogue trailers this entails detailed investigation of, again, hundreds of Polaroid prints, whereas the digital crews pore over many computer printouts.

During this period I alternate between the trailer park and the control point (CP), some 20 miles north of Mercury. We are beginning the daily dry runs, which simulate the real shot countdown that is getting closer and closer. The countdown for this particular shot is 30 minutes, relatively long. During this time, various signals are sent to the device and detectors, which subsequently translate the nuclear outputs to electric volts and amperes along the copper cables. Relevant output and status signals from the device, detectors, and the trailer recording instrumentation are back monitored to CP, and it is one of my responsibilities to monitor these, understand their significance, and advise mitigating actions should one or more go to the unexpected or abnormal state.

On one occasion, Professor Sir Ron Oxburgh (chief scientific adviser of the Ministry of Defence) joined me, asking me to explain the significant features of the countdown. All was going well until the signal monitoring the scope camera shutters in 984 went to an abnormal status state. This could have serious impact on the gamma reaction history, a very important measurement, so although I have practiced this before and advise a temporary halt to the count with the necessary corrective action to be taken, the situation demanded the utmost attention and my pulse raced. The countdown continued, and the remainder of the run was without incident. Nevertheless, I measured my pulse rate at time zero to be still at 130 counts per second. Ron thanked me profusely and offered all the best wishes for the weeks to come and shot day!

In parallel, there is extensive activity on the rack, the experimental laboratory about 100 long and almost 8 feet in diameter, to the bottom of which the device under test is fitted before lowering down the hole. The rack contains all the lines of sight the nuclear gammas and neutrons would travel along to be incident on the myriad of sensors that convert nuclear signals to electrical volts and amperes.

The U20az vertical emplacement hole (2,500 feet deep and 8 feet diameter) was drilled months ago, and it is time to lower a video camera down the entire length to assess its status and uniformity. At the weekly meeting, Ron Cosimi announces that this test has indicated there is a "kink" in the hole and, unless remedial action is taken, the rack will not go down the hole! A slightly larger-diameter rack is hastily constructed in North Las Vegas, delivered to the test site, lowered down the hole as far as the kink, and, none too gently, raised and lowered to knock the offending corner off!

The device engineers have been on site for some time, painstakingly assembling the many components of the device under test. Activity is definitely on the increase now, the copper pigtail cables from each sensor are connected to the signal cables to the trailers at the rack connector plate. Lines of sight and voids within the rack are filled with lead shot to avoid cross talk from the vast amounts of neutron, gamma, and X-ray outputs when the device is detonated.

Signal day runs are now becoming much more representative of the real thing. All trailers are functioning, and detector bias volts are being switched on. The days are long for all the trailer crews. I discuss a temperature measurement termed DART (diagnostics addressing radiation transport) one day with the shot physicist, Reg Smith, who disagrees with the recording coverage of the signal the particular designers of the experiment have suggested. He asks how long it would take to reconfigure the scope coverage to make what he believes are vital changes. Some very long days and nights later, the rework is complete but it does mean, for this time, that several of us do not make it to the Mercury cafeteria before it closes in the evening. We eat instead with the miners at area 2 camp.[2]

The device is now assembled, attached to the rack, and the downhole lowering is in full flow. When the device reaches the bottom, the readings from the "whoopee cushion" indicate there has been no flooding in the hole, and the backfill and gas-blocking procedures commence. The trailer park infrastructure has been removed, leaving only the cable runs snaking from the hole across the desert to the recording trailers. The trailer containing the device firing systems is in position. The day runs are sometimes two a day now, virtually the same as on the real run.

The day for the final dry run is now upon us. When the kinetic ion temperature experiment (KITE) detector voltages are switched they immediately go into runaway state, consuming large currents. My screams to hold the countdown are upheld by Ron Cosimi, and I hastily convene a review panel to determine the best way forward. The group reaches a realistic working solution, the trailer crew hastily modifies the bias voltages and makes minor modifications to the scope coverage, and we hold a successful formal, final-day run. Most of us do not leave the trailer park until 10:00 p.m., when we make our way back to Mercury, utterly exhausted but confident that shot day tomorrow will be a successful conclusion to three months of hard work for us at the end of a two-year period when most areas of the Aldermaston and Burghfield sites have played a significant part.

Then I return to my dormitory in the green Los Alamos block to find that note on my door from Harry Powell: DON'T FORGET THE WEATHER BRIEFING AT CP AT 3:30 a.m.!

NOTES – "A PERSONAL PERSPECTIVE"
This perspective is dedicated to the hard work and endeavors of a great bunch of people: Gerry Risley, Eddie Lyford, Barry Frith (now sadly departed this world), Mike Roper, John Donald, Kevin McKenzie, Bill Clements, Mike El-liott, Jeff Wilkinson, Mark Ashley, Stuart Hedges, Stuart Murdoch, Martin Firth, Phil Smith, Steve Eatwell, Calvin Seymour, Richard Baldock, and many others from Aldermaston, Lawrence Livermore, Los Alamos, and Sandia Na-tional Laboratories. Call us Cold War warriors, short-trousered enthusiasts (as the *Daily Telegraph* science correspondent observed), or whatever, no one can take away the tremendous pride we have all taken from being part of a little piece of history. I have taken some poetic license in the narrative here: the events depicted are all true but occurred during several tests in Nevada.

1. The United States was so impressed by the digital alpha technique that a U.S. version was being developed by Clayton Smith at Los Alamos, the prototype of which was ready for development when President Clinton's 1993 moratorium on tests came into effect.

2. Reg was absolutely correct. The signals for the experiment came in spot on within the reconfigured amplitude dynamic range.

20

GOVERNMENTS, SCIENTISTS, AND THE UK NUCLEAR WEAPONS PROGRAM

FRANK PANTON

It is now 50 years since I first became involved with the United Kingdom's nuclear weapons program. In this contribution I will offer a personal overview of the UK nuclear weapons scene from 1957 to 1976. In that process, I shall attempt to describe the part played by particular scientists in the program, their relationships to governments at the high policy and political level, as well as the dominating role played by the Mutual Defense Agreement (MDA) from 1958 onward and the U.S.-UK special nuclear relationship.

In 1957, after some years in Berlin attempting to obtain intelligence on matters such as the Russian exploitation of uranium ore mining in East Germany, I was posted to London to be the deputy head of a small unit in the Ministry of Defence (MOD) tasked with the collection and evaluation of intelligence on the Soviet nuclear weapons program. One of the unit's major activities, code-name Music, attempted the assessment of Soviet plutonium production through the amount of krypton 85 in the atmosphere generated by Soviet production reactors. This had started in the late 1940s and used a worldwide network of ground-based collection stations and aircraft sampling the atmosphere. For detection of nuclear explosions, the unit also ran a number of seismic and acoustic monitoring and debris collection stations both overseas and in the United Kingdom.

Within the MOD the unit reported directly to the chief scientific adviser (CSA), Sir Fred Brundrett. Its activities were overseen by a high-level scientific panel composed of the CSA, Sir John Chadwick,

Sir John Cockroft, and Sir William Penney. These activities were close-ly coordinated through the unit's representative in the Washington embassy with similar, but much larger, programs in the United States. Periodic U.S.-UK meetings were organized to discuss and review oper-ations, evaluations, and results. At these meetings, scientists from Har-well and Aldermaston would discuss with their U.S. opposites nuclear weapons programs, short of warhead design details.

The United Kingdom's contribution to the collective effort to obtain intelligence and information on the USSR's nuclear weapons program and assess its progress was highly thought of by the U.S. nuclear com-munity. The contacts between UK and U.S. nuclear scientific commu-nities, which this necessarily required, provided a valuable link in the lean time before the 1958 MDA. These relationships helped to ensure that U.S. nuclear scientists had had sufficient contact with their UK counterparts over the years in order to welcome deeper contacts with them on device design. The significance perceived in these contacts for the negotiation of the MDA is illustrated by the United Kingdom's decision to suspend action on both the cessation of the Music pro-gram and an internal reorganization of the other activities until after the MDA had been concluded and became operative.

By 1957, production and deployment of the United Kingdom's first fission weapon was under way, work was proceeding on the develop-ment of a thermonuclear device, and the United Kingdom had by its own efforts become an operational nuclear power. The impact on U.S.-UK nuclear relations of the discovery of nuclear spies in the United Kingdom in the early 1950s had subsided. Amendments in 1954 and 1955 to the U.S. Atomic Energy Act had already facilitated a slight ex-pansion of U.S.-UK cooperation, particularly over the joint assessment of Soviet nuclear capabilities. Sputnik had raised doubts in the Ameri-cans' minds about the superiority of their own technology. In the wake of the Suez crisis, a combination of President Dwight D. Eisenhower's willingness to be generous to the United Kingdom and Prime Minister Harold Macmillan's astute diplomatic exploitation of his old wartime friendship with the president contributed to significant progress to-ward full cooperation on nuclear warhead design.

As these exchanges were proceeding, negotiations on a Comprehen-sive Nuclear Test-Ban Treaty (CTBT) with an associated moratorium on nuclear testing began to gain momentum. Macmillan was as ar-dent a proponent of a comprehensive test ban as he was for a U.S.-UK nuclear design exchange agreement, and in 1958 he had the difficult task of pursuing simultaneously these two interconnected aims. The Americans had made it clear to Penney that this agreement would be possible politically only if the United Kingdom could demonstrate it had mastered the design of thermonuclear warheads. The United Kingdom's Grapple tests of 1957–1958 were mainly directed to that end.

The U.S.-USSR-UK experts meeting in autumn 1958 on methods of monitoring a CTBT concluded that such a treaty could be satisfactorily monitored, and test ban negotiations and a testing moratorium began. By that time, the 1958 MDA had been signed, providing the United Kingdom with satisfactory understandings on a nuclear submarine reactor purchase and the fuel to power it, in addition to design exchanges. These coveted results were attained through a combination of factors: Macmillan's relationship with the president, Eisenhower's willingness to impose his will on dissident factions within the U.S. government, and the recognition by the U.S. nuclear scientific community of the excellence and ability of their UK counterparts.

The role of Sir William Penney, director of Aldermaston Atomic Weapons Research Establishment (AWRE), was pivotal in both sets of technical negotiations. Assisted by his deputy, Sir William Cook, he achieved a thermonuclear design shortly before the test moratorium commenced. He was the leading UK member of the experts group that concluded that a test ban could be effectively monitored, bridging the gap between widely differing U.S. and USSR proposals and subsequently playing an important role in the working group on seismic detection capabilities. He was called upon on numerous occasions to advise Macmillan and his cabinet directly on both matters, advice that was invariably accepted by them. Penney's high standing in Macmillan's eyes was matched by the affection, trust, and high regard in which U.S. nuclear scientists held him: altogether the right man for the occasion.

Dr. Robert Press, then head of the UK nuclear monitoring organization, was the United Kingdom's expert adviser on the CTBT in 1958–1959. He went on to be Zuckerman's right-hand man on nuclear matters in the MOD and in the Cabinet Office, and after Zuckerman's retirement he continued to advise the Secretary of the Cabinet until he died in 1984. I myself succeeded Press in the Geneva negotiations and was in turn followed by Robert Snelling, also a member of the UK nuclear monitoring organization. Victor Macklen, as Sir Fred Brundrett's assistant in nuclear matters, played a key MOD headquarters role in the run-up to the 1958 agreement and in the first years of its implementation.

Thus, by the end of 1958, Macmillan had both achieved his "great prize"—the 1958 U.S.-UK agreement—and played a major part in the start of the CTBT negotiations. This situation lasted until September 1961, during which time a moratorium on testing was observed by the three countries. The arrangement came to a rather abrupt end when the USSR embarked on a huge series of nuclear tests in two locations.

ENHANCED COOPERATION

The initial flow of information from the United States to the United Kingdom under the MDA fully confirmed Eisenhower's statement to Macmillan that he would be as generous as possible in determining what could be exchanged. Not only designs but also detailed engineering drawings of U.S. warheads were handed over, and transactions for the supply of nuclear materials were satisfactorily agreed. The United Kingdom decided in the light of all this information that it would save time and possibly expense if it were to "Anglicize" proven U.S. designs to meet existing UK military requirements. This proved more difficult than first thought, owing in part to the need to substitute UK materials and practice for what the United States was doing, but it was satisfactorily accomplished. After 1961 both the United States and, with some hesitation, the United Kingdom resumed testing; after 1963 the testing was underground only, with the United Kingdom using the Nevada Test Site under the provisions of the 1958 agreement.

From 1958 to 1963 significant changes in the requirements for UK nuclear ordnance took place. Before 1958, AWRE was tasked with a range of requirements from the three services, including warheads for battlefield and tactical applications. Work on artillery shells, free-fall bombs, missiles of various types, and underwater depth charges proceeded under a bewildering number of code names, some of which may have referred to the same basic warhead design. By 1963, this had all changed. The United Kingdom's nuclear weapon program had been reduced to two systems only: the submarine-borne Polaris and the WE177 family of free-fall bombs (three varieties: 400 kilotons, 10 kilotons, and underwater depth charge).

An obvious factor contributing to these changes was the cancellation of the Blue Streak and then the Skybolt strategic delivery systems, with the subsequent U.S. agreement in 1962 to sell Polaris to the United Kingdom (Macmillan charmed another president!). This met the requirement for a UK strategic deterrent. The Royal Air Force was left equipped with U.S. bombs supplied under Project E, together with a supply of WE177s against targets mostly coordinated with, or integrated into, U.S. strike plans. No provision existed for UK-designed and -manufactured nuclear weapons for the British Army. Tactical and battlefield nuclear warheads were supplied by the United States to the United Kingdom and NATO under key-of-the-cupboard arrangements.

In 1964, Eric Younson, then in Zuckerman's section in MOD, visited the United States and told an assembled throng of interested representatives of U.S. nuclear weapons organizations that the United Kingdom had decided that its nuclear weapons program would consist of Polaris and the WE177 family. I had organized the meeting for him, at his request, and we both expected that there would be no more than about a dozen people present. More than 50 crowded in, and I think most of them were somewhat surprised at the modest size of the UK program compared with that of the United States and in the light of the aspirations voiced in 1958.

Nevertheless, the exchanges between AWRE and the U.S. nuclear laboratories proceeded apace until the Labour Party came to power in 1964. The party's manifesto of September 1964 cannot have encouraged the United States to view the continuation of the MDA exchanges with enthusiasm. It said of the UK Polaris force that "it will not be independent and it will not be British and it will not deter. . . . We are not prepared any longer to waste the country's resources on endless duplication of strategic nuclear weapons. We shall propose renegotiation of the Nassau Agreement." However, no wholesale renegotiation took place. Instead, it was proposed that internationalization of the UK strategic deterrent should be achieved through a new UK initiative, the Atlantic Nuclear Force (ANF).

In November 1964 Harold Wilson, the new UK prime minister, briefed the full cabinet on a decision to commit the Polaris submarine to the proposed ANF:

The precise number of these submarines would be for further consideration; but it was relevant to a decision that the construction of them was already sufficiently advanced to make it unrealistic to cancel the orders. On the other hand the number to be retained would be smaller than the number which the previous Government had envisaged and would be such as to make it clear that we no longer contemplated the maintenance of an independent nuclear force.

The Labour Party manifesto in March 1966 committed the party to stand by "its pledge to internationalize our strategic nuclear forces" through the proposed ANF. Unfortunately, or perhaps fortunately, this never materialized: it had been supported by the United Kingdom as an alternative to the Multilateral Force (MLF), which also did not materialize. It would seem that the one nuclear force—the ANF—sank another—the MLF—as well as itself without trace.

As a consequence, in August 1967, Denis Healey when he was secretary of state for defence implemented a decision and stated:

> In accordance with the Nassau Agreement our Polaris missiles will be assigned to NATO's supreme Allied Commander, as soon as the first submarine becomes operational, i.e., in 1968. Ultimate United Kingdom control of the Polaris Force will not be affected, since control of the firing chain will remain in UK hands; in particular, no submarine commander will be authorized to fire the Polaris weapons without the PM's specific authority.

Despite its 1964 pre-election manifesto to renegotiate the Nassau Agreement on UK Polaris, the Labour government finally in 1967 acted in accordance with that agreement while in effect retaining the UK finger on the button.

Other developments in the mid-1960s had a more direct impact on nuclear exchanges at the technical level. Zuckerman, the senior UK member of the technical exchanges under the MDA, told the U.S. participants at a U.S.-UK stocktake meeting in 1965 that the United Kingdom had no interest in research into new nuclear warhead systems beyond Polaris. From that point, up-to-date information from the United States under the joint working groups and exchange links began to dry up and then effectively ceased for a time in 1967 after Prime Minister Wilson stated that the United Kingdom had no interest in Poseidon as a potential second-generation submarine-launched ballistic missile deterrent.

This situation was exacerbated by two additional problems. The first was AWRE's need for an ongoing research program, including nuclear tests, to keep abreast of developments in nuclear design and the science of deterrence and to make sufficient contributions to the nuclear exchanges to ensure that the U.S. interest in them would continue. Apart from one UK test explosion in Nevada in 1964 related to the Polaris warhead, the planned nuclear testing program proposed by AWRE to the incoming Labour government was canceled. This decision was a disappointment not only to AWRE but also to the U.S. nuclear laboratories. The second problem was that antiballistic missile (ABM) developments in the United States and the USSR raised questions about the continuing capability of the UK Polaris force to penetrate possible future Soviet ABM defenses. To assess how serious this problem might be, basic data on vulnerability were needed from the United States. This had been specifically excluded in the Polaris Sales Agreement (PSA), and the drying up of up-to-date information from the United States under the MDA in the second half of the 1960s precluded obtaining it through that channel.

In the wake of disagreements with Denis Healey over what measures might be taken to maintain AWRE's expertise and to sustain exchanges with the United States under the MDA, a fresh approach became possible in 1967 when Sir Solly Zuckerman moved to the Cabinet Office. Sir William Cook took his place, and he brought back Victor Macklen from the UK Atomic Energy Authority at Risley to replace Dr. Robert Press as assistant chief scientific adviser (nuclear). With Healey's support, and despite determined opposition from Zuckerman in his new role as scientific adviser to the cabinet, Sir William set in train an examination of the vulnerability of the UK nuclear deterrent force and how to improve its ability to penetrate possible USSR defenses. The work was headed by AWRE, under the leadership of Peter Jones, who subsequently became its director. U.S. cooperation was obtained with some difficulty and, as a consequence, exchanges under the MDA were effectively resumed by the early 1970s, assisted by the outgoing Labour government's decision in 1970 to opt for Super Antelope as the system to improve Polaris.

The incoming Heath government in 1970 spent three years in a fruitless exploration of the possibilities of collaboration with the French.

This was managed and conducted on the British side at high levels. Because of the extremely close links with the United States on nuclear weapons and associated technology, the United Kingdom recognized that it would need to gain U.S. acceptance before it discussed with the French any topics involving U.S. information. This prevented discussions from going much further than political and doctrinal issues. For their part, the French were unwilling to contemplate any arrangements they perceived as threatening the independent control of their nuclear forces and programs. When it became clear that no formal agreement could be concluded with the French, assessments were made in the United Kingdom of various modes of enhancing the capabilities of the UK submarine-based deterrent, including Poseidon and Super Antelope, through cooperation with the United States. The decision by the Heath government in 1973 to opt for Chevaline effectively terminated thoughts of nuclear cooperation with the French in the short and medium terms although some form of longer-term cooperation was not ruled out.

With hindsight, it may be thought that time was not entirely wasted on this exploration of possibilities for cooperation with the French. Edward Heath achieved his aim of taking the United Kingdom into the European Economic Community (EEC), with no opposition from the French. The Chevaline program made progress, albeit on drip funding; and the UK attempt to explore cooperation with the French may have stimulated the United States to begin to offer advice—without strings attached—on some aspects of the U.S. nuclear program, so the French may also have gained something from these exchanges.

CHEVALINE

It is both useful and interesting to review in some detail the Heath government's convoluted path toward the Chevaline decision. In November 1972, when the MOD reported on both the Super Antelope Project Definition Programme and two other options for Polaris improvement, it seemed premature to pass over these alternatives—Poseidon and Stag (a Poseidon without its multiple independently targetable reentry vehicles [MIRVs])—without sounding out the United States to see whether the MIRV technology could be made available. Henry Kissinger, at the time the national security adviser to President Richard M. Nixon, produced the expected answer that in the present climate of détente there would be congressional difficulties over the release of a fully MIRVed Poseidon, but he was far more positive about the sale of a de-MIRVed version. A UK request was subsequently made to the president for the purchase of the de-MIRVed Poseidon.

In February 1973, at a meeting between Dr. James Schlesinger, then head of the U.S. Atomic Energy Commission, and Sir Herman Bondi, CSA, MOD, further complications were generated when Schlesinger increased the range of options to six, including the three already under consideration. One new option was to fit up to ten U.S.-designed warheads manufactured in the United Kingdom into a de-MIRVed Poseidon. This option M solution began to be favored by MOD, partly because it was based on proven U.S. designs and partly because it would offer a capability of penetrating possible USSR endoatmospheric defenses. Supporting data on costs and timescales of four of the options (Poseidon and Chevaline being the exceptions) were relatively sketchy, however, and in March 1973 and again in July 1973 Victor Macklen was sent to Washington with a small team of UK experts to obtain further information.

It emerged that a new dispenser system would have to be developed to fit warheads and decoys to a de-MIRVed Poseidon M, thus increasing its cost and complexity. Option M thus appeared to be no more than a concept, based on little or no feasibility or development work. Doubts were also arising at this time about the reliability of the Poseidon missile itself. The uncertainty of these matters made technical evaluation and comparative costs of solutions involving Poseidon, MIRVed or de-MIRVed, difficult to arrive at. In December 1973, a decision finally to opt for Chevaline was made, but it was left to the new Labour government in February 1974 to decide whether that decision should be implemented.

Sir William Cook and Sir Solly Zuckerman retired from their posts in the MOD and in the Cabinet Office, respectively, by 1971. Sir William abstained from further involvement in the debate on Polaris improvement, but Sir Solly retained an office in the Cabinet Office and continued intermittently to make interventions on the subject well into the 1980s. Wilson's incoming Labour government in March 1974 again reviewed options for improvement of UK Polaris (not including Poseidon, consideration of which was ruled out by MOD), to see whether a cheaper solution could be found or whether savings could be made on the increasing costs of the Chevaline program. Cheaper alternatives were judged unable to meet the "Moscow criteria" for deterrence despite the limits of USSR ABM deployments specified by the 1972 Anti-Ballistic Missile Treaty and the 1974 protocol. One more year of funding for Chevaline was authorized, pending a MOD review.

It is fascinating to read how Prime Minister Wilson explained to the full cabinet in November 1974 his decision to proceed with Chevaline and retain a credible nuclear deterrent:

> . . .If we were to retain the strategic nuclear force it must be a credible deterrent. The improvements necessary to ensure the continuing credibility of the present force were relatively cheap; they would not involve either a new generation of missiles or the introduction of Multiple Independently Targeted Re-entry Vehicles. The essential question was whether to retain the Polaris force or to reverse the policy followed in the past and abandon it. The Defence and Overseas Policy Committee had unanimously decided that it should be retained. For our European allies it represented an insurance against a breakdown in the credibility of the United States Strategic Nuclear Guarantee. If we abandoned our deterrent France would be the only country in Europe with a strategic nuclear capability and this was not committed to NATO. Such a situation would be particularly disquieting to other members of NATO and especially to the Germans. In normal times, our possession of the nuclear deterrent gave us a unique entree to United States thinking and the possibility of influencing this, not only in nuclear matters, including strategic arms limitation, but over a very wide politico/strategic field. In times of tension, it provided us with a unique opportunity to influence events both in Washington and in Moscow and counsel moderation. For this country it provided, in the worst case, the best protection against risk of nuclear attack or blackmail. . . .

As a set of cogent political arguments for retaining and improving UK Polaris, this was convincing, albeit coming from the leader of the party that a few years previously had declared in its policy manifesto the intention not to waste the country's resources any longer on endless duplication of strategic nuclear weapons.

This review of the years 1957 to 1976 should also acknowledge three other factors that impinged on the United Kingdom's nuclear weapons program. First, in the late 1950s and in the 1960s the possibility of an international agreement on a cutoff of the production of fissile material production for weapons purposes, together with an inspections regime to ensure the operation of such an agreement, was a constant source of worry. The United Kingdom was having difficulty in meeting the fissile material demands generated by its production program. Barter and supply arrangements made with the United States and the emphasis in the testing program on proving designs that would reduce fissile material requirements were two methods of softening the blow if a cutoff should occur. Also, implementing an acceptable cutoff inspection regime would have been difficult because of the dual civil-military nature of the United Kingdom's production facilities. Although much time and energy were spent by the UK departments concerned with the matter, a cutoff was never agreed.

Two other problems of great potential significance to the United Kingdom loomed in the period from 1969 to 1973. There was a danger that U.S.-USSR agreements arising out of the bilateral SALT negotiations might result in a no-transfer clause that might prohibit or limit UK-U.S. cooperation under the MDA, the PSA, or both. There was also a danger that agreed ABM deployments might inhibit the ability of UK Polaris, or its improvement, to penetrate their targets in the USSR. Again, much effort on various levels was made by the United Kingdom to ensure that the United States would keep British interests firmly in mind in pursuing the negotiations with the USSR. This effort paid off. No no-transfer clause emerged, and the number of ABMs permitted to be deployed could be overcome by Chevaline.

CONCLUSION

In reviewing the progress of the United Kingdom's nuclear weapons program during 1957–1976, what broad observations have I to offer?

Despite what may have been said in pre-election manifestos, no UK government wanted to move toward relinquishing possession of a credible independent nuclear deterrent. The principal reason was the international standing and leverage the possession of a nuclear deterrent provided, especially the possible influence over U.S. policy. Factors relevant to reaching decisions on maintaining the deterrent included costs in relation to overall defense costs; possible effects on relations with France, the EEC, and NATO; the need to sustain a program of work at AWRE sufficiently relevant to maintain exchanges with the United States under the MDA; the need for the UK deterrent force to maintain its credibility; and the need to pursue in parallel an active program of a nuclear test ban, arms control, and disarmament.

Essential to the UK program in these years were the 1958 MDA and the 1963 PSA. It is doubtful whether a credible independent UK nuclear deterrent would have survived the 1960s without them. Nuclear disarmament and arms control measures were supported in varying degrees by successive UK governments, but not to the extent that the continued possession of a credible nuclear deterrent was, or might have been, challenged. Each government discussed nuclear weapon policy issues within a small group of ministers, mostly those immediately concerned. Rarely was the whole cabinet involved, except perhaps to approve decisions reached within the small group. This was particularly true of Labour governments, which always had to reckon with a significant number of unilateralists and antinuclear members within the party, the parliamentary party, and the government.

Transitions between UK governments required briefing of, and further investigation by, fresh ministers. It usually took at least about six months before the views of the new government could be obtained. Such downtime was not conducive to the efficient and cost-effective work of the nuclear warhead and weapon program. In the period from 1965 to about 1971 little or no new information on subjects such as vulnerability was transmitted to the United Kingdom from the United States. Had this shutdown proceeded much longer, and had a vulnerability study by the United Kingdom with U.S. cooperation not started in 1970, AWRE's capabilities would have become suspect and the operational aspects of the MDA could have been terminated.

Throughout the time under review, a relatively small number of scientists in the higher levels of the scientific civil service kept the UK nuclear warhead and weapons program alive and relevant in difficult circumstances, supplying technical advice and guidance in an impartial manner to enable political decisions on the program to be taken. Among these may be noted Lord Penney, Sir W. Cook, Dr. R. Press, V. H. B. Macklen, assisted by F. H. Panton and D. Fakley. Among the key players at AWRE were E. F. Newley, J. Challens, P. G. E. F. Jones, and S. Orman; and from RAE, F. East and R. Dommett.

21

THE ROLE OF NUCLEAR
SUBMARINE PROPULSION

STEVE LUDLAM

Although the Mutual Defense Agreement (MDA) is probably best known for providing Britain access to U.S. nuclear weapons technology and test sites, nuclear propulsion technology was also a vital part of the arrangements. The agreement provided for the export to the United Kingdom of a complete submarine nuclear propulsion plant and its uranium fuel. If the United Kingdom were to develop a nuclear propulsion program, could it have been done alone? Was the mutual respect that had been formed in wartime the catalyst for the exchange of nuclear propulsion technology, or was it forged by personal respect between individuals, well documented over the years?

FORMATIVE YEARS

In world history 1945 was a remarkable year and was particularly so for U.S.-UK nuclear relations. The untimely death of President Franklin D. Roosevelt in April was met with sadness and shock on both sides of the Atlantic and was a severe blow to Winston Churchill. Their friendship, forged over the previous five years, had set the pattern for the whole joint war effort and was the foundation of "the most comprehensive unification of military effort ever achieved by two allied states."[1] It extended beyond the normal military collaboration to take in the building of the atomic bomb, a project so well guarded by the two leaders that their successors knew little or nothing about it.

By the end of August 1945, World War II was over and the overwhelming power of the atomic bomb had been witnessed for the first time. In 1941 Britain had transferred its nuclear work (mostly theoretical) to the U.S. project, and when, in 1946, Congress passed the U.S. Atomic Energy Act, better known as the McMahon Act after its sponsor, ". . .the door to collaboration was almost, though not quite, hermetically barred."[2] This effectively prevented any supply of nuclear information or materials to other countries, including Britain.

The British government of the time quickly realized that it would have to plough its own furrow on nuclear research if it were to achieve membership of the world's nuclear nations. This power did not have to be used destructively; it could also be harnessed to replace coal, difficult to extract and a major pollutant. "Atoms for peace" became the slogan of the hour, accompanied by dreams of limitless, clean, cheap power. Britain started its own research program based at Harwell, near Oxford, and in 1947 the first graphite-moderated research reactor went critical. Work then began on fuel production, and the decision was made that gas-cooled reactors would be the type used for British commercial energy production. By the end of 1950, the first Windscale reactor was critical, and the United Kingdom's energy program was gaining pace.

With the outbreak of the Korean War that year, various programs were accelerated, and in 1952 the first UK atomic bomb was detonated. The British Ministry of Supply had learned of the experiments with nuclear propulsion for aircraft then being carried out in the United States, and the Ministry suggested a leading British aero-engine manufacturer should be associated with the Harwell group, but there were also other possibilities. Rolls-Royce formally started nuclear propulsion studies in the same year.

The Admiralty, through the department of the Engineer in Chief, had maintained since the end of the Second World War a watching brief on the possibility of nuclear propulsion for warships. When President Harry S. Truman announced to the world in 1952 that the keel had been laid for the U.S. Navy's first nuclear-powered submarine and that he had awarded the Legion of Merit to the project's leader, Captain Hyman G. Rickover, the Admiralty's enthusiasm significantly increased for a project of Britain's own. They strengthened the Royal Navy team at Harwell, where theoretical studies had already persuaded them that the pressurized water reactor (PWR) was the most suitable for a submarine, independently reaching the same conclusion as the

Lord Louis Mountbatten, 1st Earl Mountbatten of Burma, was appointed First Sea Lord in 1955.
© Getty Images, Hulton Archive.

U.S. team. Separately, Lord Hives, the Rolls-Royce Chairman, widened his Derby-based team's terms of reference to include a marine dimension as well as aircraft nuclear systems. He could then bring the project to the Admiralty's attention—and they, it appeared, were prepared to invest in a nuclear submarine program.

The task before the team was a challenging one, as Alex Smith, a key member of the team, said at the time: "Trying to design something when you have the knowledge that somebody else has already done it is a very different proposition from probing around trying to assess the feasibility of an idea. There is no question of whether or not it is possible. You know it can be done. It is knowledge which both helps a designer, and yet raises apprehension in him that he may be found wanting, that he may be unable to find out how it can be done."[3]

DEFINING ROYAL NAVY POLICY

Lord Louis Mountbatten, 1st Earl Mountbatten of Burma, appointed First Sea Lord in 1955, had already devoted much time to a review of possible future roles for the Royal Navy. He had concluded that, of several proposed new warships, only the nuclear submarine provided sufficient improvement in performance over existing designs to justify the very high costs involved.

In October 1955 Mountbatten visited the United States to meet Admiral Arleigh Burke, the U.S. Chief of Naval Operations, and to discuss Anglo-American naval cooperation. Burke intended to take Mountbatten for a trip in the newly commissioned USS *Nautilus,* the U.S.

Rear Admiral Hyman G. Rickover (circa 1955), acknowledged by many as the visionary behind the successful U.S. nuclear propulsion program. Photo courtesy U.S. Naval Historical Foundation.

Navy's first nuclear submarine. Rickover—nominally Burke's subordinate—vetoed the plan.

This was probably the first time anyone from Britain had experienced the formidable, and now promoted to Rear Admiral, Hyman Rickover. No doubt Rickover would have cited the 1954 Atomic Energy Act, a slight watering down of the McMahon Act, if anyone had dared question his decision. Those who knew him say he was a staunch Republican who distrusted all aristocratic titles, especially royal ones.

With the increasing pressure of the Cold War, early in 1956 the U.S. government amended the 1954 regulations. Information and advice as well as the specialized materials needed for nuclear energy research and development could now be supplied to friendly countries. This relaxation of the rules and access to some of the technology was to be invaluable to Britain.

Rickover visited London in August 1956 for his first personal meeting with Mountbatten. To everyone's surprise, these two strong-minded individuals got on very well together. Sources in the U.S. Navy reported that ". . .the introvert iconoclast from the Ukraine . . . fell under the spell of Queen Victoria's great grandson. . . ." It also seems likely that Rickover had learned that Mountbatten was a professional engineer and member of the Institution of Electronics and Radio Engineers, as well as a fighting sailor. Lord Hood, at the British embassy in Washington, later described Rickover's reaction to their meetings as "the decisive factor in our cooperation" and said it was largely due to "the personal efforts of the First Sea Lord."[4]

In the autumn of 1957 the USS *Nautilus* took part in the NATO Rum Tub exercise, escorting the British aircraft carrier HMS *Bulwark,* defending it from conventional submarine attacks. At the conclusion of the exercise Admiral Sir John Eccles, Commander in Chief of the Royal Navy home fleet, reported that "so long as *Nautilus* behaved in a conventional manner, our equipment came up to expectations, but just as soon as she developed her full capabilities she had the freedom of the seas . . . the only real answer to a nuclear submarine is another one . . . time is not on our side."[5] In 1958 *Nautilus* became the first submarine to travel beneath the ice at the North Pole.

FIRST RESEARCH REACTOR

In January 1956 the Admiralty sent a letter of intent to place a contract for a prototype set of nuclear submarine machinery to Vickers Armstrong (Engineers) Ltd. as the main contractor; it named Rolls-Royce Ltd. for design and production of the reactor and Foster Wheeler Ltd. for the steam-raising units. The Admiralty defined their requirements as a land-based prototype with a complete propulsion system installed in a section of submarine hull, with a target date for criticality of January 1960. The first production plant for a submarine would follow with criticality by mid-1962.

The Derby-based nuclear reactor team was now able to focus on a project that involved the production of a piece of nuclear engineering hardware, a naval reactor plant for research purposes. It was to be built to a properly defined specification, with delivery by a date agreed in advance. The construction of the Neptune zero-energy research reactor and the associated test rigs at Harwell involved the theoretical knowledge and practical experience of all disciplines represented by the company. It was first taken critical in November 1957 and had cost £233,000 (at 1957 prices). Neptune was subsequently moved to Derby and recommissioned in 1963.

In early 1957 a Contractors Derby Team was formed, to be the focus of the design and procurement work for the prototype plant that would be later known as the Dounreay Submarine Prototype (DSMP). At around the same time Harold Macmillan became Prime Minister and U.S.-UK relations returned to near their wartime high. He and President Dwight D. Eisenhower had been involved in the allied landings in North Africa in 1942 and were firm friends. The two concluded a conference in Bermuda in March by signing an agreement to deploy intermediate ballistic missiles on British soil: ". . .the two elderly gentlemen relished their reunion . . . chatting of old times and new challenges. Eisenhower . . . later said the meeting had been 'by far the most successful international conference I had attended since the close of World War II.'"[6]

Admiral Rickover returned to the United Kingdom in May 1957 to review the current state of the British project at Rolls-Royce, Foster Wheeler, and, particularly, at Harwell. One positive outcome was an invitation for a team from the British project to visit the United States a month later, to tour the various establishments involved in the U.S. Navy's nuclear program. Rickover arranged the schedule personally to ensure they had a thorough but extremely grueling trip.

In July 1957 Vickers was instructed to proceed with the building of Britain's first nuclear submarine, with the reactor plant and a second core to be manufactured by Rolls-Royce. The submarine would be named *Dreadnought,* after the modern capital ships that had been the ultimate expression of sea power in the early twentieth century.

RICKOVER'S PROPOSALS

Rickover's next visit was early the following year. Before his first meeting with senior members of the nuclear submarine project, he joined Mountbatten for a private discussion. In his own words, "I asked Mountbatten whether the British Admiralty wanted to satisfy its pride, or whether it desired to build a nuclear submarine as quickly as possible. He replied that he wanted to get a nuclear submarine as quickly as possible."

As is now well documented, he suggested that Britain should have access to all available U.S. information and, in addition, should be allowed to purchase a complete submarine reactor. Lord Mountbatten accepted his offer on the spot, but his decision met with general disapproval from senior members of the Admiralty and the Royal Navy, who were reluctant to agree to the implied increase of Rickover's influence.

Rickover had insisted that negotiations for the design and manufacture of the U.S. Navy's nuclear submarines should be handled by commercial companies rather than by government agencies. Moreover, he believed that conventional shipbuilding organizations were too conservative in their outlook and so preferred to place orders for nuclear work with engineering companies. After all, he was himself an engineer! He indicated that he expected the Royal Navy to adopt the same practice and appoint a British engineering company to lead Britain's nuclear project.

In fact, this was not such a revolutionary proposal as it seemed. Within the Admiralty it had already been suggested that Rolls-Royce, an engineering company with a track record in the design and manufacture of small engines, should lead the British project. Rolls-Royce was already contributing nuclear engineering expertise to the Vickers nuclear engineering organization and had demonstrated competence with engineering hardware such as the Neptune reactor that Rickover would have seen during his visit to Harwell. There was already a bilateral agreement between Westinghouse and Rolls-Royce, signed in 1953, for the exchange of classified data concerning gas turbine engines; this, it was hoped, would be both a precedent and a model for any similar agreement on nuclear power.

Following the London discussions, Rickover went to meet senior Rolls-Royce and Admiralty personnel. Having explained his proposals for increased Anglo-American cooperation to the research group in the splendid surroundings of Duffield Bank House in Derby, Rickover went for more detailed discussions with the management. He always insisted on dealing with a company's chief engineer, at the time a title held by Adrian Lombard, a respected pioneer of gas turbines. By his own admission he knew little of nuclear power and was therefore supported by the chairman, Lord Hives. Rickover distrusted any company director with an aristocratic title, but fortunately he learned that Hives was not an administrator but an experienced engineer—or, as Hives himself put it, "a bloody mechanic"—who had initiated the nuclear submarine project from the start. At this, Rickover gradually relaxed and listened to the explanations of the company's standards and the methods employed to maintain them.

It was during this time in Derby that Rickover damaged his electric razor and asked his hosts whether they could get it repaired. The razor was sent to the electronics laboratory, where it was a routine task to rewind the burnt-out coil; it was handed back to the admiral as he went to lunch. He thanked the company, expressed surprise at their promptness, and admitted that he had temporarily forgotten the warning not to use the device on the British 240-volt mains.

This visit was followed almost immediately by a return British visit to organize the agreement's implementation. A member of the team was particularly impressed by two aspects of the trip—the tight security imposed by their U.S. hosts at all times and the genuine panic at the Westinghouse plant when they learned Rickover was planning a visit.

At some stage the British team was advised that the U.S. offer had been revised. Instead of the S3W reactor, they would have the option of purchasing the latest S5W reactor, as installed in the USS *Skipjack,* lead ship of its class and recently launched. However, there would no longer be an unconditional supply of technical information, only what was necessary to construct, operate, and maintain the plant.

1958 BILATERAL AGREEMENT

In the aftermath of the first Sputnik launch and the increasing sophistication of the Soviet threat, the most urgent task now rested with the diplomats to organize the necessary changes to the Atomic Energy Act of 1954 to allow the commercial negotiations for the S5W reactor procurement to proceed.

By 1958 the relationship between the U.S. and UK governments had returned to near its wartime high. The Bilateral Agreement for Cooperation on the Uses of Atomic Energy for Mutual Defense Purposes, better known as the 1958 Bilateral Agreement, between the governments of the United Kingdom and the United States was drawn up and passed into law by Congress on August 4, 1958.

Following these prolonged meetings and discussions, it was announced that Rolls-Royce had negotiated a contract with Westinghouse to purchase the completed submarine machinery and that a license agreement gave them and the Admiralty the design philosophy and detailed information concerning the reactor portion of the propulsion machinery.

After nearly ten months of negotiations, Rickover had managed to persuade all interested parties to implement the policies he had agreed with Mountbatten in 1957. It reveals a side to his character that is seldom mentioned—his considerable political skills, often involving a great deal of patience and tolerance to ensure that everyone was satisfied. He seems to have been an excellent judge of those he could provoke and insult safely—and of those whom he needed to placate! There is a general agreement among his contemporaries that he was anxious that Britain, with its limited resources of materials and money, should benefit from the U.S. knowledge and at the same time learn to "stand on her own feet," as Mountbatten wished. He did not believe it was in

HMS *Dreadnought*, Britain's first nuclear-powered submarine, was launched in October 1960. Photo courtesy Royal Navy Submarine Museum.

Britain's best interest to become too dependent on continued support from the United States.

It was recognized that new working arrangements would also be needed to undertake the work. The Westinghouse Electric Company would negotiate and give licenses to no one other than Rolls-Royce, and it was essential to bring shipbuilding and steam-raising knowledge into the project. It was decided by the three partners (Rolls-Royce, Vickers, and Foster-Wheeler) that they would form a joint company that would manage not only the procurement of the machinery from the United States but also the procurement and design of future nuclear propulsive equipment for the Royal Navy. This company would be known as Rolls-Royce & Associates Limited (RR&A).

With the agreement signed, the pace of progress in the U.K. nuclear propulsion program changed completely. The supply of one complete (S5W) reactor plant meant that the Royal Navy's first nuclear submarine, HMS *Dreadnought,* could be completed two or three years early and would be a composite design. From the reactor compartment aft would be the U.S.-supplied equipment, with the UK design forward. The U.K. prototype program DSMP would continue at Dounreay in Scotland.

In 1959 RR&A was formed to manage the supply of the Westinghouse reactor; Babcock & Wilcox (pressure vessels) joined in 1967. Rolls-Royce was in charge of supply of the overall system design, reactor core, and control equipment, with Foster Wheeler responsible for component supply. Vickers-Armstrong (Shipbuilders) Ltd. was responsible for the hull and integrating the systems. The employees of three different companies had to be united into a single group. Over time, the partners withdrew their support, and RR&A became a wholly owned subsidiary of Rolls-Royce, taking full control of the nuclear technology and development and becoming the design authority for the naval nuclear reactor in 1992.

With such a complex plant there were inevitable delays, some owing to acts of generosity from Westinghouse, which exceeded the terms of its agreement by advising the Royal Navy of all modifications learned from the U.S. Navy's experience with the S5W plant in service. But the Royal Navy's first nuclear submarine was a well publicized and prestigious project; it was therefore afforded the highest priority to ensure all work was completed to program. HMS *Dreadnought* was launched on schedule by Queen Elizabeth II at Barrow-in-Furness on Trafalgar Day, October 21, 1960, and commissioned there in 1963.

POLARIS AND THE FIRST ALL-BRITISH NUCLEAR SUBMARINE

In 1959 doubts had begun to surface about the "concept of ballistic rockets fired from a fixed and therefore vulnerable site,"[7] and in 1960, while visiting Washington for test ban negotiations, Prime Minister Harold Macmillan had meaningful talks with President Eisenhower that concluded with no firm offer of Polaris submarine-launched missiles (then under development) but an informal agreement that it might be arranged later if necessary. Reminded of this fact in 1962, President John F. Kennedy, perhaps influenced by the bond forged between them during the Cuban missile crisis, eventually agreed to supply Polaris missiles to Britain. In a letter to Macmillan after illness had forced him to stand down as Prime Minister, President Kennedy wrote: "In the three years of cooperation, we have worked together on great and small issues, and we have never had a failure of understanding or mutual trust. I believe the world is a little more safe and the future for freedom more hopeful than when we began. . . ."[8]

In early 1963, the Polaris Sales Agreement was signed. The United States would provide the missiles and Britain would build its own deterrent submarines and develop a new generation of warheads: the U.K. strategic deterrent would transfer from the Royal Air Force to the Royal Navy. The success of the collaboration led to the amendment of the Polaris Sales Agreement in 1980 to facilitate the sale of Trident missiles. The agreement remains in place today and is set to continue long into the twenty-first century.

Knowledge of S5W, extensive training, U.S. data on ship nuclear propulsion, experience with the Dounreay prototype, together with commitment and innovation were all pooled to produce the PWR1 plant and the first British-built submarine reactor core. The first submarine PWR1 plant with a UK core was destined for HMS *Valiant,* the first nuclear submarine completely built in the United Kingdom and commissioned in 1966. But with the Cold War at its height, the cancellation of the Skybolt air-launched weapon, and the change to Polaris, four submarines capable of launching the new deterrent had to be designed and built very quickly. To meet the Royal Navy's aggressive build program, two build yards had to be used, each building two submarines. In what can only be viewed as a remarkable achievement, HMS *Resolution* was launched in September 1966 and Polaris patrols commenced in June 1968, a strategy that put Britain's nuclear deterrent at sea and has remained a cornerstone of government naval policy ever since. Before the turn of the decade, all four Polaris submarines were in service, and by 1971 a total of ten nuclear submarines were operational.

The quest for continual improvement was a key program driver and had seen work on longer-life reactor core designs start in 1962. A series of new reactor cores was developed, with each new concept of reactor design being built and tested in the Neptune zero-energy reactor to prove the design before being tested at power in DSMP at Dounreay.

THE DETERRENT AND PWR2

During the late 1970s it became apparent that a second-generation and much larger deterrent submarine would be required to carry the significantly larger Trident D5 missiles. Therefore, a more powerful reactor would be needed, and developments in nuclear technology together with changing safety standards had to be incorporated. Design of PWR2 began in 1977, and with the project's arrival the need for a specific prototype was also recognized. A new shore test facility (STF) was built to house the PWR2 plant at Dounreay alongside the existing DSMP. STF, or Vulcan (its more widely used naval name), was completed to program and budget in 1986. HMS *Vanguard,* the first submarine to be powered by a PWR2 plant and equipped with a significantly larger core, was commissioned in 1993. Its submerged displacement of

16,000 tons was twice that of the earlier Resolution-class Polaris submarines. The original PWR2 reactor core has now been replaced with the long-life core designed to last the life of the submarine and is the standard fit for the Astute class. Work is now under way to develop the nuclear propulsion plant for a new class of successor submarine that is scheduled to replace the Vanguard class beginning in 2024.

The Polaris and now the Trident submarine deterrent, powered by Rolls-Royce nuclear reactors, has kept unbroken deterrent patrols since it took over the RAF's strategic role in the late 1960s. This continuous service is testament to the British and U.S. ability to work together in the nuclear submarine community.

CONCLUSION

The long-standing relationship between the United States and the United Kingdom facilitated a nuclear submarine solution for Britain. I have no doubt that, based on the evidence, Britain could have done it alone. However, the foresight, friendship, diplomacy, and drive of a few outstanding individuals ensured the timely introduction of Britain's nuclear submarine flotilla, an achievement that helped deliver some balance in the evolving strategic circumstances of the 1960s and continues to contribute today.

NOTES

1. John Baylis, *Anglo-American Defence Relations 1939-1980: The Special Relationship* (London: Macmillan, 1981), p. 9.
2. Sir Roger Makins, ambassador to Washington from 1953 to 1956 and chairman of the UK Atomic Energy Authority from 1960 to 1964; quoted in Ibid., p. 28.
3. Sir Alex Smith, *Lock Up the Swings on Sunday* (London: Memoir Club, 1998).
4. P. Zeigler, *Mountbatten, The Official Biography* (Glasgow: William Collins and Sons, 1990), p. 557.
5. J. O. Coote, "The Only Answer to a Nuclear Submarine Is Another One," *The Submariner's World,* 1983.
6. Martin Walker, *The Cold War and the Making of the Modern World* (London: Fourth Estate, 1993), p. 118.
7. Harold Macmillan, *Pointing the Way 1959–1961* (London: Macmillan, 1972), p. 255.
8. Harold Macmillan, *At the End of the Day 1961–1963* (London: Macmillan, 1973), p. 517.

Part Four

STRATEGIC PERSPECTIVES THROUGH ORAL HISTORY
ABSTRACTS OF INTERVIEWS WITH CURRENT AND FORMER SENIOR OFFICIALS AND SCIENTISTS

AUDIO FILES OF INTERVIEWS ARE AVAILABLE AT
WWW.CSIS.ORG/ISP/PONI/US-UK

DES BROWNE
UK SECRETARY OF STATE FOR DEFENCE

Des Browne began his parliamentary career in 1997, after being elected as member of parliament for Kilmarnock. Following the 2001 general election, he was appointed to the Northern Ireland Office as parliamentary under-secretary, with responsibility for the criminal justice system and issues of human rights. In 2003, Browne was promoted in a cabinet reshuffle to minister for work, at the Department of Work and Pensions. One year later, he became minister for immigration. In 2005, Browne entered the general election as minister of state for citizenship and immigration. Following the election, Browne became the chief secretary for the treasury. In 2006 Browne became secretary of state for defence, where he remains today.

Browne, appreciating the strength of European alliances, is acutely aware of a uniquely significant relationship across the Atlantic. "We consistently are more comfortable with the United States as an ally than almost any other country in the world," he remarked. This special relationship is therefore premised upon more than merely a common history. "We have that relationship for very obvious historical reasons but it is sustained by our shared values and the trust that we have in each other, which is quite substantial." This confidence in one another, he asserts, has always been at the heart of the Mutual Defense Agreement (MDA). "It seems to me," Browne continued, "that the MDA came about because the politicians both here and in the U.S. recognized that mutually there would be defense benefits from close cooperation. We both had something to bring to this."

The benefits that cooperation, under the auspices of MDA, continues to provide are a source of great pride for Browne. A notable highlight was the recent exchange of letters, regarding the future of the UK's deterrent requirements, between the prime minister and the president of the United States, in 2006. The ease with which both countries were able to conclude and determine such an important exchange was of major significance. "I think that is a particularly important achievement for us and was underpinned by these 50 years of cooperation." This cooperation is, however, much more than just an agreement to disseminate knowledge. Cooperation, according to Browne, is extremely useful for the maintenance of safe, secure, and reliable nuclear warheads. "We live in an environment of the Comprehensive Nuclear Test-Ban Treaty, so we accept that obligation to rely on stewardship of a stockpile by the development of a science-based program, because we deny ourselves live testing."

It is important, however, to appreciate the limits within the MDA. Beyond the obvious difficulties of opening up an exchange of sensitive national security information there remain more inherent challenges to cooperation. "At the end of the day, we have a strategic requirement, and I think a political requirement also, to maintain a sovereign capability in certain areas, and that will limit the degree of mutual interdependence," Browne said. Further, although the MDA predates other agreements, such as the Nuclear Non-Proliferation Treaty (NPT), it has to remain consistent with these wider restrictions. "Nuclear collaboration," he continued, "is aimed at harmonizing potential requirements and solutions, but it has to be carried out in the context of each party's own laws."

Accepting that the Anglo-American relationship has evolved, Browne strongly rejects simplified assessments of the MDA's development. "I don't actually think the character of it has changed. The implementation of it has, because the environment in which we are working has changed." He continued, "The focus in the early years was about gaining the maximum yield for the minimum warhead size and weight. But now, what we seek to do with this agreement is to maximize the confidence in the safety, security, and operation of nuclear weaponry." Thus, although broader ambitions remain the consistent focus of the MDA, Anglo-American nuclear relations retain a strong degree of flexibility. "The agreement has stayed true to its character in terms of cooperation but been flexible enough for us to be able to modify what we do, to address the different strategic environment," he explained.

As the world has changed, Browne emphasizes that Britain's nuclear commitments have not. "Our ambition is to use the dynamic of the NPT and our privileged position in that," he said. "But we take responsibility that we have to drive the world forward to a world free of nuclear weapons." The MDA thereby serves to empower Browne's recent speech in Geneva, regarding the pressing need for international cooperation regarding the twin challenges of disarmament and proliferation. "We have this collaboration and 50 years of it with the U.S. to our mutual advantage to point, interestingly, to other countries to say this is what working together generates."

Looking to the future, Browne is confident in the strength of the MDA and the significant degree of common purpose moving forward. "As far as our nuclear relationship is concerned, the relationship between the United States and the United Kingdom has never been as good," he said. "It is really important that we continue jointly to address the challenges that we face as policymakers of today and those of the future . . . and that we work together to realize our shared ambition of a world free of nuclear weapons." He concluded, "I would expect collaboration to continue, but frankly, I would expect it to grow, because I think that the challenges that we face going forward to maintain our stockpiles in a safe and secure fashion are going to become greater."

—*David Gill*
Aberystwyth University

JAMES SCHLESINGER

FORMER U.S. SECRETARY OF ENERGY

James Schlesinger became chairman of the Atomic Energy Commission (AEC) in 1971; during his tenure the United States conducted the nuclear test at Amchitka Island—Cannikin—to test the warhead for the Spartan missile. In 1973, he served as director of Central Intelligence for a brief period before he became secretary of defense from 1973 to 1975. In 1976, President Jimmy Carter appointed him to form the Department of Energy, which absorbed the responsibilities of the AEC. Dr. Schlesinger was the nation's first secretary of energy, from 1977 to 1979.

Dr. Schlesinger emphasized that the special nuclear partnership established between the United States and the United Kingdom is a relationship that should continue to be fostered in spite of any difficulties posed by current proliferation challenges. The historical nuances of the special nuclear relationship can be analyzed according to problems and successes but, most important, this relationship can provide future lessons for nonproliferation and partnership.

According to Dr. Schlesinger, Cold War considerations influenced the special partnership, but they did not define the relationship. In fact, the partnership between Great Britain and the United States that had been established during World War II was equally important in paving the way for the Mutual Defense Agreement of 1958. "The MDA was not a driving force behind the cooperation between the British and the United States," said Dr. Schlesinger. "It was a reflection of wartime association, most particularly in the case of General Eisenhower who led a combined British-American army into Europe." During this period, the special relationship was not only aided by wartime partnership but by an "institutional, organic, emotional relationship" that would have been difficult to forge with any other country.

The United Kingdom played a vital role as a U.S. nuclear ally and in the NATO alliance, although at times the British had reservations regarding U.S. strategy during this period. On the one hand, Great Britain was a nuclear partner of the United States that benefited from exchanges of nuclear information and materials. On the other hand, Great Britain refrained from being "wholly coalesced with U.S. strategy" because it "would have in a sense undermined the independence of their nuclear deterrent which was the driving motivation for its creation," functioning as an independent deterrent to the Soviet Union.

The British, for example, were hesitant to adapt to the changes in strategic doctrine that were advocated by the United States regarding the Soviet Union. In the mid-1970s, the Soviets had developed a counterdeterrent that could target U.S. cities. The United States responded by announcing that "the strategic forces of the United States were thoroughly integrated into the defense of Western Europe and that, as a consequence, the United States would respond, should conventional forces be overwhelmed, with nuclear attacks on the Soviet Union itself," including economic and military targets. This was a change in strategy because, at the time, the United States had been more focused toward implementing the strike plan of the Supreme Allied Commander Europe (SACEUR) that focused on targets in Eastern Europe. According to Dr. Schlesinger, the British were concerned that the United States was trying to substitute conventional defense for the nuclear deterrent. This strategy was eventually accepted once the British felt that the United States was not intending to limit the United Kingdom's ability to pursue a nuclear capability and they saw that the change in strategy improved deterrence.

Dr. Schlesinger recalls that, during his time in government, the interactions he had with his UK counterparts were "always very warm" despite periods of diplomatic tension in other areas of policy such as the Middle Eastern war of 1973. Regarding the exchange of nuclear information, Dr. Schlesinger states, "It was at the personal level a very open relationship with a good deal of camaraderie despite certain limits to information sharing." He cited as an example General Hyman Rickover's initial reluctance to share information on nuclear propulsion for submarines. The fact that this information was ultimately shared is further testament not only to the borderlines of cooperation but to the willingness to further nuclear partnership.

Dr. Schlesinger participated in both diplomatic and scientific aspects of the special relationship. As director of Central Intelligence, he traveled to the United Kingdom to discuss U.S. assessments of the Soviet antiballistic missile system around Moscow. This was important because there was a concern about the effectiveness of British missiles against the Soviet threat. He also traveled to Dounreay, Scotland, to witness the British breeder reactor construction after President Richard M. Nixon and Prime Minister Edward Heath agreed in 1971 to cooperate on the construction of breeder reactors. Although breeder reactors turned out not to be economically viable, the positive technical and diplomatic relationships that had been established during the Manhattan Project continued through this type of cooperation during Dr. Schlesinger's time in government.

Dr. Schlesinger emphasized that the special partnership is dependent on factors that go beyond the nuclear realm. He emphasized the importance of the nuclear aspect, however, by stating that the "nuclear relationship and the relationship with regard to intelligence exchanges between the Americans and the British are twin pillars which support the overall political relationship." Regarding the future, Dr. Schlesinger stated, "the relationship between the United States and the United Kingdom has a degree of intimacy that exceeds that within the NATO alliance, and I see no reason why that should ever come to an end."

—*Tara Callahan*
Center for Strategic and International Studies

PETER CARRINGTON
FORMER UK FOREIGN SECRETARY

Peter Carrington, 6th Baron Carrington, took his seat in the House of Lords in 1938 and thereafter embarked upon a political career spanning seven decades. After serving in the Second World War, during which he received the Military Cross, Lord Carrington returned to political life within the Conservative governments of Winston Churchill, Anthony Eden, Harold Macmillan, and Sir Alec Douglas-Home. Between 1954 and 1956 he was parliamentary secretary to the Ministry of Defence, and between 1959 and 1963 he served as First Lord of the Admiralty. Lord Carrington returned to government as secretary of state for defence between 1970 and 1974 under Edward Heath. Between 1979 and 1982 he served as foreign secretary under Margaret Thatcher. Later, from 1984 to 1988, he was secretary general of NATO. Lord Carrington continues to sit in the House of Lords.

Lord Carrington was well acquainted with, and equally appreciative of, the friendship and spirit of cooperation that existed between Great Britain and the United States throughout his political career. "One had a very great admiration, respect, and gratitude to America," he recalled. "There was that very close relationship." Despite this rapport, however, he considers the phrase "special relationship" to be somewhat questionable. Instead, Lord Carrington stressed that the nuclear relationship between the United States and Britain was one based on necessity. "If our national interests didn't coincide, it wouldn't last very long," he stressed. "It's always been national interests. People like to bang on about the special relationship but it's always interests."

The close nuclear relationship between the United States and Great Britain, Lord Carrington suggested, was a remnant of military cooperation during the Second World War. This relationship was sustained in the postwar period by America's growing anxiety regarding economic depravation and political instability throughout Europe. As Lord Carrington explained, "The Americans needed us because Europe at that time hardly existed. . . . We needed them because we were in a poorish way ourselves." These issues were exacerbated and in many cases perpetuated by the growing tensions of the Cold War. Lord Carrington contends that Britain's eventual nuclear cooperation within NATO was based on a shared interest in ensuring that "Europe was not submerged under the Communist regime." It was this collection of broader strategic issues across Europe that defined the Anglo-American nuclear relationship. As Lord Carrington explained, "Without each other's help it would be difficult to see how Europe would have survived."

Consequently, notable diplomatic events such as the Mutual Defense Agreement of 1958 and the Nassau conference of 1962, although important, served only to influence the form of this cooperation. In and of themselves both had a limited impact on the larger course of Anglo-American nuclear relations. Despite this, Lord Carrington was resolute in his belief that cooperation had been strengthened by factors other than just national interest. He suggested that "there are a whole lot of reasons why there is a relationship. Not least language and not least the position we have vis-à-vis Europe and not least the Second World War." A spirit of friendship, a history of shared experiences, and strong personal relationships between presidents, prime ministers, technicians, and statesmen had a notable influence on the nature of the Anglo-American relationship.

Personal relationships primarily served to facilitate a largely functional relationship. This is not to deny the significance of these personal relationships but rather to temper their influence. Lord Carrington argues that "one should never suppose that personal relationships ever in the end take precedence over national interest because they don't, but they oil the wheels and certainly they did with Macmillan and Kennedy, and Churchill in his postwar days." During periods of cooperation and conflict between both governments, Lord Carrington always considered his U.S. colleagues easy to work with. This was as true throughout Kennedy's meetings with Macmillan during the Nassau

Conference as it was during Nixon's anxious discussions with Edward Heath during the latter's continued flirtations with Europe.

As the Cold War thawed and memories of a bipolar world faded, the broader character of Anglo-American cooperation changed. "The Americans have become infinitely more dominant," said Lord Carrington. "We were all, in a sense, hangers on." U.S. hegemony corresponded with a marked decline in British international authority. Britain's eventual withdrawal of troops from the East of Suez served to highlight the extent of this disparity. "Although this was fairly obvious in 1945, it didn't filter through in the same way, partly because there was still the British Empire. . . . I think we felt then that we really were a world power." Despite this growing British dependency, a series of shared ambitions continues to remain prominent within Anglo-American relations.

Looking to the future of the Anglo-American nuclear relationship, Lord Carrington was cautiously optimistic. Although steadfast in his belief that "in the end national interests prevail," this need not be considered an inherent obstacle to future collaboration. Nor is there any reason to believe that national interests must undermine the successful history of interdependence born out of the Second World War. Instead, Britain is likely to retain a distinctly unique relationship with the United States. Lord Carrington suggested that Britain was a companion to the United States. The spirit of Anglo-American cooperation, he concluded, was based on national interests, but it's also togetherness. "It's nice to have friends."

—*David Gill*
Aberystwyth University

HAROLD BROWN
FORMER U.S. SECRETARY OF DEFENSE

Harold Brown completed his doctorate in physics at Columbia University in 1949 and began working at the University of California radiation laboratory. From 1952 until 1961, he worked on nuclear weapons design and testing at the Lawrence Radiation Laboratory in Livermore, California, eventually becoming director. In 1961 he became director of defense research and engineering at the Department of Defense, and in 1965 he became secretary of the Air Force. In 1969 he left government to become president of the California Institute of Technology, returning to the DOD in 1977 as secretary of defense during the administration of President Jimmy Carter.

As a scientist at the Livermore Laboratory, Dr. Brown regularly met with British scientists. He thought that coordinating research made sense because "the more independent nuclear weapons programs there are, the more chances there are for mistakes." After the Mutual Defense Agreement was signed in 1958, Dr. Brown traveled to London twice annually to meet with counterparts in the UK Atomic Energy Establishment and the Ministry of Defence. "It was a matter of interest to interact with a group that had worked essentially independently beginning in the late 1940s when the wartime collaboration between the UK and the U.S. actually ended," he said. "The U.S. nuclear weapons designers had worked essentially on their own. There was, of course, cooperation and competition between Livermore and Los Alamos, so there were two sets of designers, but working with the British gave a completely new look at how the concepts—especially the concepts of thermonuclear designs—had evolved. . . . The leadership of the British nuclear weapons program, Bill Penney in particular, was well known to the people who worked on the Manhattan Project, and he and his colleagues had obviously made considerable progress."

Dr. Brown believed, however, that the technical benefits gained by the United States through the cooperation were minimal. "The British were substantially farther behind us than they had let on, so I don't think we learned very much from them, except that they had come to the same key insights as to how to design a thermonuclear weapon as had the U.S. side," he recalled. "But they had not proceeded nearly as far on calculations of details and had not in fact carried out such a test."

To Dr. Brown, the MDA was not an attempt on the U.S. side to gain technical insights; it was a way of strengthening the alliance. "It was really a policy decision, not a technical decision," he said. "It was a symbol more than anything else." The MDA strengthened the alliance by forging relationships between scientists that carried over when these individuals moved into positions of political influence.

Dr. Brown became acquainted with many of the Britons involved on both the political and the technical sides in the late 1950s. He said of Solly Zuckerman:

> When I got to Washington he was already the chief scientific adviser to the cabinet, and so he was involved in the policy side, as was I when I was in Washington. So that relationship and corresponding ones with the senior military people did make it a lot easier to implement the purpose of those agreements. For example, in the Kennedy administration the British ambassador, Lord Harlech, was involved in the discussions. I had met him during 1959 and 1960 when he was the head of the British delegation at the Conference on the Discontinuation of Nuclear Tests. He was only David Ormsby-Gore before his father died and he became Lord Baron Harlech. And when Lord Mountbatten came over to the United States, I had lunch with him at the British embassy; we got to know each other. We on the U.S. side and the British side clearly had gained a closer relationship from the work that had happened during the late 1950s.

Though the United Kingdom likely benefited more from the technical cooperation with the United States, the United Kingdom's staunch support of U.S. positions in NATO and elsewhere is portrayed as part of the exchange. Dr. Brown valued the United Kingdom's support in NATO because it was accompanied by its views on the subject matter: "It is good to have an ally who will generally support you but who will give advice that you don't always get from inside."

Dr. Brown said that the MDA would become more important in the event of a future strategic arms reduction treaty:

> There are perfectly good reasons for the U.S., the UK, and others of the P-5, all of which have nuclear weapons, to reduce the numbers, to deemphasize nuclear weapons. . . . In that process I think the MDA agreement with the UK will play a useful role because if the U.S. and the UK can agree on a path, it'll make it easier—although not easy—to get the P-5 to move towards much lower levels of nuclear weapons, and, more important, to deal with the issue of control of fissionable material, whether plutonium or U235, in a way that minimizes the risks of proliferation, by urging other countries not to have their own fuel cycle, their own reprocessing cycle, their own enrichment cycle. How far that will go, how successful that will be, remains to be seen.

—Cassandra Smith
Center for Strategic and International Studies

MICHAEL QUINLAN
FORMER UK PERMANENT UNDER-SECRETARY OF STATE

After more than five decades of experience in matters of British defense policy, Sir Michael Quinlan remains a leading authority in the field. In 1954, following service in the Royal Air Force, he began a career in the civil service. Between 1956 and 1958 Sir Michael served as private secretary to the parliamentary under-secretary of state for Air and then to the chief of Air Staff between 1962 and 1965. In 1968 he acted as a one-star civilian in the Defence Policy Staff, before becoming defence counsellor in the United Kingdom delegation to NATO between 1970 and 1973. Sir Michael served in the Cabinet Office from 1974, becoming in 1977 the UK policy director in the Ministry of Defence, where he was closely involved with nuclear force modernization in the United Kingdom and NATO. In 1988 he returned to the Ministry of Defence as permanent under-secretary of state until his retirement in 1992. Between 1992 and 1999 he was director of the Ditchley Foundation and later acted as a special adviser to parliamentary committees on international security issues. Sir Michael is a visiting professor in the Department of War Studies, King's College London, and an honorary *ancien* of the NATO Defense College.

Acknowledging the difficulty of generalizing about such a lengthy period of cooperation, Sir Michael considers the Anglo-American nuclear relationship to have been, in the main, particularly close. "I think there is a very good degree of understanding and a good degree of trust," he suggested. "It is enormously robust, and it has been for us enormously fruitful, and I think it has been good for the United

States, too." This cooperation was founded upon on a shared history and largely perpetuated by congruent ambitions. Thus, Sir Michael suggested, the relationship rested predominantly on "the habits and memory of World War Two alongside the fact we spoke the same language, both in the literal linguistic sense and more generally in ways of thinking."

For Britain, the Anglo-American nuclear relationship proved crucial. Sir Michael suggested, "Certainly if we had not had that cooperation we would have faced some very awkward decisions: to get out of the business; to stay in it in a pretty third rate . . . way; or to stay in the business, spend a lot of money, and have severe opportunity costs elsewhere in the defense budget." U.S. cooperation therefore meant that these difficult decisions were ultimately avoided. It would be wrong, however, to assume nuclear cooperation was founded solely upon notions of friendship. Instead, the United States gradually came to recognize that "it was useful to have somebody else, as it were, to carry at least a bit of the moral and intellectual load of the nuclear business." This shared burden was largely grounded in an appreciation of strategic considerations, and particularly an awareness of the need for a strong military presence in Europe during the Cold War. Sir Michael suggested that the United States came to appreciate that "if you squeeze the British out of the business, quite apart from the fact you lose a friend, you may lose British willingness to pull its weight in NATO."

These national interests meant that personal relationships were, according to Sir Michael, rarely of critical importance. Although he considered the U.S. mind-set as generally sympathetic, it was never altruistic. "When the chips are down, though the civilities are observed, America, like any other country and perhaps more than most, pursues pretty rigorously its own advantage, its own national interest; and the idea that some sentimental consideration is going to move it off its perception of that interest is romantic," he said. Yet, despite such motivations, Sir Michael stated, "I never saw any sign in either the nuclear field or any other field of an American attempt to manipulate or leverage the cooperation they did give us to secure our compliance in policies on which we were not at one." Despite the necessities driving this relationship, Sir Michael considered the relationship to be based upon an almost unlimited willingness to cooperate.

A sudden breakdown in the relationship is therefore considered quite beyond the realm of reasonable policy insurance. "It does seem to me that a sundering of the relationship would be a nuclear event itself," Sir Michael said. "Something very extraordinary would have to happen." There is a distinct confidence in Sir Michael's considerations of future cooperation across the Atlantic. "In some ways I think there is at least as strong a case as ever there was for us to stay close together and talk," he said. Since the interests of the United Kingdom and the United States are very similar, "there is every reason why we should stay close and talk closely, and so far as I know we do."

Looking to the future, Sir Michael encourages the next generation of policymakers on both sides of the Atlantic to better understand the history and the thinking that has already been developed within the realm of nuclear policy. "I am sometimes dismayed by the extent to which, as it were, the intellectual inheritance tends to have faded away, perhaps not so much within government, but certainly in public discourse," he said. Sir Michael ultimately wishes, therefore, to foster a greater appreciation of the progress that has already been made in nuclear history. "There's a lot of wisdom out there and a lot of mistakes made and lessons learned from them."

—David Gill
Aberystwyth University

JOHN FOSTER
FORMER DIRECTOR
LAWRENCE LIVERMORE NATIONAL LABORATORY

John Foster was director of the Lawrence Livermore National Laboratory from 1961 to 1965. Before he was appointed director, he served as a division leader and associate director while he led the laboratory's efforts to develop low-yield fission warhead designs.

Dr. Foster's career began in 1942 at Harvard's Radio Research Laboratory; he was then assigned to the Fifteenth Air Force as an adviser on radar and radar countermeasures during World War II. After the war he finished his undergraduate degree at McGill University and completed his graduate studies at the University of California, Berkeley, while working at the Lawrence Radiation Laboratory. Foster left his post as Livermore's director in 1965 to become director of defense research and engineering at the U.S. Department of Defense. He joined TRW Inc. in 1973 and retired in 1988 as the company's vice president for science and technology. He served on TRW's board of directors until 1994 and is currently a consultant to government and private industry.

Foster recalled that when he began his work designing fission warheads at the Livermore laboratory "the instructions that I received at the time were that these fission weapons were not to be like Los Alamos, so they were to be different. That turned out to be quite a challenge." Of the Los Alamos designs, Foster stated that he knew "nothing, in fact, other than what I read in the government releases after Hiroshima and Nagasaki." After he was placed in charge of developing fission weapons, Foster said, however, that he "spent every waking moment thinking of ways to provide a device superior to what Los Alamos came up with." Despite the rivalry, "we had complete cooperation from Los Alamos. So it was intense competition and full cooperation. . . ."

After the signing of the Mutual Defense Agreement (MDA) in 1958, the scientists from the United Kingdom became an integral part of this competitive venture. "What was delightful about the interaction with the folks from Aldermaston was that their design was not like either of ours," said Foster, "so I think that was perhaps the essential ingredient of being able to work constructively together as well as competitively, to the advantage of both countries." More specifically, Foster recounted how "we used to say that the UK did not have the resources that were made available in the United States and, therefore, they had to think more. And that's what made the difference: they had to think of clever ways to get the job done more efficiently, and every bit as effectively."

After he heard about the UK idea for a fission weapon, Foster recollected, he asked the scientists at Livermore to imagine how the United States could improve on it. "So we actually produced designs along the concept of the United Kingdom designs," he said, "and, at the same time, hopefully, made some improvements in effectiveness, production feasibility, and so on."

Reflecting on the time of his interactions with Sir William Penney, Nyman Levin, Edward Newly, Victor Macklen, John Corner, and others, Foster noted that "the pace was rapid . . . and so there was a never-ending list of challenges and exchanges, and it was always interesting. It was competitive, stimulating, good."

In the wake of the Soviet Union's successful test of the massive Ivan bomb, Foster recalled, "It was clear that the Soviets had prepared for several years for that test series, and so that was a big shock to us. But it was also clear that the Soviets were on a different course. . . . We did not feel that very high yield nuclear weapons were the direction where we should go." Although the new special relationship between the United States and United Kingdom did not, in Foster's view, have a major bearing on how the United States viewed the Soviets, "I do remember . . . that a hundred megaton warhead could wipe out the British Isles," he noted. "And so, while it was abhorrent to us, it was far more abhorrent to the UK folks."

The benefits of collaboration accrued to the United States as well as the United Kingdom. "It seemed to me an opportunity, a challenge, to exchange views and developments and to have both sides gain," he said. The independence of the laboratories also helped preserve the benefits of collaboration. "It's interesting in retrospect, to realize that by and large Los Alamos, Livermore, and UK folks each stayed on the course they were on for a long time," said Foster. "But there were improvements in all three as a result of the progress of the other laboratories in their pursuit of their design."

In Foster's view, the MDA is still very important because the United States and the United Kingdom face different sets of threats, challenges, and opportunities. "All of these things change the requirements of the nuclear deterrent," he said, ". . . so there's room for value to come from collaboration." This is also true for intelligence operations, which he describes as the "leading edge of our national security."

—Mark Jansson
Center for Strategic and International Studies

David Owen became parliamentary private secretary to the minister of defence in 1966. Between 1968 and 1970 he was parliamentary under-secretary of state for the Royal Navy. In 1974 Lord Owen served as minister of state for health before becoming secretary of state for foreign and commonwealth affairs in February 1977, a position he held until the general election of May 1979. In early 1981 Lord Owen, along with Roy Jenkins, Bill Rodgers, and Shirley Williams, established the Social Democratic Party. Lord Owen was the deputy leader of the party from 1982 to 1983 and the leader of the party from June 1983 until August 1987. After the 1992 general election Lord Owen was made a life peer of the City of Plymouth and currently sits as a crossbencher.

During Lord Owen's tenure as foreign secretary, Britain was confronted with several challenges to retaining a credible nuclear deterrent. Lord Owen, however, emphasized that "Britain benefited massively" from Anglo-American nuclear cooperation during this period. On the subject of the Chevaline program, the British top secret project to upgrade its Polaris missile system, Lord Owen emphasized that he agreed to the project continuing but secured the caveat that it was not being endorsed because of the strategic rationale of the "Moscow criterion." "Throughout my period as foreign secretary I challenged the need for the British deterrent to take out Moscow and thereby have to penetrate their antimissile defenses," he stated. "I believed it was sufficient for a minimum nuclear deterrent for the British that we would be able to hit a number of major Soviet cities."

Lord Owen added that when the Ministerial Committee of four discussed a possible future purchase of a successor system to Polaris, he personally favored the acquisition of cruise missiles over the Trident system, but he encountered opposition from the Ministry of Defence, briefed by the U.S. Department of Navy. "If we were strong and rich, we could afford to continue in the ballistic missile business, but it struck me that the Chevaline cost overrun had indicated that AWRE [Atomic Weapons Research Establishment] was not really up to it," Lord Owen said. A possible British purchase of cruise missiles "was being discouraged by the Ministry of Defence and, indeed, its accuracy and ground-hugging capability downplayed deliberately by the U.S. Naval Department because they wanted to go for the Polaris successor, Poseidon and Trident, and they did not want to boost the alternative case, which was the cruise missile," he said. "But they knew and Peter Jay in our Washington embassy knew that it was getting to be a very effective weapons system." The possibility of Britain collaborating with France on a successor system to Polaris was not considered a viable option during Lord Owen's time as foreign secretary. As he described it, "minimal discussion under the Callaghan period" occurred concerning Anglo-French nuclear cooperation.

Lord Owen was of the opinion that personalities did make a significant difference in the conduct of Anglo-American relations. In the context of the relationship between President Jimmy Carter and Prime Minister James Callaghan, Lord Owen explained that "Jim Callaghan had a very good relationship with him [President Carter]" and had on occasion been able to influence the president. On the specific issue of the possibility of President Carter proposing a new NATO doctrine of "no first use" of nuclear weapons against the Soviet Union, Prime Minister Callaghan was consulted and was so concerned about the possible ramifications within the NATO alliance regarding the confidence of the U.S. nuclear guarantee that he privately wrote to the president in order to dissuade such a course from being pursued. Lord Owen believed that this was "a very good example of where a prime minister has a good working relationship and indeed a good deal of affection in his relationship with the president, so that they could have a private exchange, and the British could exercise their influence quietly, not even being known to their European colleagues."

On the prospects of future nuclear disarmament, Lord Owen was skeptical that it could ever be realistically achieved. He was of the opinion that Britain could "slowly and steadily get our nuclear weapons down to a minimum, and then if we can get ours down to a minimum and the ones of China, Russia, and the United States down to a much reduced level, we should consider giving up nuclear weapons. But it should be a collective UK-U.S. judgment, and I think it's pretty unlikely."

Lord Owen emphasized his strong support for a continuation of the Atlantic alliance and the importance it holds for British national security. "I think we should definitely retain it," he said. "It's an alliance that brings Canada and America across the Atlantic. It is a thoroughly important thing for us [Britain]. So it seems to me past experience demonstrates the need for American forces in Europe, to do anything in the EU to encourage the Americans to go out of the Atlantic alliance would be absolute folly." Lord Owen then rounded off his support for NATO by declaring, "I'm a strong supporter of NATO, today in 2008 as much as I was when I first became involved in the issue when I was a young student in the arguments over the Campaign for Nuclear Disarmament."

—Thomas Robb
Aberystwyth University

PETE NANOS

ASSOCIATE DIRECTOR, RESEARCH AND DEVELOPMENT, DEFENSE THREAT REDUCTION AGENCY, U.S. DEPARTMENT OF DEFENSE

Vice Admiral George Peter Nanos began his naval career in 1967 managing the technical development effort for the U.S. Navy's high-energy laser program. He then became deputy director of warfare systems engineering in the Space and Naval Warfare Systems Command, guiding the completion of the submarine inert navigation system to support the Trident II weapon system. In 1994, he became commander of the strategic system programs. There he was accountable for the design, development, and performance of the submarine-based strategic missile systems for the United States and the United Kingdom. He then served as principal deputy associate director for Los Alamos National Laboratory's Threat Reduction Directorate and, after four months in this position, was appointed as director. Dr. Nanos is currently the associate director for research and development at the Defense Threat Reduction Agency.

According to Admiral Nanos, the U.S. and UK navies have shared a particularly strong relationship since the 1963 signing of the Polaris Sales Agreement, which provided U.S. Polaris missiles to the United Kingdom. He described how the agreement involved plenary meetings on both sides of the Atlantic that brought both sides together and helped to cement personal relationships. He stated that the United States built Polaris missiles for the British and transferred U.S. technology to the United Kingdom in exchange for a depot in the United Kingdom on the coast of Scotland. The United States put a submarine tender in Holy Loch from which it operated its Polaris boats. UK

Polaris submarines operated out of Faslane, and the British supplied their own Polaris magazines, assembly, and maintenance facility with equipment provided by the United States. This relationship has continued to include the Trident II missile system.

Dr. Nanos emphasized that Trident is a mingled program. "In the Trident system there's no such thing as a purely U.S. or UK missile," he said. "The UK buys missiles, but parts of those missiles go into a common pool, and when a British submarine comes to Kings Bay to pick up its load of Trident missiles, they are presented with a list of all the missiles that have been assembled, and they can select any missile from the list." The missile may have come off of a U.S. submarine in its previous iteration before being passed onto a UK submarine. Essentially it is a completely mingled population of missiles, so British and U.S. test data come from the same pool; making the weapons statistics and diagnostics more thorough and effective. Dr. Nanos emphasized that during his period as the program director "I did for the British Navy exactly what I did for the U.S. Navy. I provided them the Trident system and fully supported it with all the same rigor and all the same quality and essentially an identical system to what I provided for the U.S. Navy."

As director of Los Alamos National Laboratory, Admiral Nanos was directly involved in the stockpile stewardship program, which was commonly pursued by the United Kingdom in the 1990s. Cooperative experimental programs associated with building and validating codes were incredibly successful, he said. The United States and United Kingdom shared calculations and reviewed each other's work to the point where the United Kingdom had "essentially become almost like a third weapons laboratory." Both sides have seen positive results from nuclear trade, information sharing, and security through the stockpile stewardship program.

Although the United States has a moratorium on nuclear testing and has signed the Comprehensive Test Ban Treaty and the United Kingdom has ratified the treaty, which prohibits them from conducting nuclear tests, the special partnership has become an effective way for the United States and United Kingdom to compare separate approaches to technical problems and use information exchange to bolster confidence in each country's ability to maintain its deterrent posture. Currently, this partnership has resulted in "a tremendous confidence in the reliability of weapons without having to test them," making the nuclear partnership, in this case, a tremendous success.

Dr. Nanos believes that the naval tie is the strongest in the special partnership because not only did it bring the United Kingdom fully into the realm of submersible naval warfare, but it brought the U.S. and UK nuclear deterrents very close together technically. Although Dr. Nanos stressed the importance of recognizing that the relationship "is not a relationship between individuals but a relationship between nation-states," he also stated that personal relationships greatly facilitated the common interests of both countries. In addition, military-to-military exchanges also helped to foster strong rapport. The Mutual Defense Agreement helped to foster "a tremendous period, that goes on to this day, of cooperation on key nuclear matters which has served to strengthen both nations."

—Tara Callahan
Center for Strategic and International Studies

GEORGE ROBERTSON
FORMER UK SECRETARY OF STATE FOR DEFENCE

George Robertson became a member of the House of Commons in 1978 and served in this capacity until 1999. During this period, he became interested in matters of British defense and foreign policy. In 1997 Lord Robertson was appointed Defence Secretary under the newly elected administration of Tony Blair and served in this capacity until October 1999. In August 1999 Lord Robertson became the secretary general of NATO, a position he retained until 2004.

Lord Robertson was of the opinion that the United Kingdom benefited significantly from its cooperation with the United States in the nuclear realm. "Given that the deterrent is such an important part of Britain's defense posture, collaboration with the Americans is absolutely critical," he said. He pointed out that the nuclear relationship between the two countries was also beneficial to the United States. "There is a degree of expertise in the UK they can draw on," he noted. "The United States benefits, inasmuch as sharing responsibility is critical in the way things are done. It establishes a relationship of trust at the very highest level and therefore makes sure we are bound together by a common endeavor."

When asked whether he believed there were any negative consequences for the United Kingdom in undertaking nuclear cooperation with the United States, Lord Robertson emphatically replied that there were not. "In essence, the fact that it has worked for so long is a clear indication that it is based on something that is fundamentally workable," he said. Theoretical problems, which some have suggested are apparent in the United Kingdom's nuclear relationship with the United States, such as the British dependence on U.S. missiles were in Lord Robertson's opinion just that: theoretical issues. This was because such a strong degree of mutual trust exists between the countries that any potential problems occurring over the British dependency on U.S. missiles are negligible.

Lord Robertson firmly believed that Britain has to retain its strategic nuclear deterrent into the twenty-first century and described it as an "insurance policy" of sorts. He explained, "Their [nuclear weapons'] primary function is to stop people thinking they can win a conventional war, and that is as relevant today as it was in the past." Lord Robertson further explained that even though the Cold War was now finished, the rationale for a nuclear deterrent was just as prevalent as it ever was. "In an uncertain world where the ability to gain a nuclear capability is not impossible, even for nonstate actors, clearly having the nuclear deterrent as a part of the wide range of military policy is all the more critical," he stated. Lord Robertson concluded, "If you were to give it up [the nuclear deterrent], first of all it would not be understood and in many cases it would not be believed. But you would have to start again if some other threat needing the ultimate deterrent was to come along; the fact that one opponent, one enemy, has gone does not mean the argument for deterrence has gone."

NATO is just as relevant today as it was when it was first created, Lord Robertson believes. "It is a living organization that deals successfully with security issues on a transatlantic basis," he said. The institutional mechanisms "force people to come together and solve problems." Lord Robertson also firmly supported NATO's new role in operating in "out of area" action and stated that NATO has to be able to go to wherever the threat is going to be.

On the issue of arms control, Lord Robertson was confident that regarding certain types of arms control issues, notably dealing with proliferation by new states, there is a growing prospect of having relevant new agreements and that "we should be able to see progress on that matter." He believed that Britain has an extremely important part to play in reaching such agreements, and he highlighted that during his time in office Britain had taken several important steps in leading the way in reducing its own nuclear weapons. "We [Britain] got it [nuclear weapons] down to the lowest level necessary to establish deterrence," he said. However, Lord Robertson warned against unilateral disarmament and explained that within the context of his time in office "it was right to do it, in the changed circumstances, but doing away with it completely would leave you with no flexibility."

Lord Robertson's parting advice for future nuclear weapons planners, strategists, and policymakers was that they have to keep their policies and strategies relevant to the changing environment and evolving threats that they face. "It has to be kept relevant," he said. "One of the great problems we have today in the military arena, especially in a lot of the NATO nations, is that people are looking on the enemies of the past rather than the threats of tomorrow."

—*Thomas Robb*
Aberystwyth University

SIEGFRIED S. HECKER

**CODIRECTOR, CENTER FOR INTERNATIONAL SECURITY
AND COOPERATION, STANFORD UNIVERSITY**

Siegfried S. Hecker has had the opportunity to interface with the British under the 1958 Mutual Defense Agreement (MDA) in a myriad of roles as scientist, facility manager, and laboratory director. Dr. Hecker began his career at Los Alamos National Laboratory (LANL) as a summer student in 1965. His first interactions with the British began in the early 1970s when he met colleagues at a conference and later through the joint working groups (JOWOGs) set up to bring representatives from laboratories in the Department of Energy complex together with their counterparts from the United Kingdom, where they discussed, in Dr. Hecker's case, topics of plutonium metallurgy and plutonium science.

During the 1980s in his role as Chemistry Metallurgy Baker division leader, Dr. Hecker had extensive interactions with his British colleagues about the construction of A-90, their plutonium facility. As director of the LANL from 1986 until 1997, he interfaced with both the Ministry of Defence and Aldermaston on topics directly related to the MDA. In addition, the lessons learned from the building of A-90 were relayed back to the operators of the LANL plutonium facility, TA-55. From 2000 to 2005, Dr. Hecker served on the Atomic Weapons Establishment (AWE) corporate advisory panel.

The highlight of Hecker's interactions was the ability to have colleagues he could talk to regarding classified plutonium metallurgy and plutonium science: "Since there are few places that do plutonium research and even fewer that can discuss classified results, personal interactions with the British plutonium metallurgy researchers was extremely productive and fruitful since they have a lot of capability in this area dating back to the 1950s," said Dr. Hecker. "From a broader standpoint . . . specific collaboration between British and Americans on warhead and missiles systems for Trident submarines is certainly one of the most important accomplishments. Secondly, over the entire test history [we] learned a lot in both directions, as the United Kingdom for the most part after the 1950s conducted its nuclear testing at the Nevada Test Site. . . . So there was a lot of exchange related to the testing program, and [we] saw the benefits as mutual." Finally, Dr. Hecker said, the ability to exchange information on respective plutonium facility and production experience proved invaluable in building A-90 and creating a plutonium production capability at TA-55.

Dr. Hecker felt that some of the biggest contributions of the MDA have been the peer reviews, not just on nuclear weapons design and manufacturing, but also on health safety, facility operations, and other topics. He felt the British served this role extremely well and also brought a level of impartiality to U.S. programmatic disputes. Often he felt the two sides brought significantly different approaches to looking at problems, which helped both sides advance. He believed that this collaboration aided when investment in a country's capabilities ebbed and flowed. "There was a period of time when the Brits were doing very little plutonium metallurgy . . . but they came back just in time as we were scaling back and focusing on our production activities, so there was give and take over the years."

During the past 50 years, Dr. Hecker believes, the quality of interaction has remained high, although he acknowledges that the nature of the interactions changed at the end of nuclear testing in 1992. Instead of an emphasis on actual nuclear tests, the interactions had to move on to modeling and calculations and subcritical tests. He believes that future collaboration under the agreement will be primarily a function of what the British decide to do. "Peer review becomes significantly more important in the world we currently live in, which is this world without nuclear testing. . . From that standpoint, technical interdependence will increase. Programmatic interdependence is mostly a British call."

With the changing global world, increased alliances, and a continuing push to reduce nuclear weapon stockpiles, Dr. Hecker acknowledged the agreement may have to change in the future. In the current climate, however, he sees no impact on the framework or implementation of the MDA.

Dr. Hecker disagrees with the notion that there is a missing generation. Though the early leaders and pioneers in the field were young, that was a reflection of the newness of the field of nuclear science. The emphasis by Congress, DOE, and, as a result, lab management on risk avoidance means science and technology decrease. This naturally skews to an older crowd. He believes the U.S. government must make working at the national laboratories attractive in order to revitalize the technical and policy communities and to attract the best and the brightest next generation of scientists and policymakers to interact under the MDA.

Dr. Hecker has observed during the past 43 years that it is getting increasingly difficult to do science at national laboratories as the emphasis on risk aversion continues to grow. He feels a particular calling to attract both physical and social scientists to look at nuclear policy problems and to ensure that adequate funding is provided, which is why he accepted his position at Stanford. He believes it is up to the older generation to transfer not only their knowledge, but their enthusiasm as well, to younger folks in real time and on real problems.

—Donna Smith
Los Alamos National Laboratory

PETER MARSHALL

ALAN DOUGLAS

FORMER HEADS, FORENSIC SEISMOLOGY GROUP,

ATOMIC WEAPONS ESTABLISHMENT, BLACKNEST, UK

Alan Douglas and Peter Marshall, CMG, OBE, successive heads of the Atomic Weapons Establishment (AWE) Seismology Group at Blacknest, together spent more than 70 staff-years in the group. Now, as semiretired distinguished scientists, they continue to carry out research, publish papers, and coach the next generation in observational seismology and its application to the detection, location, and assessment of underground nuclear tests and in test-ban verification. Their account portrays the disagreements as well as the harmonious side of the Mutual Defense Agreement of 1958.

Professor Douglas remembers that as a junior AWE scientist, "there were many stories about interactions with the U.S., and initially I thought, well what has the UK got to contribute?" In his view, the joint working group (JOWOG) meetings could be a bit of a burden to the small UK group if the meetings were too frequent because they allowed little time for the British to conduct new research and get ready for the next meeting. However, by the time Douglas was leading the group as chairman of the seismology JOWOG he was sure that the exchanges were mutually beneficial.

Marshall and Douglas recall how the seismology JOWOG, formed in 1962, uncovered in the early 1970s differences in yield estimates of foreign nuclear tests that led to what became known as the "yield wars" between the United Kingdom and the United States. This term referred to the discrepancies between the Soviet declaration of compliance with the Threshold Test Ban Treaty (TTBT) and U.S. analysis of seismograms from the Soviet tests. The UK interpretation of the seismograms compensated for differences in geology in Russia and therefore agreed with Soviet declarations. These differences were not finally resolved until the U.S.-USSR joint verification experiment in 1988, but they proved contentious in the discussions surrounding TTBT compliance verification.

Marshall recalled his effort to persuade the United States to change its approach to testing threshold verification. "I spent a year at Livermore trying to explain why the Americans were not going to be able to verify Soviet compliance with the Threshold Test Ban Treaty, but I think it took 16 years before the Americans accepted that we were right," he said. "We addressed the National Security Council, again, through the JOWOG agency." Marshall believed that the JOWOG was a stimulus in his work, and his collaboration with Lawrence Livermore National Laboratory researchers Don Springer and Howard Rodean resulted in a definitive joint publication, "Magnitude Corrections for Attenuation in the Upper Mantle," on the estimation of yield from seismic magnitude, which was published in the *Geophysical Journal* of the Royal Astronomical Society in 1979.

Douglas also identified one of the early areas of substantial cooperation under the MDA—the setting up of Pole Mountain, an array station about 1,000 kilometers from the Nevada Test Site—that led to a watershed moment in nuclear explosion verification. "It was the recordings at Pole Mountain from the distant Russian and French (Saharan) test sites that changed the whole UK program," he said. "So, indirectly through this contact with the U.S., we refocused on long range rather than for close in; and that has been a division [between the two programs] for the whole time." However, the new thinking by the United Kingdom paid dividends by 1962, as Douglas described a "very famous meeting in which Sir Solly Zuckerman, chief scientific adviser at the Ministry of Defence, led a group to the U.S. and said, 'we have these results from Pole Mountain from long range; it suggests a totally different way of going about verification.'" Zuckerman invited the United States to refocus its program but encountered hesitance in his U.S. colleagues. "They were very resistant to it in the beginning," he said. "Their main complaint was that the UK plan involved larger arrays, so the processing would be more difficult, [as the required] computing power would be two supercomputers of that time. And the UK came back rather bruised I believe, but determined to press ahead."

Subsequent developments in computing rapidly eroded this objection. Marshall noted that the initial U.S. reluctance also had political dimensions, as this breakthrough meant that "the Americans would not [need] stations within the Soviet Union, and that was not what the Americans really wanted. It was a bloodletting occasion apparently."

Dr. Marshall also pointed to differences in the instrumentation used by the United States and United Kingdom that led to early differences of opinions and contributed to resolution of the yield wars. "Another major difference between ourselves and the Americans was the recording instruments," he said. "The United States was much more concerned with detection than with source identification with regard to seismology." By contrast, "we [the AWE group] had to detect the event, we had to locate it, then we had to make a yield assessment." This led to the United Kingdom developing unique capabilities utilizing an expanded pass-band (the range of frequencies that can pass through filters without being weakened) that the United States had not yet accepted. "The United States seismological community was primarily concerned with just detecting—and it meant that their instrumental pass-band [was a] very narrow band system," he said. However, in the United Kingdom, "we had a system which had a much higher frequency response so when we showed some seismograms, the Americans would say, 'well we don't see that in our seismograms,' ergo, it doesn't exist. And this proved a running battle because of this very narrow band."

According to Marshall, the first time the idea of using a wider pass-band for detection and verification purposes was introduced to the Americans, "they sort of laughed us out of court on it and said, 'well, all you are going to record is background noise' [with] no interest at all in broadening that band." This was to the detriment of the United States during the yield wars following entry into force of the TTBT. Marshall attributes the United Kingdom's advanced understanding of detection to experience gained in the United States through the MDA. "Our wide band system allowed us to see high frequencies from Soviet tests, which was completely absent in the seismograms from American tests," he said. "And we put it all down to differences in the attenuation between the Soviet test site and the American test site." Eventually this was accepted by the United States and the wider verification community following the joint verification experiment.

Although the seismology JOWOG was disbanded in the 1990s, the friendly rivalry over the science continues today. Eventually, upon their retirements at the beginning of the millennium, Douglas's and Marshall's contributions were recognized by senior U.S. colleagues and officials, including, in Marshall's case, the secretary of the U.S. Air Force. In their view, the fact that the contributions of the United Kingdom have been much appreciated bodes well for the future of the relationship that was started under the MDA.

Because Blacknest is an open facility that hosts world-renowned researchers, Dr. Marshall recalled the positive and negative impacts on the MDA relationship. "The program in this country was completely unclassified . . . so that we could [host] Americans, Russians, Chinese, whoever, without all the problems with getting clearances from the main site," he said. And, I think, in the early 60s we had Keilis-Borok and Igor P. Bashilov [from the USSR], who spent six weeks here." However, he added, "you had to be very careful, because when you had contact with the Russians, there was usually a rebound with the Americans; they stopped talking to you for a period of time." This was patently clear after Sir Solly Zuckerman took Blacknest founding head Dr. Hal Thirlaway to Moscow to discuss Comprehensive Nuclear Test-Ban Treaty (CTBT) issues. "We were blacklisted for quite some months and communications between ourselves and the United States were at a real low during that time. I don't know what circumstances turned it around . . . but we carried on as if nothing had happened."

Dr. Marshall joined the AWE Ground Shock Division in which Eric Carpenter, a founding member of the AWE seismology group at Blacknest, was already a prominent figure. Dr. Marshall described the very beginning of the UK interest in seismology and early success with "decoupling," the method of attenuating seismic impacts by conducting nuclear test explosions in a cavity or porous rock. "We did conduct the very first decoupling experiments and demonstrated with a working paper in Geneva that decoupling did actually work," he said. "And the success of that program led Sir William Penny [the first AWRE director] to set up a group to look at the problems associated with seismic discrimination and detection of nuclear explosions."

In the early days, Dr. Douglas recalled, the Americans were generous in sharing their research reports and data, providing "a torrent of reports on all aspects of verification [and] contractors' reports, which we are currently scanning, as probably one of the few places with a large collection." Access to live feeds of raw data was offered, but at the time the UK group did not have enough resources to work on the data to justify accepting the generous offer. The new forum for exchanges became the CTBT negotiations and open academic conferences, where the relationship of scientific peers, founded under the MDA, continued to be clearly valuable. Both Dr. Marshall and Dr. Douglas noted that collaboration and co-publication between the two programs continues, and the exchanges between the United States and United Kingdom were mutually beneficial, with many long-lasting friendships being made.

—Owen Price
Atomic Weapons Establishment

JOHN HARVEY
DIRECTOR, POLICY PLANNING STAFF,
NATIONAL NUCLEAR SECURITY ADMINISTRATION,
U.S. DEPARTMENT OF ENERGY

John Harvey began his career in 1978 at the Lawrence Livermore National Laboratory, where he worked on intelligence estimates of the Soviet nuclear program, oversaw treaty monitoring activities, served as a technical adviser to the Strategic Arms Reduction Talks, and led advanced warhead concept studies for U.S. strategic ballistic missile systems. From 1995 to 2001 he served as the deputy assistant secretary of defense for nuclear forces and missile defense policy. In this capacity, he had extensive engagements with the United Kingdom on nuclear planning and operations. Since 2001, he has maintained frequent contact with the United Kingdom in his position as director, policy planning staff at the National Nuclear Security Administration. Dr. Harvey's cooperation with UK counterparts has spanned the range of nuclear issues, including technical cooperation, policy development, nuclear planning, and operations.

The U.S.-UK nuclear relationship that Dr. Harvey cultivated was "much closer than most realize . . . and probably a more intimate relationship on nuclear weapons matters than we had even with other U.S. government agencies like the State Department." While at the Pentagon, he participated in annual "home and home" visits in which U.S. and UK delegations would brief each other on their activities and host comprehensive tours of their respective nuclear weapons facilities. During the course of these visits, Dr. Harvey commented, he had "pretty much seen and heard everything" regarding the UK nuclear weapons program. One of the highlights of these interactions was at

Cape Canaveral in August 1995 when he participated in a "dry run" of a UK Trident missile launch. He recalls "going out in the morning on the submarine with the UK crew and going through all the pre-launch procedures without actually launching . . . and the next day we'd go out on the observation ship to watch the launch itself. . . . It was really exciting."

The level of transparency in nuclear weapon design authorized by the Mutual Defense Agreement (MDA) requires an extraordinary level of trust. "We built that trust over more than just the 50 years since the MDA," he said, "but the MDA took it to a new level." Remarkably, this happened despite the revelations that a British spy at Los Alamos, Klaus Fuchs, had provided the Soviets the design for what would be their first nuclear test. For Dr. Harvey, the fact that the relationship could survive that and enter into "the most transparent cooperation we have with any country in nuclear weapons matters" testifies to the extraordinary strength of the special relationship.

Despite the risks inherent in cooperation, the scope of the relationship has been broadened because the "benefits that we've received have well exceeded the risks." To Dr. Harvey, the core benefit to cooperation is the value of an "independent voice." He commented: "We get to understand how a relatively independent set of nuclear designers and engineers think about problems." This creates an interesting paradox: As the scope of cooperation expands, the two sides start thinking more alike and "you put in jeopardy the independence" that motivated the expansion at the outset. According to Dr. Harvey, the British are sensitive to this tension and strive to maintain an independent set of expertise.

Driven by a mutual curiosity that transcends borders, Dr. Harvey has seen this scientific bond flourish even among U.S. and Russian scientists who, despite having no classified exchanges, "are still fascinated with even the unclassified elements of nuclear weapons work." Still, the intimacy of U.S.-UK cooperation has created a dynamic that is "more one way than the U.S.-French relationship" because the United States shares less and because the French have retained more of their independence in thinking about design.

To Dr. Harvey, the most significant technological impact of the MDA has accrued to the United Kingdom: "Without the MDA, there would be a much different UK deterrent, probably heavy designs for bomber delivery. . . . If the UK wasn't able to conduct nuclear tests in

Nevada, its systems would be much more primitive and probably not as safe or secure." Although there has been less of an impact on the U.S. deterrent, Dr. Harvey finds tremendous value in the MDA: the intimacy of the "technical cooperation that evolved from the '58 agreement facilitated the broader set of cooperation in the nuclear planning and employment area . . . beginning in the 80s under Frank Miller . . . and it may not have happened without [the MDA]."

Dr. Harvey foresees a number of potential developments in the nuclear relationship. "As we consolidate our complex for the post–Cold War mission, we're looking for opportunities to scale back in some areas and may actually decide to become more dependent on UK analysis for certain things." For example, the British have "great capabilities in nuclear weapons effects, an area fertile for further cooperation." In addition, should the United States go forward with the reliable replacement warhead (RRW) initiative, the scope of cooperation will have to be expanded if UK scientists are to contribute meaningfully to that effort, and "we are taking steps to amend the MDA to allow for that. . . . How we secure warheads against unauthorized use is an integral part of the RRW effort and has so far not been an area of cooperation." These prospects suggest a deepening level of intimacy for the future of the nuclear relationship as "there is no secret held more closely than the types of things we do to prevent our warheads from unauthorized use."

—Jessica Yeats
Center for Strategic and International Studies

DAVID PARKES

FORMER CHIEF DESIGN ENGINEER,

ATOMIC WEAPONS ESTABLISHMENT, UK

David Parkes completed a Ph.D. at Nottingham University in structural analysis and the application of finite element modeling before he joined the Ministry of Defence (MOD) at the Admiralty of Underwater Weapons Establishment in 1976. He initially conducted submarine structures shock analyses and later ran a section involved in shock and materials research. In the late 1980s, Dr. Parkes became director of intelligence, science and technology at Whitehall, responsible for intelligence related to missiles; electronics; and nuclear, chemical, and biological weapons. In 1992, Parkes became head of weapon engineering at AWE, and he was promoted to chief design engineer shortly thereafter.

"When I came in 1992, I was immediately made chairman of a JOWOG [joint working group], which was weapon engineering," he recalled. "Up until then there had been a very long period of active underground testing, but the Hatfield agreement had basically stopped it. So the JOWOG was very much an exchange of UGT veterans. . . . If we went back into the early years of it, people were designing a new bomb every year; and we've now got down to the world since arms control, a lack of underground tests, and no new warheads required. What happens?"

The answer according to him was that "everybody becomes very focused on the systems they've got . . . and you suddenly find your exchange changes dramatically. The constraints that are put onto you by system owners [become more salient because] the people working in the labs that you used to work with are now working on specific problems associated with [their particular system]." Parkes considers one of his major collaborative achievements to be getting the labs properly involved.

Parkes sought to "move from what was a test environment to something which was more like a research and good exchange type of environment." So he tried to align similarly focused scientists in groups that could benefit from targeted exchanges with their counterparts in the United States. "One of the problems that I always found in the U.S. labs was to find the right people to actually link up with, particularly at LANL," he said. "So you'd find odd people who would pick it up, but they were very focused in their own little area."

There were additional pressures—in particular the U.S. desire to preserve the independence of its labs—that limited collaboration. Parkes recalls that "the big pressure I always found was the U.S. guys were always working on one of their [labs'] systems and, as such, they couldn't talk to us and couldn't give you a paper about it, and so [we] found it very, very difficult to get anything out of them." However, as chairman, Parkes was able to arrange "informal chats" with his U.S. counterparts that enriched the overall collaboration, especially with the scientists at Lawrence Livermore, who were not closely linked to the Los Alamos–designed Trident system, which the United Kingdom had purchased. "We'd actually share a few things—obviously not declare system things—but just a few interesting things, and I found with Lawrence Livermore that this was particularly beneficial." To that end, the United Kingdom became "very reliant on the 1958 agreement to maintain [links with Lawrence Livermore National Laboratory because] we weren't able to formally through the Trident agreement."

Challenges notwithstanding, Parkes believes that both sides have indeed benefited greatly from the MDA, because "when you're working together, you can spin off each other ideas and knowledge." For instance, the United Kingdom benefited from "early warning" of new ideas in the United States. Likewise, "when [the United States] was having some real problems with their design, basically we offered a load of information to them about the alternative design that we've pursued. Because we had different approaches, we came with independent and fresh ideas," which helped the Americans, and vice versa.

Mr. Parkes headed Trident Systems Support from 1998 until retirement in 2005, and he is now a consultant to the MOD on Trident-related issues. Looking toward the future, Parkes stressed the importance of removing system barriers to cooperation and noted that mutual trust was critical, despite the political hurdles. To strengthen the partnership, Parkes posited that "if you can identify people who are good and enjoy the exchange, [then] they are going to have a really decent relationship." In his view, the United States and United Kingdom should therefore seek to identify and develop these people early, as they will comprise the "seed core of a lasting relationship."

—Owen Price
Atomic Weapons Establishment

FRANKLIN C. MILLER
FORMER U.S. SPECIAL ASSISTANT TO THE PRESIDENT
FOR DEFENSE POLICY AND ARMS CONTROL

Franklin Miller is both the father and the architect of the U.S.-UK dialogue on nuclear weapons policy and operations. Although technical cooperation under the Mutual Defense Agreement (MDA) had been in place for nearly 30 years, it was not until 1985, under the stewardship of Mr. Miller, then serving as director of nuclear targeting at the Office of the Secretary of Defense (OSD), that U.S. policymakers began "to explore with British officials how to establish a dialogue where each side could talk about its deterrent philosophy and plans." The relationship quickly flourished, embodied in twice yearly nuclear policy staff talks that continue to this day.

For the next 20 years Mr. Miller oversaw the expansion and evolution of the dialogue as he held successively senior-level posts at OSD and the National Security Council. After he left government in March 2005, Mr. Miller's service and contribution to the U.S.-UK relationship was rewarded in 2006 with an honorary knighthood. Although his involvement was limited mainly to the policy side of nuclear cooperation, he also played a significant role in the extension of the MDA in 1998 and 2004, and he recalls a number of bureaucratic hurdles that nearly caused the MDA to expire "just by accident."

The impetus for the dialogue was born out of two converging developments in the early 1980s: the U.S. agreement to sell to the United Kingdom the Trident II missile, initially designed to be equipped with 12 warheads; and the subsequent compromise reached with the Soviet Union during the Strategic Arms Reduction Talks (START) to limit the warhead capacity of the U.S. Trident II missile to eight. This prompted a series of questions within the administration: Ought the UK missile be subject to the restrictions of START? Why does the UK need 12 warheads? Mr. Miller recalls: "We realized that our ignorance of UK targeting policy and doctrine was enormous and that there was in fact no dialogue at the policy level between NATO's nuclear powers. And that struck us as a very bad thing. So we changed that."

In response to questions concerning the independence of the UK deterrence, the United States released a formal statement to the Soviets in the early 1990s that placed the UK force outside the bounds of the START agreement and reaffirmed the open-ended commitment by the United States to support British nuclear modernization "in perpetuity." To Mr. Miller, the intimate technical and policy cooperation "in no way" infringes on the sovereignty of the UK deterrent. Although they spoke extensively of the philosophies that governed the British national plan and the U.S. single integrated operational plan, the British and U.S. participants never discussed specific aim points or "desired ground zeros."

Mr. Miller finds enormous value for U.S. strategic interests in an independent UK deterrent. First, sharing the "intellectual, moral, and political burden of providing the NATO nuclear deterrent. . . . It's enormously helpful when operating in the world of government to have a friend." Mr. Miller also believes that the "dual centers of decision-making" reduce the likelihood of a miscalculated Soviet first strike: "The Soviets might have convinced themselves on the basis of some intelligence that Washington would not respond, but they could never convince themselves that both Washington *and* London would not respond." While some may argue that that logic is antiquated and does not suit the twenty-first-century security landscape, Mr. Miller argues that this view makes the dangerous "assumption that historical change is irreversible."

The dialogue enriched both sides' intellectual capacity with regard to a number of policy and operational issues: "Deterrence means that you have to threaten your adversaries' vital assets, holding and resources— all elements of state power. And the UK looked at things differently, so we had an excellent dialogue about the nature of the Soviet system and what the leadership in Moscow valued."

The British also enhanced U.S. thinking about nuclear weapons effects with their more sophisticated understanding of the effects of fire.

With the demise of the Soviet Union, a new set of issues entered the dialogue: the evolving nature of deterrence, the role of NATO's strategic forces, the possibility that separatist elements might take over an intercontinental ballistic missile base in Russia, and other "hypotheticals and nuclear exercises." As the scope of the relationship expanded, Mr. Miller said, "the nuclear staff talks, which had originally just been two people from my team and three people from the UK, grew until we had Joint Staff people and people from the Trident project office and from Omaha . . . and they didn't only talk to each other when the groups met twice a year—they had each other's phone numbers. I probably talked to my British counterpart at least every two weeks. You get people comfortable with the fact that they can talk, and the space just keeps expanding."

Mr. Miller has learned that to make a partnership function—whether it's a marriage or a relationship between U.S. government agencies or your foreign counterparts—"you've got to work at it . . . and more than anything else you've got to listen. You cannot be in broadcast mode all the time. When you have absolute confidence that the person sitting next to you at the table is a close friend and someone you trust completely there is no limit to what you can get done."

—*Jessica Yeats*
Center for Strategic and International Studies

PETER SANKEY
HEAD OF THREAT REDUCTION,
ATOMIC WEAPONS ESTABLISHMENT, UK

Peter Sankey's career at the Atomic Weapons Establishment (AWE) spans nearly four decades. After Sankey joined the Atomic Weapons Research Establishment (AWRE) in 1970, he worked on intelligence-related projects; he then took charge of diagnostics for the underground tests conducted at the Nevada Test Site under the Mutual Defense Agreement. He continued in this role until the moratorium on nuclear testing. After that he served as a technical consultant to the Comprehensive Nuclear Test-Ban Treaty negotiations in Geneva, and he now serves as head of threat reduction at AWE.

"Being involved in underground testing was the absolute highlight of my career and one of the most important areas that anyone at AWE could have ever been involved in," he stressed. To him, the benefit of UK cooperation on testing was twofold. "Not only did it show us the way forward, how we are going to demonstrate credibility to the outside world, but it brought the whole of the capabilities of AWE together."

Similarly, in Mr. Sankey's view, "one of the UK's virtues in the 1958 agreements on underground tests was we actually helped to bring the U.S. laboratories together," even if there was a healthy competition among them. ("We each said we were better than they were.") Mr. Sankey took pride in getting both the Los Alamos and Livermore labs to adopt the same trailer park and down-hole grounding for UK shots. "It was a big achievement as it meant that they got together."

In this relationship, Mr. Sankey ranked the UK contributions to the peer review process as one of the most important UK contributions. "[The United States] had internal peer review with Los Alamos and Livermore and Sandia . . . but we thought differently, we did things differently, and they benefited greatly from that."

As the person responsible for making sure that all the diagnostic equipment was functioning properly, Mr. Sankey needed to get the most out of each experience; this meant that everything needed to be accounted for during the dry runs. "During the countdown they used to throw things at me to see how I would react," he said, "and it was right, as I had to be able to react in a split second." Once he had to stop the countdown because of a problem with detectors. "We worked almost through the night," he recalled, "because once you get the thing down the hole and stemmed you really don't want to leave it; you just want to get on and do it."

He also noted that because the United Kingdom tested far less frequently (one or two shots per year versus about 24 per year for the United States), the scientists at AWE introduced new ideas, which made the UK experiments interesting to the U.S. scientists. "We had a little more time between tests; therefore, we could put whatever extras we were testing on it, or whatever special features we were testing, and always had exciting experiments." With a great deal riding on each test, this also meant that the planning on the UK side was intense and meticulous, spanning up to two years.

The policy of maintaining absolute secrecy until after the test was, in Mr. Sankey's view, virtually impossible to maintain. "When tens of UK people turned up in Vegas and would stay in the same grotty motel and go to the same bar," he recalled with humor, "the same Americans in the bar would say 'the limeys are here again to let off a nuke' and the chances were it was going to be a test."

Indeed, by the time the UK team arrived at the test site, they had already spent months in collaboration with their peers in the United States. "We planned the diagnostics together, planned all the recording together, shared what we would do in trailers; and so there was a group of people who knew each other very well." The close contact with each lab continued during test preparations and created a "brilliant environment for innovation," according to Mr. Sankey. "We all wanted to get 100 percent" out of each experience.

According to Mr. Sankey, there was concern that the extended stays in the United States could affect personal relationships for UK scientists, especially because tests were scheduled in late autumn. It also meant that the radiochemists were always working through the Christmas holiday, away from their families. "They never thanked us for that, but it was just one of those things, and I had a young family," he said. However, the personal commitment and willingness to endure separations from loved ones were, to him, evidence of the great dedication and satisfaction that the UK scientists derived from their accomplishments and the "tremendous relationship" that had been forged with the United States.

"It was the materials, it was the diagnostics, it was the recording, it was the physics, it was absolutely everything," he concluded. "And [thus] not only a test of capability of AWE, which is vital, but a test of that relationship, and that's why it worked."

—*Stephen White*
Atomic Weapons Establishment

GLENN L. MARA

PRINCIPAL ASSOCIATE DIRECTOR FOR WEAPONS
PROGRAMS, LOS ALAMOS NATIONAL LABORATORY

Glenn L. Mara has been involved in the U.S. nuclear weapons program for more than 33 years. His weapons experience has spanned the materials science, design, engineering, testing, production, and dismantlement of nuclear weapons. Mara's most significant contributions to work under the UK-U.S. Mutual Defense Agreement (MDA) came as a result of his leadership in the Stockpile Stewardship Program (SSP) as well as elements of numerous underground tests at the Nevada Test Site for Lawrence Livermore National Laboratory. Several of these tests were either in collaboration with or led by the United Kingdom's Atomic Weapons Establishment.

After the cessation of testing, Mara was a central player in shaping the U1a complex where joint U.S.-UK subcritical experiments are performed. Mara has been involved in shaping the SSP and has been an integral player in the MDA. During the past five years, Mara has helped develop the "enhanced collaboration" agreement with the United Kingdom, in which both countries work together on fundamental science through experiments, theory, and computation.

After receiving his master's degree in the materials science of welding engineering from Ohio State University in 1971, Mara began his career at Lawrence Livermore National Laboratory as a materials scientist welding engineer in the Chemistry Division. He was the Test Engineering Program leader from 1987 to 1989 and oversaw aspects of fielding underground tests. From 1989 to 1998, Mara served as Livermore's Nevada Program leader, during which time he continued to coordinate underground tests until the testing moratorium was imposed in 1993. He became the principal deputy project manager for the National Ignition Facility in 2001, before he was selected as the associate director for engineering at Livermore. In 2002, Mara was named Livermore's deputy director for operations. In June 2006, as a member of the new management team selected to operate Los Alamos National Laboratory, Mara assumed the position of principal associate director for weapons programs.

"Over the past 50 years, the motivation for the continued U.S. support of the MDA has been to enhance the technical performance of the U.S. scientists, peer review of classified work, and partnership on experiments that are fielded at unique facilities like U1a, DARHT, NIF, and LANSCE," said Mara. "The MDA provides critical interactions for each country's nuclear stockpile certification enterprises. It has an influence on the U.S. role in nuclear deterrence within NATO. The United States benefits from the interactions with the United Kingdom on many levels."

In Mara's opinion, the most significant contribution from the agreement has been learning the value of planning and detailed analysis, which was the United Kingdom's core approach to weapons experiments. Mara explained, "The low number of experiments available to the UK scientists trained them to exercise more forethought in the experimental preparations. . . . This included preparing detailed pre-shot calculations and fully exploiting the acquired data." The British also introduced many advanced diagnostics that helped both countries better understand basic physics. In contrast, the United States was able to use a more empirical method of experiment design because of the somewhat abundant availability and frequency of underground testing. The U.S. methodology allowed evolutionary experiments and concepts to be tested quickly and arguably less expensively.

As a consequence of the cessation of underground testing, the past 15 years of weapons certification without testing have driven the weapons physics laboratories to seek a first principles understanding of weapons performance and led to increased emphasis on peer review of the technical work. "The past UK planning and detailed analysis methods are now equally important to the U.S. program," Mara said. The complexity of executing today's stockpile science and engineering experiments at complex facilities like DARHT and NIF has placed greater emphasis on measurements of properties that could not have been examined through testing. The principal goal for both nations now is to validate their individual predictive computational abilities. This effort requires higher precision measurements than were ever required during the years of testing. In addition, "the British approach to [data mining and] exploiting every measurement in the experiments has helped motivate the U.S. to perform more in-depth examinations of the data acquired over four decades of atomic testing," Mara noted. Thus, "the methodology the British had to learn because of their limited access to test and experiment facilities became the standard approach to stockpile stewardship without testing." The modern U.S. stewardship approach has adopted many of the UK scientific review methods and project preparation in dedicated weapons science experiments, Mara noted. "Both nations still reserve their principal interests and individual requirements for assessing the operability of their weapons systems," Mara said, "but the overall needs are similar enough to drive the technical collaborations."

The grueling 12- to 15-hour days preparing for nuclear tests or stockpile stewardship experiments indisputably led to improved science and engineering as well as to lasting friendships. Mara described how the collegiality of the work led to interactions on a more personal level and even to friendly competition. While setting up for experiments, the UK scientists and engineers engaged their U.S. counterparts in cricket matches, and in turn the U.S. scientists and engineers shared softball games with their UK counterparts. The collegial interactions led many of the UK and U.S. scientists and engineers to take up residence in each other's countries. These vital interactions helped reduce the stress and hardship of the complex work while they brought elements of each nation's deterrent community closer together.

—Tom Tierney
Los Alamos National Laboratory

Note: This work has been authored by an employee of Los Alamos National Security, LLC, operator of the Los Alamos National Laboratory under Contract No. DE-AC52-06NA25396 with the U.S. Department of Energy. The United States government retains and the publisher, by accepting this work for publication, acknowledges that the United States government retains a nonexclusive, paid-up, irrevocable, worldwide license to publish or reproduce this work, or allow others to do so for United States government purposes.

Kevin Tebbit joined the Ministry of Defence (MOD) in 1969, was appointed assistant private secretary to the secretary of state for defence, Lord Carrington, in 1972 and was the MOD's nuclear "desk officer" between 1976 and 1979. From 1979 to 1982 Sir Kevin was seconded to the diplomatic service as first secretary in the UK delegation to NATO until 1982, when he began service in the East European and Soviet Department in the Foreign Office. In 1987–1988 he served as director of cabinet to the secretary general of NATO, Lord Carrington, and from 1988 to 1991 he was the political and military counsellor at the British embassy in Washington. Sir Kevin returned to head the Foreign Office Economic Relations Department in 1992, and in 1997 he became the deputy under-secretary of state for defence and intelligence.

Sir Kevin was of the opinion that Anglo-American nuclear cooperation throughout the past 50 years has been beneficial to both powers and that the 1958 Mutual Defense Agreement (MDA) has been of "fundamental importance" to the bilateral relationship, both nuclear and more generally. This was because the relationship has been based on shared interests, with the nuclear interest at the heart of them.

On the British side, Sir Kevin noted, "Clearly in a narrow sense the UK benefited enormously because we were able to benefit from U.S. technology and U.S. expertise." He added that financially Britain had substantially reduced the cost of maintaining a nuclear deterrent and estimated that compared with pursuing a purely independent deterrent, in the fashion of France, Britain had only had to endure a fraction—perhaps one-third—of the financial burden. From the U.S. perspective, Sir Kevin opined that it is "very lonely if you're a sole superpower" and that the U.S. management of the NATO alliance and the NATO strategy of flexible response was "eased enormously by having the UK as a nuclear partner."

Further, Sir Kevin pointed out that because Britain was the "second center of decisionmaking," it reinforced deterrence against the Soviet Union because the Soviet Union could not rely on being able to "decouple" the United States from Europe and engage successfully in nuclear blackmail because another nuclear power, Britain, was available to ensure any necessary "recoupling."

On the issue of choosing a successor system to Polaris in the later years of the 1970s, Sir Kevin highlighted that the Ministry of Defence was against the idea of cruise missiles. "The problem with anything other than a ballistic missile, including cruise missiles, is that they did not have a guaranteed way of getting through defenses and they did not have a guaranteed failure rate as low as ballistic missiles," he said. "The whole point of nuclear deterrence is that the adversary should be uncertain as to whether you might use nuclear weapons, but very certain that if you did, the effect would be both achieved and devastating." But cruise missiles could not guarantee the same level of "certainty of arrival" as a ballistic missile system. Sir Kevin concluded that cruise missiles would have been a "dangerous way of trying to signal one's determination" to a potential adversary that Britain could ensure that the risks of aggression would outweigh any presumed benefits.

On the possibility of Britain engaging with France in nuclear cooperation, Sir Kevin made it clear that for both political and technological reasons "France could never replace the United States" and that "France was never seen seriously as an alternative pole." Further to this, Sir Kevin noted that under the terms of the 1958 MDA, "Our relationship with the United States meant we could not share certain information with a third country," which was a major obstacle to Anglo-French nuclear cooperation.

Sir Kevin noted that although Anglo-American nuclear cooperation was institutionalized by the 1958 MDA, "the lesson I would draw is that you can never take even close friends for granted" and that continuous work had to be applied to the management of the alliance in order for it to work successfully. He emphasized his belief that a very strong trust was built between the two countries at all levels among scientists, military officers, diplomats, and government officials, which enabled the relationship to remain strong, even when there were strains at head-of-government level from time to time.

On the subject of arms limitation, Sir Kevin raised his skepticism over Britain unilaterally disarming and stated, "I think we still need to be able to influence the debate and you can't do that from a position of unilateral disarmament." He argued that the priority was for both the United States and Russia to work harder toward reducing their nuclear stockpiles, but it was not seen as a wise objective to create a world where proliferation remained unchecked or where disarmament meant that the utilization of conventional weapons was more likely. Sir Kevin also expressed his belief that "nuclear weapons helped us win the Cold War and secure peace for Europe. Society should not forget that."

—*Thomas Robb*
Aberystwyth University

LINTON F. BROOKS
FORMER ADMINISTRATOR,
NATIONAL NUCLEAR SECURITY ADMINISTRATION,
U.S. DEPARTMENT OF ENERGY

Linton Brooks began his career serving as a seagoing U.S. Navy officer before he was assigned to the office of the Assistant to the Secretary for Atomic Energy in the Department of Defense. While at the DOD, Ambassador Brooks was responsible for the Navy's nuclear portfolio and cooperation with the United Kingdom, and he advocated the U.S. decision to support the UK's move to the Trident weapon system. He served in the State Department as head of the U.S. delegation on nuclear and space talks, and he was chief Strategic Arms Reduction Talks negotiator during the administration of President George H. W. Bush. During the 1990s he left government to become vice president at the Center for Naval Analyses. During the administration of President George W. Bush, Ambassador Brooks served until 2007 as the under secretary of energy for nuclear security and administrator of the National Nuclear Security Administration. During the George W. Bush administration, Ambassador Brooks was one of the two senior U.S. officials managing the 1958 Mutual Defense Agreement (MDA) with the United Kingdom.

Ambassador Brooks worked with chief scientific advisers (CSA) at the UK Ministry of Defence, Sir Keith O'Nions and Professor Sir Roy Anderson, during his tenure at the NNSA. "It is hard to imagine a better professional relationship," Ambassador Brooks recalled. CSAs are distinguished members of the academic community who are contracted to provide advice to the UK Ministry of Defence although they formally report to the prime minister, and the CSA is the British custodian of the 1958 agreement.

Ambassador Brooks credits the technical nature of the MDA with its success. The real cooperation is between laboratories, formally operated through joint working groups known as JOWOGs. The Foreign Office and the State Department are not present at most meetings about the MDA and come together only intermittently for large policy decisions. This insulates the technical cooperation from broader policy issues. Of the 1958 agreement, Ambassador Brooks says, "The amount of technical data exchanged with the UK has no analogue." He acknowledges that at times during its 50-year history, "there were probably more years when the two-way traffic was going one way," pointing to the early 1980s as an example when "the British weapons establishment was being starved for funds and, looking at a year-by-year basis, the benefits were mostly here to there. However, in recent years, that has not been the case . . . a tit-for-tat analysis misses the fundamental point of the special relationship, and in aggregate cooperation has benefited both countries hugely."

The special relationship between the United States and the United Kingdom has endured many changes in perceptions of threats in the international environment. The relationship was forged during World War II and solidified during the Cold War, and the United Kingdom is the most staunch ally of the United States in the war on terror and the Iraq War. In the 1980s, the United States was interested in nuclear strategic defenses, which bothered its UK ally because the United Kingdom feared that competition with the USSR in the field of defenses would lead the USSR to develop the ability to blunt a small attack from the UK, thus lessening the effectiveness of its deterrent. However, the relationship survived this and other trials presented by the changing international environment in the immediate aftermath of the Cold War and the erosion of the Soviet threat.

During the 1990s the United Kingdom and the United States embraced the negotiations for the Comprehensive Test Ban Treaty although the United States did not ratify it. Relations remained strong because "we generally have a commonality of views and a commonality of values." Ambassador Brooks cites the long tradition of cooperation between the two countries, noting that, although friendships are not impervious to changes in national perceptions, he would not be surprised if the special relationship lasted far into the future.

The British government has devoted funding to updating the submarines carrying the Trident system and has resolved to discuss updating the Trident weapon system. Speaking of the United Kingdom's 2006 white paper, "The Future of the UK's Strategic Deterrent," in which the government clearly outlined the debate on maintaining a nuclear arsenal in the post–Cold War era, Ambassador Brooks said:

> We lacked a document with the clarity of the white paper. To some extent this was easier in Britain because the British view of the purpose of nuclear weapons is narrower; they focus on deterrence as the only thing that weapons do. They don't feel a need to emphasize extended deterrence—what we now call assurance; they don't think it is their role to discourage others from an arms race—which we now call dissuasion; and they tend to be a little more convinced that deterrence will work, so they don't get into the issues about the role of defenses that we've gotten into.

Although Ambassador Brooks believes a U.S. white paper would be harder to write, he laments the fact that the attempt was never made. He believes that the lesson of a clearly articulated policy is a valuable one.

Ambassador Brooks believes that recently the United Kingdom has been more successful than the United States in modernizing its arsenal because it has a clearly defined and articulated policy, and, in every major weapons development decision the British have taken, they have in parallel made some kind of arms control or nonproliferation decision. For example, when the British decided to update the Trident system, they also committed to a reduction of the number of deployed warheads, demonstrating that their nonproliferation and security obligations are linked. He believes that the United States has done that less well.

—Cassandra Smith
Center for Strategic and International Studies

TIM HARE

FORMER DIRECTOR, NUCLEAR POLICY,

UK MINISTRY OF DEFENCE

Commodore Hare joined the Royal Navy in 1965 and thus began a career in the realm of British defense. In 1970 he joined the submarine service and in 1982 was appointed to the Polaris submarine HMS *Resolution,* where he served at the front line of Britain's nuclear deterrent force. Commodore Hare's later appointments were in the procurement executive at the Ministry of Defence (MOD), where he was responsible for the policy, procurement, and development of submarine weapon systems and in the MOD providing advice on strategic nuclear submarine (SSBN) operations and effectiveness. In 1993 he was promoted to captain and became project manager for the Vanguard-class SSBN tactical weapons system.

His final appointment was as a commodore in March 1999, when he became director of nuclear policy in the MOD and took responsibility for the development and promotion of the United Kingdom's nuclear deterrence policy in Britain, NATO, and the wider international community. Commodore Hare went on to contribute to nuclear force planning in the United Kingdom, and he provided ministerial advice on the U.S. missile defense initiative. Commodore Hare retired from the Royal Navy in 2002 and joined the international defense company, Thales, where he remains today.

According to Commodore Hare, the Mutual Defense Agreement of 1958 is one of two fundamental agreements underpinning Britain's nuclear deterrent capability, the other being the Polaris Sales Agreement of 1963. "Those two taken together," he suggested, "are pivotal to us being able to maintain an affordable deterrent capability in this country." He argued that political and popular support in Britain rested on an effective deterrent at an affordable cost. Without U.S. cooperation, the existence of a British nuclear state would have been much more questionable. "I would go so far as to say that without those two agreements the road by which we have maintained an independent nuclear deterrent capability would have been much more rocky than it has been."

Commodore Hare is, however, skeptical with regard to more romantic assessments of the Anglo-American relationship. "I think there is a quid pro quo here," he commented. "There are political and geostrategic benefits to both sides in the agreement." This evaluation has a direct bearing on his interpretation of Anglo-American nuclear cooperation. "I don't use the term special relationship, I don't use the term bridge to Europe," he stated. "But I do think that there are benefits to the United States in ensuring that they have alongside them a second decisionmaking center on nuclear matters." Commodore Hare stresses that this is particularly true "when debating nuclear issues within NATO and with other allies." He therefore considers this cooperation as essentially a product of the political and geostrategic relationship with the United States. "I think there is a common interest in ensuring the spread of democracy and the defense of freedom throughout the world," he said.

Commodore Hare is keen to note, however, that as cooperation filters down below these higher-level common interests, some differences in perspective emerge. These differences range from the dramatically different force levels involved to the more subtle divergences of declaratory policy and approaches to global disarmament. Commodore Hare was equally aware of such differences at the practical level during his time aboard the British deterrent. Despite the sharing of the Polaris technology, for example, there were two distinct ways of operating submarines. Consequently, he sees the relationship as somewhat of a mixture: "In some areas we are clutched in, almost at one, and in others there are recognized differences which, in the policy area, you just learn to manage because those differences are subtle."

Commodore Hare believes that the Anglo-American relationship is affected by personalities: "The relationship is very much governed by the nature of the two administrations that are in power at any one time, the personal chemistry between president and prime minister is crucial and sets the tone for lower-level exchanges."

Looking toward the future, Commodore Hare is optimistic regarding continued cooperation while the case for a nuclear deterrent capability remains sound. "Whilst nuclear disarmament remains a mutual long-term objective, there are subtle differences in approach towards working with international institutions and core disarmament treaties such as the NPT," he said. "For example, whilst the U.S. has not ratified the Comprehensive Test Ban Treaty (although it follows the implied principle) and approaches the NPT with some caution, Britain has ratified the treaty and implemented a number of other de-alerting, stockpile reduction, and transparency measures called for by the NPT."

Notwithstanding this, the twin issues of proliferation running out of control and stockpiles remaining high all in a highly volatile global security environment form a strong case for the retention of a minimum nuclear deterrent capability. "I think the U.S. sees the benefit of us maintaining that capability as well, not only in today's security environment, but in the project scenarios of the future," he said. "So I do believe that the MDA/PSA will continue to provide the necessary channel for technical and acquisition exchange." Not only does he believe that these agreements will continue to operate in a positive way but, looking toward the future, Commodore Hare remarked, "I see the working relationship warming quite a bit as affordability issues on both sides of the Atlantic mitigate for stronger technical ties between the two countries."

—*David Gill*
Aberystwyth University

HERBERT YORK
FORMER DIRECTOR
LAWRENCE LIVERMORE NATIONAL LABORATORY

Herbert York completed his bachelor's degree and master's degree at the University of Rochester in 1943 at the age of 21. He then joined the Radiation Laboratory at the University of California, Berkeley, where he earned his doctorate while contributing to the laboratory's work with particle accelerators. His work there brought him into contact with Ernest Lawrence, who would later call on him to explore the idea of establishing a second laboratory to help drive U.S. atomic weapons research and then to serve as the first director of this new laboratory, which was located at Livermore. Serving as director from 1952 to 1958, York oversaw Livermore's emergence as a vital center of atomic weapons research and helped lead its innovative thinking in developing smaller and more versatile warheads.

York attributes his selection to run the Livermore laboratory to his previous exposure to Ernest Lawrence at Berkeley. "I was usually one of the few people who was there in the evening," he remembers, "Ernest knew more about me, or was more aware of me, than he was perhaps of the average graduate student. . . ." Upon completing his doctoral studies, York received offers to work elsewhere, but he resolved to stay at Berkeley's renowned Radiation Laboratory because, he said, "I'd rather be a little frog in a big puddle."

Following his tenure at Livermore, York accepted government positions that included service as the chief scientist of the Advanced Research Projects Agency and as director of research and engineering at the Department of Defense. His career in academia included a position as professor of physics at the University of California, Berkeley; two stints as chancellor of the University of California, San Diego, where he currently serves as the chairman of the Scientific and Academic Advisory Committee that oversees the work of Lawrence Livermore and Los Alamos National Laboratories; and director emeritus of the university's Institute on Global Conflict and Cooperation.

When York was asked about establishing a second national laboratory, he realized that he could frame the discussion in Washington "in highly negative and pejorative terms, such as Los Alamos is much too stuffy and they've just got to have competition; or it could be put into more reasonable terms, which is that two laboratories will provide competition for each other, and that's a good thing, in the American spirit." Ultimately, he chose the latter perspective.

As the idea for a new laboratory took shape, York dealt with the developers, Ernest Lawrence and Edward Teller, in a "slightly conspiratorial way." Lawrence, with his entrepreneurial zeal and the belief that "if you do a good job, everything else will take care of itself," embraced the idea of a second laboratory. Teller, however, "was very suspicious of everybody" and questioned the intentions of the government and the true relevance of a second laboratory to the U.S. atomic weapons program. As York summarized, once work began at Livermore, "Ernest knew we would get into the bomb business, but he didn't have to have that [guarantee] as part of the program to start with. Edward did."

The laboratory's first few explosions resulted in very low yields and drew some "horselaughs" from the establishment in Los Alamos. "Looking back on it," reflects York, "it ought to have been more discouraging than I remember it being . . . so, although we were embarrassed, we were not really disheartened."

The young scientists remained undaunted, thanks largely to Lawrence's leadership, according to York. "He was remarkable with young people . . . a father figure for me, I suppose." According to York, Lawrence was exceptionally fond of the physicists and frequently remarked that his "physicists didn't need [specific] titles; the best title . . . was physicist at the Radiation Laboratory. That was the best title in the world, not just in the laboratory or in the University of California."

Although Teller wasn't present at the Livermore lab for several of its first years, "he was always an inspiration to people, especially the theoretical groups." So the young scientists at Livermore pressed on after their early failures, in some ways disregarding the government's direction, testing themselves and the new technology. Boldly, and perhaps even naively, "we did keep charging ahead," said York. "The policy was to push extremes in order, consciously, to make technology as challenging as pure science." In fact, after testing the limits of size and power, York recalled that "it was Eisenhower himself who said, 'Stop.'"

By York's account, "the spirit was one of Edward always interested in trying to invent things, and Ernest with the notion of building a floor, and the sky's the limit. . . ." With John ("Johnny") Foster and Harold Brown leading teams for small and large weapons, respectively, Livermore soon achieved critical breakthroughs in atomic weapon design. York unambiguously credits the laboratory's "adventurous spirit" for these advancements. "It wasn't as if Lawrence and Teller were telling us to do these things; it was natural for us to do them, and they participated with a lot of boyish enthusiasm."

—Mark Jansson
Center for Strategic and International Studies

STEVE DEARDEN

DIRECTOR, NUCLEAR PROPULSION,

UK MINISTRY OF DEFENCE

Commodore Dearden commented that in respect of U.S.-UK nuclear propulsion technology exchange, the 1958 Mutual Defense Agreement had been, and continues to be, of vital strategic importance. "The MDA is the single enabler for nuclear propulsion technology exchange with the U.S. Naval Nuclear Propulsion Program and allows both of us to take advantage of a unique opportunity to talk with a like-minded, responsible nuclear power on some quite sensitive material," Commodore Dearden explained, and continued by stating, "The 58 MDA provides us with the legal cover to exchange on nuclear propulsion design and development work; we interpret to mutual agreement how we control the exchange and security of each other's information and technology."

In the field of nuclear propulsion the United Kingdom is totally responsible for its own reactor plant design and operation. "We don't buy wholesale from the US," he emphasized; "they'd probably not want to do that sort of business; our business is built on the ability to share ideas and consider each other's work." Further, Commodore Dearden made clear that one of the objectives behind nuclear propulsion technology cooperation between the United Kingdom and United States was to make sure that Britain fully contributed to the nuclear program between the two countries. "Part of the original agreement on the exchange of nuclear reactor technology was that the UK would stand on its own two feet in terms of its ability to discharge responsible nuclear ownership, so we developed our own processes, systems, and technical understanding; we developed our own technology base," Commodore Dearden explained. "We had to have the capability ourselves without leaning on the US."

Furthermore, the working relationship with the United States gave the United Kingdom "considerable cost leverage" in Commodore Dearden's opinion: "Bang for your buck we get a great deal from working with the US." The United States, for its part, similarly benefits from nuclear cooperation with the United Kingdom, as it provides an opportunity for an intellectually independent body to review and evaluate its work on extremely sensitive material. Overall, Commodore Dearden believed that "the MDA is an enabler; it's facilitated by political considerations: what the shared ideals of the two countries are. What you do under that is about engineering and technology exchange, so we do what we need to do to support our national programs in a manner that is mutually beneficial, particularly where we can avoid duplication and spending for the sake of it."

As for the continuation of nuclear cooperation under the terms of the 1958 MDA, Commodore Dearden saw no reason as to why this should stop. "We have a robust technical exchange currently," he said. "I suppose the question would be why would we want to jeopardize that relationship?"

His advice for future policymakers involved in all aspects of the use of nuclear technology for defense purposes is that they cannot neglect educating future generations in scientific and engineering matters if the United Kingdom wishes to remain a credible nuclear power. "There is no substitute for technical excellence and engineering competence. You cannot ignore your responsibility as a nuclear operator. If you're in the nuclear game you've got to understand what you're dealing with and be demonstrably able to manage the risks; so you've got to have the best people, enough of the best people, and this has got to be the case in both the government and industry, if you are to manage a program safely, and to appropriately spend the significant sums of public money that come with that program." Commodore Dearden was concerned that, "We (the UK) have a fragile industrial base capability for complex engineering" and that this could negatively impact on future collaboration with the United States because the UK's credibility as a nuclear owner could potentially be undermined. He concluded by saying, "Strategically, the 58 MDA is a tremendous asset for the United Kingdom because without it we would not be able to exchange with the United States and we could become stagnant and introspective."

—*Thomas Robb*
Aberystwyth University

.

JOHN T. MITCHELL
REAR ADMIRAL, U.S. NAVY (RETIRED)

The U.S.-UK Mutual Defense Agreement (MDA) created close ties between the military officers tasked with the operational and technical aspects of nuclear cooperation. For Rear Admiral John T. Mitchell, the MDA was an important and influential component of his extraordinary navy career. As a member of the U.S. Navy's Strategic Systems Programs (SSP) office, including service as director of the office from 1992 to 1994 after promotion to flag rank, Admiral Mitchell spent a significant portion of his naval career advising, working with, and supporting the United Kingdom's submarine-based nuclear weapons program.

Admiral Mitchell's cooperation and collaboration with the United Kingdom began early in his career. In 1966, after he graduated from Rice University and spent a few years at sea, the U.S. Navy sent him to Sunnyvale, California, where Lockheed Martin was working on the development of the Polaris A-3 submarine-launched ballistic missile. Because the United Kingdom had decided to use the Polaris missile in its submarines, a group from the United Kingdom was stationed in Sunnyvale. Admiral Mitchell worked with the United Kingdom on a variety of technical matters related to the new missile, including work on penetration aids that they had planned to install to defeat what was believed to be an emerging antiballistic missile system in the Soviet Union.

In Admiral Mitchell's view, the close U.S.-UK collaboration codified in the Mutual Defense Agreement was a natural outgrowth of the close relationship created during the Second World War. America's early support to the British in the form of the Lend-Lease Act created in the post–World War II world an important pathway for even closer cooperation with agreements such as the MDA. Mitchell and his colleagues at Sunnyvale were "fully committed" to helping the United Kingdom with its nuclear weapons program, and Mitchell's early work on the Polaris A-3 made a long-lasting impression on him. "It was extraordinary how close the cooperation was, not only technically but in a managerial sense—how we made the two programs support each other and help each other," he recalled. "It was an extremely professional and open working relationship in that environment."

The close U.S.-UK nuclear relationship is exemplified by the continued support of the United States for the United Kingdom's Polaris program long after the United States had moved away from Polaris in favor of other missile systems. When the United Kingdom decided to extend the service life of Polaris into the early 1980s—long after its intended life span—the United States was instrumental in helping to keep the missiles operational. This required that the United States essentially reinvent old manufacturing techniques and redevelop materials that no longer existed in order to maintain and replace the missiles' aging rocket motors. "We kept A-3 in service for them well longer than we kept it in service for ourselves," Mitchell said. "They were totally dependent on us for the technology of the missile itself. They operated it, but if you wanted to do anything different to it than the way it came, we had to do that for them." In this area, as well as in many others, the United States willingly served as the United Kingdom's "logistics support team."

Admiral Mitchell joined the main office of SSP in 1978, and for the next 16 years his duties and responsibilities included collaboration with the United Kingdom. As director of SSP from 1992 to 1994, Mitchell was the U.S. counterpart of the United Kingdom's chief strategic systems executive (CSSE), the Royal Navy's primary liaison to the U.S. Navy on nuclear matters. Admiral Mitchell's team met formally with the CSSE every four months as part of the Joint Steering Task Group, and Mitchell describes these meetings as carefully orchestrated and scripted. According to Mitchell, these meetings continue today.

Frequent meetings between the United States and the United Kingdom created close relationships and deep mutual respect. Admiral Mitchell's work with his UK counterparts developed into long-lasting personal friendships. "When we would make these trips back and forth [between the United States and the United Kingdom], we would spend a few days at our counterparts' homes," Mitchell said. "You worked with these people for 10 or 15 years, as they go up through the ranks, so did you." The personal relationships that were created as a result of the MDA were so strong that they continued even after people were transferred out of their assigned posts.

Admiral Mitchell is quick to point out that the MDA benefited the United States as much as it benefited the United Kingdom. In his view, the creation and continuation of the nuclear partnership created pathways for mutually beneficial collaboration in other areas. Through close cooperation, the United States gained insight into the Royal Navy's operational procedures and consequently received operational test data for free. By observing how the Royal Navy worked, the U.S. Navy could compare its procedures with theirs and potentially adopt best practices. Mitchell also notes that having a professional counterpart in the same business helped create better leaders. The opportunity to observe practices and discuss important issues with a foreign counterpart provided new ways of thinking about pressing nuclear matters and enhanced leadership skills. Finally, and perhaps most important, close U.S.-UK nuclear cooperation contributed to the U.S. Navy's ability to operate forward, that is, to conduct sea patrols far away from U.S. territorial waters.

—Michael S. Gerson
Center for Naval Analyses

GERRY WILMOTT
FORMER SUPERINTENDENT OF
(WARHEAD) MECHANICAL DESIGN,
ATOMIC WEAPONS ESTABLISHMENT, UK

Gerry Wilmott joined the Atomic Weapons Establishment (AWE) from the Ministry of Defence (MOD) as a development engineer in 1981. His early work focused on research and development for engineering systems before he was promoted to take charge of one of the two underground testing teams. In this role he came into close contact with his counterparts from Los Alamos through the joint working groups (JOWOGs) forged under the Mutual Defense Agreement of 1958. He returned to the MOD in 2001 and now works on safety and peer review.

During the early 1980s AWE was a computerless environment until Dr. Wilmott went and brought the first computer into his department (an Amstrad purchased with petty cash from Boots Pharmacy). Designs were done on paper, and there was a strong emphasis on testing in the lab, where he recalls experimenting with washing liquid under high pressure and accidentally filling a lab with foam. He worked closely with the physics department on underground tests (UGTs), which led to an involvement from an early stage in the JOWOGs. Dr. Wilmott was quickly promoted to be in charge of one of the two UGT engineering teams, and he looked after three of the shots fielded by Los Alamos. This meant he was on the sharp end for both safety and deadlines, which brought him into a much closer working relationship with Los Alamos. "It was a great honor then to go out on the exchanges with the U.S. labs," he said. "We had to convince ourselves and the Americans that the tests would be safe. If there had been an incident of any type, then it would have finished UGTs in the short term and soured our relationship with the U.S.; and that was something that we sought to avoid at all costs."

"I became engrossed in the JOWOG community," said Dr. Wilmott. "They forged a far more constructive relationship between the two design communities that understood better one another's constraints." His involvement with the JOWOGs also benefited him personally throughout his 20 years at AWE. "The JOWOG exchange did my career the world of good," he said. "It gave me the technical confidence I needed to hold my own with the physicists because I didn't just want to be the tame engineer who did what he was told."

During this time he got to know many of the U.S. engineers personally, recalling that "meeting people outside of work was psychologically very important when you were away from home and family for six to eight weeks at a time." And so "I would go out cycling and running with my U.S. counterparts, and this made our trips extremely pleasurable. You form very strong relationships with these people when you're working hard alongside them."

Dr. Wilmott acknowledged that the AWE program was somewhat underresourced compared with its U.S. counterparts, and sometimes there was frustration that the UK scientists seemed to be "drip-fed" information. After the first few JOWOGs, however, he "realized that the UK did have something to offer. The U.S. didn't have a better intellectual capability, just more if it, more horsepower. [But] we had original ideas, and we received recognition for that."

Indeed, Dr. Wilmott found the exchanges to be a two-way street of information in which scientists who respected one another would learn from and challenge each other's ideas. During these exchanges, he noticed that "new people who came in afresh were somewhat surprised, and perhaps shocked at the brutal honesty." In his view, however, the competition and challenge helped strengthen the relationships. "It's very important to have others of a similar ilk crawl all over your work and ask honest hard questions, and for the person subjected to not be offended and learn from it. We grew in this throughout the '80s and the bond with the U.S. continued to grow. I'd like to think that they gained from this tin-pot little nation!"

Although the challenge was healthy and important, Dr. Wilmott found that it was often the strength of the personal relationships created through the JOWOGs that provided the backbone for the collaboration under the MDA. According to him, dialogue with the United States through the JOWOG loop continued even after specific projects were canceled or sidelined as a result of reductions in funding.

After transitioning away from his work on underground tests, Dr. Wilmott remained in contact with his colleagues in the United States and eventually chaired one of the JOWOGs. In his words, this involved "lots of visits to the U.S., whistle-stop tours around the labs, making new friends and contacts, [as] my relationship with U.S. colleagues continued to be strong and robust throughout my career at AWE."

—Owen Price
Atomic Weapons Establishment

ROBERT G. JOSEPH
FORMER U.S. UNDER SECRETARY OF STATE FOR
ARMS CONTROL AND INTERNATIONAL SECURITY

Robert Joseph served as the under secretary of state for arms control and international security from 2005 to 2007. Before holding that position, he was the special assistant to the president and the senior director for proliferation strategy, counterproliferation, and homeland defense at the National Security Council (2001–2005). During that time, he worked closely with UK counterparts on a number of major initiatives, including the successful efforts to disarm Libya's programs for weapons of mass destruction (WMD). In the Reagan administration, he held various high-level nuclear planning positions in Brussels, including the director of theater nuclear forces policy (1985–1987). In that capacity, he worked closely with the British and other NATO allies on modernizing the nuclear force posture in the alliance and implementing the Intermediate-Range Nuclear Force (INF) agreement. He has held other positions involving the bilateral nuclear partnership, including in the Office of the Undersecretary of Defense and as ambassador to consultative commissions on the Anti-Ballistic Missile Treaty and nuclear testing.

To Dr. Joseph, the Mutual Defense Agreement is both a perpetuation and a reflection of the special relationship with the United Kingdom that predates World War II, a partnership he describes as "truly unique" and "joint in every sense of the word." He recalls close cooperation with many NATO member states, but with the United Kingdom he believes that "the difference is a reflection of our very close technological and operational interactions in the nuclear field." The 1958 agreement was very important in sustaining the relationship through the complexities that attended the Cold War and the evolution of deterrence. "It continues to provide a foundation and legal framework for the special relationship and the fusion of operational and technical cooperation," he said.

Contributions from the United Kingdom were instrumental to nearly every foreign policy success that Dr. Joseph played a role in achieving. On theater and strategic missile defense, British radar capability and political support for the "strategic logic of missile defense" was critical to its deployment. The UK partnership was also pivotal in the joint and ultimately successful effort in 2003 to compel Libya to dispose of its WMD programs. Dr. Joseph, who led the policy negotiations leading up to the disarmament announcement, contends that this "major intelligence and policy success story could not have happened without the British being full partners, and it could only have happened with the British."

In deterrence policy and NATO operational issues writ broadly, contributions from the British "had a major impact on the end of the Cold War" and the ultimate demise of the Soviet empire. In part, these contributions to the policy dimension of nuclear planning were born out of the integration of the UK strategic capability into NATO, which was greatly influenced and enhanced by the technical exchanges in warhead design taking place under the Mutual Defense Agreement. As a clear leader in the alliance as well as an integral basing country, the United Kingdom worked closely with the United States in INF decisions and was "very important in the decision to deploy the ground launch cruise missiles and Pershing II missiles in the early 1980s, which held the alliance together." The United Kingdom also played a prominent role in advancing the arms control track to the INF agreement. "I will never forget the briefing that the U.S. provided to the high-level group on nuclear requirements," said Dr. Joseph. "The results were unsettling. They certainly didn't meet the expectations of the other partners in the alliance, and the British were instrumental in their own analysis, which resulted in the number of 4,000 nuclear weapons in Europe."

The nature of the partnership that Dr. Joseph witnessed with the United Kingdom on nuclear issues both informed and reflected his model for effective multilateral cooperation. "Where interests intersect, you ought to do everything you can to cooperate," he said. This model of mutually beneficial partnerships can be seen in other multi-lateral initiatives he has spearheaded, including the Proliferation Security Initiative, the Global Initiative to Combat Nuclear Terrorism, and the G-8 Global Partnership against the Spread of Nuclear Weapons. "The traditional nonproliferation way of doing business is to seek universality often at the expense of the best outcome, so in some cases you get the least common denominator," he said. "This approach is much different. You get together with a small group of people that share the same interests and are willing to act proactively, and you develop a set of standards and commitments. And what you see over time is that participation in these coalitions becomes a standard for good nonproliferation behavior."

—Jessica Yeats
Center for Strategic and International Studies

MALCOLM JONES
DESIGN AUTHORITY SCIENTIFIC ADVISER,
ATOMIC WEAPONS ESTABLISHMENT, UK

Malcolm Jones began working for the Atomic Weapons Establishment in 1967, after completing his Ph.D. at Swansea University. His distinguished scientific career has included developing firing circuits and explosive to energy transducers; modeling firing detonators, reentry plasmas, and radiation effects; and designing arming, fuzing, and firing (AF&F) architectures. Throughout his career, he has maintained a focus on safety, from developing and assessing items, assessing systems, to assisting the Ministry of Defence with top-level safety requirements such as the Ordinance Board Procedures and the Safety Principles and Safety Criteria document.

Much of Jones's work has been collaborative in nature, and his first involvement with the United States was through a joint working group (JOWOG) working on AF&Fs. He traveled to the United States to discuss MHD (magnetohydrodynamics) and the modeling work he had done on flux compression devices. "We weren't particularly successful in building them," he recalled, "but at the time, we were more successful than the Americans in being able to model the outputs." Using information on some of the U.S. devices, Jones's group performed predictive analyses that were "remarkably on the ball."

In 1992 Jones and several other U.S. and UK colleagues decided there was a gap in the JOWOG system. While there were various technical JOWOGs that looked after safety aspects in their own areas, there was nothing that looked across the board in terms of assessment methodologies and bringing all of the information together in a systems context, either for weapons system design or safety cases for operations. As such, they set up a new exchange, first under an EIVR (Exchange of Information by Visit and Report) framework, which was more recently elevated to a full JOWOG that Jones now chairs.

Jones has also collaborated under the auspices of the Mutual Defense Agreement (MDA) through the British scientists who first went to the United States during the early stages of the United Kingdom's Trident system procurement. Jones recalled that "it was a very hectic week of [absorbing] all the information that was given to us and then of course coming back and trying to make head or tail of it, looking at the strengths and weaknesses and all the follow-on arena of questions that needed to be asked."

However, in the case of Trident procurement and with nuclear cooperation in general, Jones believes the MDA benefits both sides. In sum, the United Kingdom benefits from the fact that the United States "covers a wider range of potential applications . . . [while the United States benefits when] the United Kingdom is able to concentrate in-depth on certain areas." Furthermore, Jones speculates that the United States has taken an interest in observing how the United Kingdom maintains its system with fewer resources. Whereas in past years the U.S. nuclear weapons program had virtually unlimited resources, Jones noticed that "in recent times, they are contracting and are wondering what the model should be in a contracting organization—so they look towards us, our model, why we are successful spending so little on it . . . and presumably looking to see how far they can go down that sort of route and use us as a template."

Jones also finds particular value in U.S.-UK cooperation following the moratorium on underground tests (UGTs). "Obviously on the design of physics packages without UGTs, both sides have a slightly different methodology; and that's of benefit to both sides because two approaches put together are obviously going to be better than the two approaches in isolation." Thus, Jones adds, "my impression has been that the amount of cooperation has increased over the last decade or so and there seems to be a lot more [openness about] wanting to extend this cooperation." Jones further indicated that the quality—as well as the quantity—of cooperation tends to improve over time, because when "you're meeting with people you know and you both know the rules, there's sort of a track record of trust" that solidifies and improves working relationships.

Jones concedes that certain constraints on collaboration remain, as the United States does not disclose information about systems that are currently in service, and so "there's a lot of juggling around about how to keep the flow of research information healthy and, still, for the balancing act make sure that nothing has slipped across the border."

Looking to the future, Jones can see increased cooperation, yet he doesn't think that "the Americans would ever want to be in a position where they were dependent on another country. By that I don't mean [that it is not] useful to get research knowledge from another country; but if it was related to something that went into one of the U.S. weapon systems that was produced in some form outside the United States, then that becomes a bargaining chip" that the Americans would have to deal with.

From the UK side, Jones believes that "the situation is pretty straightforward [because] we see that there is more to gain than lose in [collaboration]." To that end, he expressed some concern about U.S. indecisiveness on nuclear weapons issues and the future of the U.S. stockpile. "There is a lot of enthusiasm on the lab side," he noted. And if decisions could be made on key modernization issues in the United States, "then certainly our collaborations would look healthier."

—Owen Price
Atomic Weapons Establishment

RICHARD L. WAGNER
FORMER U.S. ASSISTANT TO THE SECRETARY OF
DEFENSE FOR ATOMIC ENERGY

Richard Wagner began his career at the Lawrence Livermore National Laboratory in the early 1960s in nuclear weapon design, and by the end of the 1970s he was deputy director of the laboratory and had led a major part of the design and underground testing programs. During those years he worked intimately with UK nuclear scientists, holding numerous meetings with the Atomic Weapons Research Establishment (now the Atomic Weapons Establishment) representatives in the United Kingdom and in the United States. In 1981 he left Livermore for the Pentagon, where he served as assistant to the secretary of defense for atomic energy and was, in his words, "the keeper of the technical side of the MDA." He has since worked at the Los Alamos National Laboratory and continued his involvement with the policy dimension of the Mutual Defense Agreement (MDA) by membership on the Defense Science Board, the Defense Intelligence Agency Advisory Board and the Threat Reduction Advisory Committee for the Office of the Secretary of Defense. Dr. Wagner's extensive history with the MDA offers an illuminating account of the nuclear relationship, from the political negotiations that codified it to the technical exchanges that formed the core of it.

Permeating all of his interactions with UK counterparts, whether at Livermore or in the Pentagon, was a sense of common purpose that they were "in this Cold War thing together." There were disagreements, but, "the way those disagreements worked out always ended up strengthening the relationship," he said. "We wouldn't be doing anything as well as we are today without the UK relationship."

To Dr. Wagner, the nature of the benefit was different on the two sides. "If you think of technology transfer, there was more flow from us to the UK," he said. "But if you think of insight transfer, it was at least equal and maybe the flow ran from them to us." It was perhaps precisely because they lagged in technological capability that they contributed with such insight. "There were knotty, difficult problems in nuclear weapon design, and time and again we found that our British counterparts, despite not having the computers and codes and experimental facilities that we did, would think deeply about the physics and had a good sense of intuition, and often more insightful views on these problems."

Because of the larger and more capable computers available to U.S. scientists, there was a tendency to orient U.S. design work more around the calculations rather than think more deeply about the physics. In fact, witnessing this type of thinking from their UK counterparts spurred speculation among U.S. scientists that the Soviets, too, thought more like physicists, and it was always a nervous surmise that "because the UK scientists were better than they ought to have been, given their tools, maybe we were underestimating the Soviet capability."

While at Livermore, Dr. Wagner led a program that included developing new machines to take flash radiographs, an important ancillary nuclear weapon technology that took very short snapshots of the implosion of nuclear weapon primaries without the fissile material. According to Dr. Wagner, UK engineer Charlie Martin had very innovative ideas about how to build these X-ray machines, and it was "the challenge of his ideas that led to the resurgence of electron accelerator technologies in the late '70s which, later, also assisted in the recent development at Los Alamos of dual-axis radiographic hydrodynamic testing (DARHT)."

Dr. Wagner found that his UK counterparts had different and frequently broader positions within their defense establishment. For example, the chief scientist to the Ministry of Defence contributed to the interchange with a broader look into everything that was going on technologically, whereas Wagner's position was more narrowly nuclear.

The benefits to the United States from the cooperation sanctioned by the MDA extended far beyond the technical exchanges that were expressly part of the agreement. Wagner described an implicit quid pro quo, that the two-way benefits of the technical interchanges helped to cement the already close U.S.-UK political relationship. This was evident, for example, in the 1980s controversy about intermediate nuclear forces involving deployment of the Pershing II and ground-launched cruise missiles in Europe and, later, the INF treaty that limited both the earlier Soviet and the NATO deployments of INF missiles.

Dr. Wagner recalls his British colleagues as "wonderful people to work with, insightful, entertaining people as well as valued colleagues. We had close relationships with many NATO allies, but it was different with the British . . . I found it inspiring."

—Jessica Yeats
Center for Strategic and International Studies

Everet Beckner, after holding senior positions at the Sandia National Laboratories in New Mexico, served as the deputy administrator for defense programs at the Department of Energy's National Nuclear Security Administration (NNSA) from February 2002 until April 2005. Previously, he served as the DOE's principal deputy assistant secretary for defense programs from 1991 to 1995. He joined Lockheed Martin in 1996, and, while serving as vice president, the UK government issued a request for proposal permitting U.S. defense firms to bid for the contract to manage the United Kingdom's Atomic Weapons Establishment (AWE). His company won the bid, and in 2000 Beckner became the first American to be appointed deputy chief executive at Aldermaston.

Everet Beckner's career attests to the nature of the special relationship between the United States and the United Kingdom: he has worked for both countries' nuclear weapons establishments. Dr. Beckner said it was "quite revolutionary" for the UK government to hire a U.S. company for a defense job at AWE; he acknowledged that this could never have happened without the 1958 MDA between the United States and the United Kingdom and the allowance for the exchange of people.

"It took exposure from both the UK and the U.S. view for me to develop an appreciation for what the UK scientists bring to the relationship," Dr. Beckner said. When he left his position at AWE to return to the NNSA in 2002, he pledged that he would work on broadening and strengthening the relationship between the two programs. His experience had showed him that the U.S. program could benefit more from the relationship with the UK than was realized. "I knew from my exposure at AWE that it had to be a two-way trade; otherwise you can't really get the work done that you want to get done," he said. "In the joint working groups, each side pays their own way. It's done on a sort of collegial, you-both-will-benefit basis."

Early in his career in research and engineering at Sandia, Dr. Beckner was not involved with the nuclear weapons program. As he moved into the field at Sandia, he was involved with test effects and thus came to learn about the United Kingdom's nuclear weapon tests at the Nevada Test Site. He became more involved in Sandia's mainline nuclear weapons program and the technical cooperation among the scientists. "I'm sure I would have said that the Brits got a lot more out of this than we did," he said, although he acknowledged that this had a lot to do with the relative sizes of the two weapons programs. "The reality is, the interaction provides a good check and balance on ideas . . . which otherwise would go largely unreviewed by an external technical body of some sort."

Beckner says that, as a participant in the joint working groups, he believes the relationship between the technical experts has been helpful to both countries. "The problems are the same," he said. "In both case you're talking about the design, the development, the production, the fielding, the maintenance, the surveillance of a nuclear weapon. And, not surprisingly, our nuclear weapons and theirs are in some ways similar."

After the Cold War, the nuclear weapons establishments of both the United States and the United Kingdom went through similar downsizings, yet the information sharing continued. Both countries were replacing their testing and development programs with science. Side by side, they developed similar stockpile stewardship programs. "Now, in 2008, more than any time since the early 1990s, both countries are finding it to their advantage to have technical experts from outside their own program give them a second opinion," according to Dr. Beckner. "The whole question of certification without testing when you make changes to the stockpile, when you do life extension programs, when you contemplate developing more secure and more easily maintained weapons (called RRW in the United States) . . . the programs continue to move in parallel paths, and it is very useful to both sides."

Dr. Beckner said that despite the technical benefits, cooperation was not always easy: "It requires conscious effort on the part of the senior people in the U.S. program to recognize the benefits of the relationship. . . . The UK knows they need help from the U.S. program more than the U.S. knows it needs help," he said. "So it takes effort, but it will pay off all the more over time, because we are confronted with a common problem. . . . As long as there are nuclear weapons, this country has to be first among equals . . . and history tells us that our most reliable partner in defense and in nuclear matters is the UK. We'd better guard this relationship, first of all, politically. . . . The most valuable thing you have is the ability of smart people to analyze problems."

—*Cassandra Smith*
Center for Strategic and International Studies

Richard Mottram was the secretary of the Duff-Mason study group that investigated the rationale for the British nuclear weapons system in the late 1970s. From 1982 to 1986 he served as private secretary to a number of secretaries of state for defence, including John Nott, Michael Heseltine, and George Younger. Subsequently, Sir Richard served as the under-secretary responsible for the British defense program until 1989, when he became the deputy secretary responsible for British defense policy until 1992.

Sir Richard was of the opinion that Britain had benefited substantially from its cooperation with the United States in the nuclear realm. "The particular benefit of the MDA [Mutual Defense Agreement] was that it enabled a sort of peer review about the nuclear weapons effort, and that had to be an advantage to us to be joined up to a much bigger player," he said. Sir Richard emphasized that the United States also gained from the joint collaboration: "Equally, it had to be an advantage to the United States to have someone on the inner track within a very tight circle who could peer review what they were doing, so it was mutually beneficial." In a strictly financial sense, Sir Richard pointed out that Anglo-American nuclear cooperation significantly lowered the burden for Britain in maintaining a nuclear deterrent. Sir Richard asserted, "Quite clearly the path we went down to procure our nuclear deterrent was a lower-risk, cheaper option than to have gone down a route of independence, where every time we tried to be more independent we discovered the costs and the risks."

When British policymakers were faced with the task of choosing a successor system for Polaris, Sir Richard emphasized that within British circles differing options were discussed, with one group suggesting that the acquisition of the U.S. Trident system was the desirable route to pursue. Sir Richard articulated that "anyone who wanted a low-risk approach to life could immediately see the attraction of accessing a successor system, which was the standard U.S. model." However, as he made clear, this brought a number of political problems to the forefront, such as the question of Britain being granted a fully MIRVed system. An alternative course was the cruise missile, but Sir Richard remarked, "The official system was quite cautious about it [cruise missiles] essentially because of doubts about whether over time it would have the same penetration capability of ballistic missiles." Eventually it was decided that Britain should acquire the U.S.-built Trident system.

Sir Richard noted that at varying times throughout his time in government differing degrees of enthusiasm existed for Anglo-French nuclear cooperation. "There was an institutional drive usually coming out of the Foreign Office and the Ministry of Defence that was quite sympathetic to Anglo-French cooperation," he said. However, he noted, "the military were pretty unenthusiastic and the Royal Navy could never see a rationale for why would you do something with the French when you could do something with the Americans." Coupled to these problems, Sir Richard also made it clear that "in the context of the '58 agreement [MDA] there was always very, very great caution about our doing anything in relation to the French which might lead the Americans to believe that we were not fulfilling our obligations under the '58 agreement. And so that was an absolute constraint in the way we all worked. We mustn't compromise our relationship with the Americans, and we suspected that the Americans themselves had a dialogue with the French." Sir Richard concluded that the MDA was a very "serious bar" in the face of Anglo-French nuclear cooperation and that "the natural habits of cooperation and the overall political frame, and the low risk associated with working with the Americans tended to trump any alternative."

Sir Richard also believed that Britain should retain its strategic nuclear deterrent, arguing that "once you're in this game, getting out of it is a very, very big statement, and getting out of it in unilateral circumstances and in circumstances where there is another power in Europe which is a nuclear power might also be quite a big ask for any government." Sir Richard was also skeptical as to whether British nuclear disarmament would have any impact upon the actions of other states wishing to obtain nuclear weapons.

Sir Richard doubted the likelihood of future U.S.-Russian arms control agreements being undertaken even though he thought that "the Russians and Americans could operate with a much smaller number of nuclear weapons and have confidence in their security." He believed that the British should not be "caught up in this" because the British number of weapons was a negligible amount in contrast with the U.S. and Russian arsenals.

Being a strong supporter for the continuation of the NATO alliance, Sir Richard expressed the belief that NATO's existing mechanisms to organize and deploy forces on a multilateral basis meant that one would only attempt to dismantle such an organization with "great reluctance."

—Thomas Robb
Aberystwyth University

Throughout Steve Henry's career, nuclear weapons and deterrence have been a central focus of his work. From his time in the field artillery branch of the U.S. Army, up to his current position as the deputy assistant to the secretary of defense (nuclear matters), Mr. Henry has been involved in the technical, operational, and political aspects of U.S.-UK nuclear cooperation. Henry's career experiences—both in the army and as a high-ranking civilian defense official—provides insight into the inner workings of the U.S.-UK nuclear partnership.

Beginning in the 1990s, Mr. Henry worked closely with the United Kingdom on a wide range of technical and operational issues related to nuclear weapons. Henry recalls that discussions and information exchanges frequently focused on technical practices, delivery platforms, and ensuring the safety and security of the warheads. In other areas, such as the life extension of existing weapons systems and platforms, the United States played a critical role in supporting the UK's nuclear program. The central question was how to maintain confidence in its aging weapons systems and platforms, and Henry, then working for the U.S. Department of Energy, examined whether the service life of the weapons could be lengthened. He worked with the United Kingdom to create programs to extend the life of warheads, share surveillance information, and devise more innovative methods of production.

Military officials from both nations viewed the MDA as an important collaborative partnership, and many of the intricacies of nuclear operations were handled as a joint effort. Through the MDA, both countries could "look to see how much is enough, who can do what, and how to maximize what is available." U.S. and UK officials would work together to determine which weapons system would best engage a particular target, and final decisions on these issues were the result of teamwork, rather than one side leading the other. From his viewpoint, "both countries learned from each other, [such as] how to leverage our resources and take advantage of each nation's strengths." During the Cold War, the United Kingdom's nuclear weapons systems were particularly useful in covering the growing target list in the Warsaw Pact. These capabilities, Henry notes, were especially useful for covering long-range targets. By leveraging British nuclear capabilities, NATO greatly improved its standoff strike capabilities.

Mr. Henry said he was "very impressed with the level of cooperation and the level of exchange between both nations, both on operations and technical [issues]. Those relationships are closely tied and mutually beneficial to both parties." In his view, the relationship was very professional and close, and both nations respected the limits and boundaries of the nuclear relationship. The historic nuclear partnership enshrined in the MDA did have limits, as both nations were pursuing nuclear developments that were kept secret from all foreign governments. The fact that the United States and the United Kingdom carefully worked within certain limitations in the relationship reflects the profound mutual understandings and respect that characterize U.S.-UK relations.

In Mr. Henry's view, the MDA was important in creating trust between allies, and the formation and continuation of long-lasting mutual trust have allowed both countries to benefit from each other's assets and expertise. "You can't work with folks as we have day-in-day-out and not develop relationships," he said. "I think that also builds trust and confidence . . . and this continues on past job assignments and changes in location." Henry believes that the U.S.-UK relationship has strengthened over time, and the unique qualities of the transatlantic partnership benefited other areas of global security by creating pathways for additional cooperation. For example, the MDA has helped build a strong relationship in nonproliferation and counterproliferation, such as cooperation on detection and nuclear forensics capabilities. In addition, both countries face similar questions regarding nuclear warhead design and production without testing, and Henry notes that the United Kingdom has been useful in helping answer the myriad of scientific issues associated with warhead certification without tests.

The continued relevance of nuclear weapons in international politics indicates that there is an ongoing need for technical and strategic expertise on nuclear matters, Henry believes. "Nuclear issues are always going to be on the table," he said, and therefore the United States, United Kingdom, and other allies "need people to look at the threat of nuclear weapons, and look at deterrence and how it applies." Henry suggested that U.S. views of deterrence and credibility may be different from our adversaries' views, and therefore the United States must better understand their strategic calculations in order to strengthen deterrence. The United States needs to be able to demonstrate the continued credibility of its nuclear stockpile through scientific analysis, and the nuclear infrastructure must be flexible and adaptable to emerging threats. Because countries will continue to make decisions based on their own national interests—which could include relying on weapons of mass destruction to counterbalance U.S. conventional superiority—the United States and its allies require the necessary capabilities and expertise to help ensure stability and security.

—*Michael S. Gerson*
Center for Naval Analyses

STANLEY ORMAN

**FORMER DEPUTY DIRECTOR, ATOMIC
WEAPONS ESTABLISHMENT, UK**

Stanley Orman began his career in 1961 as a junior scientist at the Atomic Weapons Research Establishment at Aldermaston, spending several years serving on U.S.-UK joint working groups (JOWOGs). In 1975, he transferred to the Chevaline project, working for seven years on the British program to counter Russian antiballistic missile defenses; he completed the project as the chief engineer. From 1982 to 1984 Dr. Orman served in the British embassy in Washington as the minister responsible for defense exchanges between the United States and the United Kingdom. He returned to Aldermaston as the deputy director and chaired several JOWOGs under the Mutual Defense Agreement (MDA) before returning to the British Ministry of Defence as the founding director general of the Strategic Defense Initiative (SDI) participation office, heading the British involvement with the missile defense program.

Some critics of the MDA believe that the United Kingdom would have been incapable of acquiring or maintaining nuclear weapons without U.S. assistance. Dr. Orman would challenge this critique by outlining the numerous ways in which the U.S. program has also relied on UK technology and scientific expertise. Both sides have benefited from their close working relationship.

Historically, there is no doubt that the MDA gave Great Britain unique access to U.S. nuclear information, technology, and materials. Dr. Orman believes that the British have gained from exposure to the U.S. program, saying that "the American teams brought much greater breadth." The United States also provided the Nevada testing facility for British nuclear weapons tests. In addition, the British "took the concepts of the Super Antelope (an American decoy program) and modified it to produce the UK Chevaline program." However, Dr. Orman also cited many uniquely British contributions that helped to develop and improve the U.S. nuclear program.

One area where this is apparent is in the study of the behavior of nuclear materials in a nuclear warhead. During the 1960s, neither the United Kingdom nor the United States could obtain uniform data on the corrosion rate of uranium. While studying this reaction, Dr. Orman discovered that minute traces of oxygen, in parts per thousand, inhibited uranium water reaction, slowing it by a factor of 50-fold. This was important because filling a warhead with nitrogen gas led to a much faster corrosion rate than filling it with air. More important, with no oxygen present, the uranium-water reaction generated hydrogen, which could permeate into other warhead components and, in some cases, prevent them from functioning in the way in which they were designed. Because the U.S. design used nitrogen, these findings caused U.S. scientists to make changes to their design, which resulted in a more reliable warhead with a longer life span. By running the experiment in more depth using parts per thousand, British scientists were able to make a scientific discovery that benefited the U.S. weapons program.

Dr. Orman also highlighted some cases in which the United Kingdom developed a specialized niche capability. For example, the British scientist Charlie Martin developed X-ray capabilities that could measure implosion characteristics inside large steel containers, a discovery that helped with the analysis of the implosion characteristics of a nuclear bomb. In addition, British scientists also developed a technique to implode a nonfissile plutonium isotope. U.S. law prohibited this kind of development because it involved the implosion of plutonium even though it was nonfissile. Therefore, U.S. scientists used British laboratories for these types of experiments. In essence, independent of U.S. nuclear programs the British developed several capabilities that were eventually incorporated by the U.S. side.

British scientists were also the first to discover an inhibitor that could sufficiently slow a plutonium-hydrogen reaction that would maximize the functionality of a nuclear weapon. This was important to both U.S. and British programs because both sides were concerned by the degradation of plutonium once it was exposed to an isomer of hydrogen (tritium). It is crucial that plutonium is not degraded too quickly. By exposing these findings through the JOWOGs, "the Americans did the necessary underground tests and confirmed the effectiveness," and the British designers benefited from this testing to incorporate this design change. In this case, the United States benefited from a British discovery, and the British benefited from U.S. verification, which eventually allowed both sides to improve their nuclear weapons design.

Scientists from both sides of the Atlantic contributed to the success of the partnership through their participation in JOWOGs, information sharing, and the British nuclear tests conducted at the Nevada Test Site. Dr. Orman, who believed the JOWOG format had been such a critical tool in the development of the close partnership under the MDA, established a similar format under the SDI memorandum of understanding, when he became the director general of the SDI program. Dr. Orman stated: "It was these close special relationships that built up individual bonding which helped enormously to get things done . . . mainly because as scientists both sides tended to want to find a solution. . . . And if someone had a better idea than your side had, you were most interested in exploring it."

—*Tara Callahan*
Center for Strategic and International Studies

WALTER B. SLOCOMBE
FORMER PRINCIPAL DEPUTY ASSISTANT
U.S. SECRETARY OF DEFENSE

Walter B. Slocombe graduated from Harvard Law School in June of 1968 and went on to clerk on the Supreme Court for Justice Abe Fortas until 1969. He spent a brief time working for Donald Rumsfeld on the U.S. poverty program during the administration of President Richard M. Nixon. Mr. Slocombe then went to work on the National Security Council staff from 1969 to 1970, which was headed at the time by Henry A. Kissinger. When President Jimmy Carter was elected, Mr. Slocombe received an appointment at the Defense Department as the principal deputy assistant secretary of defense for international security affairs, and he became the director of the staff that worked on the Strategic Arms Limitation Treaty process for the Office of the Secretary of Defense. After the Carter administration, Mr. Slocombe returned to his law practice for several years until President Bill Clinton appointed him, first, as principal deputy under secretary of defense for policy in 1993 and, later, as under secretary, a post he held from 1994 to 2001. He spent six months in 2003 in Iraq as the director of national security and defense in the Coalition Provisional Authority.

During his time at the Department of Defense and the National Security Council, Walter Slocombe was deeply involved with policy decisions concerning U.S. nuclear programs, which necessitated forging close relationships with his British counterparts. In Mr. Slocombe's opinion, the U.S.-UK Mutual Defense Agreement is "not something we do just to be nice and to be good friends. It is something we do to support an ally that is supportive of us in other areas. The United States gets an advantage in terms of deterrence and, particularly under the conditions of the Cold War, from there being what the British call the second center of decision." In his opinion, having the Soviets worried not just about what the United States might do but the Europeans as well contributed to deterrence in ways that were mutually beneficial. While the net flow of technology has gone to the British, Mr. Slocombe noted that one of the major advantages of the cooperation was that U.S. nuclear scientists had someone to talk to. "Scientists and technologists tend to work to a remarkable degree by exchanging ideas and trying out different approaches," he said, "and it's to our advantage to have an ongoing parallel British weapons development program."

In 1977, the British were genuinely concerned that President Carter would not be willing to continue with the cooperative agreement. However, according to Mr. Slocombe, the Carter administration was only doing what lawyers would refer to as "due diligence," weighing the advantages of the cooperation to make sure it was in the best interest of the United States. "It is fair to say that all American administrations have regarded the alliance with the British as very important and have regarded the nuclear cooperation as being part of that," he said.

There were, however, two significant points of contention over the years. During the Cold War, the U.S. government (especially the Carter administration) worried that the Europeans were not devoting enough resources to their conventional forces. Many U.S. policymakers thus believed that it was ill advised for the British to be devoting 10 percent to 15 percent of their defense budget to their nuclear deterrent. In Mr. Slocombe's opinion, the issue most fought over was money. "We got a huge advantage out of the relationship with the British, and to some degree we haggled a little bit too much about the money," he said. The British believed in chipping in for incremental costs, but when it came to development costs, they argued that they should not have to pay for something the United States was going to do regardless of Britain's financial participation. "On the other hand, America will always maintain that the British got a bargain," he contended.

Mr. Slocombe expressed his belief that the United States government is going to have to decide in the coming years what exactly the strategic rationale is for maintaining nuclear forces. "There's no question that the Russians under Putin are not the Soviet Union under Brezhnev, [however] Russia is still by orders of magnitude the second-largest nuclear power in the world," said Mr. Slocombe. "Nobody says [they are] a current threat, but times change. Things which seem fine go bad. The NATO position, as we all know, is that NATO reserves the right to use nuclear weapons if necessary. We hope it will never be necessary, it shouldn't be necessary; we do things to make sure it will not be necessary. However, if push comes to shove, we're going to maintain our capacity for deterrence, for nuclear deterrence as well as diplomacy, as well as conventional deterrence."

Although Mr. Slocombe maintains that some of the best cooperation he saw between governments during his time in government was between the United States and the United Kingdom, he still admits that even among friends diplomacy was often difficult. "The secret to British diplomacy," said Mr. Slocombe, "is that the British have figured out that Americans love to be liked, and if you're so friendly, the Americans won't notice when sometimes they're being stabbed in the back."

—Jeremy White
Center for Strategic and International Studies

ROBERT WALMSLEY
FORMER CHIEF OF DEFENCE PROCUREMENT,
UK MINISTRY OF DEFENCE

Robert Walmsley joined the Royal Navy in 1958 and went on to develop an expertise in nuclear propulsion. During his naval career, he served as chairman of the Naval Nuclear Technical Safety Panel and, as a rear admiral, as director general, submarines. He also was the assistant chief of the defence staff for communications, command, control, and information systems; and he completed his naval service as controller of the Royal Navy with the rank of vice admiral. On leaving the Royal Navy in 1996, he was appointed chief of defence procurement at the Ministry of Defence and retained this position until 2003.

Sir Robert made it clear that there was a significant difference in the actuality of cooperation between the United States and United Kingdom on nuclear propulsion and nuclear weapons, although both were founded on the 1958 Mutual Defense Agreement (MDA). "It appears to me that there has been far less ongoing, detailed cooperation or exchange of information or ideas on nuclear propulsion than on the weapons program," Sir Robert said. On matters relating to nuclear propulsion, Sir Robert stated his understanding that Admiral Rickover, representing the U.S. authorities in matters of naval nuclear propulsion, had deliberately "cut the apron strings" once the initial *Dreadnought* plant, together with manuals, spare parts, and some training, had been delivered. Furthermore, "the United States Navy's commitment was to inform us if there were any safety issues of which we would otherwise be unaware but that in all other respects we should be independent." Sir Robert believed that this was a positive course of action because it left the United Kingdom in "extremely good stead. It forced us to become self-reliant."

On the subject of cooperation on nuclear weapons, Sir Robert made it clear that the United Kingdom had benefited from its relationship with the United States, that the exchange was two way, and that moreover there was a level of cooperation that would generally be "completely unrecognized" by those working on nuclear propulsion. Sir Robert emphasized his belief that the cooperation between the two powers in the weapons field was of mutual benefit in several aspects. "You don't want to be marking your own homework in this business," he said. "The great advantage of being able to bring in someone from a different culture, say Los Alamos, is that they don't come with a UK institutional orientation." Sir Robert believed that the 1958 MDA was likely to be just as relevant today as it has ever been, not least given the continuing debates surrounding the long-term future of the United Kingdom's strategic nuclear deterrent. "My guess is that this treaty [the MDA] is absolutely essential to genuine cooperation because it promotes the exchange of information within prescribed security arrangements but without subjecting the exchange to the defense export controls which would otherwise have to be obtained," Sir Robert said.

Sir Robert was skeptical about the United Kingdom involving its own strategic nuclear deterrent in multilateral nuclear arms discussions because of the negligible quantities of weapons it possessed in comparison with the two predominant nuclear weapons owners. On the issue of Britain undertaking unilateral disarmament, Sir Robert was even more unconvinced. "It's an odd time to give it up when lots of other people are getting it or may be trying to get it," he stated. Further, on the subject of whether the United Kingdom should provide a successor to its own strategic nuclear deterrent system, Trident, Sir Robert was firmly of the belief that this was imperative. "If you decide not to [replace the current strategic nuclear deterrent], at some future date, I think you are virtually saying from the moment you announce that decision or promulgate it within the community that you are not serious about strategic deterrence," he declared. "You are really sounding the death knell of the existing deterrent."

Sir Robert believes that there is great value to the United Kingdom in the current relationship with the United States in nuclear weapons, in that the United Kingdom buys a standard U.S. missile that is then fitted with a UK nuclear warhead and is deployed in Royal Navy submarines. One of the particular benefits of such an off-the-shelf system is that it gives UK nuclear planners the comfort of knowing the system they are purchasing actually works. It also cuts down the financial burden of a strategic deterrent in not having to spend money on development, including numerous tests, as well as on inherently small-scale production and ongoing system validation. Sir Robert, although of the firm belief that the United States would continue to cooperate with the United Kingdom on nuclear weapons and would retain its own submarine-launched ballistic missile (SLBM) fleet, warned, "If they don't, then all bets are off, as we can't possibly do it ourselves. We don't have the missile technology, we don't have the money, and things get disproportionate within the UK defense budget if we had to find it." However, as Sir Robert emphasized, for the United Kingdom to continued to base its SLBM deterrent on U.S. cooperation was a "really good buy." He concluded, "If you want a deterrent, I can't think of a better one."

—Thomas Robb
Aberystwyth University

After graduating from the United States Naval Academy in 1945, Admiral Robert Wertheim was assigned to the Pacific Fleet just before the end of World War II. He received an master's degree in nuclear physics from the Massachusetts Institute of Technology and was summoned to Washington to work in the Special Projects Office on the submarine ballistic missile program. The Special Projects Office was formed to take the U.S. Army's Jupiter missiles to sea. The logic behind this operational transformation of the missiles was that it tried to correct a perceived imbalance in the U.S.-Soviet arms race. At the time, it was believed that the Soviets had an advantage in the development of intercontinental ballistic missiles, and there would be no way to deter the Soviets from using a ballistic missile against U.S. cities. By deploying these intermediate-range missiles at sea, the United States could bring more Soviet targets in range. This project later developed into a submarine program using solid-propellant ballistic missiles launched underwater.

In January 1957, Wertheim was given the responsibility for the development of the payload for this new missile called Polaris. Wertheim became a military assistant to the secretary of defense, Robert McNamara, and to McNamara's deputy for science and engineering, Harold Brown. In 1962, Admiral Wertheim was tasked to write a report on the Polaris missile system as one of the options to substitute for the Skybolt that the United States had planned to sell to the British but then canceled.

Wertheim retired from the U.S. Navy in 1980 as director of the Special Projects Program; his career had spanned the transition from Polaris to Poseidon missile systems. After his retirement from the navy, he entered the private sector as a senior vice president for science and engineering at Lockheed Martin. He retired in 1987 but continues to serve as an adviser to many government and nongovernmental organizations and committees.

U.S.-UK naval relations were strengthened as a result of the cooperation on Polaris and subsequent projects. The Cuban missile crisis, which resulted in the acceleration of the program, also made cooperation stronger, emphasizing the "importance of nuclear deterrence." Admiral Wertheim recalls that his interaction with his British counterparts was "a very constructive and rewarding experience." There were open exchanges and regular meetings, and relations were social and professional. "The association was a very positive one, and I think that both the Royal Navy and the U.S. Navy's relations were strengthened."

While the United States benefited tremendously from the cooperation with the British, Admiral Wertheim believes the United Kingdom benefited more than the United States strategically because the Polaris system gave the United Kingdom an independent nuclear deterrent. The dynamics of the relationship changed slightly as the United States transitioned from the Polaris to the Poseidon missile, which was able to carry more warheads. The strategic logic of multiple warheads was to assure target penetration by overwhelming or saturating Soviet defense systems.

Yet, many voices in the UK scientific community preferred a different approach: the development of penetration aids, such as decoys. The Royal Navy did not share this view and supported the Poseidon missile because the Royal Navy did not want to go down a path of development separate from the United States. After skipping over the Poseidon missile system, the United Kingdom eventually adopted the Trident system.

Since the end of the Cold War, the primary change in the nuclear realm has been in the reduction of arsenals and delivery systems. Admiral Wertheim contends that the U.S. Navy's responsibility for maintaining U.S. strategic capability is far greater today than in the past: more than 50 percent of U.S. strategically deployed nuclear weapons are on submarines. Meanwhile, the British are completely dependent on the Royal Navy for the delivery of their nuclear weapons.

Admiral Wertheim believes the big issue for the United States and the United Kingdom has centered on the maintenance and development of the U.S. and UK arsenals. Since the end of the Cold War, development of new systems has slowed down. Wertheim believes "the nuclear production complex needs to be modernized and the people retiring with expertise need to be replaced with a new generation of scientists and designers." The cessation of testing has also negatively affected the recruitment of young nuclear scientists. "It is difficult to maintain an atmosphere that would attract and challenge a new generation of scientists if all of their designs . . . were going to be simulated and modeled." The British are facing the same issues.

There is, however, one unintended positive consequence of the cessation of testing: namely, there is now an even greater need for the United States and United Kingdom to cooperate and share data. The United States and the United Kingdom share test data on a common population of Trident missiles. "There have been over 120 successive successes without a single failure," he said. "The cooperation has increased since the Cold War rather than decreased. The benefits on the whole were mutual in that it strengthened the ties between the navies."

—Lawrence Rubin
University of California, Los Angeles

PAUL TAYLOR
DIRECTOR GENERAL FOR EQUIPMENT,
UK MINISTRY OF DEFENCE

Paul Taylor joined the Ministry of Defence (MOD) science and engineering "fast stream" in 1988 and embarked on a career in the management and procurement of research. Mr. Taylor has held posts responsible for aspects of defense research policy and participated in major reviews within the MOD. Currently Taylor is the director general for equipment and is responsible for some 40 percent of the British defense budget in the form of the equipment and support plan. He is also the two-star senior responsible for the United Kingdom's future strategic deterrent, which involves the task of ensuring that Britain's strategic nuclear deterrent is upgraded on time and within budget.

Paul Taylor was of the opinion that Anglo-American nuclear cooperation benefited both the United States and Britain. He argued that militarily Britain gained little from nuclear cooperation with the United States because Britain's nuclear deterrent was a "political weapon." Politically Britain gained "enormously" from Anglo-American nuclear cooperation, he said. In the technical field, Taylor suggested that Britain, via its working arrangements with the United States, accesses a wide array of scientific data that greatly helps Britain to sustain a credible strategic nuclear deterrent. Taylor made it clear that Britain enjoys an "extremely good working relationship" with its U.S. counterparts. The United States, in Taylor's opinion, has also received substantial benefits from Anglo-American nuclear cooperation. Taylor made clear that America wanted a "second center of decisionmaking," as this enhanced the credibility of deterrence. Further, Taylor suggested that

Anglo-American nuclear technical and scientific cooperation presented an opportunity for other experts to "mark their homework," which enhances the safety of Britain's nuclear warheads, allows for Britain to derive information from previous nuclear tests without having to undertake them, and moreover, from the perspective of both countries, to know whether they are on the "right track."

On the subject of nuclear arms limitations, Mr. Taylor noted how Britain had taken major steps since the end of the Cold War to limit its nuclear weapons by eliminating all of its tactical nuclear weapons systems. However, he argued that Britain should continue to retain its independent strategic nuclear deterrent. Regarding multilateral nuclear disarmament, Mr. Taylor argued that Britain could only "give it up once" (its strategic nuclear weapons) and that little would be achieved from British unilateral disarmament. He supported the idea that both the United States and Russia should undertake further reductions in their nuclear arsenals and was optimistic that such actions would come about in the near future.

Mr. Taylor was a strong supporter of the continuation of NATO in the twenty-first century, as he was when the Cold War finished with the collapse of the Soviet Union. He stated that NATO brought both the United States and Canada "across the Atlantic," which acted in part to counterbalance some of the isolationist sentiments prevalent in U.S. domestic politics. Further, NATO as an organization "forced countries to talk," even when bilateral relations between two countries were not particularly warm.

Mr. Taylor hoped that Anglo-American nuclear cooperation would continue for "another fifty years," and suggested that he saw no reason why it should not. He pointed out that Britain could potentially see benefits from nuclear cooperation with third parties, but the fact remained that the United States had "more to offer" and as such Britain should retain its nuclear cooperation with the United States. However, he warned that nuclear cooperation between the two countries, although institutionalized by the Mutual Defense Agreement, could be halted if a president or prime minister wanted it stopped. That said, Mr. Taylor noted that this appeared an unlikely scenario, pointing to the complete absence of debate within U.S. domestic politics regarding the continuation of Anglo-American nuclear cooperation.

—*Thomas Robb*
Aberystwyth University

KENNETH C. MALLEY
VICE ADMIRAL, U.S. NAVY (RETIRED)

Throughout Vice Admiral Kenneth Malley's distinguished naval career, cooperation with the United Kingdom on nuclear weapons matters was a significant component of his duties and responsibilities. As a high-ranking member of the U.S. Navy's Fleet Ballistic Missile Program, including directing the Navy's Strategic Systems Programs (SSP) office as a one- and two-star admiral, Admiral Malley was frequently in close contact with the Royal Navy.

As U.S.-Soviet tensions were heating up in the early 1950s, Admiral Malley attended the United States Naval Academy, graduating in 1957. After earning a master's degree in electrical engineering from the Naval Postgraduate School in 1960, Admiral Malley's navy career was characterized by successive promotions to senior positions in the Navy's fleet ballistic missile programs. In May 1994, Malley, having risen to the rank of three-star admiral in charge of the Navy's Sea Systems Command, retired after 42 years of service.

Admiral Malley's increasingly close interactions with the Royal Navy occurred during his 15 years in the Navy's SSP office. From 1976 to 1983, he was head of the office's Missile Branch, and from 1985 to 1991, after promotion to flag rank, Malley served as director of the office. As the director of SSP, Admiral Malley was the U.S. counterpart to the United Kingdom's chief strategic systems executive, the UK admiral tasked with overseeing the Royal Navy's nuclear cooperation with the U.S. Navy. In this capacity, one of Malley's primary duties was to participate in and manage U.S.-UK technical exchanges pertaining to nuclear submarines and missiles.

Admiral Malley fondly recalled the close working relationship with his UK counterparts. The men and women in uniform "knew that it [the Mutual Defense Agreement] was a very important project and everybody put proper attention to it," and they focused on "how to best work with the UK." Malley described these frequent exchanges as well-managed, frank, and very professional. He said his team was deeply committed to working with the United Kingdom, and they worked hard to provide the UK representatives with the systems, research, and expertise needed to operate and maintain their strategic deterrent.

"The UK mirrored the architecture and structure we set up in SSP for running and manning the program," he said. "We met with them on a routine basis at the technical level." Admiral Malley emphasized, however, that although the United Kingdom was largely dependent on the United States for technical assistance, the United Kingdom felt that its strategic deterrent was "very independent" from the United States. The United Kingdom had its own operational procedures and targeting packages, and Malley's interactions with the United Kingdom were strictly technical and did not cover war plans, submarine patrol operations, or targeting.

The substance of the U.S.-UK partnership focused on many critical technical aspects of operating and maintaining a sea-based strategic deterrent. The United States provided the United Kingdom with highly sensitive information and assistance as well as advice and guidance on future weapons systems and platforms. For example, when the United Kingdom expressed interest in upgrading its forces from the Polaris A-3 missile to the Poseidon, the United States suggested that it would not be in the United Kingdom's interest to make the switch because by the time the full capability would be in operation it would be outdated technology in the U.S. arsenal. In other areas, the United Kingdom expressed more concern about procedure and operations than the United States, and consequently asked for additional cooperation and information. Admiral Malley recalls that his UK colleagues were especially concerned about safety, in particular regarding the loading of warheads onto submarines and operations while at sea.

The professionalism and civility that characterized these frequent meetings to discuss technical nuclear matters planted the seeds for long-lasting personal friendships. The social interactions were an important part of the U.S.-UK relationship. "We would get together for joint meetings and then have very good social get-togethers before and afterward," Malley recalled. "It was a superb relationship." These close professional as well as personal connections demonstrate how the MDA evolved into more than just a defense agreement—this unique partnership also forged common bonds and shared understandings between the men and women tasked with ensuring the security of their respective countries. In his view, no other cooperative defense agreement between the United States and another nation has been as close, both professionally and personally, as the U.S.-UK nuclear partnership. Admiral Malley reflected that his work with the United Kingdom "was the most rewarding time in my naval career because of the things we accomplished."

Today, Admiral Malley believes that the relative inattention to strategic nuclear programs in the United States could create a dangerous gap in U.S. deterrence capabilities. In his view, the nuclear genie is out of the bottle, and the need for deterrence will not go away. Therefore, the United States must maintain the military capabilities and technical expertise to maintain and develop weapons systems for deterrence, and this will require continued investment in organizations and people in order to respond to emerging nuclear threats.

—*Michael S. Gerson*
Center for Naval Analyses

ROBERT HILL
FORMER CHIEF NAVAL ENGINEER OFFICER,
ROYAL NAVY

Robert Hill dealt with matters concerning nuclear propulsion through-out his career in the Royal Navy, initially in a diesel-powered subma-rine and then in the Polaris submarine, HMS *Repulse.* He also served at Chatham Naval Base as nuclear power manager; as captain of the Roy-al Navy's new entry training establishment; and at the fleet operational headquarters as chief staff officer (engineering). Between the years 1989 and 1993 Sir Robert served as the chief naval engineer officer.

Sir Robert made it clear that in the field of nuclear propulsion the Anglo-American "special relationship" came to an end in 1963, once the initial delivery of the SW5 propulsion unit for HMS *Dreadnought* had been concluded under the terms of the 1958 Mutual Defense Agree-ment (MDA). Thus, throughout Sir Robert's time serving in the Royal Navy on matters relating to nuclear propulsion, "there was no contact as contact was broken off in 1963" between the United Kingdom and United States. Sir Robert did, however, emphasize that, although co-operation between the United States and United Kingdom lasted only for the relatively short period of five years under the terms of the 1958 MDA, these years were of enormous benefit to the United Kingdom's nuclear propulsion project. He described the 1958 MDA terms for the United Kingdom as a "fantastic deal" and said that the SW5 plant was "effectively a gift of a proven reliable propulsion plant for *Dreadnought,* which acted as Admiral Rickover said it would for subsequent UK de-signs," enabling the UK to stand on its own feet thereafter.

Further, Sir Robert suggested that the United Kingdom "acquired a focus on core safety" because Admiral Rickover's stringent nuclear safety standards had a beneficial impact on the United Kingdom's nuclear propulsion project. "Without Rickover we would not have done this [impose such stringent safety measures]," Sir Robert suggested. He described the safety standards transferred to the United Kingdom under the 1958 MDA as the "greatest thing we inherited." Sir Robert was of the opinion that the United States gained few physical benefits from cooperating with the United Kingdom on nuclear propulsion, but he suggested that when Admiral Rickover saw that the UK submarines "radiated a much lower noise signature," he acted to improve the U.S. nuclear submarine fleet.

Sir Robert said that the United Kingdom sent a delegation to the United States to try to ensure that cooperation on nuclear propulsion continued after 1963, but that the approach was "rejected out of hand." This should not have surprised UK officials, according to Sir Robert, who stressed that the terms of the 1958 MDA, as interpreted by Rickover in the Westinghouse–Rolls-Royce supply contract, only allowed for an initial transfer of nuclear propulsion technology. Admiral Rickover's refusal to continue nuclear propulsion cooperation with the United Kingdom was, in Sir Robert's opinion, the correct decision, as it prevented a situation where the United Kingdom would forever be reliant upon the United States for technical assistance. Moreover, it avoided the temptation to approach the United States in order to cut the financial costs involved with nuclear propulsion.

Sir Robert stated that this lack of Anglo-American cooperation on propulsion did not upset those in the United Kingdom tasked with such matters. "For those within the program actually it was quite a relief not to be expected on every occasion to get an American opinion on our decisions or to save money by getting something American," Sir Robert said. "It released us from a great weight of extra bureaucracy and burden to actually get on with the job with the money we had available."

Sir Robert believed that the initial transfer of the SW5 plant coupled to the fashion in which the UK company, Rolls-Royce, and the other companies in the nuclear submarine program conducted themselves have enabled the United Kingdom to now possess "world-class submarines." "Rolls-Royce did an absolute superb job" with the limited financial and technical resources at its disposal, Sir Robert noted. The initial technology transfer to the United Kingdom under the 1958 MDA was important because certain specific components of the nuclear reactors currently in use in the United Kingdom today are "fundamentally based" on the first SW5 plant.

—Thomas Robb
Aberystwyth University

APPENDIX

AGREEMENT BETWEEN THE GOVERNMENT OF THE
UNITED STATES OF AMERICA AND THE GOVERNMENT
OF THE UNITED KINGDOM OF GREAT BRITAIN AND
NORTHERN IRELAND FOR COOPERATION ON THE USES
OF ATOMIC ENERGY FOR MUTUAL DEFENSE PURPOSES

AS AMENDED, 23RD DAY OF MAY, 1994*

ORIGINAL AGREEMENT SIGNED, WASHINGTON,
JULY 3, 1958

The Government of the United States of America and the Government of the United Kingdom of Great Britain and Northern Ireland,

Considering that their mutual security and defense require that they be prepared to meet the contingencies of atomic warfare;

Considering that both countries have made substantial progress in the development of atomic weapons;

Considering that they are participating together in international arrangements pursuant to which they are making substantial and material contributions to their mutual defense and security;

Recognizing that their common defense and security will be advanced by the exchange of information concerning atomic energy and by the transfer of equipment and materials for use therein;

Believing that such exchange and transfer can be undertaken without risk to the defense and security of either country; and

Taking into consideration the United States Atomic Energy Act of 1954, as amended, which was enacted with these purposes in mind,

Have agreed as follows:

---

*The Mutual Defense Agreement was amended again on June 14, 2004, extending the agreement from December 31, 2004, to December 31, 2014. Reproduced with the permission of the British American Security Information Council (BASIC), http://www. basicint.org/nuclear/1958MDA.htm.

ARTICLE I ∿ GENERAL PROVISION

While the United States and the United Kingdom are participating in an international arrangement for their mutual defense and security and making substantial and material contributions thereto, each Party will communicate to and exchange with the other Party information, and transfer materials and equipment to the other Party, in accordance with the provisions of this Agreement provided that the communicating or transferring Party determines that such cooperation will promote and will not constitute an unreasonable risk to its defense and security.

ARTICLE II ∿ EXCHANGE OF INFORMATION

A. Each Party will communicate to or exchange with the other Party such classified information, sensitive nuclear technology, and controlled nuclear information as is jointly determined to be necessary to:

1. the development of defense plans;

2. the training of personnel in the employment of and defense against atomic weapons and other military applications of atomic energy;

3. the evaluation of the capabilities of potential enemies in the employment of atomic weapons and other military applications of atomic energy;

4. the development of delivery systems compatible with the atomic weapons which they carry; and

5. research, development and design of military reactors to the extent and by such means as may be agreed.

B. In addition to the cooperation provided for in paragraph A of this Article, each Party will exchange with the other Party other classified information concerning atomic weapons, sensitive nuclear technology, and controlled nuclear information, including special nuclear materials properties and production or processing technology, when, after consultation with the other Party, the communicating Party determines that the communication of such information is necessary to improve the recipient's atomic weapon design, development and fabrication capability.

ARTICLE III ∿ TRANSFER OF SUBMARINE
NUCLEAR PROPULSION PLANT AND MATERIALS

A. The Government of the United States will authorize, subject to terms and conditions acceptable to the Government of the United States, a person to transfer by sale to the Government of the United Kingdom or its agent one complete submarine nuclear propulsion plant with such spare parts therefor as may be agreed by the Parties and to communicate to the Government of the United Kingdom or its agent (or to both) such classified information as relates to safety features and such classified information as is necessary for the design, manufacture and operation of such propulsion plant. A person or persons will also be authorized, for a period of ten years following the date of entry into force of this Agreement and subject to terms and conditions acceptable to the Government of the United States, to transfer replacement cores or fuel elements for such plant.

B. The Government of the United States will transfer by sale agreed amounts of U-235 contained in uranium enriched in the isotope U-235 as needed for use in the submarine nuclear propulsion plant transferred pursuant to paragraph A of this Article, during the ten years following the date of entry into force of this Agreement on such terms and conditions as may be agreed. If the Government of the United Kingdom so requests, the Government of the United States will during such period reprocess any material sold under the present paragraph in facilities of the Government of the United States, on terms and conditions to be agreed, or authorize such reprocessing in private facilities in the United States. Enriched uranium recovered in reprocessing such materials by either Party may be purchased by the Government of the United States under terms and conditions to be agreed. Special nuclear material recovered in reprocessing such materials and not purchased by the Government of the United States may be returned to or retained by the Government of the United Kingdom and any U-235 not purchased by the Government of the United States will be credited to the amounts of U-235 to be transferred by the Government of the United States under this Agreement.

C. The Government of the United States shall be compensated for enriched uranium sold by it pursuant to this Article at the United States Atomic Energy Commission's published charges applicable to the domestic distribution of such material in effect at the time of the sale. Any purchase of enriched uranium by the Government of the United States pursuant to this Article shall be at the applicable price of the United States Atomic Energy Commission for the purchase of enriched uranium in effect at the time of purchase of such enriched uranium.

D. The Parties will exchange classified information on methods of reprocessing fuel elements of the type utilized in the propulsion plant to be transferred under this Article, including classified information on the design, construction and operation of facilities for the reprocessing of such fuel elements.

E. The Government of the United Kingdom shall indemnify and hold harmless the Government of the United States against any and all liabilities whatsoever (including third-party liability) for any damage or injury occurring after the propulsion plant or parts thereof, including spare parts, replacement cores or fuel elements are taken outside the United States, for any cause arising out of or connected with the design, manufacture, assembly, transfer or utilization of the propulsion plant, spare parts, replacement cores or fuel elements transferred pursuant to paragraph A of this Article.

ARTICLE III BIS ～ TRANSFER OF MATERIALS AND EQUIPMENT

A. The Government of the United States shall transfer to the Government of the United Kingdom the following in such quantities, at such times prior to December 31, 2004, and on such terms and conditions as may be agreed:

1. non-nuclear parts of atomic weapons which parts are for the purpose of improving the United Kingdom's state of training and operational readiness;

2. other non-nuclear parts of atomic weapons systems involving Restricted Data which parts are for the purpose of improving the United Kingdom's state of training and operational readiness when in accordance with appropriate requirements of applicable laws;

3. source, by-product and special nuclear material, and other material, for research on, development of, or use in atomic weapons when, after consultation with the Government of the United Kingdom, the Government of the United States determines that the transfer of such material is necessary to improve the United Kingdom's atomic weapon design, development or fabrication capability.

B. The Government of the United States shall transfer to the Government of the United Kingdom special nuclear material, and authorize the transfer of other material, for research on, development of, production of, or use in utilization facilities for military applications, in such quantities, at such times prior to December 31, 2004, and on such terms and conditions as may be agreed.

C. The Government of the United States shall transfer enriched uranium, and shall arrange enrichment and other uranium services for the Government of the United Kingdom, for military purposes, in such quantities, at such times prior to December 31, 2004, and on such terms and conditions as may be agreed.

D. The Government of the United Kingdom shall transfer to the Government of the United States for military purposes such source, by-product and special nuclear material, and equipment of such types, in such quantities, at such times prior to December 31, 2004, and on such terms and conditions as may be agreed.

E. 1. With respect to by-product material, special nuclear material and other material transferred from one Party to the other under this Article, the recipient Party agrees not to use any such material for purposes other than those for which it was received, provided that material which has lost its identity as a result of commingling with other material of the recipient Party may be put to other uses if the recipient Party retains an equivalent amount of its own material for the purpose for which the other Party's material was received.

2. For material or equipment transferred from one Party to the other Party, the recipient Party shall pay or reimburse, as may be agreed, all packaging, transportation and related costs. Packaging, shipping containers and methods of shipment shall be as may be agreed.

3. Should either Party desire to acquire materials or components for use in the manufacture or in preparation for manufacture of atomic weapons from any source within the jurisdiction of the other Party, the procuring Party shall inform the other Party of the proposed procurement in order that such other Party may determine whether the proposed procurement involves classified information and if so whether the proposed procurement is in compliance with its applicable laws and regulations.

ARTICLE IV ～ RESPONSIBILITY FOR USE OF INFORMATION, MATERIAL, EQUIPMENT AND DEVICES

The application or use of any information (including design drawings and specifications), material or equipment communicated, exchanged or transferred under this Agreement shall be the responsibility of the Party receiving it, and the other Party does not provide any indemnity, and does not warrant the accuracy or completeness of such information and does not warrant the suitability or completeness of such information, material or equipment for any particular use or application.

ARTICLE V ～ CONDITIONS

A. Cooperation under this Agreement will be carried out by each of the Parties in accordance with its applicable laws.

B. Under this Agreement there will be no transfer by either Party of atomic weapons.

C. Except where specifically authorized by this Agreement or, as may be agreed for civil uses, the recipient Party agrees not to use the information communicated or exchanged, or the materials or equipment transferred, by either Party pursuant to this Agreement for other than the preparation or implementation of defense plans in the mutual interests of the two countries.

D. Nothing in this Agreement shall preclude the communication or exchange of classified information, sensitive nuclear technology, or controlled nuclear information, which may be transmissible under other arrangements between the Parties.

ARTICLE VI ~ GUARANTEES

A. Classified information, materials and equipment communicated or transferred pursuant to this Agreement shall be accorded full security protection under applicable security arrangements between the Parties and applicable national legislation and regulations of the Parties. In no case shall either Party maintain security standards for safeguarding classified information, materials or equipment made available pursuant to this Agreement less restrictive than those set forth in the applicable security arrangements in effect on the date this Agreement comes into force.

B. Sensitive nuclear technology and controlled nuclear information transferred pursuant to this Agreement shall be accorded at least the same level of protection by the recipient party as that accorded to such information by the transferring Party. The Parties shall consult with each other regarding the appropriate protections for such information.

C. Adequate physical security shall be maintained with respect to any source material, special nuclear material and equipment transferred pursuant to the Agreement, and with respect to any special nuclear material used in or produced through the use of any material or reactor so transferred. Such protection shall be commensurate with the importance of the material or equipment involved.

D. Classified information, sensitive nuclear technology, and controlled nuclear information, communicated or exchanged pursuant to this Agreement will be made available through channels existing or hereafter agreed for the communication or exchange of such information between the Parties.

E. Classified information, sensitive nuclear technology, and controlled nuclear information, communicated or exchanged, and any materials or equipment transferred, pursuant to this Agreement shall not be communicated, exchanged or transferred by the recipient Party or persons under its jurisdiction to any unauthorized persons, or, except as provided in Article VII of this Agreement, beyond the jurisdiction of that Party. Each Party may stipulate the degree to which any of the information, materials or equipment communicated, exchanged or transferred by it or persons under its jurisdiction pursuant to this Agreement may be disseminated or distributed; may specify the categories of persons who may have access to such information, materials or equipment; and may impose such other restrictions on the dissemination or distribution of such information, materials or equipment as it deems necessary.

F. Adequate materials control and accountability shall be maintained with respect to any nuclear material (including source material and special nuclear material) transferred pursuant to the Agreement, and with respect to any nuclear material used in or produced through the use of any nuclear material or equipment transferred pursuant to the Agreement. Each Party guarantees adequate materials control and accountancy shall be maintained so long as such nuclear material or equipment remains under its jurisdiction or control. As may be mutually agreed, the Parties shall consult with each other regarding methods and technology for providing such materials control and accountability.

ARTICLE VII ⌁ DISSEMINATION

Nothing in this Agreement shall be interpreted or shall operate as a bar or restriction to consultation or cooperation in any field of defense by either Party with other nations or international organizations. Neither Party, however, shall communicate classified information, sensitive nuclear technology, and controlled nuclear information, or transfer or permit access to or use of materials, or equipment, made available by the other Party pursuant to this Agreement to any nation or international organization unless:

A. it is notified by the other Party that all appropriate provisions and requirements of such other Party's applicable laws, including authorization by competent bodies of such other Party, have been complied with as necessary to authorize such other Party directly so to communicate to, transfer to or permit access to or use by such other nation or international organization; and further that such other Party authorizes the recipient Party so to communicate to, transfer to or permit access to or use by such other nation or international organization; or

B. in the case of communication of classified information, sensitive nuclear technology, and controlled nuclear information, and access to materials or equipment, such other Party has informed the recipient Party that such other Party has so communicated such classified information to, or permitted access to such materials or equipment by, such other nation or international organization; or

C. in the case of material which has lost its identity as a result of commingling with other material of the recipient Party, the recipient Party retains an amount under its jurisdiction equivalent to that made available to it by the other Party under this Agreement.

ARTICLE VIII ⌇ CLASSIFICATION POLICIES

Agreed classification policies shall be maintained with respect to all classified information, materials or equipment communicated, exchanged or transferred under this Agreement. The Parties intend to continue the present practice of consultation with each other on the classification of these matters.

ARTICLE IX ⌇ PATENTS

A. With respect to any invention or discovery employing classified information which has been communicated or exchanged pursuant to Article II or derived from the submarine propulsion plant, material or equipment transferred pursuant to Articles III or III bis, and made or conceived by the recipient Party, or any agency or corporation owned or controlled thereby, or any of their agents or contractors, or any employee of any of the foregoing, after the date of such communication, exchange or transfer but during the period of this Agreement:

1. in the case of any such invention or discovery in which rights are owned by the recipient Party, or any agency or corporation owned or controlled thereby, and not included in subparagraph 2 of this paragraph, the recipient Party shall, to the extent owned by any of them:

(a) transfer and assign to the other Party all right, title and interest in and to the invention or discovery, or patent application or patent thereon, in the country of that other Party, subject to the retention of a royalty-free, non-exclusive, irrevocable license for the governmental purposes of the recipient Party and for the purposes of mutual defense; and

(b) grant to the other Party a royalty-free, non-exclusive, irrevocable license for the governmental purposes of that other Party and for purposes of mutual defense in the country of the recipient Party and third countries, including use in the production of material in such countries for sale to the recipient Party by a contractor of that other Party;

2. in the case of any such invention or discovery which is primarily useful in the production or utilization of special nuclear material or atomic energy and made or conceived prior to the time that the information it employs is made available for civil uses, the recipient Party shall:

(a) obtain, by appropriate means, sufficient right, title and interest in and to the invention or discovery, or patent application or patent thereon, as may be necessary to fulfill its obligations under the following two subparagraphs:

(b) transfer and assign to the other Party all right, title and interest in and to the invention or discovery, or patent application or patent thereon, in the country of that other Party, subject to the retention of a royalty-free, non-exclusive, irrevocable license, with the right to grant sublicenses, for all purposes; and

(c) grant to the other Party a royalty-free, non-exclusive, irrevocable license, with the right to grant sublicenses, for all purposes in the country of the recipient Party and in third countries.

B. 1. Each Party shall, to the extent owned by it, or any agency or corporation owned or controlled thereby, grant to the other Party a royalty-free, non-exclusive, irrevocable license to manufacture and use the subject matter covered by any patent and incorporated in the submarine propulsion plant, spare parts or equipment transferred pursuant to paragraph A of Article III or paragraphs A, B, C or D of Article III bis for use by the licensed Party for the purposes set forth in paragraph C of Article V.

2. The transferring Party neither warrants nor represents that the submarine propulsion plant or any material or equipment transferred under Articles III or III bis does not infringe any patent owned or controlled by other persons and assumes no liability or obligation with respect thereto, and the recipient Party agrees to indemnify and hold harmless the transferring Party from any and all liability arising out of any infringement of any such patent.

C. With respect to any invention or discovery, or patent application or patent thereon, or license or sublicense therein, covered by paragraph A of this Article, each Party:

1. may, to the extent of its right, title and interest therein, deal with the same in its own and third countries as it may desire, but shall in no event discriminate against citizens of the other Party in respect of granting any license or sublicense under the patents owned by it in its own or any other country;

2. hereby waives any and all claims against the other Party for compensation, royalty or award, and hereby releases the other Party with respect to any and all such claims.

D. 1. No patent application with respect to any classified invention or discovery employing classified information which has been communicated or exchanged pursuant to Article II, or derived from the submarine propulsion plant, material or equipment transferred pursuant to Articles III or III bis, may be filed:

(a) by either Party or any person in the country of the other Party except in accordance with agreed conditions and procedures; or

(b) in any country not a party to this Agreement except as may be agreed and subject to Articles VI and VII.

2. Appropriate secrecy or prohibition orders shall be issued for the purpose of giving effect to this paragraph.

ARTICLE X ∼ PREVIOUS AGREEMENTS FOR COOPERATION

Effective from the date on which the present Agreement enters into force, the cooperation between the Parties being carried out under or envisaged by the Agreement for Cooperation Regarding Atomic Information for Mutual Defense Purposes, which was signed at Washington on June 15, 1955, and by paragraph B of Article I bis of the Agreement for Cooperation on Civil Uses of Atomic Energy, which was signed at Washington on June 15, 1955, as amended by the Amendment signed at Washington on June 13, 1956, shall be carried out in accordance with the provisions of the present Agreement.

ARTICLE XI ∼ DEFINITIONS

For the purposes of this Agreement:

A. "Atomic weapon" means any device utilizing atomic energy, exclusive of the means for transporting or propelling the device (where such means is a separable and divisible part of the device), the principal purpose of which is for use as, or for development of, a weapon, a weapon prototype, or a weapon test device.

B. "Classified information" means information, data, materials, services or any other matter with the security designation of United Kingdom 'Restricted' or United States Confidential or higher applied under the legislation or regulations of either the United States or the United Kingdom, including that designated by the Government of the United States as "Restricted Data" or "Formerly Restricted Data" and that designated by the Government of the United Kingdom as "ATOMIC".

C. "Sensitive nuclear technology" means any information (including information incorporated in a production or utilization facility or important component part thereof) which is not available to the public and which is important to the design, construction, fabrication, operation or maintenance of a uranium enrichment or nuclear fuel reprocessing facility or a facility for the production of heavy water, but shall not include information designated as Restricted Data by the Government of the United States."

D. "Controlled nuclear information" means information protected by the Government of the United States from unauthorized dissemination pursuant to sections 57.b. or 148 of the United States Atomic Energy Act of 1954, as amended.

E. "Equipment" means any instrument, apparatus or facility and includes any facility, except an atomic weapon, capable of making use of or producing special nuclear material, and component parts thereof, and includes submarine nuclear propulsion plant, reactor and military reactor. 'Equipment' also includes non-nuclear parts of atomic weapons and other non-nuclear parts of atomic weapons systems involving Restricted Data.

F. "Military reactor" means a reactor for the propulsion of naval vessels, aircraft or land vehicles and military package power reactors.

G. "Person" means:

1. any individual, corporation, partnership, firm, association, trust, estate, public or private institution, group, government agency or government corporation other than the Department of Energy and the Ministry of Defence; and

2. any legal successor, representative, agent or agency of the foregoing.

H. "Reactor" means an apparatus, other than an atomic weapon, in which a self-supporting fission chain reaction is maintained and controlled by utilizing uranium, plutonium or thorium, or any combination of uranium, plutonium or thorium.

I. "Submarine nuclear propulsion plant" means a propulsion plant and includes the reactor, and such control, primary, auxiliary, steam and electric systems as may be necessary for propulsion of submarines.

J. "Non-nuclear parts of atomic weapons" means parts of atomic weapons which are specially designed for them and are not in general use in other end products and which are not made, in whole or in part, of special nuclear material; and 'other non-nuclear parts of atomic weapons systems involving Restricted Data' means parts of atomic weapons systems, other than non-nuclear parts of atomic weapons, which contain or reveal atomic information and which are not made, in whole or in part, of special nuclear material.

K. "Atomic information" means information designated 'Restricted Data' or 'Formerly Restricted Data' by the Government of the United States and information designated 'ATOMIC' by the Government of the United Kingdom.

ARTICLE XII ⌢ DURATION

This Agreement shall enter into force [n1] on the date on which each Government shall have received from the other Government written notification that it has complied with all statutory and constitutional requirements for the entry into force of this Agreement, and shall remain in force until terminated by agreement of both Parties, except that, if not so terminated, Article II may be terminated by agreement of both Parties, or by either Party on one year's notice to the other Party.

NOTES

n1 Aug. 4, 1958.

IN WITNESS WHEREOF, the undersigned, duly authorized, have signed this Agreement.

DONE at Washington this third day of July, 1958, in two original texts.

SIGNATORIES:

FOR THE GOVERNMENT OF THE
UNITED STATES OF AMERICA: JOHN FOSTER DULLES

FOR THE GOVERNMENT OF THE
UNITED KINGDOM OF GREAT
BRITAIN AND NORTHERN
IRELAND: HOOD

ABOUT THE EDITORS AND AUTHORS

ROY M. ANDERSON

Professor Sir Roy Anderson, FRS, FMedSci, served as chief scientific adviser in the Ministry of Defence from 2004 to 2007 before becoming professor of infectious disease epidemiology at Imperial College London. He will be rector at Imperial College in July 2008. His previous academic positions include the Linacre Professorship and head of zoology, University of Oxford; professor of parasite epidemiology and head of biology, Imperial College; and director of the Wellcome Trust Centre for Infectious Disease Epidemiology, University of Oxford. Sir Roy has published more than 450 scientific papers on infectious disease agents, including HIV, BSE, foot and mouth virus, vCJD, SARS, dengue virus, parasitic helminths and protozoa, and respiratory tract viral and bacterial infections.

LINTON F. BROOKS

Ambassador Linton F. Brooks is a consultant on national security and a senior adviser at CSIS. From 2002 to 2007 he was administrator of the Department of Energy's National Nuclear Security Administration, where he was the senior U.S. official responsible for cooperation under the 1958 Mutual Defense Agreement. Previously he served as chief negotiator for the Strategic Arms Reduction Treaty, director of defense programs on the staff of the National Security Council, director of the U.S. Navy's Strategic and Theater Nuclear Warfare Division, and vice president at the Center for Naval Analyses. Ambassador Brooks is a graduate of Duke University, the University of Maryland, and the U.S. Naval War College, and he is the author of several award-winning articles on naval and nuclear strategy.

ANDREW BROWN

Dr. Andrew Brown is a fellow at the Belfer Center's project on Managing the Atom, Kennedy School of Government, Harvard University. He trained and worked as a physician in London and has been in practice as a radiation oncologist in New Hampshire since 1990. He has written about the Cambridge University scientists of the twentieth century (including major biographies of James Chadwick and Desmond Bernal), examining their influence on political decisionmakers. He is currently writing a book on Eisenhower's nuclear policies, *Ike's Global Nuclear Deals.* He holds degrees from Bristol University, University of London, and Harvard University.

TARA CALLAHAN

Tara Callahan is the special assistant to the chief of staff at the Center for Strategic and International Studies. She graduated in June 2007 with a bachelor's degree from the University of Washington in Seattle, where she finished two majors, in international studies and French. She also received an international diploma from the Institut d'Etudes Politiques in Paris in 2006. Her areas of interest include nonproliferation issues, transatlantic relations, and global security studies.

ALAN B. CARR

Alan B. Carr serves as laboratory historian for the Los Alamos National Laboratory, a position he has held since 2003. Before joining the staff at Los Alamos, he studied at Texas Tech University, earning a master's degree in modern history with an emphasis on interwar Soviet military doctrine. Carr's publications include *The Forgotten Physicist: Robert F. Bacher, 1905–2004; Science in the National Interest: Photographs Celebrating Six Decades of Excellence* (coauthor); and several articles and reports on atomic history and various Cold War topics.

PAUL CORNISH

Paul Cornish has served in the British Army and the Foreign and Commonwealth Office, has taught at the Joint Services Command and Staff College and at the University of Cambridge, and was director of the Centre for Defence Studies at King's College London. He is Carrington Chair in International Security and head of the International Security Programme, Chatham House. His recent publications include *The Conflict in Iraq, 2003* and *The CBRN System: Assessing the Threat of Terrorist Use of Chemical, Biological, Radiological and Nuclear Weapons in the United Kingdom.* He holds a doctoral degree from the University of Cambridge.

TIM HARE
Commodore Hare served in the Royal Navy from 1965 to 2002, specializing in submarines. He held a variety of appointments at sea and in the Ministry of Defence, with a major focus on the management and operation of the United Kingdom's submarine-based nuclear deterrent force. His last appointment was as director of nuclear policy in the MOD from 1999 to 2002, where he was responsible for the formulation of the United Kingdom's nuclear deterrence policy at home and abroad and the conduct of the U.S.-UK bilateral relationship on nuclear issues. He has written articles on nuclear matters for the Royal United Services Institute (RUSI) and the Oxford Research Group. He now works for the international defense company, Thales.

BRIAN P. JAMISON
Brian P. Jamison is a postdoctoral research fellow at the Mountbatten Centre for International Studies, University of Southampton. He earned his doctoral degree in Scottish studies from the University of Glasgow, and he is the author of two books and several articles dealing with the United Kingdom's nuclear weapons program and with Scottish security dynamics. His current research focus includes Scotland's experiences with the Trident system, its relationship with NATO, and the possibility of establishing an independent Scottish defense force.

MARK JANSSON
Mark Jansson is a master's degree candidate in the field of conflict resolution at Georgetown University, and he holds an internship with the Project on Nuclear Issues at the Center for Strategic and International Studies. His areas of academic concentration include nuclear weapons issues, international security and arms control, political development, and structural causes of conflict. He has also worked in the nonprofit sector as a grant writer, administrator, program developer, and founda-

tion relations specialist. He received his bachelor's degree with honors from Roanoke College and holds a graduate certificate from the Institute for Conflict Analysis and Resolution at George Mason University.

KEN JOHNSTON

Ken Johnston was awarded a first class honors degree in chemistry from St. Andrews University before he joined the Atomic Weapons Research Establishment in 1958, where his early work focused on safeguards monitoring techniques. He later worked on the UK Polaris and Chevaline upgrade programs. During the 1970s Mr. Johnston held a succession of senior AWRE and Ministry of Defence science and research management positions prior to being appointed head of the Atomic Coordinating Office Washington. Subsequently he assumed responsibility for all Atomic Weapons Establishment research and development programs in warhead physics, engineering, and materials. From 1992 to 2000 he held the post of AWE chief scientist. Mr Johnston is now retired and works as a consultant to the MOD.

ROBERT G. JOSEPH

Robert Joseph is a senior scholar at the National Institute for Public Policy. Until March 2007, he served as under secretary of state for arms control and international security, overseeing the bureaus of International Security and Nonproliferation; Political and Military Affairs; and Verification, Compliance, and Implementation. Previously he served on the National Security Council as special assistant to the president and senior director for proliferation strategy, counterproliferation, and homeland defense. He has held senior positions related to nuclear testing and international security at the Department of Defense. He was also professor and director-founder of the Center for Counterproliferation Research at National Defense University.

STEVE LUDLAM

Steve Ludlam is president of Submarines, Rolls-Royce, which provides the nuclear reactor plants for the United Kingdom's submarine flotilla. He joined Rolls-Royce and Associates as a graduate apprentice and has held several engineering management positions. On January 1, 1996, he became general manager of Vulcan Naval Reactor Test Establishment in Scotland. He was appointed director–Submarines in October 2000 and subsequently became director–Europe, responsible for all submarines and naval surface ship activity in Europe. Mr. Ludlam is a member of the AWE-ML Programme Advisory Committee. He has a master's degree in nuclear reactor technology from Royal Naval College, Greenwich.

JENIFER MACKBY

Jenifer Mackby is a fellow in the CSIS International Security Program. She has worked in France on European, biological, and strengthening-the-global-partnership projects, and she has served as rapporteur for international conferences. Previously she was a senior political officer at the Conference on Disarmament, responsible for the negotiations on the Nuclear Test-Ban Treaty, the Group of Scientific Experts, and the Biological Weapons Convention. She also worked for the CTBTO Preparatory Commission in Vienna. Ms. Mackby has coauthored a number of books and has written articles for publications such as the *New York Times, Newsweek,* and the *Bulletin of the Atomic Scientists.*

CLIVE MARSH

Clive Marsh, CBE, graduated in mathematics at Leeds University in 1964 and earned a doctoral degree in astrophysics in 1967. As an associate at the U.S. National Academy of Sciences, he modeled solar wind phenomena in anticipation of data collected in the vicinity of the moon by the Explorer satellites. He joined the Atomic Weapons Research Establishment in late 1968 to work on high-temperature phenomena, including theoretical treatments of nuclear fusion and laser-created plasmas. He then managed the physics design of the UK Trident warhead. In 1983, as head of design mathematics, he carried responsibility for nuclear warhead research and development and for technical coordination of the United Kingdom's underground test program. He became chief of warhead physics in January 1989 and was appointed chief scientist in April 2000.

FRANKLIN C. MILLER

Franklin C. Miller is an independent consultant and a senior counselor at The Cohen Group. His 31 years of government service included positions as special assistant to the president and senior director, defense policy and arms control on the National Security Council staff; principal deputy assistant secretary of defense; acting assistant secretary of defense; and other senior posts in the Department of Defense. He received his bachelor's degree from Williams College and his master's of public affairs from the Woodrow Wilson School of Public and International Affairs, Princeton University. In 2006 he was awarded an honorary Knight Commander of the Order of the British Empire (KBE) by Queen Elizabeth II in recognition of his many contributions to U.S.-UK relations during his decades of government service.

KEITH O'NIONS

Sir Keith O'Nions, FRS, was chief scientific adviser at the Ministry of Defence from 2000 to 2004 and subsequently, until 2008, director general, science and innovation in the Department for Innovation, Universities and Skills. Currently he is a visiting professor at Oxford University. Previously he followed an academic career as head of earth sciences at Oxford, professor of geology at Columbia, and Royal Society Research Professor at Cambridge. He was a member of the Council for Science and Technology Research Council and has participated in Research Council committees as chairman or member for the past 25 years. He is a graduate of the University of Nottingham and the University of Alberta.

FRANK PANTON

Frank Panton, CBE, MBE, has been a leading figure in the United Kingdom's development of weapons technologies, including the advanced Chevaline system. He was technical adviser to the UK delegation at the nuclear test ban negotiations in Geneva and counselor (defense) at the British Embassy in Washington, D.C. In the Ministry of Defence he served successively as assistant chief scientific adviser (nuclear), director of the Propellants, Explosives and Rocket Motor Establishment, and director of the Royal Armament Research and Development Establishment. He has been a consultant on nuclear defense policy in the Cabinet Office and on nuclear safety in the MOD.

ROBIN PITMAN

As head of Nuclear and Strategic Defence, British Defence Staff (United States), since 2003, Robin Pitman has been responsible for UK-U.S. cooperation on nuclear warhead and nuclear propulsion matters under the Mutual Defense Agreement. Following a number of years of responsibility for the nuclear warhead research and capability maintenance program, he completed a major review of the United Kingdom's nuclear warhead capability. His career has included plutonium metallurgy, nuclear warhead design physics, high-power lasers, and scientific and technical intelligence. Mr. Pitman graduated from the University of Kent at Canterbury with a bachelor's degree (with honors) in physics, and he is a member of the Institute of Physics.

MICHAEL QUINLAN
In his civil service career Sir Michael Quinlan held several posts concerned with nuclear weapons policy, including as private secretary to the chief of Air Staff, defence counsellor in the UK delegation to NATO, policy director in the Ministry of Defence, and finally permanent under-secretary of state there (the senior nonpolitical civilian). After leaving government he served as director of the Ditchley Foundation. He is a visiting professor at King's College London and a consulting senior fellow at the International Institute for Strategic Studies. He has written many articles on nuclear weapons policy and other defense themes.

JEFFERY H. RICHARDSON
Jeffery H. Richardson is a technical adviser on change of station from Lawrence Livermore National Laboratory, assigned to the Directorate of Space and Nuclear Operations at Air Force Headquarters. He received his bachelor's degree from CalTech and his doctoral degree from Stanford University, and he has been at Lawrence Livermore National Laboratory for more than 34 years. His assignments at LLNL include chemical sciences division leader and proliferation and terrorism prevention division leader; and he has contributed to several weapons, energy, nonproliferation, and homeland security programs. He has authored more than 100 papers, mostly on chemistry and materials science.

ERIC RIDGE
Eric Ridge is a research assistant for the CSIS International Security Program, where he works on defense policy issues and conducts research for projects, including Beyond Goldwater-Nichols. Previously, Ridge was program coordinator for the CSIS Homeland Security Program. He has coauthored "Planning for Stability Operations: The Use of Capabilities-Based Approaches" and has written a chapter on U.S. domestic security in *Five Years After 9/11: An Assessment of America's*

War on Terror. Ridge holds a bachelor's degree from the Johns Hopkins University, where he majored in international relations with a concentration in global security.

PETER ROBERTS

Peter Roberts is the technical strategy manager in the stockpile management at the Atomic Weapons Establishment. In the mid-1970s he worked on design aspects of the UK underground test program, writing a major simulation code and demonstrating the ability of high-power lasers to address weapon physics. In 1984 he became superintendent of physics design, responsible for all aspects of UK weapon design. In 1988 he was promoted to head of the Design Mathematics Department, which included responsibility for algorithm, code development, and material property data. Roberts was seconded in 2003 to the Ministry of Defence to work on technical aspects of defence policy. He returned to AWE in 2005 and is working on improving warhead design processes.

PETER SANKEY

Apart from a brief spell in industry in the mid-1970s, Peter Sankey, OBE, has worked at the Atomic Weapons Establishment since graduating in mathematic physics from King's College London in 1970. He became the AWE deputy trials director for UK underground testing in Nevada from the mid-1980s until the 1992 nuclear test moratorium. Sankey then provided technical support to the UK ambassador during the Comprehensive Nuclear Test-Ban Treaty negotiations in Geneva (1994 to 1996). Since 2001 he has been head of threat reduction, managing both resource and program and also providing radiological and nuclear technical advice to defense and intelligence services, nuclear treaty verification, and weapon accident and counterterrorism radiological and nuclear incidents.

GLEN M. SEGELL

Glen M. Segell is the editor of the *London Security Policy Study*. He has worked and published more than 100 articles on arms control for the U.S. Naval Postgraduate School and the Institute of National Security Studies at the U.S. Air Force Academy. He has taught and researched in Britain, Iraq, Ireland, Israel, South Africa, Spain, and Sudan. He has held elected positions in the British International Studies Association, the Political Studies Association of the United Kingdom, and the U.S. International Studies Association. He was educated at the University of Witwatersrand South Africa, Hebrew University Israel, King's College London, and Canterbury University.

JOHN SIMPSON

John Simpson, OBE, is a professor of international relations and director of the Mountbatten Centre for International Studies at the University of Southampton. An international authority on nuclear issues, Professor Simpson has represented the United Kingdom at UN meetings and advises the UK delegation to review conferences for the Nuclear Non-Proliferation Treaty. He served as program director of the Programme for Promoting Nuclear Non-Proliferation and has authored *The Independent Nuclear State: The United States, Britain and the Military Atom* and "The United Kingdom and the Nuclear Future." Professor Simpson holds a master's degree in economics from the University of London and a doctoral degree from the University of Southampton.

KRISTAN STODDART

Kristan Stoddart is a research fellow at the Mountbatten Centre for International Studies. He is the author of two books to be published in 2008 on the subjects of Anglo-American nuclear weapons policy and the relationship with NATO—*Losing an Empire and Finding a Role* and *The Sword and the Shield*—as well as a number of articles dealing with national and international nuclear weapons policy. Mr. Stoddart holds both a bachelor's degree and a master's degree in history, a master's degree (economics) in European politics, and a doctoral degree from Swansea University.

TROY E. WADE II

Troy Wade is chairman of the Nevada Alliance for Defense, Energy and Business; president and chairman of the Nevada Test Site Historical Foundation; and president of Wade Associates. He also serves on the Department of Energy panel examining the appropriate role for the Nevada Test Site in the stockpile stewardship program. Mr. Wade served for 31 years on nuclear programs in the U.S. Department of Energy, finishing as assistant secretary of energy for defense programs. Previously he was deputy manager of the Nevada Operations Office and director of the Idaho National Engineering Laboratory. He was a member of the Secretary of Energy's Openness Advisory Panel and Committee on the Safety of Nuclear Facilities.

MICHAEL J. WEAVER

Michael J. Weaver is the nuclear nonproliferation deputy director at Los Alamos National Laboratory, providing technical direction to a professional staff of more than 250. He has more than 20 years of experience in the U.S. nuclear weapons program. Mr. Weaver was the lead weapons planner for the first joint nuclear weapon accident full-field exercise conducted in the United Kingdom, and the senior technical adviser to the deputy assistant secretary for military applications at the National Nuclear Security Agency. He graduated from Montana State University with bachelor's and master's degrees in mechanical engineering.

RICHARD WEITZ

Richard Weitz is a senior fellow and director of program management at the Hudson Institute. Weitz holds a doctoral degree in political science from Harvard University and has written for journals such as the *National Interest,* the *Washington Quarterly, NATO Review, Studies in Conflict and Terrorism, Defense Concepts,* and the *Journal of Strategic Studies,* as well as for the *International Herald Tribune,* the *Baltimore Sun,* and the *Washington Times.* His books include *Reserve Policies of Nations: A Comparative Analysis; Revitalising US–Russian Security Cooperation: Practical Measures;* and *Mismanaging Mayhem: How Washington Responds to Crisis* (coeditor).

INDEX

Page numbers followed by the letter f *refer to figures. Page numbers followed by the letter* n *refer to chapter endnotes.*